Agrarian Reform & Agrarian Reformism

In Memory
of the Unknown Dead
in Chile

11th September 1973—

Agrarian Reform & Agrarian Reformism

STUDIES OF PERU, CHILE, CHINA AND INDIA

Edited by David Lehmann

Faber and Faber 3 *Queen Square London*

First published in 1974
by Faber and Faber Limited
3 Queen Square London WC1
Printed in Great Britain by
Western Printing Services Ltd

ISBN 0 571 10603 x (paper covers)
ISBN 0 571 10486 x (hard bound edition)

Contents

Preface

The origins of this volume lie in a study seminar held at the Institute of Development Studies at the University of Sussex in early 1971, on the subject of 'Land Tenure, Distribution and Reform'. The seminar was attended by officials and academics concerned with land reform from a number of Asian and Latin American countries. Except for Ramón Zaldívar, all the contributors to this book took part in the seminar.

In the path from the idea to the act of writing and publishing I have incurred many debts. The first is to the contributors themselves, who have suffered much chevying and pestering, and whose capacity for team-work is quite unusual for members of their profession. As a result, this is as nearly a co-operative volume as anyone could hope; we do not all agree on the solutions to the problems we raise, but we have been able to write our papers in the light of a common set of issues. The one paper which was not specifically written for this volume – that on Peru – offered such an original interpretation of the Peruvian process, that it obviously had to be published. The paper originally appeared in Peru in *Cuadernos Agrarios* in 1971; a number of those involved in this publication have since been sacked from their university posts or imprisoned, or both. I wish here to express my thanks to Ramón Zaldívar for allowing his work to be included.

The production of this volume has been particularly smooth for the authors thanks to the efforts and bewildering patience of Margot Cameron, Rosemary Irving, Geraldine King and Carrie Stait.

We owe much to the generosity of the Institute of Development Studies at the University of Sussex, and to the encouragement of its present and former Directors, Richard Jolly and Dudley Seers. Thanks to the Institute, the contributors were able to meet in December 1972, and the volume has thereby become much more close-knit than would otherwise have been the case.

The following also attended the meeting, and recognition is due to them for their enthusiasm and interest which enriched both our discussions and our thoughts: Lionel Cliffe, Biplab Dasgupta, Scarlett Epstein, Jack Gray, Abdul Hameed, Colin Harding, Rodrigo Sanchez and Robert Wade.

Finally, two personal words of thanks: to Roland Penrose and to Clive Bell, to whom I can but return the compliment paid to me in his first footnote.

Chiddingly,
February 1973. A.D.L.

Contributors

Clive Bell and Michael Lipton are Fellows of the Institute of Development Studies at the University of Sussex.

T. J. Byres is Lecturer in Economics and Geoffrey Shillinglaw a former Lecturer in Political Science at the School of Oriental and African Studies, London.

D. P. Chaudhri is a Professor of Economics at the University of New England, Armidale, New South Wales. He was formerly a Lecturer at the Delhi School of Economics.

David Lehmann is Assistant Director of Development Studies at Cambridge University.

Ramón Zaldívar is the pseudonym of a student of the Peruvian Agrarian Reform. His essay has been translated by Maggie Harding and Miguel Sanchez Padrón. The editor would like to thank Colin Harding and Rodrigo Sanchez for their valuable help in bringing some of the information up to date.

One

Introduction[1]

David Lehmann

When doctrines command widespread agreement, the time has usually come for a re-examination; when men who otherwise disagree on fundamental political values agree on an issue of importance, they are probably using crucial terms in widely differing senses; when radical rhetoric becomes fashionable, it may well acquire non-radical implications.

So it is with land reform today, and the aim of publishing this book is to lay the way for a reappraisal. Some say that land reform is the way to preserve political stability and 'democracy' (Ladejinsky, 1969; Huntington, 1968, pp. 374–5); others, on the left, say that it is a 'reformist' measure designed to preserve a society's essential institutional and economic features; some say that it is a threat to democracy and free enterprise, others that it is the best way of sustaining and feeding capitalism (Gutelman, 1971); some say socialism destroys the peasantry, others that land reform can succeed only in a revolutionary context. Few are against reform, but while some proclaim it as the dawn of a new era, others are apprehensive and uncertain about its outcome, and the reasons for each view can vary widely.

The divergences arise largely from varying ideological viewpoints and class interests, but to say that is already to imply that the significance of land reform varies enormously in different contexts. Those most open to criticism are writers who seem to think that land reform is a magic formula which will solve a host of problems irrespective of the relationships among the problems and the phenomena they refer to.

'Blanket' justifications (or, one should say, mystifications) of land reform, tend to be formulated in such a way as to please readers of all ideologies, and as a result they cover up the conflicts of interest, within the peasantry and between sections of the peasantry and members of the urban working class and

1. I am indebted, to all the contributors, with whom the eventual content of this Introduction was discussed, and to Terry Byres, R. P. Dore and Jon Sigurdsson for comments on an earlier draft.

middle class, which arise from the redistribution of land: 'there seems now to be general agreement that a much higher performance could be expected from Latin American agriculture – if land-ownership were more diffused so that more farms were of "family-type" or medium-size, if there were more owner-operator entrepreneurs, if clear land-titles were generally the rule, if higher wages were paid to farm labour, if credit were not concentrated in the hands of a few, and if markets were accessible to all producers . . . only an increase in rural purchasing power can sufficiently enlarge domestic markets for manufactured goods and associated services.' (Carroll, 1964.) The cascade of 'if's' may be useful for airborne narodniks attempting to convert AID officials and Latin American politicians to the idea of reform, but they leave wide open central questions which are of concern even to narodniks – airborne or on the ground. Is there enough land to be distributed to *all* peasants; if not, which peasants are to benefit? How would higher wages affect mechanization and hence the unemployment situation? How would an increase in rural purchasing power affect capital formation in the economy as a whole? We must face up to the question whether what is good for 'the peasants' is good for other underprivileged groups in town and country. Predictions about the consequences of a redistribution of land are vacuous unless it is first specified which élites inspire it or carry it out, what their long-term aims are, and what class interests they represent. And even this will only tell us about intentions, for it is quite possible that the actual outcome will be far different from the original intention.

Much of the confusion is due to the ideological factors we have mentioned: people think they are talking about the same thing, when in fact they define crucial terms in radically different ways. More perverse still, there are those who use terms precisely on account of their ambiguity in order to persuade governments to adopt measures whose consequences will be more – or less – radical than it is convenient to predict. Whatever its political functions, such manipulation confuses the issues for those who seek to interpret the world – in order, later on, to change it, perhaps. But the close relationship between accounts, interpretations and advocacy has not helped our understanding. Value-freedom may be undesirable as well as unattainable, but to base analysis directly on a classification of phenomena according to moral and political criteria of goodness bears witness to a regrettable lack of sophistication. The consequences, with reference to the subject of agrarian reform,[1] reveal themselves at

1. I use 'land reform' and 'agrarian reform' interchangeably.

two points: firstly in the analysis of agrarian structures, which often begin by asking why some desirable process is *not* at work, rather than explaining what is happening in reality, and secondly in the analysis of agrarian reforms, where the issue becomes 'has the reform provoked an increase in production' or 'has the reform gone as far as was hoped in reducing inequality – in brief, has it "succeeded"?' A parallel, separate source of confusion, arising from the ultimately emotional observation of wickedness and hunger, is the belief that the elimination of the exploiters at any given moment will lead, almost by itself, to the disappearance of hunger. Unfortunately, the diagnosis of moral responsibility does not always point directly to the core of the evils it engenders. As long as our analytic formulations follow lines of these kinds, our understanding of the social and economic processes at work will be seriously impaired, and the answers even to these 'value-laden' questions will be limited. All too often we speak of the 'failure' of an exercise on policy application, where we should be inquiring into the sociology of the mystification which permitted anyone ever to take the policy seriously in the first place (the Indian land reform, the Peruvian 'revolution').[1] In this volume we seek to approach a framework for the analysis of agrarian change, of which agrarian reform is one sort; the reader will indeed find a number of different approaches, but all, even the more descriptive contributions, contain an implicit or explicit analytical framework which, however crude, is nonetheless an advance on previous work. This means renouncement of the role of judge – but not of the role of critic. The phenomena studied are ordered in the light of a theory – more or less sophisticated – about the relationships among them; the theory is critical in the precise sense that it challenges the conceptual ordering applied by politicians, planners, bureaucrats, airborne narodniks and the like.

The primary message, which was indeed the primary aim in the

1. The essentially speculative nature of much recent writing on this subject is highlighted by a recent review (Laporte et. al., 1971) of some of the literature which concludes that 'most writers contend that the effects on agrarian reform, their extent and intensity, stem from the forces that create the reform in the first place more than from the reform itself.' A somewhat elliptic phrase if you reflect upon it, but nonetheless interesting to us for a simple reason: few of the studies quoted were concerned to analyse these forces – to which they attached so much weight – except in a somewhat circumstantial way: they concentrated on production and on abstract categorizations about social structures and politics, not on social processes.

conception of this volume, is the condition for asking any relevant questions at all: agrarian reforms vary in content and meaning. They operate to the benefit of different groups in different situations, at the national level and within agrarian society. They have varying effects on the political system, sometimes contributing to its continued or restored stability, sometimes upsetting that stability. Readers might be struck, for example, by the resemblances between the egalitarian, distributist reform advocated with very much verve by Michael Lipton, and the practice of the Chinese Communists described in Geoffrey Shillinglaw's illuminating account. Yet evidently the ulterior implications of such a redistribution would be fundamentally different if it was implemented by the Indian Congress – a hypothesis analysed in detail by Clive Bell, despite its inherent unlikelihood.

The national class structure also appears in all our papers: urban bias versus rural bias, rich peasants versus urban bourgeoisie, urban proletariat versus the peasantry, and so on. All have interests at stake in the process of reform, and no analysis should ignore them. It may be that the models we use are overly static, that we do not always take into account sufficiently the ways in which these interests are articulated, the dynamics of class conflict and political bargaining. This element is absent in particular in the papers on India, but we must remember that the study of Indian villages has for long ignored manifestations of class conflict, confining itself to the study of caste, and of class only in the static manifestations which emerge as the caste system comes into contact with the forces of capitalism.[1] Thus our premonitions as to which groups might provide active support for, or present active resistance to, land reform in India are based on precious little evidence, and overlaid by an irresistible impression of continued stagnation. D. P. Chaudhri's warnings of social unrest are apt, but we are singularly powerless to predict whether the 'green revolution', with the changing patterns of inequality it brings in its trail, will in fact provoke a mass movement among one or another stratum of the peasantry.

The conflict of interests most fully analysed in the Indian papers is, as the reader will quickly perceive, that which supposedly opposes town to country, industry to agriculture. We have been fortunate in bringing together two notable exponents of

1. For one interesting analysis of the peasant movement in West Bengal, however, see Dasgupta (1972). For studies of 'class' emerging from caste see, *inter alia*, Gough (1955) and Béteille (1965).

diametrically opposed views, Terry Byres and Michael Lipton. In the event, it was Lipton who could see Byres's paper before writing the bulk of his, and who therefore had the opportunity of replying to Byres's arguments; lack of space, and consideration for the reader's patience, precluded allocating further space for further rejoinders, but the polemic will no doubt continue, and those who are interested will be able to follow it up in the journals. In the meantime one remark is perhaps in order: neither Byres nor Lipton has a monopoly of concern for the peasants' long-term welfare. However, in differing fundamentally over the means to achieve it, and over the issue of which groups should pay the price, their explicit or implicit strategies do lead to different final goals. In the absence of a revolutionary situation, Byres believes that the peasantry with or without further land reform, will continue in a large measure to be exploited; he would welcome reforms such as those which eradicate share-cropping and otherwise promoted rural capitalism, but in general, the impasse leads him to favour what he sees as the one available progressive path of change, industrialization; presumably this would eventually liberate resources to return to the peasantry from which a surplus was at first painfully elicited. For Lipton, all urban social classes are privileged in relation to most rural classes. The greatest possible reduction of rural poverty is the immediate issue on the agenda. Like Byres, he readily admits that everyone cannot benefit from short-term change: if we follow up his implied preferences, the strategy implicit in Byres's paper would maintain urban living standards at a more or less constant level (the additional surplus hypothetically released going, presumably, to investment) but probably depress those of certain rural groups, while Lipton would benefit the small peasants, rather than the landless, at the expense of the landlords. (See Clive Bell's paper for some relevant calculations.) Many issues remain unresolved: there are conflicting judgements – of value to be sure, but also of evidence – as to whether 'urban bias' really is a feature of the Indian polity (for it is in the polity that prices and terms of trade are largely decided upon) and as to the effects of distributist reform on the marketed surplus (on which Clive Bell's note on 'perverseness' again provides some theoretical illumination) but in the end the argument is unfortunately based on conjecture pending implementation of reform. . . . A question mark nonetheless continues to hang over the ulterior consequences of either path: to what use would an increased marketed surplus be put? If, as D. P. Chaudhri pointed out in our discussions, such a use were not of general social benefit, is it worth imposing such social costs? Conversely, we must ask whether, after the inevitable social upheavals which would accompany an egalitarian, distributist reform, if the forces of differentiation of the peasantry were to be renewed, would the effort, again, have been worth it? Lipton's defence of his reform against renewed inequalities depends on relevant action being taken by government with respect to new technologies and consolidation. In the absence of such action, Bell's inclination to the view that population growth would tend to have a polarizing rather than an equalizing effect – in an unreformed setting, true – appears relevant. Should one encourage measures whose consequences are, to put it mildly, and on the admission of the authors themselves, not at all certain?

The argument will no doubt continue for a long time. Meanwhile, having advanced in our appreciation of the interests of the various groups involved, maybe we should begin to seek out ways in which those groups we favour could more effectively articulate their interests in the Indian polity. To this I shall return.

A further common theme echoed throughout the book concerns the illusion of bureaucratic or technocratic omnipotence which tends to overtake advocates of one policy or another – an illusion rampant in the entire field of development studies. (What would the development jet-set do if they found that the governments they advise are incapable of carrying out any 'policy' at all?) However apparently powerful a political party (China) or an army (Peru) may be, it is evidently very difficult to control what happens on the ground, within the agrarian society, especially where relationships among the peasants themselves are concerned. We cannot take intentions as given when they involve some form of administrative control. The bureaucracy, need we emphasize it enough?, is not an 'autonomous' force, it is subject to strong political influences and internal contradictions, and carries out measures arrived at on political grounds at various levels. The measures may be distorted, cancelled out, or defeated by their administration and the political effects will depend greatly on the relationship between the peasantry and a bureaucracy on which they depend increasingly for inputs, public works, etc. Bureaucracy, like 'the government', is a dependent variable. Michael Lipton offers some sane remarks on the subject, and his inclination to the use of market mechanisms where the bureaucracy fails is not to be dismissed out of hand on the charge of 'neo-classicism'.

Finally, the pre-existing agrarian structure emerges in all our papers as essential to the understanding of patterns of reform. The point may seem obvious, but it is surprising how often predictions of a coming El Dorado ignore the simple observation that measures of reform interact dynamically with a given situation: Shillinglaw emphasizes how the agrarian structure in Southern China, for example, placed singular constraints on the implementation of a policy laid down by the Chinese Communist Party – a policy which had met with considerable success in the North of the country. The reader will notice how much easier it is to isolate a landed élite in a latifundist situation than in a land-scarce one where the rich peasants and landlords can resist far more effectively the encroachments of political parties or central governments on their political clientele.

Many of our papers – especially those on China, Peru and Chile – mention and analyse rural social movements. This is a currently fashionable topic, of which too little is as yet understood, despite the spate of literature. Certain kinds of reform can be implemented without mass rural mobilization – indeed, mass mobilization might seriously impede the achievement of their stated, or unstated, objectives. Think of Iran, of Peru. Some reforms are intended to stem or reverse the tide of agrarian unrest. Think of Italy (Tarrow, 1967). But in many cases peasant mobilization seems an inescapable condition – not only of the redistribution of rights in land, but also of a change in the political status and consciousness of the people.

Michael Lipton, in his paper, criticizes those who would postpone reform until a rural mass movement has emerged; stated thus baldly, the criticism seems justified, yet the baldness of the statement hides complex questions. Surely where the implementation of reform is evidently out of the question in the absence of such a movement, the study of techniques and strategies of mass mobilization, of *concientização* as the Brazilians call it, appears as much a priority as the elaboration of projects for land reform. In the post-reform situation, further complexities emerge: the peasantry may be subjected to exploitation by a new class of traders, or by urban and industrial classes, in a capitalist or in a socialist framework, and they may also be the object of political repression or manipulation. One or the other may, under certain conditions, be desirable, but the most difficult political decision requires an assessment of future social trends which is almost certainly 90 per cent guesswork: is it worth postponing reform in favour of subsequent revolution when we are uncertain whether that revolution is forthcoming, or when there is an outside chance that a capitalist reform will itself create a revolutionary situation by, say, dividing the ruling class?

This last question can be approached on the basis of class analysis, and I have tried to do so elsewhere (with hindsight: Lehmann, 1971). On the relationship between pre-reform organization and post-reform manipulation and exploitation the evidence, on the surface, is contradictory. In Mexico, even a massive and violent uprising (though not uniformly spread through the country, see Womack, 1968) was not a sufficient condition to protect the beneficiaries of reform, and the rest of the peasantry, from armed repression by their 'allies' before and after the early post-revolutionary reform, or from persistent political manipulation and economic exploitation for the benefit of Mexican capitalism and industrialization (Stavenhagen, 1970b; Flores, 1970).

In Venezuela the peasantry were well organized before reform (Powell, 1971) yet are subject to skilful political manipulation today (Pugh, 1970), while in Bolivia, the peasant organization which led a violent and spontaneous seizure of lands in 1952, later provided crucial political sustenance to right-wing régimes such as that of Barrientos. In Iran, economic exploitation of the peasantry has developed new patterns after the land reform (Khosrovi, 1969). One might even advance a tentative generalization to the effect that under an ongoing capitalist system the peasantry are bound to be subject to either economic exploitation or political manipulation or both, after – if not as a result of – agrarian reform. Under socialism this eventuality is not by any means excluded, but it is far less common than is sometimes thought: witness the case of Poland, where the peasants remain peasants and seem to possess a good deal of (negative) political leverage (Korbonski, 1965) and other Eastern European countries such as the German Democratic Republic where collectivization was 'bought' by credits, and cheap inputs, at a cost to the urban proletariat, rather than imposed as was the case – under very different conditions – in the Soviet Union. In China the leadership seems to have been unable to impose onerous levels of surplus extraction, perhaps on account of its own unwillingness to use excessively violent means. (Remember Mao's phrase to describe the Soviet experience: 'draining the pond to catch the fish'.)

The issue is not only whether the peasantry are exploited, but also, if this is to be, in favour of whom? We know the crucial role of class alliances which lie behind a reform and we have the frequently observed inability of the peasantry, or any particular stratum thereof, to mobilize effectively without outside support and often outside leadership. Thus, the issue is both whether to await a rural mass movement, and whether the class alliances this inevitably implies are likely to favour either the peasants' long-term interests or those of other social classes. Whether it is decided that the peasantry ought to be exploited, in favour of socialist industrialization for example, or that it should protect itself from the kind of successful exploitation and manipulation by capitalist forces which would postpone indefinitely the possibilities of a transition to socialism, the need for mass organization remains, in both cases. The peasantry, left to their own devices in the early post-distribution situation, are particularly vulnerable to the siren songs of private property – the private property which will eventually permit renewed exploitation, as in Mexico, or which will hinder socialization. Now it is noticeable that all the cases of post-reform exploitation and manipulation of peasant movements under capitalism have occurred where the movements were under the influence of, or dependent upon, political forces of the middle-class urban intelligentsia or of the bourgeoisie. Thus, we find not that the mass organization of the peasantry in the abstract is essential, but that such organization, specifically in alliance with the proletariat, is essential to protect the benefits of reform from erosion by certain very common patterns of capitalist development. Too many organizations of struggle have been transformed into patronage networks for bourgeois politicians. Those who seek capitalist development without an exploited peasantry, or without the exploitation of the proletarianized mass of the peasantry by the enriched few, may be trying to have their cake and eat it. Socialist development, too, has its short- and medium-term burdens, but some may find the distribution of these burdens more palatable. If socialist development is sought, then the argument for a rural mass movement under strong working-class influence is all the stronger; if such a movement is not forthcoming, the peasantry may be so alienated from socialist aims that if it is not repressed it may endanger forever the prospects for a transition to socialism. It is on account of the early concern for peasant organization, for 'penetration of the natural village', that the Chinese experience emerges in a far more favourable light than that of the Soviet Union (Bernstein, 1967; Schurmann, 1971; Lewin, 1968), where the Communist Party showed so little capacity for peasant organization.

The scope of this volume is limited to capitalist land reforms. Even the Chinese Reform – in the period covered by Geoffrey Shillinglaw – was very much a capitalist one, liberating productive forces and human beings from the extra-economic constraints exercised by landlords. But a few words of clarification must be said, in conclusion, about land reform and socialism.

Under capitalism, the redistribution of rights in land is eventually succeeded by the rise of capitalist farming, and of a rural proletariat; under socialism it is succeeded by collectivization or strong state control of the circulation of commodities and of investment. In both cases a change in the structure of production is sought. Redistribution of rights in land does not imply redistribution of economic roles among individuals;[1] rather it allows them to continue in the same roles as before, under less onerous conditions. This applies as much to the lifting of feudal constraints as to the transformation of a latifundium into a production co-operative. As far as collectivization is concerned, it is only in a relatively advanced capitalist agriculture, such as Cuba's, that the 'individualist' stage can be realistically skipped. Collectivization implies that the family loses its role as the unit of decision-making, and the father loses his unquestioned authority as primary decision-maker. The rationality of Chayanov's non-capitalist peasant family economy, yields, at least, to that of the labourers on the farm as a whole, and at most, to the interests of the society as a whole, interpreted more or less democratically by a Planning Commission.

Collective agriculture is not, however, a sufficient defining characteristic of socialism, nor is peasant farming an insurmountable stumbling block to be avoided at all costs in the period of transition. In Peru, production co-operatives are conceived as one basis of an emerging corporate state – in China peasant farming was the first step on the road to socialism. Indeed a capitalist system need have little difficulty in harbouring production co-operatives, while premature collectivization might well create unnecessary obstacles in a transition to socialism (cf. Chile). In both cases, it is essential to consider the laws of circulation of commodities in the economy, and the exercise of political power. What is the class basis of that power? How is it exercised? The Chinese concentration on psychological procedures such as 'speak bitterness', 'unleashing', 'free flowing', *fanshen* (see Shillinglaw's paper and Hinton, 1972) tells us that the political perspective imprinted on the process of redistribution of land counted for much in the transition to socialism: right from the start emphasis was given to mutual education of peasants and cadres,[2] and to the

1. I am indebted to R. P. Dore for this phrasing.
2. One of Hinton's chapters is entitled: 'Who shall educate the educators?' Despite Herculean efforts at interpretation of what

development of various forms of co-operation, starting from the most elementary – the Mutual Aid Teams. Conversely, in Chile one finds the existence of forms of co-operation apparently more 'advanced' than in post-liberation China, but, despite strenuous efforts, a sense of political perspective is missing and there is insufficient success in changing the peasants' consciousness.

If the perspective imprinted on the process of land reform by political forces is important, so must be the general path of development. Even reforms which bear superficial resemblances to one another can carry fundamentally different meanings. It is otiose to discuss alternative methods of redistribution of income and structural change in agriculture on grounds of 'efficiency' without taking into account the prevailing ideology of development in the society as a whole, without considering the interests of the ruling élites and the classes they are likely to defend: to proceed thus is to encourage those who would seek to install the 'Jugoslav model' in Chile, the 'Swedish model' in Peru, the 'kibbutz model' in the Ecuadorian Andes, or indeed the 'American model' in Vietnam.

References

Bernstein, Thomas, 'Leadership and Mass Mobilization in the Soviet and Chinese Collectivization Campaigns of 1929–30 and 1955–6: a comparison', *China Quarterly*, **31**, July–September 1967.

Béteille, André, *Caste, Class and Power*, Berkeley, 1965.

Carroll, Thomas, 'Land Reform as an Explosive Force in Latin America', *Explosive Forces in Latin America* (eds. John J. Tepaske and Sydney N. Fisher), Ohio State U.P., 1964; reprinted in Stavenhagen (ed.), 1970.

Dasgupta, Biplab, 'Gandhism in West Bengal', *Journal of Contemporary Asia*, **2**, 3, 1972.

Feder, Ernest, 'Societal Opposition to Peasant Movements and its Effects on Farm People in Latin America', *Peasant Movements in Latin America* (ed. Henry Landsberger), Cornell U.P., 1969.

---

little evidence there is, ignorance remains the hallmark of much of what is said in favour of and against the Chinese revolution; we must guard against the recent tendency to convey an idealized picture of China seen through the rose-tinted spectacles of vicarious North American puritanism.

Feder, Ernest, 'Counterreform', *Agrarian Problems and Peasant Movements in Latin America* (ed. Rudolfo Stavenhagen), Doubleday, New York, 1970.
Flores, Edmundo, 'The Economics of Land Reform', *International Labour Review*, **42**, 1, July 1965; reprinted in Stavenhagen (ed.), 1970.
Gough, Kathleen, 'The Social Structure of a Tanjore Village', *India's Villages* (ed. M. N. Srinivas), Asia Publishing House, Delhi, 1955.
Gutelman, Michel, *Réforme et Mystification Agraires en Amérique Latine: le cas du Mexique*, Paris, 1971.
Hinton, William, *Fanshen: a Documentary of Revolution in a Chinese Village*, New York, 1966; Penguin, Harmondsworth, 1972.
Huntington, Samuel P., *Political Order in Changing Societies*, Yale U.P., 1968.
Khosrovi, K., 'La réforme agraire et l'apparition d'une nouvelle classe en Iran', *Etudes Rurales*, **34**, April–June 1969.
Korbonski, A., *The Politics of Socialist Agriculture in Poland: 1945–1960*, Columbia U.P., New York and London, 1965.
Ladejinsky, Wolf, 'The Green Revolution in Bihar: the Kosi Area', *Economic and Political Weekly*, **4**, 39, September 1969.
Laporte, Robert, James Petras and Jeffrey C. Rinehart, 'The Concept of Agrarian Reform and its Role in Development', *Comparative Studies in Society and History*, **13**, 1, October 1971.
Lehmann, David, 'Political Incorporation versus Political Stability: the Case of the Chilean Agrarian Reform, 1965–1970', *Journal of Development Studies*, **7**, 4, July, 1971.
—, 'Generalizing about Peasant Movements', *Ibid.*, **9**, 2, 1973.
Lewin, Moshe, *Le Paysannerie et le Pouvoir Soviétique*, Mouton, Paris and The Hague, 1966.
Powell, John Duncan, *Political Mobilization of the Venezuelan Peasant*, Harvard U.P., 1971.
Pugh, Ramón, 'Venezuela: el caso de Barbecho', *Estudios de la Realidad Campesina: Cooperación y Cambio* (ed. Orlando Fals-Borda), United Nations Research Institute for Social Development, Geneva, 1970.
Schurmann, Franz, *Ideology and Organization in Communist China* (revised edn.), Berkeley, 1971.
Stavenhagen, Rodolfo (ed.), *Agrarian Problems and Peasant Movements in Latin America*, Doubleday, New York, 1970.
Stavenhagen, Rudolfo, 'Social Aspects of Agrarian Structure in Mexico', in Stavenhagen (ed.), 1970.
Tarrow, Sydney, *Peasant Communism in Southern Italy*, Yale U.P., 1967.
Womack, John, Jr., *Zapata and the Mexican Revolution*, New York, 1968.

Two

Agrarian Reform and Military Reformism in Peru

Ramón Zaldívar

I. Introduction

1. *Political Background*

We begin with a short résumé of political events in modern Peru, beginning at the turn of this century, when the country was slowly recovering from the effects of the war with Chile. With the First World War came the eclipse of the British Empire and the penetration of North American imperialism. As a result of the economic vacuum left by this change, and, as an economic alternative to American penetration, there arose new strata of the bourgeoisie, independent of the traditional agrarian bourgeoisie and therefore also, to some extent, of imperialism, with which they had conflicting interests; thus, the way was laid open for capitalist development based on radical reforms.

These nationalist strata found a political expression in APRA,[1] whose programme, aimed basically at 'the cotton and sugar barons', envisaged reforms for the achievement of capitalist development. As lack of capital impedes such development, APRA accepted the need for foreign capital, but sought to limit its freedom, calling for the development of a Latin American front to counter-balance imperialism.

Yet APRA was to be prevented from coming to power and applying its programme by the modern land-owning sector of the bourgeoisie, who were strengthened by their ever-increasing commitment to American imperialism, in return for which they obtained export quotas, loans and technical assistance; and also by the military veto, arising apparently from the killing of soldiers by APRA,[2] but more fundamentally from the military's desire to preserve the traditional order.

1. *Alianza Popular Revolucionaria Americana.*
2. During the Trujillo uprising, 1932.

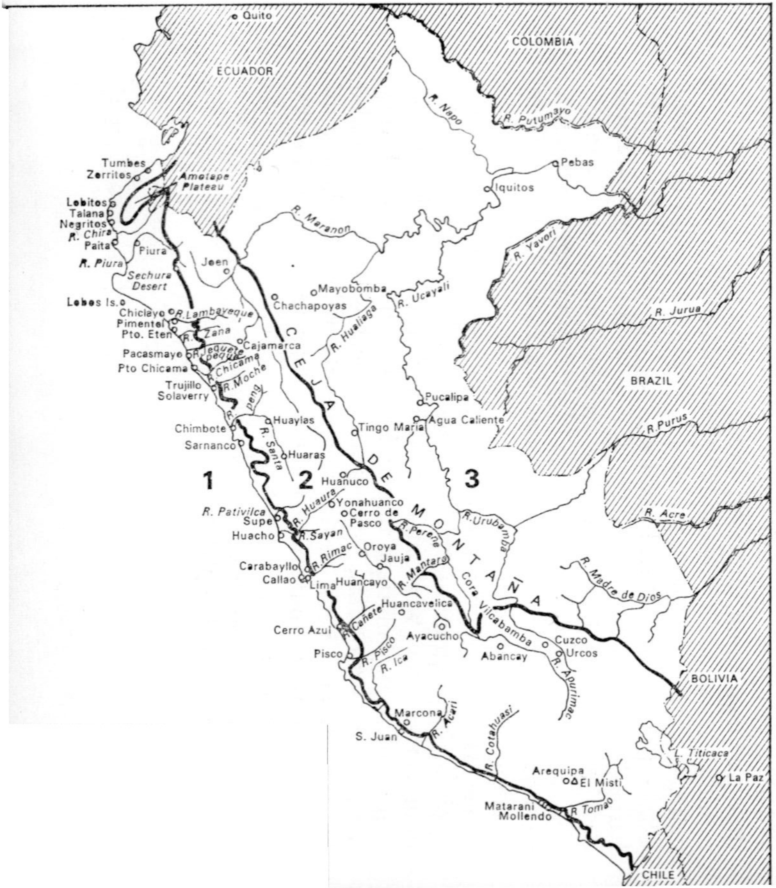
Quito
ECUADOR
COLOMBIA
BRAZIL
BOLIVIA
CHILE
R. Napo
R. Putumayo
Pebas
Iquitos
R. Maranon
R. Yavori
R. Ucayali
R. Jurua
R. Purus
R. Acre
R. Hualiaga
Tumbes
Zerritos
Amotape Plateau
Lobitos
Talana
Negritos
R. Chira
Paita
Piura
R. Piura
Sechura Desert
Jaen
Lobos Is.
Chiclayo
R. Lambayeque
Pimentel
Pto. Eten
R. Zana
Cajamarca
Pacasmayo
Pto Chicama
R. Chicama
Trujillo
Solaverry
R. Moche
Chachapoyas
Mayobomba
CEJA DE MONTAÑA
Chimbote
Sarnanco
Huaylas
R. Santa
Huaras
Tingo Maria
Pucalipa
Agua Caliente
1
2
3
Huanuco
Yonahuanco
Cerro de Pasco
R. Pativilca
Supe
Huacho
R. Huaura
R. Sayan
R. Rimac
R. Perene
R. Urubamba
Oroya
Jauja
Carabayllo
Callao
Lima
Huancayo
R. Mantaro
Huancavelica
R. Cañete
Cerro Azul
Cora Vilcabamba
R. Madre de Dios
Ayacucho
Abancay
Cuzco
Urcos
R. Apurimac
Pisco
R. Pisco
R. Ica
Marcona
R. Acari
S. Juan
R. Cotahuasi
L. Titicaca
La Paz
Arequipa
El Misti
Matarani
Mollendo
R. Tomo

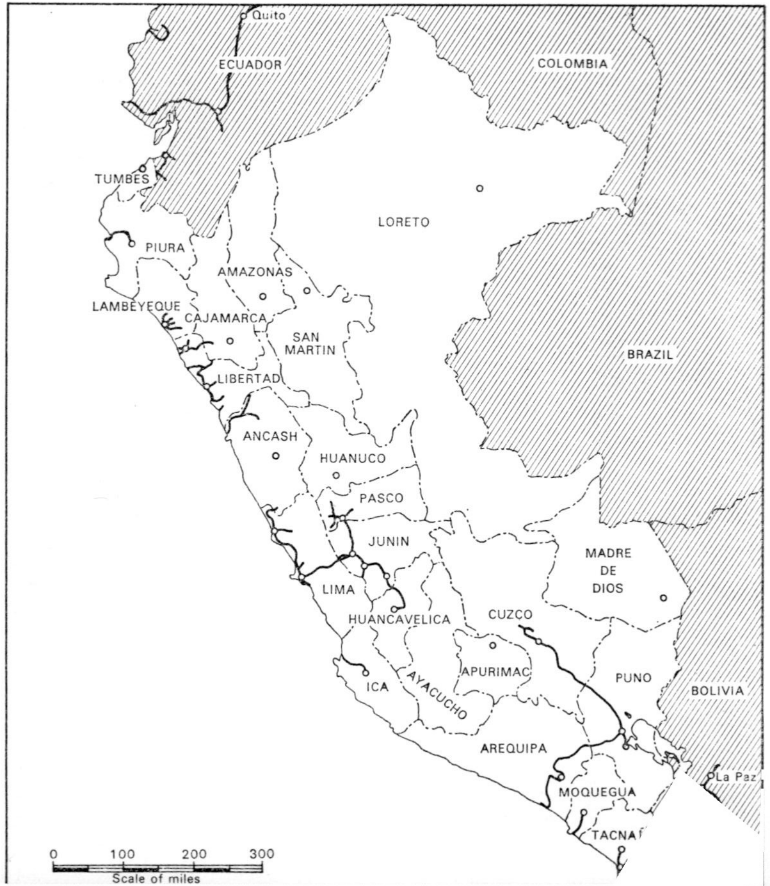
Quito
ECUADOR
COLOMBIA
BRAZIL
BOLIVIA
La Paz
TUMBES
LORETO
PIURA
AMAZONAS
LAMBEYEQUE
CAJAMARCA
SAN MARTIN
LIBERTAD
ANCASH
HUANUCO
PASCO
JUNIN
LIMA
HUANCAVELICA
MADRE DE DIOS
CUZCO
APURIMAC
AYACUCHO
ICA
PUNO
AREQUIPA
MOQUEGUA
TACNA
0
100
200
300
Scale of miles

The agrarian bourgeoisie showed enough vitality to resist the crisis of 1929–34, thanks to the expansion of technically advanced export crops and American aid. During the Second World War and the Korean War, and under the Odría dictatorship (1948–56), with its land-owning ministers such as Guimoye, this hegemony was preserved and reinforced. By 1956, after years of repression and exclusion from power, APRA made a pact with Prado, the candidate of the bourgeoisie, and in 1963 with its old persecutors, the Odriístas, thus renouncing its long-standing radical programme. Yet the APRA-Prado alliance also reflected the disappearance of the enmity between landowners on the one hand, and industrialists and financiers on the other, as the agricultural sector lost its dominant position in the economy.

Once the export boom produced by the Second World War and the Korean War was over, the radicalized sectors reappeared as an alternative as the economic and social problems of the country again became acute and the issue of social reform returned to the forefront. It had been raised already, albeit timidly, at the Punta del Este Conference in 1962, under the auspices of the U.S.A.[1] Liberalization and structural reform were now seen as the best ways to enlarge the market for American capital and the development of certain industrial activities, one way of achieving them.

Thus, *Acción Popular* (AP) arose as the instrument of the new wave of radical bourgeois groups in their search for power. APRA having joined the reactionaries and the most servile pro-imperialist groups, AP received support from the Social Progressive Movement, a group formed by the intelligentsia of the nationalist bourgeoisie, of the petit-bourgeois Christian Democrats (DC) and of the equally petit-bourgeois revisionist left (PC *Unidad*, FLN, etc.).

Since 1953, the ideas of the national bourgeoisie had found their way into the army through CAEM (the Centre of Advanced Military Studies). Soldiers who passed through this school began to take up positions which, at other times and with a different emphasis, had been favoured by APRA. Senior officers seized power in 1962, cutting off the advance of APRA who had won the elections and, during their one year of government, carried out an agrarian reform in La Convención valley, with the aim of neutralizing the peasant movement.[2] Then, in 1963, they handed over power to the alliance of AP and the Christian Democrats led by Belaúnde (AP–DC), new standard-bearers of bourgeois

1. Charter of Punta del Este, 'Aims', 4 and 6.
2. Associated with the name of Hugo Blanco; see Hobsbawn (1969).

reformism, who, unlike APRA, enjoyed the benefit of military support.

The inability of AP and the Christian Democrats to carry out their programme of reforms soon became apparent, and the opposition, made up of APRA and the Odriístas, forced them to defend the interests of the traditional bourgeoisie. Thus, the second attempt at bourgeois development was frustrated around that time and the AP–DC alliance broke up, and sub-divided. AP split into a big-bourgeois group and a radical bourgeois one (led by Edgardo Seoane) and DC, in its turn, split into a big-bourgeois group, representing the large Lima businessmen and another petit-bourgeois one. This split opened the way for the triumph of APRA, now the defender of the traditional bourgeoisie. It would have meant once again the death of a reformist programme, so desired by the nationalist bourgeoisie, the supporters of capitalist industrial development in Peru, despite the existence of favourable economic conditions provided by the fishing boom and the copper mining. Two similar great opportunities had been lost in the past century, and now a third was to be lost, thus disappointing those liberal bourgeois intellectuals and their disciples, the military, who believed that autonomous capitalist development was possible in Peru.

The *Acta de Talara* scandal[1] was the last straw in a series of sell-outs by Belaúnde, and presented the military with an opportunity to intervene. So it was that in October 1968, led by President Velasco Alvarado, they carried out a *coup d'état* distinguished from previous ones by a number of characteristics: (1) it was carried out by representatives of all sectors of the Armed Forces; (2) their programme contained 'structural reforms' directed 'against privileged groups'; (3) the coup was not followed, as was the custom, by the immediate repression of radical or leftist sectors; on the contrary, the army sought to attract them; (4) among the first acts of the government were the military take-over of Talara and the establishment of diplomatic relations with socialist countries. These actions provoked doubts both on the left and on the right, but eventually it became clear that the military represented but a new version of bourgeois developmentalism.[2]

1. An agreement between the Belaúnde government and the International Petroleum Company resolving an age-old dispute over oil-rights. The agreement was reputed to be highly prejudicial to Peruvian interests, but the crucial final page of the document was 'lost'.
2. *Desarrollismo*: a term used to describe the development theories

The unexpected take-over of Talara, a highly nationalist measure, brought about an abrupt realignment of political forces. The bourgeois parties could not keep quiet, much less oppose such an act of restitution, and pronounced themselves in favour. The Communist Party, who had hoped a thousand times for a bourgeois-democratic revolution, and had failed to understand the government's reformism at first, accusing them of being *gorilas*,[1] had to step down and give them their support, especially after the establishment of diplomatic relations with the U.S.S.R.

2. *The Political Context of the Agrarian Reform Law*

The struggles of the working class were not at their peak during this period, owing mainly to the pro-employer leadership which APRA was developing in the CTP and also to the bureaucratic leadership of the CGTP. Both unions were involved in legalistic battles and avoided mass mobilization.

The peasants, for their part, found themselves on the ebb-tide of the glorious movements of ten years ago. But the pressure they exerted has, in the long run, been the principal factor in triggering off the agrarian reform.

Between 1955 and 1965 servile relations of production were in evident decline, as a result of seizures and sub-divisions of *haciendas* (large semi-feudal estates). Likewise the sugar-workers were gaining in strength since the wave of unionization of 1956–1964. The intention of the military to avoid the rise of peasant movements at whatever cost, is shown in the repression of peasants and students at such places as Cospán, Raúl, Cañete, Cayaltí and elsewhere.

The Agrarian Reform Decree-Law (No. 17716) was passed on 24 June 1969 'Day of the Peasant'. The very radical Presidential speech which accompanied its publication seemed revolutionary to many. The Law was a great improvement over that passed by the AP-DC alliance, especially with regard to the expropriation of the land of the modern *haciendas*, together with plant for raw materials processing, since this meant the expropriation of all the large *haciendas* on the coast, the central nucleus of Peruvian agriculture. On the other hand, the government's eager defence of private property was also evident, as was its desire to develop

elaborated in the United Nations Economic Commission for Latin America (ECLA), based on structural change in a capitalist framework.

1. *Gorilas.* A term of abuse commonly used to refer to pro-American fascist military dictatorships in Latin America. (Ed.) Many terms and acronyms are explained in the glossary at the end of this chapter.

a modernized middle class in the countryside and to keep peasant movements under control.

In spite of these clues to the future, several sectors of a widely based and diffuse left, especially the pro-Moscow and the radical petit-bourgeois sectors, devoted themselves to working feverishly for the Law. Their insistence that, while this process was not itself revolutionary, it was certainly leading towards revolution, was to be put to the test in the following months.

II. A Summary of Achievements in the first two years

The character of the agrarian reform and its effect on the working class, must not be interpreted on the basis of official texts or government speeches, but rather through analysis of its application in practice. It is therefore vital to analyse the criteria, instances and social groups on the basis of which the reform is being applied. We shall do this, with reference to six different methods of application.

1. *The Transformation of the Coastal Sugar Plantations into Co-operatives*

When the reform process was set in motion the share of sugar in gross domestic product was not decreasing but fluctuating wildly, while its share in exports was decreasing. Productivity was relatively static, as a result of decapitalization by the owners. Vast amounts of foreign capital were tied up in sugar, on account not of the attractiveness of sugar production itself but rather of the processing industries annexed to it. The estates were under pressure from unions to concede higher standards of living, and wage concessions made by the estate owners after 1964 were sustained by the distribution of the Cuban sugar quota among satellite countries; however, by 1968, exports had fallen appreciably and the prosperity which made such concessions possible had disappeared. Furthermore, all the plantations had a transient or under-employed population, made up either of the workers' relatives or of migrants eking out a precarious existence on the outskirts of their urban centre.

Sugar dominated the agricultural sector on account of its high level of technology, of its economic power and of the foreign origin of most of its capital, but it was no longer preponderant in the national economy. Indeed the political influence of the sugar companies exceeded their economic significance. This was due to the size of these enterprises, to the presence of the most advanced forms of union organization and to the concentration within them of workers with a high degree of class-consciousness.

The sugar-based industrial complexes as a whole do not seem to have been on the verge of bankruptcy, but the sugar companies, when their accounts are considered separately from the paper mills, distilleries and factories producing plastics and paint, certainly were; since the same people owned both, they were not bankrupt.

The expropriation of the sugar complexes can be considered a nationalist action, since the majority of shares in the sugar industry belonged to foreign companies. But, under pressure from local and foreign capitalists, the government at first left untouched the industrial processing enterprises which were dependent on by-products of sugar refinery, such as bagasse, molasses and wax – the very enterprises which had the highest rates of profit. In the end these industries were taken over, but they were paid for in cash, on terms far more favourable than those governing the expropriation of the land.

The transformation of the farms into co-operatives can be divided into three stages. The first is the intervention of the estates, started in June 1969. This involved state control of the companies, with the purpose of carrying out the technical, legal and political plans drawn up by the government in accordance with the criteria of maintaining order and productivity. It is this stage which has the revolutionary image, because it came by surprise and brought with it 'revolutionary' agents and priests, to stir up the workers' consciousness with the idea that they had been liberated for ever and that a new era had begun; they used radical Christian language but were careful not to 'fall back' into Marxism. In October 1969 a great meeting in Trujillo, centre of the sugar region, was seen by the large number of people present as the ultimate proof of the death of APRA, which had hitherto dominated the unions.

But the revolutionary image had a bourgeois reverse-side to it: of the twenty-eight *interventores* (managers appointed by the State), the majority were former employees of the Grace Company which owned three enormous plantations. Grace was the first foreign company to declare its satisfaction with the Agrarian Reform Law. The government pressed the workers to hold reconciliation meetings with the engineers, long-standing enemies of the unions, seeking thereby to preserve the symbols of exploitation. The workers were told that now they were owners, the continued existence of the union was pointless: police vigilance became more marked and many *interventores* began to behave like the former bosses.

The workers who had the use of a piece of land – and thus tended to support the bosses – were given the choice of handing it over or leaving the co-operative; this forced them into the arms of APRA which was keeping up a steady flow of criticism of the government. In the interests of efficiency and sound administration, it was decided that only permanent workers could be members of the co-operative, thereby perpetuating the internal divisions among the workers.

At this stage the organizing committees of the co-operatives were set up. They worked on the premise that the engineers and administrators, as well as the workers, would be members and, in the total absence of mass mobilization and power, this meant confirming the advantages enjoyed by the former group. The results of the elections for these committees can be seen in the following table:

TABLE 1 *Results of the Elections of Organizing Committees in 3 Plantations*

	Engineers	*Administrators*	*Workers*	*Total*
Cayaltí	14	—	1	15
Laredo	7	4	25	36
Paramonga	3	5	6	14

Several engineers were always elected to the committees due to government pressure, but also because the majority of labourers accepted the premise that a labourer is not and never will be able to run an enterprise; and in all the committees the president was an engineer or high-level technician; the workers were generally in a minority on the committee and these were *apristas* and pro-employer, even more reactionary than the government.

In this phase the Co-operative Development Office (ONDECOOP) and the Agrarian Reform Office clashed head-on, the former favouring co-operativization of a petit-bourgeois socialist variety, and sponsored by the government as a means of hitting at APRA; and the latter favouring the conversion of the *haciendas* into SAIS,[1] which, although as yet ill-defined, would clearly emerge as some kind of co-operative, possibly with non-workers and even capitalists as members. The battle was won in November by ONDECOOP,

1. 'Agricultural Social Interest Societies' – see below, Section II, 4.

when the regulations governing agrarian co-operatives were published, establishing that:

a the plantations were not to be split up and were to be converted into production co-operatives;

b ownership of land and capital was to be in the hands of the co-operative;

c all permanent workers were to be members, including engineers and administrative staff;

d casual labourers were not to be members; casual labour was to be limited, giving the criterion of profitability preference over that of full employment;

e individual plots were to be forbidden within the co-operative (this had still not been applied by April 1971);

f the co-operative fund was to be used for annual payments to the former owners;

g each member was to have a certificate of contributions to a central fund, the initial payment for which was to be the total amount of social benefits accumulated by each individual member (*Agricultural Co-operative Regulations*, Section III);

h the Agrarian Reform Office was to supervise the co-operatives. (A provision which they later took advantage of to edge out ONDECOOP.)

A second stage starts with the publication of the co-operative regulations and ends with the setting-up of the co-operative and the handing-over of the plantation to it.

When the organizing committees were already in being, the government appointed special temporary administrative committees made up of delegates from the Ministry of Agriculture, the Agrarian Reform Office, the Agricultural and Industrial State banks and a few delegates from the workers, which always meant engineers. Co-operative training was carried out under these organizing committees, extremely quickly and with the following aims in view:

a to consolidate and prolong ONDECOOP's victory over the Agrarian Reform Office, blocking any ideas about forming SAIS;

b to explain the functioning of the co-operative to the different sectors of the expropriated enterprise;

c to strictly control and detect 'saboteurs', meaning *apristas* (as extreme right-wingers) and revolutionaries;

d to promote the emergence of leaders who were neither *apristas* nor *vanguardistas*,[1] because the latter were the only group seeking to mobilize the masses in the area.

1. Members of *Vanguardia Revolucionaria*, a left-wing revolutionary movement.

During this period the 'Agrarian Reform Control System' (*Sistema de Conducción de la Reforma Agraria*) took shape, made up of soldiers from the Military Intelligence Service, entrusted with the ideological control which, although the government denies it, was simply a policy of repression of the left, since APRA presented only the vaguest opposition.

This phase ended with the establishment of the co-operatives of Tumán, Cayaltí and Laredo, as experiments. The experiment seems to have gone wrong. Assemblies were formed with 120 delegates, but not all of them were elected by the workers. In Tumán the government took it upon itself to appoint ninety-eight out of the 120, in Cayaltí twenty-eight and in Laredo seventy-six. The justification of this procedure was that by guaranteeing the redemption of the bonds, they had put the national interest at stake, and therefore had to appoint the delegates in order to safeguard it. By drawing this distinction between the 'country' and the workers, the government demonstrated that it was in fact pursuing the imposition of state control in the sugar complexes. Table 2 shows us this 'combination' of elected delegates and government appointees.

TABLE 2 *Composition of Delegates to Co-operative Assemblies*

		Elected by the Sugar-Workers	*Appointed by the Government*	*Total*
Tumán	(June 1970)	22	98	120
Cayaltí	(,,)	98	22	120
Laredo	(,,)	44	76	120
Paramonga	(Sept. 1970)	32	88	120
Cartavio	(,,)	55	65	120
Casagrande	(,,)	24	96	120
		275	445	720

Long-standing unionists were prevented from standing as candidates in the elections. On futile and far-fetched pretexts, it was laid down that 25 per cent of the delegates had to be engineers or staff technicians. This, on top of big wage increases for engineers, and the despotic and disdainful policy of the military 'controllers', finally exasperated the workers who, in Cayaltí and particularly in Tumán, provoked a series of incidents when the

Minister of Agriculture came to formally hand over the complexes.

Blame for the incidents was placed on ONDECOOP, which had had the audacity and vision to use university students in Lambayeque in the co-operative training courses. The students had been used by the government in its fight against APRA – a task made more difficult by the very political narrowness of the military 'controllers' and the vast apparatus of repression deployed in the complexes. When they were no longer useful, the students were sent home. Some of them managed to carry out important work in awakening revolutionary consciousness, but only in so far as they came into open conflict with the government. Not surprisingly in the light of the underlying similarities between them, the military have, wherever possible, arrived at a *modus vivendi* with young *apristas*.

And so the first year of agrarian reform in the sugar zone came to a close. The government worked out its policy for the other complexes on the basis of what it had learned in the first three. An administration with a three-branch system of authority was established: (1) the Control System (*Sistema de Conducción*) staffed by the military, generally from the Intelligence Service; (2) the Control Committees (*Comités de Vigilancia*) formed by management and technical staff, whose outlook was bureaucratic and technocratic and which were directly linked to the Executive Secretariat of the agrarian reform where the crucial decisions to do with the co-operativization process were in fact taken; (3) an Administrative Council with no real executive capacity in the co-operative, elected by the assembly.

However, in Cayaltí the members of the Control Committee were on the point of being expelled from the co-operative for criticizing the conduct of the Administrative Council, which is dominated by engineers; furthermore a strike was called to prevent the union leaders' exemption from normal duties from being abolished. Something similar happened in Pucalá, where the leaders went to prison because a strike was regarded as sabotage of the agrarian reform and hence punishable by law. At Christmas and New Year the worker-members of Paramonga demanded a rise from 1,000 to 2,000 soles in their end-of-year bonus, agreeing that this should be regarded as an advance on the profits. When the Administrative Council – also dominated by engineers – refused, they called a stoppage which led to the imprisonment of their leaders and humiliation for the workers. The leaders were released from prison in May 1971.

As early as the summer of 1971, the Tumán assembly, in which progressive delegates have a strong influence, showed that appreciable increases in workers' wages are no obstacle to the realization of an investment plan worked out by technicians. They obtained substantial increases, but their legal adviser ran the risk of being seized by the police, and there were serious incidents in March which led to the imprisonment of the leaders, who were only released after a week of 'intensive explanations' designed to intimidate them.

Thus, early in 1971 the workers became aware that the co-operatives, as established, enabled them to be grossly exploited, in order to guarantee payment of the debt to the former owners and to increase the State's tax receipts. It is clear that there is a class struggle between worker members and engineer members. The ridiculous increase of 4 soles a day[1] that the government fixed as a maximum reveals its desire to hold down wages so that the amount received as a share of profits (8,500 soles in Laredo at the end of 1970) equals what they would get if wages had gone up as in the years when there was still a right to strike. Since the sugar co-operatives were set up any claims arising there pass directly to ONDECOOP, and ONDECOOP will only deal with individual claims. Can more proof be given that the government is seeking to destroy the unions and return to the times when everything was settled directly and individually with the employer?

At the root of these conflicts is the increase in wage differentials. The manager of Pomalca, the former administrator and faithful servant of the De la Piedra clan, raised his own salary from 18,600 soles in February 1970 to 40,927 soles in October of the same year,[2] and Table 3 opposite offers further evidence for Paramonga.

In contrast to these increases which get larger at the top of the scale, the workers only got a rise of 4 soles a day. In Tumán the technicians, members of the co-operative, earn an average of 7,032 soles a week, ranging from 2,604 to 18,334 soles. Tumán is in the best financial circumstances of all the complexes, thanks to an exceptional rate of capitalization. Nonetheless we show the distribution of their surplus or profits, in order to show the relative shares of the State, the employers (who receive payment of the debt) and the workers.

The State is the biggest beneficiary, together with the land-owners who receive payments on the debt; then come the workers. Taking into account that there are 2,100 workers, the 33,123,000

1. 44 soles = U.S. $1.00.
2. *Bulletin*, 3, of the Education Committee of Sugar Co-operative 38, Pomalca, March 1971.

TABLE 3 *Wage and Salary Increases in Paramonga*

Size of present wage/salary	*Size of increase*
(soles)	
under 4,000	600
4,000 – 6,000	700
6,000 – 8,000	800
8,000 – 10,000	1,000
10,000 – 12,000	1,200
12,000 – 15,000	1,300
15,000 – 20,000	1,400

(Source: *El Cañero Combatiente*, 5, 23 March 1971.)

TABLE 4 *Distribution of Gross Profits*[1] *in the Tumán Sugar Co-operative* (in soles)

I. Gross Profits:		228,411,000
Less: Land tax	76,000,000	
Agrarian Debt[2]	42,000,000	118,000,000
Net Profit[1]		110,411,000
II. Net Profit is distributed thus:		
Reserve Fund	12,206,000	
Co-operative Education Fund	5,520,000	
Social Security Fund	11,042,000	
Investment Fund	43,000,000	
Co-operative Development Fund	5,520,000	77,288,000
Remainder, to be distributed among members:		33,123,000

1. The original term is *remanente bruto*, meaning the difference between income and expenditure. The term *utilidad*, which means 'profit', is avoided because the enterprise is not classed as a capitalist one. A more faithful translation might be 'surplus', but this gives rise to further confusion in English. (Ed.)
2. Payment of land to former owners, in annual instalments. (Ed.)

soles will amount to an individual surplus of 15,500 soles. The government hopes that this surplus, being much larger than that distributed in other co-operatives, which may have none at all, will appease the workers.

To these economic trends should be added changes in the mechanisms of decision-making within the co-operatives. The Executive Secretariat of the agrarian reform, which acted as a sort of dictator over the Administrative Councils, has been replaced by the Central Organization of Sugar Co-operatives of Peru (CECOAAP), constituted under a new set of rules by the same men and characterized by the same neo-paternalist tendencies of the technicians.

As far as unions are concerned, the government, in its eagerness to destroy them, has set up 'circles' of workers and technicians under the leadership of a delegate and advised by the government, with the purpose of imparting instruction in co-operativism and of channelling demands, in the hope of removing the unions' basic function. The reply from the workers has been one of almost total indifference, the delegates have shown no interest and the technicians do not like to attend. Thus, this corporativist technique, which sets out to join opposing classes harmoniously in a single multi-class body, and to destroy the class organizations of the workers, such as unions, has so far met with no success.

Finally, with the establishment of the co-operatives, the System of Control ceased to be necessary, and was abolished in December 1970. In its place a new structure has been assembled to maintain 'vigilance'. It consists of a *Sistema de Asesoramiento y Fiscalización de Cooperativas Agrarias de Producción*[1] which places a military representative, not only in the sugar complexes, but also in the SAIS in the Central and Southern Sierra. At departmental[2] level, this system functions through a committee presided over by a senior military officer and made up of the local heads of ONDECOOP, the Chief of the Police Investigation Department and others.

Thus in the second year, the co-operatives acquired their shape to come, and the actions of the workers reflected an increasingly clear understanding of the situation. The process is none other than a form of State control, since the control exercised by the CECOAAP technicians and the technicians who dominate the administrative councils, as well as the repressive character of the vigilance committees, are designed to ensure the payment of high taxes to the State, and to maintain a bigger bureaucracy (Education Fund for ONDECOOP, Co-operative Development Fund for the same purpose and a large number of

1. 'Advisory and Control System for Agricultural Production Co-operatives'. In mid March 1972 this body passed under the control of SINAMOS (see glossary). (Ed.)
2. Provincial level, as in the French *département*.

CECOAAP functionaries paid by the co-operatives). At the same time the process is in the interests of the bourgeoisie, in that it sets out to guarantee the punctual payment of the agrarian debt to the local and foreign capitalists, who owned most of the shares in the sugar enterprises. The workers, as partners of the State, receive part of the profits, which is the price paid by the bourgeoisie and its government to pacify and hopefully to 'bourgeoisify' the working class, but it hardly compensates for inflation.

The workers on the plantation remain the principal obstacle to the success of this ambiguous approach. In 1970–1 they have shown that they understand that the conflict is no longer between the owner of the *hacienda* and the workers, but between these and the technical staff, who have always served the bourgeoisie and its State. The tacit ban on strikes with the fairy story about 'sabotaging the agrarian reform' has obliged the workers to undertake new forms of resistance, which seem to express a demand for genuine and truly autonomous co-operatives, in which the union participates as a body for protecting the 'proletarian members' against the arbitrary behaviour and bad faith of the 'white collar members'.[1]

2. *Private Parcelization of Land*

Article IX of the Reform Law laid down that the owners of *haciendas* could, on private initiative, that is, without State intervention, parcel up their *haciendas*, in order to reduce them to the size set as unexpropriable limit for the various provinces.[2] As the Law states that the agrarian reform will be carried out gradually, by areas, owners could parcel out the land before their region was declared an agrarian reform zone. The then Minister of Agriculture urged them to do this on his visits to Piura and Ica.

The 'floor' for expropriation varies between 150 and 200 hectares on the coast and between 15 and 330 hectares in the sierra. For cattle-farming areas it is fixed by the number of animals, ranging from 5,000 to 20,000 sheep or the equivalent in other species. These limits are pretty comfortable: an owner of 200 hectares of cotton on the coast is still a 'cotton baron'.

1. On 16 April 1972, SINAMOS organized new elections to the administrative bodies of the sugar co-operatives, abolishing government appointees, and introducing proportional representation for each (geographical) sector. Some old union leaders were elected to the Committees, and everything seems to have been quiet there since then. (Ed.)
2. A province is an administrative district within the department.

The size of properties regarded as unexpropriable is similar to, though larger than, what is known in the CIDA report as the large multi-family farm. We have tried to calculate the agricultural area affected by private sub-divisions, using the concept of 'multi-family' property. There were approximately 3,792 large properties in the country, occupying something like 76 per cent of the agricultural land (CIDA, pp. 35 and 41). Discounting 500 properties which could be converted into co-operatives and SAIS, and jungle land not liable to expropriation, some 35 per cent, or perhaps a little less, of the agricultural area of the country, could be affected by private sub-division. The number of proprietors who have actually carried out this operation is easy to estimate, but it is difficult to estimate how many workers suffered the consequences of this style of agrarian reform.[1]

In the period between June (when the Law was passed) and November 1969 when the section dealing with private parcelization was modified, an extraordinary number of lightning parcelizations took place, which exhibited the following characteristics:

a the parcelization could be by means of division of the land belonging to a limited company, according to the number of shares held by each member; by sub-division of the land, for sale; by splitting off parcels, and by other means;

b the sub-dividing enterprise was obliged first to dismiss all its workers, paying them the corresponding severance pay;

c the dismissed workers might or might not be rehired by the owners of the farms created by this process. A law passed by the previous government, which has not been rescinded by the present one, allows the employer to re-employ only those whom he chooses. Those who were not rehired but whose labour was needed, continued to work as temporary hands without social security benefits;

d the new *haciendas* tried to group the workers in small new housing compounds, thereby dispersing the larger old compounds and creating problems concerning schools, transport and so on;

e the unions were divided up into as many pieces as there were new properties and in some of them the number of rehired permanent workers was no longer sufficient to form a union or a union-organizing committee within the scope of the Law;

f the former permanent workers who had now become casual labourers were turned out of their houses, which the owner then tried to demolish or even burn down;

1. Figures based on CIDA, pp. 35 and 41.

g a lot of land was sold to foreign farmers, who are regarded as more dynamic;

h many parcelizations were fictitious, since in such cases the *haciendas* carry on functioning as though nothing had happened, even though now, from a strictly legal point of view, there are several different farms or companies instead of one.

It is important to point out that, owing to these escape clauses, not all the parcelizations will produce a flow of capital for industrialization (see Agrarian Reform Law, Article 181), because, since they are private contracts, the State cannot guarantee the redemption of the bonds and cannot therefore decide what happens to the funds thus mobilized. When it is a question of splitting up the company among shareholders, this simply involves dividing up the capital between several different companies, with no transfer of capital to industry at all.

This process was simply a continuation of what had been happening since 1965, under Belaúnde's law, and even before that. But during this period it received a tremendous stimulus, and practically did away with all estates above the limit of exemption. It has been said that the government was unaware of its evil effects, but this cannot be true, since outbreaks of protest were frequent and widespread. The medium-sized landowners who sub-divided their land 'conscientiously' maintain very good relations with the government, so much so that the Ministry of the Interior has appointed local authorities from among their number, such as the Mayors of Cañete, El Imperial and Quilmaná, in the Province of Cañete. News stories in the Lima and provincial dailies, popular demonstrations, and a number of peasant conferences denouncing its reactionary character, testify amply to the widespread protests aroused by the process.

The wave of protests, of which the Huando case (see below) and the fifty-day strike at Santa Catalina de Supe (neither of which was reported in the papers) are outstanding examples, obliged the government to modify Section IX, and introduce a new set of rules: (1) before the land is parcelled up, a plot must be reserved as common land for the permanent workers; and (2) a larger number of smaller properties are supposed to be formed. But, as the owners had already completed some 80–95 per cent of the parcelizations, and as the modification was not back-dated, this was merely a political gesture which did nothing to change the reactionary nature of the original provisions.

APRA had a large following and influence in the unions in this sector, particularly on the coast. But it betrayed them, by restricting itself to asking for guarantees that the workers would be rehired, and would not lose their status as permanent workers. FENCAP, a petit-bourgeois peasant organization run by APRA, pledged its support to the government in January 1970, a betrayal consistent with APRA's line in other sectors.

The Christian Democrats and the Communist Party behaved in the same way, although the latter did make a few pleas for the expropriation of the *haciendas*. Many unions, disillusioned with APRA, turned to the CGTP, which, with its neo-*Aprista* line, has got them tangled up in interminable bureaucratic negotiations, and has insisted that they support the government.

The case of Cañete will serve to demonstrate some aspects of this process.

The Case of Cañete

In the valley of Cañete there were thirty-eight estates larger than the unexpropriable limit, which in this case is 150 hectares. Parcelizations began in 1964 and were stepped up in 1969. From 1964 to June 1969, when Belaúnde's Agrarian Reform Law (No. 15037) was in force, more than half the area which is now regarded as subject to expropriation was parcelled out, and in four months in 1969 (June to November) 28 per cent of it was divided up.

Some of the political effects of this process can be judged from the following:

2,000 workers were turned into casual labourers, which meant roughly 40 per cent of the wage-earners in the valley.

There were three violent meetings of the Valley Workers' Confederation (CTV) in the four months from June to November 1969.

Seven small CTV meetings in *haciendas* and urban districts.

Two meetings organized by the government, through the Cochahuasi Co-operative, promising that a solution to the problems created by private parcelizations would be found, in order to dampen discontent.

Two appeasement meetings organized by an agrarian reform official and a member of the Intelligence Service.

Twelve leaders detained between June 1969 and January 1970.

During 1970 and 1971, those unions which still remained active in Cañete sought to have the parcelizations annulled, and they met with some success, for in late 1971 all parcelizations in the valley were annulled, along with those in several other coastal valleys.

The Case of Hacienda Huando[1]

Huando is an orange-growing *hacienda* in the Chancay valley, about an hour's journey to the north of Lima. It is the political and economic power-base of the prominent Graña family. It has 1,860 hectares and 533 workers. Parcelization began under Belaúnde's régime, with sales of land being made subject to subsequent legalization. When this government's Law (No. 17716) came out, the Graña family divided the *hacienda* into sixty-three lots, with State approval.

The workers objected to the parcelization, arguing on sound legal grounds. One of these was that at least 50 per cent of the total area, according to the Law, should be divided into lots of not less than nine hectares each, which evidently had not happened. The union called a strike in October 1970, and the workers held out bravely for 120 days, advertising their cause wherever they could. In February, one group clashed with the police on the Pan-American Highway, and another took refuge in the National University at La Molina. On 4 February 1971, the government annulled the parcelization. The protests of the sixty-three buyers, as well as those of the farmers in other valleys, were not long in coming.

The Agrarian Reform Office is wavering between alternatives: to hand the land over to the workers in a production co-operative, as in the sugar zone, or to take some of the sixty-three lots and hand them over to the workers, which would be a sort of mixed solution. The long silence, and the change of Minister of Agriculture, makes it even more difficult to find out what the final decision will be.

Private parcelization deprives the workers of any benefits and of access to the land; it establishes or consolidates the middle bourgeoisie, a weak and insecure group liable to ally with the landowners; and it means breaking up farms, which is a step backwards technologically.

Private parcelization is a common element of the Belaúnde and the Velasco régimes, and has taken on three different forms between 1964 and 1971. The former permitted unrestricted subdivision, leaving it up to the owner to decide on the number and size of the new parcels, with the single condition that they should

1. There was a very long delay while the agrarian reform authorities decided what to do in Huando. There were clashes in August 1971 between workers and the police, and the head of SINAMOS made a flying visit to calm things down. Some form of co-operative seems to be the official solution. (Ed.)

not be smallei than the family farm unit (three hectares).[1] A second variation came into force in June 1969, and lays down that all estates larger than the unexpropriable limit can divide at least half of their area into parcels not smaller than three family farm units (nine or 10·5 hectares), and that the rest can remain in units not larger than the unexpropriable limit (150 hectares on the coast, and from 150 to 330 hectares in the sierra). The third variation began in November 1969, when it laid down that before the parcelization is carried out a family farm unit shall be given to each permanent worker (casual labourers have no such right), and that it shall form a single parcel to be worked in common; then, parcels of two to fifteen family units and one large parcel not exceeding the unexpropriable limit may be formed.[2] Most parcelization took place under the first two variants, and by the time the third one came into force, only a few negligent *haciendas* were left. But the common element remains: to replace the big landowners with a middle bourgeoisie; and to weaken the permanent wage-labourers.

The November 1969 modification solved nothing, since it was not retroactive. The government has permitted escape-clauses and violations of the law all over the place, but only sees violators of the law when workers fight against it.

3. *The Conversion of Small Tenants into Owners of the Land*

This process, together with the private parcelizations, is the most consistent with the spirit of an Agrarian Reform Law which seeks to create a dominant class of medium and small private owners in rural society. Three types of landless peasants are to be turned into owners:

a *Feudatarios*, or peasants who work someone else's land and pay for it by performing personal services. They live grouped together in large traditional *haciendas*, and pay rent in labour;

b Sharecroppers, who work someone else's land and pay rent with part of the crop, in kind;

c Cash tenants, who pay the ground rent in money. Generally, these are found only on the coast, or in the most modernized areas.

In all three cases, the land under tenancy may be expropriated, provided that the parcels concerned are smaller than fifteen hectares on the coast and thirty in the sierra, and high jungle.

1. Law 15037, 15 May 1964. Article 4 of the regulations of Article 55 of Secton II. Supreme Decree No. 47.
2. Law 17716. Unified Text, Article 109.

Expropriation here affects two types of owner: (1) The owners of small parcels of land who make their living from another piece of land or activity. The law obliges them to make their living from only one piece of land or activity. The beneficiaries are satisfied, even though the police and bureaucracy make the procedure both difficult and cumbersome; (2) Owners of large traditional *haciendas* who exploit their *haciendas* without investing any capital, using the labour of their *colonos* to cultivate their land or to look after their cattle or receiving produce from share-croppers.

This process is not new, either, having formed the nucleus of the tepid Belaúnde reform. Its procedures are almost totally borrowed from the previous law, and big traditional *haciendas* have at least since 1950 been parcelling out and selling off land to the peasants, sometimes by agreement, sometimes by direct invasion of the land. Thus, the law turns out to be: (1) a legal recognition of the achievements of a long-standing peasant struggle, which has cost deaths and imprisonment; (2) a legalization of the rights of many *hacendados*, who had acquired the land illegally in the first place, since expropriation means that they will be paid in instalments for property whose ownership was in dispute; (3) a process of replacing labour-rent and rent in kind with cash payments in instalment for the land. This is still an absolute rent, but it will disappear once the land is paid for in twenty years. In certain cases, the payments on the bonds will amount to more than the former payments in services or in kind. The peasants will be bound more closely to the land, and will agree to pay up because of their desire for security, while the *hacendados* turn themselves into industrialists.

When a small proprietor is expropriated, the Law (Article 177) allows for a proportionately greater payment in cash and some in bonds. As there are hundreds of thousands of small proprietors, the government has no means of making even the first payment, which ranges from 25,000 to 50,000 soles. Thus the government has confined itself to registering the *feudatarios* (Article 188), and only in a very few cases has it completed the expropriation or adjudication process, since this would create a financial problem of truly gigantic proportions. Once they are registered *feudatarios* cannot be evicted by the owner of the land, except in very remote areas, or when the owner is very influential.

Traditional *haciendas* were already undergoing profound and critical changes, which have given rise to an enormous number of local variations. In certain areas, such as Pomabamba, Huamachuco and Huari, the owners had simply abandoned their estates, confident that the State would expropriate them and that they would duly receive their bonds as a matter of course.

In such cases, the peasants have reacted in a variety of ways, ranging from dividing up democratically the land and cattle they formerly had to tend for the owner, through numerous shady distributions favouring only the craftiest among them, often including the former administrator or local boss, to cases where neither land nor animals have been touched, for fear of being accused of 'sabotaging' the reform; in these cases, the land has remained untilled or the cattle have been slaughtered by the *hacendado*, contributing to the crisis in meat supplies to the cities in 1970.

In other cases, the peasants, after exhausting all legal channels, took over the *haciendas* and shared out the owners' lands or cattle, as in Pomacocha and Jajamarca de Huamanga. There have been attempts at co-operative work, but the dominant trend is towards private ownership. The government has been trying to extract a promise of payment, but this has been resisted.

On occasion, the government decrees an expropriation, and then casts around for a co-operative formula to include not one but several *haciendas*, and not only *haciendas* but smallholding *comunidades*[1] as well, trying to make the change-over to large modern enterprises in one single leap. This is what is happening with the co-operativization plan for the *haciendas* and *comunidades* of the Pampa de Anta, in Cuzco.

Finally, we find cases of *haciendas* carrying out a double process of sub-division and business-like modernization. This procedure is graphically illustrated by the case of the estate of the local boss of Andahuaylas, Héctor Flores Samanez. This gentleman protected himself against any possibility of being expropriated right from 1964, by starting to sell plots of land to his *colonos* in the hilly part of his property, and leaving himself with the most fertile flat land on the shores of Lake Pacucha, where prospects for irrigation are most favourable.

The *hacendado's* henchmen, local toughs and his peasant clientele, managed to convince the *colonos* that they had best buy, since when the agrarian reform came the State would take all the land for itself. The land the owner has kept is worked by permanent wage-labourers and some casual workers from among those who have bought parcels.

With a touch worthy of a past-master in the manipulation of peasant conflicts, the *hacendado* refused to sell any land at all to

1. See below, Section II, 6.

one *colono*, and instead donated his share to the *comunidad* as land on which to build a school. The buyers, who call themselves *comuneros* (which indeed they are), have retained a lawyer to remove the *colono* thus deprived of land, who already has his own lawyer and has the same rights as they do. The conflict between *colonos* and *hacendado* has thus been converted into a conflict between buyers. Now the agrarian reform is welcome to come to the area, since there are no 'anti-social' (servile) working conditions on the *hacienda*, which is worked by 'wage-earners'. With some clever management of the legal limits on expropriation (Articles 28 and 31), in the regulations concerning *sociedades de personas* (Articles 30 and 31, Supreme Deciee 163–69–AP, etc.), he will manage to save the *hacienda*. This procedure suits the government, whose main intention is to establish a small and middle bourgeoisie in the countryside, and to eliminate 'traditional' or 'pre-capitalist' forms of ownership.

4. *The Transformation of Cattle and Sheep Farms into 'Agricultural Social Interest Societies'* (SAIS)

This type of enterprise was first mooted in 1968, before publication of the Agrarian Reform Law, and it received the support of a Minister of Agriculture who was subsequently replaced on account of his obvious sympathy for anti-reformist groups.[1] In 1969 it was proposed to apply the SAIS system in the sugar plantations but since the government had already decided to convert these into co-operatives those seeking to instal the SAIS system were only able to try it out in the modernized sheep and cattle breeding areas of the sierra.

SAIS have been created only in the great wool farms of the sierra. These farms are all very advanced technically, but founded upon a 'bastardized wage-system' to use Bagú's terminology; the workers do receive a wage, in the strict legal sense, but payment for pasture on the farm is deducted, leaving only a few soles' difference. In some cases, in addition to this type of worker, there are others who earn just a wage. Typical cases of such enterprises are the cattle farms on the plateaux of Junín and Lake Titicaca.

In the SAIS two principles are combined: firstly the farm is to be handed over to its workers, and secondly *hacienda* land which had once belonged to communities is to be restored to its rightful owners. To fulfil these principles, both the farmworkers and the

1. The Minister alluded to was General José Benavides, member of a well-known land-owning family. (Ed.)

neighbouring *comuneros* (members of communities) have been included as members of the SAIS. The claims of the communities are met by making them pay for the land in instalments, thus recognizing implicitly the claims of the *hacienda* over disputed land. The members of the enterprise are not the individual persons involved, but the association of workers on the one hand, and the litigating communities on the other. Profits are distributed according to proportions fixed by the government, each member receiving a determinate share of profits and bearing a corresponding share of debts.

The regulations governing agricultural co-operatives (*Reglamentos de Cooperativas Agrarias*) lay down that the SAIS will be subject to the Law on Co-operatives 'insofar as it is applicable', and that beyond that point they will be governed by the Code of Civil Societies, which regulates the operations of capitalist companies.[1] The SAIS enthusiasts, Ministry of Agriculture officials, and enemies of ONDECOOP, claim that the Co-operative Law is too rule-bound and that it limits the freedom to create new and more flexible co-operative models. They claim that the SAIS combines the advantages of co-operatives with the flexibility of the laws governing capitalist companies. They are frightened by the tendency to convert farms into production co-operatives, which they see as a step towards communism. This flexibility, of which they are so fond, means in practice that a SAIS can have non-working members and others who invest capital in order to make a profit. In other words, theirs is a hybrid conception of co-operative and limited company, a more moderate conception than that of the petit-bourgeois reformists.

The case of a SAIS called Túpac Amaru is a typical model; it was created with the lands and the sheep of a technically highly advanced *hacienda* belonging to the Cerro de Pasco Mining Company, in 1968, when the Minister of Agriculture, Benavides, was a brother of the company manager.

In 1900, eighteen farms owned the land subsequently owned by the Cerro Company. In 1924 Cerro installed a chimney which gave off smoke and gas, destroying vegetation within a radius of some 700,000 hectares. The resulting protest forced the company to install a smoke-control mechanism, completed in 1942, by which time the company had already bought 320,000 hectares. Later, the pasture grass grew again, and some 86,000 sheep belonging to Cerro de Pasco pastured there, on a total area of 216,000 hectares (CIDA, p. 22).

1. *Reglamento de Cooperativas Agrarias*, Articles 142–55.

In recent years the long-term trend of wool prices has been downward, propped up somewhat by the 1967 devaluation. As a result of the rise of synthetic materials, demand has been declining steadily since 1952; business was looking bleak and the enterprise lacked liquid funds. One way of obtaining liquid funds was by handing over the enterprise to the government. According to the company technicians wool production could only be saved by raising productivity – in other words, by reducing the number of workers: thus, in accordance with strict capitalist rationality, the company was planning to reduce their number from 327 to 250, leaving a ratio of more than 1,000 hectares per man.

Thus, the creation of this SAIS is a response to the company's search for liquidity, to the coincidence of family ties between the manager and the Minister, and to a tacit agreement among all those concerned not to convert the enterprise into a production co-operative, though, as we shall see, both fall into the same capitalist category.

Towards the end of 1968, the Túpac Amaru SAIS was organized as follows: the 327 farm workers became members of a co-operative (called a *Cooperativa de Servidores*) which in turn became the first member organization of the SAIS. The other sixteen members are the sixteen adjacent communities, one-time owners of the *hacienda* lands. However, only the members of the *Cooperativa de Servidores* actually work the lands of the farm, on account of the authorities' concern to maintain present levels of productivity and profitability. Each sends two delegates to the Assembly, which has elected an administrative council and a board of control (*Consejo de Vigilancia*).

Thus, the surrounding communities participate through their delegates, and through the receipt of an average of 5·82 per cent of distributed profits (ranging from 4·19 to 8·99 per cent), but not through actual work on the land they benefit from. The co-operative of actual workers receives 4·85 per cent of distributed profits, which is the second lowest proportion of all.

Similarly, the debt of 215 million soles owing in payment for the land, will be paid over twenty-five years, with members paying a proportion of the debt equal to the proportion of profits to which they are entitled. Net earnings will depend on profits, but the amount owing to the respective community will be invested in public works and community services, not distributed among its members. In other words, these earnings will revert to the State, since the State carries out public works.

Furthermore, it must be recalled that the government has paid in cash for the cattle, as laid down by the Law, so that the beneficiaries are in debt to it – another step in the process of absorption by the state machine.

At one stage, the SAIS did possess more autonomy than the sugar co-operatives, although, obviously, here too the old managers stayed on as technicians, and manipulated the new enterprise – but even this distinction has disappeared now that the authority of the military Advisory and Control System is extended to the SAIS.

It is absurd to apply the term 'co-operative' to an enterprise in which only one of the members actually works. The *comuneros*, receiving profits in their capacity as former owners of the land, seem to be a variety of member-capitalists. Not only can no new workers be added to the SAIS, but also, to save the enterprise from declining demand and declining prices, and to raise productivity, investments will be made in machinery and the labour force reduced.

Various other SAIS have been created, with some variations in their organization. In Puno, during the first year of the reform, nineteen were created on expropriated farms covering several hundred thousand hectares. But here the communities had no access to them at all – for which reason their name was changed to 'production co-operative'.

Including Túpac Amaru and several others created in Puno, it is estimated that already more than a million hectares (slightly more than 5 per cent of total agricultural land) must by now be in this type of enterprise.

5. *Non-Expropriable Properties*

Here we refer to all properties falling below the minimum for expropriation, and in the case of land under tenancy or feudal arrangements, above the fifteen- or thirty-hectare maximum for expropriation for these lands. Under this heading we find all properties arising from 'private' parcelization, and, naturally, some of the most faithful allies of the government, since the owners of these properties represent both the social class and the kind of enterprise which the régime is seeking to consolidate in the countryside. Yet, in what appears to be a sign of bonapartism, the government has laid down rules which threaten this sector's level of earnings. These rules are: (1) the Resolution regulating the application of Article 45 of the Agrarian Reform Law, which establishes that a farm can be expropriated even if it falls below the minimum, if it fails to provide its workers with satisfactory living conditions;[1] (2) the Decree 18296 (26 May 1970) according to which the workers must receive 50 per cent of profits, must be considered owners of 50 per cent of the capital of the enterprise, and must receive 20 per cent of net income; and (3) Supreme Decree 264–70–AG (18 August 1970), which, in order to prevent the artificial inflation of costs by owners seeking to declare very low profits, fixes maximum monthly salaries for managers of 6,500 soles on units under fifty hectares and 12,500 soles on units over that size.

These groups had lived in expectation of a quiet life, and they responded to these three measures with numerous communiqués seeking to make 'constructive criticism', and to 'contribute to the improvement of the law'. The associations of middle-size farmers of the coastal valleys and the Lima Chapter of Agricultural Engineers have been particularly vociferous.[2]

The outcome of these pressures is easily foreseeable: when there is no mass mobilization at all, the interests of medium-sized businessmen must surely prevail. For example, the application of Article 126 of the Reform Law, under which it is possible to expropriate even properties exempted from expropriation on all other grounds, when they are adjacent to communities suffering from a scarcity of land, is very unlikely.

6. *The Transformation of Communities into Co-operatives*

Article 5 of the Statute of Peasant Communities (Supreme Decree No. 37–70A, 17 February 1970) establishes that the communities must be transformed into co-operatives, and must therefore be managed by an Administrative Board and a Control Board. The government's wish to establish larger economic units on the basis of existing communities is founded on the belief that the community, previously called 'indigenous' and now 'peasant', can transcend capitalism by forming co-operative or collective enterprises.

The Statute accepts the existence of four systems of work inside the community:

1. Resolution 184-70-TR, 31 July 1970. As a result of strong protest this regulation was subsequently modified in its application, making it possible for landowners to appeal. (Ed.)
2. The communiqués of the principal landowners' association, the *Sociedad Nacional Agraria* (SNA) came to an abrupt halt in May 1972, when it was abolished by government decree, and was placed, along with regional landowners' associations, under the control of SINAMOS.

a Family work in the parcels possessed by each member of the community in private usufruct.

b Co-operative work, when the community, in the form of a production or service co-operative, cultivates land at present used in common. Naturally, at the moment the pasture is communal but the flocks are private; the government believes that the flocks can be co-operativized. This belief is based on successful experiences in the Callejón de Huaylas and others, in the Southern Zone.

c 'Special entrepreneurial production work' – at the beginning this concept was interpreted as referring only to agricultural enterprises inside the co-operative. Furthermore Article 23 established that to be a member an individual had to derive the main source of his income from agriculture. But the government changed this interpretation and now accepts that it is possible to be a member of the community without working principally in agriculture. This implies that this special type of enterprise can be non-agricultural.

d Communal work by the members of the community for the 'preservation, improvement or construction of works of social interest or other collective activities'.

The majority of the communities have preserved intact the tradition of the common use of the natural pastures; but an increasing proportion have fenced in the pasture land. However, Article 102 states that the pastures can only be exploited in common. This means that, where pasture land has been enclosed, communities will choose to disband, a procedure allowed under Article 112.

Many communities have become 'co-operatives', but this simply means that their former leadership has adopted the title of Administrative Council. Of true co-operatives there is no sign, except in wool-producing communities. In the others, the government carries out propaganda campaigns to publicize the Statute of Peasant Communities, trying to 'raise the level of consciousness' of the members.

A further problem is raised by the so-called 'purging' of the communities (under Title IV of the Statute) which establishes qualifications for membership: a member must have been born in the community or be the son of a member, be a head of a family or have reached majority, reside permanently in the community, be principally engaged in agricultural work, and own lands neither within the community nor outside. His income from outside activities must not exceed that received within, and he cannot belong to another community. These provisions have unleashed a series of conflicts between members who earn their living from other sources (as traders, professional people and university graduates), live outside the community and, at the provincial or national level, perform certain tasks for the community; these are generally rich members and, thus, leaders of the community.

In November 1970, the government compromised, accepting that persons who were earning income outside agriculture could be considered members of the community as long as their income from those sources was less than the annual income earned by a family agricultural unit, that is, between 30,000 and 50,000 soles – which is, of course, impossible to check.

It seems that the government hopes to eliminate the disadvantages of small-scale cattle-farming by fomenting a process of concentration in the co-operatives. The *minifundio* is left untouched because it is known that under present conditions there is no force strong enough to induce the members of a community to engage in collective cultivation of the land. In general, the underlying intention is to modernize agriculture in the communities; either through the concentration of production on communal pastures, or, where the land is already divided, through the consolidation of private property.

Two Cases of Co-operative Integration of Communities and Haciendas

Among the schemes to modernize the peasant economy let us examine two cases in which the government is trying to integrate a certain number of communities and even *haciendas* within large co-operative structures. The first is the 'integrated project of rural settlement' (PIAR) of Bajo Piura. The lower part of the Piura valley has 40,000 hectares of land, cultivable, in part, in rainy years and when the river brings enough water. There we find three of the few large peasant communities which survive on the coast: Castilla, Sechura, and Catacaos, with a total of some 10,000 families and about 30,000 hectares of land. Some *hacienda* land was recently returned to the communities, after a law suit.

The government's Sectoral Planning Office for Agriculture (OSPA) designed a vast co-operative structure topped by an assembly of 338 delegates and directed by an administrative committee, which would have four management branches, seven local administrations and sixty-six enterprises; it would combine the private cultivation of the members' land, with co-operative work on recently recuperated lands. Furthermore, it would try to form new enterprises with State credits, government advisers and, of course, military advice and tutelage.

In the absence of any interest among the peasants, which might stimulate their participation, this grandiose project will remain utopian, yet another bureaucratic structure, which, believing it is at the service of the peasant, will impose the paternalism of the state technician and impede the emergence of autonomous and class-oriented forms of action. Recently the OSPA has considered that the PIAR cannot be conceived as only one enterprise but as an 'area of co-ordinated actions' within the agrarian reform.

The second case is that of the Pampa de Anta, in Cuzco, with thirty-eight communities and forty-four medium-sized *haciendas* and an area of 36,000 hectares, with 5,100 peasant families comprising community members and *hacienda*-workers. Here again the government thought of forming, in virtue of its miraculous decrees, a large central co-operative which would transform the whole region into a single large enterprise at a stroke.

Here obstacles will arise not only from obstinate attachment to small-scale enterprise, but also from the transformation of the traditional or semi-modern *haciendas* into co-operatives. Variations will be found not only in work habits, but also in well-differentiated and sometimes contradictory cultural conformations. The government will have to create an extremely complex management apparatus, dependent on the services of the former bosses and foreman. It would have to resort to the middle and small bourgeoisie, in order to keep the members of the communities under control, thus deepening the contradictions among the lower strata of the rural areas. Or else, it will have to reduce the model simply to an office which, though it neither controls nor initiates anything, preserves the formal appearance of a co-operative, and whose only task will be that of offering simple services to 'co-operative sections', which in reality will mean groups of peasants or small private managers. In this way a process of division of the land sets in, and the State provides services to modernize agriculture. The bureaucratic methods and the social perceptions of the government cannot produce any other results. No new system of property or production relations can arise within a repressive economic and political framework. To claim the reverse is but bourgeois ingenuity, which furthermore confuses the peasant.

The government and their technicians do not understand that the concentration of land has always been achieved either by usurpation and anti-peasant violence during entire centuries (as in Peru) or, in a socialist context, as the result of vast peasant mobilizations in the struggle against the landlord (for example, the twenty-two-year revolutionary war in China). There are no half-way models in the age of capitalism; we learn this from the people and their struggles – not from academics. So long as these projects of 'integration' are conceived by bureaucrats and technocrats, isolated from the dynamics of a social process, they are condemned to failure. The enormous directive apparatus required by these projects would mean preserving the mechanisms and symbols of oppression.

The underlying objective of all these plans is entrepreneurial modernization; the big landowners are to be paid for the lands belonging to the community members while the development of class-consciousness and class actions among the peasants is to be hindered.

III. Agrarian Reform and the Class Struggle in the Country

After our summary of the government's performance in the rural areas, we can analyse this agrarian reform, and relate its theoretical and legal claims to its practical application.

1. *Practical Objectives*

We have to see the government's actions as manifestations of its class basis. The agrarian reform is part of a general programme of reform but although the programme tends to benefit overall the same social class or classes, the political moment causes each item to be approached with varying degrees of radicalism. The moment at which the Agrarian Reform Law was decreed was shaped by the government's political victory over the Standard Oil Company, when the U.S.A. withdrew the threat of immediate economic sanctions on Peru. This allowed the seizure of the petrol and of the Talara refinery, charging the company's debts against compensation.[1] This may explain the revolutionary rhetoric, but we must ask whether the objectives of this law are consistent with other points in the government programme, or whether it is part of an escalating radicalism which, as is claimed by some left-wing groups, will ultimately lead to revolutionary actions.

1. The balance was heavily in favour of the Peruvian government, but IPC, a subsidiary of Standard Oil, has not paid. (Ed.)

The general characteristics of the Agrarian Reform Law are as follows:

a It affects private property in land, but does not suppress it. Thus, it is based on expropriation and distribution by private initiative, both of which are forms of compulsory sale with payment of the price of the land, and thus contain an implicit recognition of the property rights of the landowner.

b It seeks to broaden and consolidate two social classes: the middle and the lower strata of the agrarian bourgeoisie. The former benefits in particular from the private sub-division of land, the establishment of limits to the size of property that can be affected (Articles 28 to 34, Title IX) and the latter benefits from the conversion of landless farmers into owners of land they occupy (Articles 79 and 80, Title XV) and from the dissolution of the communities which is allowed under conditions we have already described.

c It forces farmers to modernize by raising the limit of expropriable land for farms using advanced techniques and for those which are up-to-date in the payment of social benefits due to the workers (Articles 28 to 34).

d It aims to finance industrialization by channelling to industry the capital produced by the peasants 'benefiting' from the process (Article 181).

e It creates a complementary sector of co-operatives and semi-co-operatives which provides the financial, political and technical means of achieving the concentration and capitalist modernization which the government seeks.

f It newly consecrates communal property, returning to the communities the land usurped since 1920, and seeks to transform the communities into co-operative enterprises.

g It represses the peasant movement, creating a special category of agrarian law and of 'agrarian' crimes.

h It departs from the agrarian policy of the former régime, under which only large traditional *haciendas* using a system of parcelled land, with serfs, and small units under tenancy or sharecropping, were affected. The present process affects, in addition, the large modern *haciendas* and all modern or traditional farms exceeding the stipulated dimensions. Neither régime has touched the vast properties of the Amazon forest.

2. *The Agrarian Reform as an Expression of the Domination of a Social Class*

The agrarian reform affects the sugar- and wool-producing

sectors of the modern and pro-imperialist agrarian bourgeoisie, and the big traditional landowners who, despite the vast extensions they possessed, did not constitute sectors of very substantial power. In contrast, however, it leaves almost untouched the cotton farmers, who, though owners of medium-sized farms, are linked to foreign capital. The majority of them held less land than the unexpropriable limit, but in innumerable cases they have evaded expropriation through fictitious divisions of land. Thus, we can say that those favoured by the reform are the middle sectors of the modernized agrarian bourgeoisie.

The principal aspects of the application of the reform law can be summed up in three points:

a Expropriation of the largest estates, such as the sugar plantations on the coast, and the wool farms of the central and south plateaux. They were expropriated quickly so that the proprietors had not time to decapitalize the estates; and there is a tendency to transform them, which, although opposed to the ideological model of the national bourgeoisie, is not against their interests, as we shall see later in analysing rent; for, in addition, the former owners, now industrialists, will be paid for the land by the proletariat.

b Division of land by private initiative, whereby a certain homogeneity is sought in the size of medium-sized agrarian enterprises; the middle strata of the agrarian bourgeoisie are strengthened while, as we have seen, the rural proletariat is weakened.

c Adjudication of ownership rights to the various types of non-owning cultivators (tenants, sharecroppers, serfs and squatters). This favours the agrarian petty-bourgeoisie, and implements objectives pursued by the agrarian middle sectors and by the liberal bourgeoisie of the cities, which are: to weaken another basis of the traditional bourgeoisie – the serfs; to raise peasant support, itself a source of power that can be used against the proletariat; and to reduce unemployment and raise peasant incomes, improving their capacity to compete in the capitalist market.

The constant effect of these three lines of action, is to reduce the intensity of rural proletarian and peasant struggles. According to bourgeois logic, now that the proletarians become owners, trade unions are no longer needed. But, contrary to all expectations, the trade unions continue to exist owing to the quasi-patronal behaviour of the military and the technicians and because their fundamental demands have not been met. However, where private distributions of land have occurred, the unions, already weak due to the small size of the enterprises, have been further debilitated and some have disappeared. The combativity of small peasants is likely to diminish now that they have received some land and more time will pass before they perceive that the distribution of land rent has not been modified as far as they are concerned.

Thus the two extremes of the social pyramid have been neutralized: the upper bourgeoisie on the one hand, and the proletariat with the peasants on the other. The middle and petty-bourgeoisie will provide a reserve of political support for the government and will also guarantee the sustained productivity which is necessary as an alternative political solution to a mass movement of the peasantry. Thus, the technocratic character of the process acquires its political and class significance. Similarly the over-generous limits on expropriable land arise from a political choice more than from a technological one, since they serve the objective of preserving the power of the conservative middle sectors of the agrarian bourgeoisie. Their participation in the exercise of power through professionals and officials, in the judiciary and in army commands, will lead, with the passing of time, to the erosion of reformist laws – and the more fervent their declarations of adherence to the 'revolution', the more intense the erosion.

Already, the process shows that the interests of these strata will prevail over those of the agrarian petty-bourgeoisie, as the balance of power between them increasingly favours the former. A number of points underpin this observation:

a The defeat of several associations of small farmers who believed that the *haciendas* might be redistributed, if not free, at least by sale to the small farmers – a procedure which, when adopted, has favoured the medium farmers.

b The technocratic character of the process which has contained the small farmers' drive to seize the *haciendas*.

c The SAIS supporters' victory over the co-operativists means that, increasingly, private capital, coming by and large from provincial moneylenders, finds its way into the expropriated enterprises.

d The control of medium-level engineers and officers over the workers, both in the SAIS and in the co-operatives.

e The vast number of legal institutions where middle farmers hold back the small farmers in their attempts to obtain more land.

However, petit-bourgeois characteristics of the process also abound, arising from a situation where, being in possession of the means of production, the worker is unable to conceive the world without that possession. Thus we find several elements of a petit-bourgeois ideology:

a The desire to create new family farms and to reinforce those already in existence.

b Co-operativization as a formula to give all the workers access to capitalist property.

c The decrees concerning distribution of profits among workers and their ownership of half the enterprise capital.[1]

However, the fact that the lower and middle strata of the rural bourgeoisie are favoured does not imply that they are in command, as large sectors of the left which currently support the government erroneously believe. In fact, control lies with the grande bourgeoisie, whose power is now centred on industry, finance, trade and its commercial dealings with imperialism. Indeed, the interests of the liberal bourgeoisie are suited by the weakening or disappearance of the land-owning class. The modernization of agriculture is in their interest since, as with all models of agrarian reform, the aim is to make agriculture play its role in industrialization: to increase the production of food for a growing urban sector, to supply raw materials to the industrial sector and to provide both a flow of capital and an expanding market for the growth of manufacturing industry. The landowners, obstinately holding on to anachronistic forms of production, constitute an obstacle to the interests of the liberal bourgeoisie, whose links with imperialism explain the coincidence of views of foreign companies – especially the sugar companies – and the government, in the context of the agrarian reform. This liberal bourgeoisie can find imperialist support (in mining and heavy industry, as much from the U.S.A. as from Japan and Europe) against more traditional groups which still cling to colonial models of raw materials production for the world market. And, of course, the modern middle sectors, both agrarian and industrial, support the liberal bourgeoisie. So that, although this government defends the interests of the bourgeoisie as a whole, because all its sectors will be favoured by the process in the long term, the programme nevertheless bears the distinctive stamp of the liberal bourgeoisie; the reforms affect the concrete interests of the agrarian bourgeoisie and of imperialism, but these contradictions are not antagonistic and do allow of a sharing of benefits on a new basis, made possible by opportunities for investment in industry.

With national industrial development, the bourgeoisie must

1. See Title VII of the Law, the Agrarian Co-operatives Regulation and the Decree of 26 May 1970.

find a new basis on which to conduct its dealings with imperialism. The attitude of immediate support that agrarian reform aroused in the foreign business community, and even in the sugar enterprises, was at first a source of confusion, but not for long. The Cerro Corporation had handed over their lands even before promulgation of the Law. At first W. R. Grace, owner of a number of great sugar plantations, preserved control and ownership of the paper and plastics industries based on sugar subproducts, while being expropriated of their land with deferred payment under the Agrarian Reform Law. However, in early 1972 the company reached an agreement with the government on this matter, and the industrial plant passed under state control. In general, the interest of foreign capital in agriculture has diminished and it now finds other sectors more attractive. This is not a novelty, for with the formation of the Alliance for Progress, on American initiative and with the acceptance of the representatives of the Latin American national bourgeoisie, it was clearly established that industrial development should be accelerated by using both the public sector (which some still regard as tantamount to socialism) and private resources, encouraging agrarian reform programmes for that purpose 'where necessary'. (*Charter* of Punta del Este, Title I, 'Aims' 4 and 6.)

Peruvian industrialization, if it is achieved, marks a belated adaptation to the new character of imperialism, which allows a degree of industrialization, but preserves and develops exploitation through financial mechanisms. The fact that, since the Agrarian Reform Law, foreign enterprises have been allowed to continue remitting profits and earnings from royalties, patent rights and interest payments, that they are also allowed to make special contracts[1] and to escape the nationalistic terms of the Law of Industries,[2] shows that the traditional capitalist structure, arising from a specific kind of relationship with imperialism, is under attack so that this relationship be changed, rather than eliminated: a new imperialist contract is being drawn up. Thus the Peruvian reform does not define a contradiction between the workers and capitalists, but rather a contradiction between the traditional, latifundista, exporter, go-between bourgeoisie and the liberal industrial bourgeoisie, between two types of dependence, of which the latter is endowed with a small dose of lukewarm nationalism. In this conflict, which has been sharpening for decades, the winners are the national bourgeoisie and their allies the lower and the middle strata of the agricultural bourgeoisie.

1. Decree on the control of foreign currency, May 1970.
2. Industries Law, Articles 16 and 18.

The Agrarian Reform Law is the legal expression of the agrarian programme of the national bourgeoisie; it arises not from a strengthening of proletarian struggle but as a direct consequence of a rearrangement of the various bourgeois groups.

3. *The Economic Content of the Peruvian Agrarian Reform*

We have said that a pattern emerges from the agrarian reform that reveals its true class character. Let us now examine this pattern. In the sugar sector, the agrarian bourgeoisie leaves a sector with a decreasing rate of profit and an unstable market. The enterprises have been formally handed over to production co-operatives but their management and authority system in fact constitutes a form of *dirigisme*, if not direct state control, and is a far cry from the self-management proclaimed by some groups on the left. But, given their declining economic importance, these few traces of socialization are of no concern to the bourgeoisie.

In the Túpac Amaru SAIS the diversion of some of the profits towards the surrounding communities appears to signify an increase of the community members' income. But since those profits will be invested in public works, they will in fact be absorbed by the government which carries them out. The element of *dirigisme* is accentuated by the fact that, by paying for the *hacienda*'s cattle in cash, the government converted the workers into debtors, and thus found a pretext to control the farm.

Where there have been privately initiated divisions of land, some funds paid for the land will be extracted from agriculture to feed industry, but in many cases there will be no flow of capital because the divisions are fictitious or involve only the formality of distributing shares. All the land in the country would not suffice to distribute among the small farmers and community members, so they will in general remain on their parcels as owners; these are insufficient to raise their incomes or to give full employment, and they must bear the aggravating burden of a debt repayment equal to, or higher than, the previous rents. With continuing under-employment, this group will provide a source of cheap labour.

The small farmers have always contributed to the formation of the product on the *haciendas* and thus should also have access to some of its land; a bold policy could integrate and employ them by harnessing the huge resources wasted by all *haciendas*, as well as bringing this *minifundio* land into the co-operative. However, the opposite is being done, by dismissing as many men as possible, in the name of 'keeping up productivity'.

We can therefore detect certain constants in the co-operativization of modern *haciendas*, in the private divisions of land and in the distribution of land to peasants. The external effects upon each sub-sector or class (medium and small owners, wage-earners) may vary, but one underlying effect remains, namely the expansion of capitalism and the development of industry. The enterprise models can vary and the supporters of SAIS or of the production co-operatives can lose or gain ground, even with the formal suppression of private property, but none of this affects the essential objective of restructuring the distribution of capitalist rent. If we systematize these economic effects, we find that whatever the degree of co-operativization, state control or division of land two features subsist which sustain capitalism: the first of these is the mercantile character of production as a dominant mechanism of the system. The more obstacles imposed by the *hacendados* to a free use and cultivation of land, are removed, the more mercantilism, and therefore capitalism, will develop (Lenin, Chap. 3). The second feature is the powerlessness of the peasantry, brought about and sustained by the government through its *concientizadores*[1] (read pacifyers), its repressive apparatus and its new agrarian legal system.[2]

The co-operatives and the SAIS also operate within a mercantile system of production. A market is a market, be it for sugar, wool, cotton or coffee. None of the government reforms change this feature of production, and the triumph of one or another type of enterprise in the conflict between the agrarian reform agency and ONDECOOP, is irrelevant to it.

The creation of co-operatives and of SAIS is also, however, a means of enabling the State to control land rent. We know the land produces two types of rent to its owner. The first is absolute rent, received by the landowner through the simple fact of possessing a monopoly over a piece of land regardless of the technology employed or of the quality of the land. This type of rent exists both in capitalism and in systems prior to capitalism. The second is differential rent, which arises only in modern capitalist agriculture. Differential rent is received only by owners of more technically advanced farms who compete successfully in the market, and earn a profit on capital invested, with the help of the quality of the land they own.

1. *Concientización* refers to the 'raising of the consciousness' of peasants or others. *Concientizadores* are essentially agitators who carry this out, often as government officials.
2. Law of Agrarian Reform, special provision No. 8. Decree on Agrarian Crimes (*Delitos Agro-penales*).

In the agrarian structure which this government seeks to change, the search for absolute rent, based on the landowners' monopoly of the land, was manifest in the speculation surrounding land and agricultural products. On the other hand, as participants in the capitalist market, the landowners also received differential rent, in amounts which doubtless were increased by their ownership of the best lands in each valley or region. But now, by putting an end to the monopoly over land possessed by the agrarian bourgeoisie, and by creating numerous small and medium owners who will compete in the market, the government will eradicate the absolute rent of the land.

The modern farms operated totally in the capitalist market and with capitalist relations of production, making a profit on capital invested and obtaining a differential rent. But the owners, by virtue of their political power, also obtained an absolute rent, expressed in inflated prices or in subsidies granted to wool and sugar production.

By transforming farms into SAIS or co-operatives and managing them with technicians, the government is gaining control of the differential rent which enabled capitalist farmers to transfer capital to the fishing, trade and banking sectors. But the government will not appropriate these resources, because the rent will continue to reach the former owners in the form of bonds. The change lies merely in the fact that the government has reserved for itself the right to decide where resources arising from that rent will be invested; and they will be invested in industry.[1]

The true objective of the government in gaining control of land rent is to secure a new pattern of distribution of the surplus value produced by the workers. And an inquiry into which class or classes are favoured by this new distribution raises the question of which class is represented by the military government.

In effect, certain changes in the distribution of surplus value can be detected. Prior to the reform, part of it went to finance capital in the form of interest payments to the Agricultural Bank, to the Interamerican Development Bank which had deposited funds in the Agricultural Bank etc. As the capital of the farms has been allowed to deteriorate during the past decade, such loans must continue and increase and thus the quota of surplus-value flowing to local and foreign financial capital will both continue and grow. A further slice went to foreign interests as payment

1. So long as a former landowner can raise an equivalent amount of counterpart funds, the government can convert his bonds into immediately investible resources in industries, before the redemption period is terminated. (Ed.)

for fixed capital (machines, etc.) and this item will also have to increase for the same reason. Furthermore, the technicians' choice of mechanization rather than an expanded use of labour, as a means of increasing productivity, implies an added increase in expenditure on production goods, which are mainly bought from abroad. Finally, the landowners' claim on surplus-value in the form of profits is protected and will even increase. In the case of Tumán, for example, as we have seen, the 42 million soles received by the former owners in the form of bonds and interest are more than the annual profit made before the reform. The government is eager to accomplish this payment, to transfer it to industry, so as to assure the agrarian bourgeoisie that it will keep its position and its resources. Finally, with an increase in some rural incomes and the consequent expansion of the market an increasing absolute amount of surplus-value is likely to accrue to the commercial sector, even if its relative share declines.

Our analysis suggests that the average return to capital will be distributed between local and foreign bankers (finance capital) and the co-operatives that own the land and the installations. Differential rent will be received in part by the former owners, by the members of co-operatives and by the government; the first because they will continue to receive a rental income equal to or higher than they received before; the second because a part of the profits will be distributed among the members, although, as is clear, debts must be paid first; the government will receive a portion in the form of a land tax, taking a higher share now because there will be no more tax evasion. Absolute rent will continue to exist for twenty years while the *hacendados* will receive payment for their lands without participating in the productive process – simply as former monopolists of the land.

In other words, the reform yields a new distribution, in which, as a result of increases in the portion paid to the capitalist class, the part to be shared among the workers is reduced, though not eliminated. The agrarian bourgeoisie is not suppressed; rather it changes its base.

As far as the more backward sectors of agriculture are concerned, the *haciendas* produced varying proportions of absolute and differential rent, depending on their degree of modernization and of connection with the market. Only a few exceptional *haciendas* functioned completely outside the capitalist system, yielding only absolute rent. Those which must have had the greatest proportion of absolute in relation to differential rent, are the traditional ones of the sierra, which had bad land and were almost totally isolated from the market. But even here, the landowners had recourse to cattle breeding in order to sell in the market despite the communications problem, and, furthermore, they had to compete with Central American cattle and Argentine beef; thus, the price mechanism did affect them despite the semi-feudal character of their labour relations and their physical isolation. Indeed, it was this very mechanism that induced them to preserve the traditional systems of labour, which made it possible for them to preserve their market position and increase their absolute rent.

The expropriation of these *haciendas* and the disappearance of servile labour, will gradually eradicate absolute rent, creating suitable conditions for the development of a fully capitalist market and for the formation of differential rent. But if obligations to bond holders are honoured, they will amount to paying absolute rent for twenty years, and the peasants on these *haciendas* will receive the worst lands, producing a minimal rent, while the State will control the richer and more modern *haciendas* producing a higher differential rent. This explains why the modern *haciendas* are being transformed into co-operatives and SAIS while the traditional and less prosperous ones are being handed over to community members for cultivation in a communal system; the ultimate objective of both procedures is one and the same. Seen in this light, the SAIS and the co-operatives are in the same category of enterprise, and conflicts concerning the two models are explained as part of the struggle for power in the Ministries, rather than as a conflict between the different approaches to economic and social problems.

In contrast, the distribution of traditional *haciendas* among individuals or groups cannot be spoken of as a guarantee of capitalist development in agriculture in the same way as can that arising on capitalist farms now converted into co-operatives or SAIS, since there is no capitalist accumulation to make reinvestment and technical progress possible. Free market prices prevent the small farmer from accumulating; and payment of the bonds will mean a drain on resources and further impede accumulation. Thus, an unregulated market and the payment of the land are in contradiction with the capitalist modernization of agriculture.

In the medium-sized farms arising from private parcelizations, differential rent is preserved, as a result of the private division of land, but it is redistributed among a larger number of entrepreneurs, less rich, less powerful politically and more attached to the industrial bourgeoisie than the previous owners; these new farmers are likely to be good clients of the industrial sector and ardent defenders of the liberation and decentralization of the economy.

The agrarian reform is the latest of many attempts which have marked Peruvian agrarian history. The perennial conflict between conservatives and liberals has reflected a struggle between those who sought to preserve the dominant function of absolute rent and those who have tried again and again to reduce or abolish it in the hope of controlling differential rent. The modern capitalist sector has continuously pressed for the following changes:

a The abolition of the monopoly control of land and thus of absolute rent in the traditional *haciendas*, in order to bring about the full participation of agriculture in the competitive economy. This is not a move from feudalism to capitalism, as sometimes is wrongly claimed, but rather the development of an incipient mercantilism, which constitutes an embryonic stage of capitalism.

b The elimination of simple mercantile production such as small barter agriculture, of the most traditional type of agriculture in which there is no absolute rent and hardly any differential rent; in other words, they seek the destruction of the communities, giving way to a free market in land and its products.

Thus we have a coherent schema within which to interpret both the colonial agrarian measures, such as the protection of indigenous lands, and the republican measures, among them the Bolivar decrees granting private property to community members, which provoked widespread usurpation of their lands, the road-building plans from Balta[1] to Belaúnde, the 1920 Law of Communities, etc. We can also now see the difference between the 1964 agrarian reform of the Apra-Belaúnde régime, which affected only traditional *haciendas* where absolute rent prevailed, and the present reform which also attempts to control the flow of differential rent produced by the modern *haciendas*.

The Peruvian agrarian reform resolves the contradiction between the agrarian and industrial sectors of the Peruvian bourgeoisie in favour of the latter. At the same time and taken together with other reforms, it delays the resolution of the contradiction between the proletariat and the bourgeoisie in general, by trying to manipulate the workers while injecting a new dynamism among the capitalists. It creates new contradictions in the countryside, of which the principal will be between the peasant, as an individual or organized in groups, and the State, as the representative of the interests of the bourgeoisie. This

1. José Balta, President 1868–71.

contradiction will arise as a consequence of the play of market forces, which will oppress the peasants, however much they modernize, and benefit the merchants, and as a result of payments of land which reduce the amount of resources available for investment in the agricultural sector.

The bourgeois reform thus creates, again, its own contradiction: the form of payment impedes the development of capitalism in the countryside. Paradoxical but true: the purpose of capitalist development in the countryside is best served by non-payment for the land, but this is precisely what cannot be done in the context of a capitalist reform.

References

CIDA (*Comité Interamericano de Desarrollo Agrícola*): *Perú: Tenencia de la Tierra y Desarrollo Socio-Económico del Sector Agrícola.* Washington, Panamerican Union, 1966.

Hobsbawn, Eric, 'La Convención: a case of neo-feudalism', *Journal of Latin American Studies*, **1**, 1, 1969.

Lenin V. I., *The Agrarian Programme of Social Democracy in 1905–1907.*

Glossary

AP **(Acción Popular):** 'Popular Action', Belaúnde's party.

APRA **(Alianza Popular para la Revolución Americana):** 'Popular Alliance for the Latin American Revolution'; founded and still led by Victor Haya de la Torre, a formerly reformist, now conservative party of the 'middle sectors' and sugar-workers.

CAEM **(Centro de Altos Estudios Militares):** Centre for Advanced Military Studies. An élite school for officers, of a remarkably meritocratic character.

CECOAAP **(Central de Cooperativas Azucareras del Perú):** 'Central Office of Agricultural Co-operatives', a state agency giving technical assistance and keeping control of sugar co-operatives.

CGTP **(Central General de Trabajadores del Perú):** 'Central Organization of Peruvian Workers'. The agglomerating Trade Union organization largely controlled by the Communist Party, which follows the Soviet doctrine of peaceful co-existence, and supports the government 'critically'.

comunidades: peasant communities of the sierra, bearing some vestiges of traditional indigenous forms of organization, in particular communal pastures.

Cooperativa de Servidores: literally, 'Workers' Co-operative'. Name given to member-co-operatives of the SAIS.

CTP **(Confederación de Trabajadores del Perú):** 'Confederation of Peruvian Workers'. This the oldest of the agglomerating trade union organizations, controlled by APRA. Two further such organizations have recently sprung up, one controlled by the government, the other by the Christian Democrats.

DC **(Democracia Cristiana):** the Christian Democrat Party.

FENCAP **(Federación Nacional Campesina):** National Peasant Federation, organizing mostly sugar-workers of the coastal region, and controlled by APRA.

feudatarios: tenants of *hacienda* land who pay labour rent, as well as rendering various unpaid personal services and operating under a varying set of constraints on their economic freedom.

FLN **(Frente de Liberación Nacional):** National Liberation Front, a front organization operating in 1965–8 under the leadership of the Communist Party.

hacienda: large estate generally with a substantial amount of land under tenancy; tenants are tied to the estate by arrangements similar to those of the *feudatario*.

ONDECOOP **(Oficina Nacional de Desarrollo Cooperativo):** National Co-operative Development Office. Represented left wing of government agricultural policy in 1969–71, but has been overshadowed since.

OSPA **(Oficina Sectorial de Planificación Agrícola):** Sectoral Planning Office for Agriculture.

PC-**Unidad:** 'Communist Party – Unity'. Communist Party re-formed after split with Maoists.

PIAR **(Proyecto Integral de Asentamiento Rural):** 'Integral Rural Settlement Project'.

SAIS **(Sociedad Agrícola de Interés Social):** 'Agricultural Social Interest Society' – variant on the co-operative model.

sierra: Andean region stretching from the western foothills to the jungle on the eastern side; the jungle is conventionally considered to start at about 1,500 metres.

SINAMOS **(Sistema Nacional de Apoyo a la Movilización Social):** The acronym means 'without masters'. This agency, created in 1971, is intended to 'stimulate participation without controlling it' and 'to co-ordinate the various government agencies which deal with social mobilization in one form or another'. Its commitment to participation is balanced by the role of providing crowd support for public appearances of Ministers etc. (Palmer, David Scott and Beruff, Jorge Rodriguez: 'The Peruvian Military Government: Problems of Political Participation', *Bulletin* of the Institute of Development Studies, **4**, 4, September 1972).

SNA **(Sociedad Nacional Agraria):** National Agrarian Society. The landlords' association, dissolved and merged into SINAMOS in 1971.

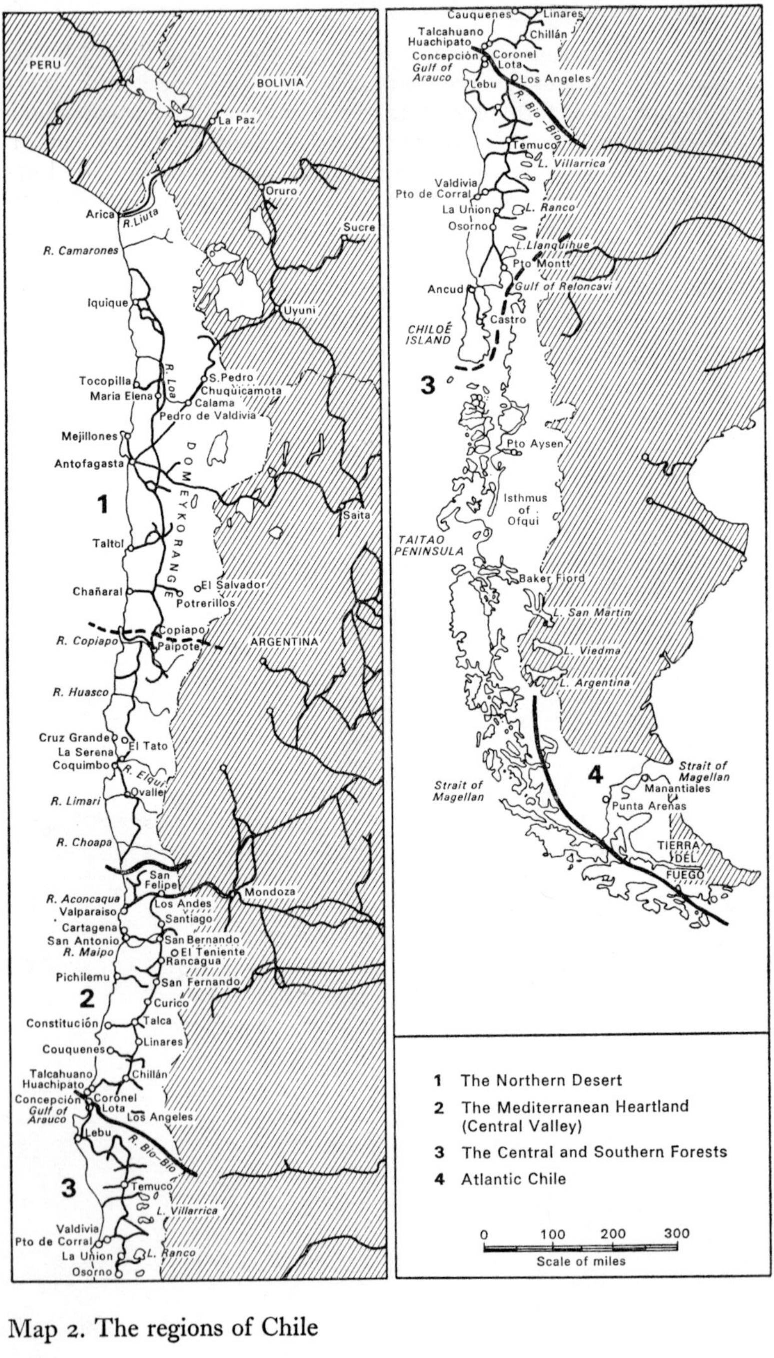

Map 2. The regions of Chile

Three

Agrarian Reform in Chile, 1965–1972: An Essay in Contradictions[1]

David Lehmann

I. Agriculture and its Crucial Role

Chilean society is highly urbanized with one-third of the total population living in the capital city itself and well under one-third of the population living in the countryside. The dominant sectors of the economy are mining, whence come over 80 per cent of the country's export earnings and 10 per cent of national product, and industry, which accounts for one-quarter of the national product. Yet the agrarian problem has accounted for some of the most bitter and fruitful polemics during the last ten years among politicians, in the Press, and among intellectuals. Moreover, such simple demographic and economic statistics conceal the enormous social and political importance of rural society. Social groups which dominate industry are formed by a combination of immigrants, and Chilean families whose recent ancestors, if not they themselves, have owned large latifundia; the land-owning groups have been prominent in the leadership of right-wing parties – the Conservative and Liberal parties, and their new incarnation the *Partido Nacional*, formed in 1966.

Until about 1958 the agrarian structure was crucial to the preservation of political order since landowners could use their power and patronage to control the votes of their workers. It

1. This work, like all my work on Chile, owes much to many people. In Chile I worked with Sergio Gomez, Emilio Klein, and Michel Langand at various times; Solon Barraclough educated me first in economics, and David Baytelman commented in detail on an earlier Spanish draft. The extent to which my ideas originate with them is impossible to disentangle, but I have benefited enormously from their patience and encouragement. This text was written at the end of 1972, and could not be changed to take account of the *putsch* of 11 September 1973. Indeed, but for changes of tense here and there, I have purposely not removed judgments which, in retrospect, may appear irrelevant, naïve or erroneous.

is since 1958, with a combination of changes in electoral legislation and agricultural organization that the stability of this order has been threatened. The agricultural sector also plays a more crucial role in the economy than its small participation in the national product (7 per cent) would first indicate. One of the main sources of weakness in the Chilean economy ever since the Second World War has been a very high food-import bill. Even by Latin American standards Chile is particularly vulnerable to fluctuations in its foreign trade situation, so that an improvement in the performance of agricultural production has been 'on the agenda' for many years now. The political obsession with the agrarian problem derives as much from the battle for the minds and the votes of the peasantry – and in particular of the workers on the latifundia – as it does from attempts to solve the economic problems of agriculture; and, far from being a criticism, this shows us the perspicacity of Chilean politicians and revolutionaries who have understood that there is no solution to the agrarian problem which is not both political and economic in content. This is not to say that the abolition of the latifundio system, brings about, as if by magic, a rise in agricultural production; indeed we shall see that agrarian reform may well create more economic problems than it solves in the short term.

However, agrarian reform remains a precondition for a change in the productive structure of agriculture, in the level of production, and in the standard of living of the rural masses. It is also a precondition for a transition to socialism in the society as a whole, even though the immediate effects of reform may be primarily to unleash capitalist forces.

Writing in 1972, and looking at the history of Chile in the last eight years, even a person who has been deeply involved during some or all of the period in the politics and frustrations of agrarian reform must surely recognize that there has been a social upheaval in the countryside. The problems today are so numerous, and it is at times so difficult to see a way of overcoming them, that Chilean intellectuals and foreign advisers tend to overestimate the element of continuity: continuity of an impossible bureaucracy; continuity of relatively low levels of agricultural production and increasingly high levels of food imports; continuous ambiguities in the agrarian policies of governments, be they committed to reformism or to revolutionary change; continuity in peasant resistance to the less subtle forms of bureaucratic control. Yet it is the upheaval which is far more striking, even if the problems today are as numerous as they were ten or twelve years ago, if not more so. Since 1964, starting almost from scratch, a rural trade union movement has grown to number some 200,000 adherents. An agrarian reform, carried out by both the Frei and Allende governments, has affected some 35 per cent of the total productive capacity in land. Even if some rural workers still prefer to work for their *patrones*[1] this is because they are receiving relatively high wages on commercial farms, and not because they are tied down by affective patronage relationships or by unending indebtedness. We set out by saying this, because in the following pages we will be placing more emphasis on problems than on achievements, on criticism rather than on praise, on the intractability rather than the solubility of many problems.

We will begin by describing the situation in Chile in late 1972. We will then return to the period of the Frei government, which forms an essential background to an understanding of the agrarian problem under Allende, and we will sum up the agrarian reform as carried out by that government. Then we shall analyse in detail the agrarian situation in particular on those farms and among those sectors of the rural population most affected by the agrarian reform since the beginning of 1971, keeping in mind the intention of the government to embark upon a period of transition towards socialism.

This is being written during a period of revolutionary struggle and political confusion, the outcome of which only the most unwary would venture to predict, yet precisely for this reason an exercise in interpretation at this moment is worthwhile; it will afford future historians the opportunity of seeing how complex the situation appears at this time and it will hopefully dissuade them from facile or rash generalizations.

II. The Difficult Revolutionary Struggle: 1970-72

The electoral victory of 1970 marked a point of culmination in the history of the Chilean labour movement, as well as the beginning of a period of particularly bitter class struggle on all fronts within the country as well as on the international front. The tripartite division of political forces of the centre, the left and the right, swiftly crystallized into bipolarity. Allende won the election with only a relative majority and the Christian Democratic candidate, Tomic, came in third with only 27·8 per cent of the votes (as against Allende's 36·2 per cent and Alessandri, the right-wing candidate's, 34·9 per cent), but the Christian Democrats were

1. A glossary of Spanish terms appears at the end of this paper.

more or less forced by circumstances to support Allende in the Congressional vote which confirmed his victory.[1]

After a period (1964–70) during which they were seeking a mass base for an essentially middle-class party, and thus incurring at times bitter conflict with the right, the Christian Democrats are now returning to the alliance with the right which gained them their 1964 election victory, concentrating on the defence of shopkeepers and white-collar workers. The party is also strong among privileged sectors of the working class such as the copper-miners and workers in some advanced industries and has a large following in the countryside, especially among the beneficiaries of the agrarian reform.

Allende's election victory was a direct consequence of the rupture of the victorious 1964 alliance between the Christian Democrats and the right. That alliance had been forged out of common fear of a victory by the socialist/communist coalition. Frei's foreign policy and his policy towards industry were not a bitter pill to swallow for the right. But his agrarian policy was more controversial. By 1970 the landowners were no longer isolated in their opposition to reform; the development of a powerful rural union movement had transformed social relationships in the countryside to such an extent that industrial capitalist groups were evidently concerned lest such a transformation should spread to industry and this is probably the best explanation available for the rupture of the alliance. (Lehmann, 1971.) Exaggerated confidence on the right in the electoral hopes of Jorge Alessandri (President from 1957 to '64), no doubt also influenced the turn of events. But, although his performance was creditable, it failed to reverse the basic trend: the Liberal and Conservative Parties, now the National Party, lost one-third of their voting strength between 1961 and 1969, and failed to retain Alessandri's remarkable support among the urban poor after 1970.[2]

1. According to the Chilean Constitution, in the event of no Presidential candidate obtaining an absolute majority, the Congress as a whole must decide between those coming in first and second. In theory it could choose the candidate which came in second. The then President of the Christian Democratic Party, when announcing his party's decision to support Allende, said that it was doing this largely in order to avoid a civil war.
2. The Conservative and Liberal Parties polled 30·4 per cent of the votes in the Parliamentary Elections of 1961, 20 per cent in those of 1969 as the *Partido Nacional*, and 18·1 per cent in the Municipal Elections of 1971.

The social base of *Unidad Popular* (UP) has been far more homogeneous. The Communist and Socialist Parties can boast a solid core of working-class support in the towns (Petras and Zeitlin, 1970) and substantial, but less solid, support among rural workers; the traditionally 'middle class' Radical Party has in recent years suffered the loss both of votes and of two successive fractions of its own parliamentary forces. The UP considers itself to be a coalition of working-class and middle-class forces, yet its programme of revolutionary change has probably eroded middle-class support. Committed to working within the constitution, and therefore to competing in the endless round of elections which characterized Chilean politics, the coalition was obviously engaged in an uphill task. Hence the slogan: *Convertir el Gobierno en Poder* ('Convert control of the government into control of power.')[1] The government barely had even the one-third of Congressmen which allows the President to push through certain kinds of measures. Thus a crucial immediate issue was how to build up mass support for a transition to socialism.

Within a short time, the UP had passed to the offensive on all fronts; on 1 January 1971 wage increases were awarded in such a way as to favour especially the lowest-paid workers in industry and agriculture, and this substantial expansion of demand forms an essential backdrop to future trends. With 40 per cent of industrial capacity lying idle industrialists could respond to the expansion of demand, in spite of the obvious uncertainty of the political situation. During 1971 Gross National Product rose by 8 per cent and industrial production by 15 per cent. The share of wages in National Income rose to 59 per cent, having stood at 51·7 per cent on an average between 1960 and 1969 (ODEPLAN, 1972). In the municipal elections of March 1971 the UP won almost 50 per cent of the vote, in contrast to the 37 per cent it had won in the previous September, on account of this expansion and other factors. During 1971 the complete and unanimous

1. The following elections have taken place since the Presidential Election of September 1970: municipal elections in March 1971, by-elections in two provinces in January 1972 and a further by-election in July 1972; election of the President of the CUT (*Central Unica de Trabajadores* – the agglomorating institution of the trade union movement), in July and August 1972; election of the Rector of the University of Chile and of the President of the Student's Union in April and July 1972. To these one could add a long list of elections in trade unions, all of which are given great importance in the press, as measures of this, or any government's popularity. Finally, in March 1973 there were parliamentary elections.

nationalization by Congress of foreign-owned or part-owned copper mines was achieved, and 130 important enterprises passed either by purchase or by 'intervention'[1] into the hands of the State.[2] By July 1972, 3,282 farms had been affected by the agrarian reform process, in addition to the 1,410 expropriated under Frei. The number of peasants benefited will eventually be of the order of 75,000 – roughly 10 per cent of the rural labour force.

The seizure of industries and farms would not have been possible without a solid working-class base on which the government could count, especially in nationalized industries. These industries are under the control of administrative councils on which workers' representatives sit side-by-side with government appointees – the latter numbering one more than the former. It would be very difficult indeed for any government to return these industries, even in those cases where legal property has not been transferred to the State. The same can be said of legally expropriated and seized farms. The UP itself was strained in its pursuit of two different and often contradictory tasks: the mobilization of the working class and a semblance of orderly government. It was difficult to control seizures of industries, and even more so to limit wage increases. The government reached agreements with the CUT in 1971 and 1972 at the national level, but the wage increases agreed were surpassed, on average, by well over 30 per cent in individual factories. Wages were rising with particular speed in the nationalized industries, and the only imaginable way of limiting them would have been through rationing or massive inflation: this latter was to come, but it could hardly be interpreted as a method of 'controlling' wages.

1. This term refers to government take-over of the management of a firm or farm without actual take-over of ownership. It is possible in virtue of a law decreed by the 100 Day Socialist Republic of 1932. According to this legislation – which had lain dormant and forgotten on the statute books – the government may, in the case of social conflict or similar difficulty, 'intervene' in the firm or farm concerned.
2. The passing of many industries into the hands of the State was a haphazard affair in some cases: groups sometimes not controlled by the UP – and perhaps not controlled by anyone – would create a *fait accompli* by occupying a factory, for example, and more or less forcing the Ministry of Labour to 'intervene' simply in order to avoid lengthy halts in production. Thus a number of firms in the *Area de Propieded Social* (State Sector) were not really 'wanted' in it, while some ninety large and important monopolies were still in private hands, awaiting more conventional constitutional procedures to be taken over – procedures for which the necessary Congressional approval did not appear very forthcoming, at least in 1972.

Against this background, the Communist Party in particular was eager not to alienate the so-called middle sectors and by mid-1972 was advocating, successfully, a policy of consolidation, involving a slow-down in nationalization and an increasingly shrill attack on the ultra-left, though it was unclear whether the middle sectors could in fact be won over under any conditions, and many factions in the Socialist Party remained sceptical about the possibilities of a successful transition to socialism which did not harm the interests of the middle class and involve a dramatic confrontation with the Christian Democrats and with the bourgeoisie as a whole.

The money supply increased by 113 per cent in 1971, and demand generated among low-income groups affected food products disproportionately, provoking an unprecedented increase in food imports at a time when world copper prices were declining and world food prices were rising astronomically, while aid- and capital-flows into the country were, for obvious reasons, drying up. Food imports, which had cost an average of 11·7 per cent of export earnings in 1965–70, rose to 15·7 per cent and 33·1 per cent in 1971 and 1972, and in absolute terms from $125 million in 1945–70 to $180 million and $364 million in the latter two years; the prices of these imports rose 8 per cent in 1971 and 41 per cent in 1972.

During the same period, domestic food-production grew by 3·5 per cent per annum in 1965–70, and by 4·7 per cent in 1970–1 and 1·3 per cent in 1971–2. Total agricultural production grew slightly more in these last years, but in any case the figure conceals marked variations in certain crops and in livestock. Wine and grape production grew by some 30 per cent in 1970–1, and crop production by 10·3 per cent, while livestock barely increased at all, partly due to contraband exports in the south, to Argentina. If the effect of the increase in wine and grape production in 1970–1 is discounted, the increase for that year is 2·9 per cent.[1] In 1971–2, cattle production declined, due perhaps to an inflationary situation which encourages farmers to keep cattle on the hoof, while livestock products such as eggs, chickens and pigs increased substantially. Thus total livestock production rose some 6·6 per cent; but crop production fell by 4 per cent (in spite of a 2·6 per cent increase in area sown). In particular, wheat declined 13 per cent, maize 12 per cent and sugar beet 14 per cent.

1. Source: UNDP-FAO-ICIRA (1972). This report was co-ordinated by Solon Barraclough and differs little in the essence of its findings on production from reports put out by the Agricultural Economics Department of the Catholic University at a similar time.

Thanks to the use of idle industrial capacity and price control, and agricultural imports, inflation in 1971 was much lower than in 1970 (22·1 per cent against 34·9 per cent). Inevitably, however, by the beginning of 1972 shortages and queues were beginning to make their appearance. Most people in all social strata were probably consuming more than they had done before 1971 but the fact that they had to queue or pay black-market prices for certain goods and that, for example, the shortage of imported spare parts for public transport was creating an almost impossible situation for Santiago commuters, eroded the government's popularity in relation to early 1971. The strategy of the then Minister of Economic Affairs, Pedro Vuskovic, had been based on the hope that there would be a far stronger political response to the redistributive measures than in fact emerged. Had forms of popular participation arisen allowing physical control over goods reaching the towns, then the fact that the upper and middle classes had not lost purchasing power in the expansion of money incomes would have been offset by the greater availability of goods among the poorer classes, and to some extent the JAP (*Juntas de Abastecimiento y Precios* – Price and Supply Boards) offered a solution. By early to mid 1972, however, the situation was almost out of control and inflation in 1972 was to be well beyond 130 per cent. The opposition, almost dormant for some six months after the 1970 election, had regrouped and re-organized and was emerging again as a powerful force capable of using against the government methods usually associated with the left: the organization and mobilization of as great a portion of the population as possible, though with the addition of provocation and para-military fascist groups. A massive effort of organization was carried out under the umbrella of civil and professional groups such as the National Confederation of Retail Trade, as well as among doctors and lawyers against the formation of the JAP, and against the government as a whole, culminating in the month-long lorry-owners' and shopkeepers' strike in late 1972, and military participation in the government.

The political choices open to UP in mid 1972 were few and nasty, but at least they were clear: the continued attempt to hold down prices would have surely involved the institution of rationing, or else the disappearance of innumerable goods away to the black market. To unleash the forces of inflation by allowing prices to return to their 'natural' levels would have meant a regressive step in the redistribution of income, yet there seemed no viable alternative. During August 1972 price increases were decreed ranging often far above 100 per cent. Whether this inflation can play the role of an 'expenditure tax' (albeit a regressive one) depends on the effectiveness of central control in the State sector.

Throughout these two years the coalition has, remarkably, held almost completely together, losing only a fraction of the Radical Party; cracks have emerged in the bureaucracy below ministerial level, and in ideological discussion. Yet most important is the political polarization which has taken place in the entire society. The spectre of civil war is now evoked quite frequently by Chilean politicians on both sides; some agitate the spectre in order to fan the flames, while others sincerely hope to avoid it.

Moderation may well achieve its immediate aim of restoring stability especially with the appointment of the Commander-in-Chief of the Armed Forces as Minister of the Interior,[1] but whether the long-term transition to socialism is still possible depends on many other factors. Among these are the tacit bargaining between government and army, the results of the parliamentary elections in March 1973 and the level of mass organization and consciousness among the working class and among rural workers; there is also the capacity of the Christian Democrats and the right to mobilize the middle class and certain sectors of the peasantry, and to complement this with provocations and para-military actions.

III. The Development of Rural Unions since 1964

Right from the start Frei encouraged the formation of rural trade unions and in 1966 the Christian Democrats and the left in Congress supported a law permitting their establishment, while in 1967 a further law was passed which protected union leaders from reprisals by landowners. The *Ranquil* Union (formerly the Federation of Peasants and Indigenous Peoples, which had existed since 1961), led by the Communist and Socialist Parties, was now able to develop more freely and rapidly. A Christian Union promoted by Jesuit priests and financed during the 1960s by funds from AID[2] had also existed since 1960 but it did not

1. A post equivalent in status to that of Prime Minister in France. The appointment was made in November 1972 in order to bring the shopkeepers' strike to an end.
2. This union had a series of precursors during the 1960s, as indeed had the *Ranquil* – though in the latter case it was only in 1961 that co-operation was achieved between socialists and communists. The Christian Union (*Union de Campesinos Christianos*, later *Confedracion Campesina 'Libertad'*, received aid from AID through the International

succeed in expanding so rapidly, because the Christian Democrats set up a new union, called *Triunfo Campesino* which benefited from the direct patronage of government agencies such as the Institute for Agricultural Development (INDAP). Between 1964 and 1970 the growth of this movement was indeed spectacular as Table 2 shows:

TABLE 1 *Expropriation under Frei and under Allende*

	Irrig. hectares exapropriated	*No. of farms*	*No. of asentados*	*Total workforce* (inc. *socios*)
1965[1]–1970[1]	290,690	1,410	26,739	32,754
1970[1]–1972[2]	344,022	2,944	29,577	36,230[3]

1. November. 2. May.
3. Estimate, assuming *asentado/socio* ratio remains unchanged.
(Source: CORA, 1972.)

TABLE 2 *Membership of Rural Unions*

	1967	*1970*	*1972*
Libertad	15,411	29,132	23,203
Ranquil	10,961	43,867	105,990
Triunfo	26,827	64,003	54,767
Unidad Obrera-Campesina	—	—	33,831
TOTAL	53,199	140,293	217,791

(Sources: For 1967 and 1970, Ministry of Labour, Union Department. For 1972, INDAP, Union Department, based on data from the Union Extension Fund.)

Strikes gradually became a customary feature of the rural scene, varying in their length and in the numbers of workers involved. The vast majority were short and limited to one or two farms, arising from wage demands, but in some cases they affected a whole province or a few municipalities in a province. Partly as a

---

Development Foundation under AID subsidy No. AID-409, June 1966. '*Libertad*' represented the right wing of the Christian Democrat ideology, and merited AID Funds because it opposed *Triunfo*, considered 'State-controlled' unionism.

result of union action, and partly as a result of the enforcement of a substantially increased rural minimum wage, and of social security obligations of the land law, the incomes of agricultural workers increased very substantially during this period. The official minimum wage increased in real terms by 50 per cent between 1960 and 1969; in some areas, especially in the southern part of the country, the minimum wage was not effectively enforced, but in most of the Central Valley, the country's most important agricultural region, it was. Unionized workers often obtained wage increases exceeding the official minimum. Despite their varying political colour, all unions pursued higher wages as their principal objective and used similar tactics. They also helped workers to exert pressure upon the Agrarian Reform Corporation (CORA) to expropriate the farms on which they were working, but it was rare for any union to engage in farm seizures. When they did, the objective was to exert pressure on wage negotiations, forcing landlords and State mediators to reach a swifter and more beneficial agreement with the workers' representatives. Seizures were adopted as frequently if not more so, by members of Christian Democratic unions as by others; perhaps because they felt more secure from repression. As with strikes, most seizures were isolated and short-lived affairs, but sometimes, as in the provinces of Coquimbo and Santiago during 1970, they were more organized and spread over a larger number of farms. In general the development of the union movement was notable for its orderly rather than its disorderly character; within the space of a couple of years the union leadership at national, provincial and local levels had become accustomed to complicated bureaucratic and legal procedures in the presentation and negotiation of wage claims, and violations were carefully calculated. The law governing strikes in Chile, curiously similar to the British Industrial Relations Act of 1971, makes it illegal for a strike to be decreed before a statutory cooling-off period, and allows the government to decree a return either on the grounds that a crop would suffer irremediably, or by compulsory arbitration. However, during a strike in the province of Colchagua, in 1969, for example, the government sought to impose a return to work. The number of strikers was great enough (3,207 on 178 farms) and the unity between the Christian Democrats and the left-wing union solid enough, to permit leaders to resist this.[1]

The membership of the unions consisted almost entirely of workers on large farms, best termed a proletariat in transition. If

1. Such united action was exceptional in the country as a whole, but seems to have been the norm in Colchagua.

they demanded increases in or simply a maintenance of their rights to land, this was regarded as part of their payment rather than as an increase in rewards for labour rent.[1] For these workers joining a union seems to have been accompanied by a fairly high degree of solidarity. If a union organization does exist on a farm it tends to include all, or almost all the wage workers thereon, and all belong to the same union. Loyalty beyond the farm limits tends to go upwards towards the union organization and political patrons, rather than horizontally towards the workers on surrounding farms.

IV. The Transformation of Social Relationships on the Latifundia[2]

The power structure of a Chilean latifundio depended for its stability upon a judicious distribution of patronage by the landlord. A core of workers and supervisors on the farm would receive substantially greater personal favours than the remainder, who might well constitute the majority. They would be allowed more pasture rights, or extra land for cultivation, or maybe the days they took off in order to cultivate their own land would simply be overlooked by the landlord or his manager. Only a few favoured individuals are required to keep the remainder in check, partly by the threat of violence and partly perhaps, by the hope that they too would come to be members of the favoured minority. The formal expression of this division is expressed by the titles *inquilino* and *voluntario*. The inquilino has usufruct of a plot round his house, pasture rights for two to five animals, and, in the irrigated areas of the Central Valley, use of three-quarters of a hectare of land for growing corn, potatoes and beans. The voluntario does not have an automatic right to a house, even if he is married, and usually lives in the house of an inquilino who may be a relative. The voluntario, in principle, has no right to land, but in practice may be allowed, say, three-eighths of a hectare.

1. The system of work on Chilean latifundia during the nineteenth century was more strictly feudal. The *inquilinos* were a relatively privileged stratum of workers who acquired rights in land or pasture according to the number of days worked by them, or by others paid by them, on 'demesne' land.
2. If the reader is taken aback by what appear to be sweeping generalizations in this section, he is referred to my articles (1971, 1972) for further clarification and evidence (especially 1972). The generalizations are based on field research in Colchagua in 1969–70.

These divisions persist, but today they frequently cut across the formal appellations. This form of organization emphasizes very strongly not just the receiving of orders from above but also ties of personal obligation and thus of loyalty, towards an individual, combined with important divisions among those of similar formal status. The *patrón* is considered by his workers to have certain moral obligations, which he must fulfil especially when unforeseen misfortunes such as disease befall them. During the 1950s and early 1960s, the terms on which workers were employed changed, gradually but steadily: the proportion of inquilinos declined and that of voluntarios and non-permanent workers increased substantially, due largely to mechanization, while total land under 'peasant' cultivation declined (Kay, 1972).[1] The bulk of union membership came from permanent workers, not from the 'most proletarianized' day-labourers – which reflected power relationships within the rural proletariat. Early measures taken by the Frei government made landlords pay higher wages, higher social security benefits, and taxes, and there is evidence that during 1965 and 1966 there was a substantial redistribution of income towards rural workers both from the landlords and from the rest of society (Echeverría, 1969). This reduced the economic capacity of landlords to allow peasants rights to land and pasture, or simply to run the farms with a degree of patronal laxity, and thus probably created fertile ground for union activists. It is unlikely that a union movement would have grown up from within the peasantry without outside agitation, patronage, and protection; in previous decades the possible desire of certain groups of workers to organize, was inhibited by their, quite correct, fear of repression either from the police or from the landlords. Although there is a long history of sporadic conflict on farms all over the country which has remained hidden in obscure records of the Ministry of Labour (Loveman, 1971) it has never yielded a sustained organized movement. Now, as from the last month of 1964, rural workers organized, because they could see that the State machine offered them an alternative source of patronage and protection. It is not surprising that, benefiting from an army of agitators paid by the State (officials of INDAP), the Christian Democrat union seems to have grown faster than

1. According to Kay (1972), on the basis of Agricultural Census data, 'peasant' cultivation covered one-quarter of the cultivated land on *haciendas* in 1955 and one-seventh in 1965, producing a third of their output in 1955, and about a fifth in 1965. Their numbers declined, between 1935 and 1965, from 107,900 to 46,500, or from 21 per cent to 6 per cent of the total agricultural labour force.

the others; perhaps what is surprising is that the left-wing union managed, with far fewer resources, to grow very fast as well.

V. Agrarian Reform under Frei and its Limitations

The 1967 Agrarian Reform Law, passed after lengthy delays in Congress, but with few changes from the original draft presented by the Christian Democrat government, may not be a socialist document, nor was it intended to be, but it certainly places far-reaching powers in the hands of a government. With minimal exceptions the government can expropriate all land belonging to landowners who own more than eighty standard hectares, paying between 1 and 10 per cent in cash and the remainder in bonds redeemable after a period of between five and thirty years according to the reason for expropriation. The value of the bonds is, in principle, readjusted by 70 per cent of the rate of inflation. However, eighty standard hectares are equivalent to eighty hectares of land in a very fertile valley near Santiago, so that this still leaves farms of a fairly substantial size in existence. Furthermore, the Law stipulates that all cattle, machinery and houses must be paid for in cash, and the owner has a right to keep a reserve of a minimum of forty standard hectares. During the Frei régime 290,000 irrigated hectares in 1,410 farms were expropriated and some 33,000 peasants were benefited thereby. It is very difficult to establish firm figures on this point, because frequently a very long period elapsed between the legal process of expropriation and the actual entry into force of new forms of tenure.

In theory, the beneficiaries were to pay for the land over thirty years; CORA was to remain owner of the expropriated land for three years and then hand it over to the beneficiaries. In practice, the *asignación* rarely took place within this time, under either government, and when it did, the relationship between *asentados* and the State, which we shall describe, hardly changed at all.

The reform, as implemented by Frei, was limited, both quantitatively and qualitatively, in the number of farms expropriated and by the absence of parallel measures which might have substantially undermined the economic dominance of large farmers. For example, the distribution of credit between large landowners and peasants remained substantially unchanged; this was particularly true for credit distributed to smallholders, but *asentados* suffered from similar inequalities. On the basis of data from the Agricultural Planning Office for 1968, it has been calculated that CORA distributed 12·1 per cent of total State credit, INDAP (the agency for small farmers' credit) 5·1 per cent, the State bank 74·1 per cent and the Development Corporation (CORFO) 8·7 per cent, the last two being credit agencies for commercial farmers; the lion's share of credit was still going to capitalist farmers. True, the total amount of credit distributed had multiplied by 2·5 since 1964, and CORA's share had increased from 0·9 per cent (Menjívar, 1969), but independent smallholders still received the same share in 1968 as in 1964 through INDAP. Thus, there was improved treatment for the beneficiaries of the reform and continued preferential treatment for capitalist farmers. The latter were receiving improved technical assistance, package deals whereby they could install enterprises breeding broiler hens and pigs intensively on a large scale, and the benefits of corn imports from the U.S.A. under PL480 which provided cheap feed for these ventures. Although they were being squeezed on the wages side, those who cared to modernize, and intensify their production could obtain ample credit at rates of interest which fell below the rate of inflation (though not as low as INDAP and CORA rates). During the Frei period the rate of growth of agricultural products rose from an average of 1·8 per cent between 1949 and 1964 to an average of 4·6 per cent between 1965 and 1968, due largely to expanded credit and technical assistance to commercial farmers as well perhaps as to the threat of expropriation on more onerous terms of particularly undercultivated farms.[1]

The landowners were indeed revitalized as an interest group by the agrarian reform. The National Society for Agriculture (SNA) which had represented them ever since 1869 had not resisted very violently the Agrarian Reform Law, but the leadership changed in 1967, when an old-time Liberal Party politician replaced the more progressive Christian Democrat sympathizer who had seen the Society through the passage of the Reform Law. But the Society was still not competent to deal with a new situation, and a National Confederation of Agricultural Employers (CONSEMACH) was formed growing within two years to a membership of over 9,000 in late 1969 as against SNA's 4,000 (Gomez, 1969, pp. 55 and

1. In practice, the articles of the Law permitting the most onerous terms of expropriation (abandonment of the farm, or poor standard of cultivation) were hardly applied at all. 37 per cent of farms taken over were offered by their owners who thereby obtained better terms than otherwise, and 46 per cent were expropriated on grounds of size, which again did not allow very onerous repayment terms (onerous, that is, from the owner's point of view). See Echeñique (1970).

59). This grouping adopted a stance of militant opposition to the government and to the agrarian reform, to the level of prices fixed for wheat, and to any other convenient issue that arose. Under Allende's government, the organization became even more militant, and some groups of members organized '*retomas*' (literally 'reseizures') of farms seized by the peasants. The CONSEMACH, for the first time, managed to incorporate medium-size farmers into political life, and sought to give them a sense of national purpose, with an agrarian and nationalist ideology, thus defining its difference from the more oligarchic and indeed exclusive SNA, which had never organized mass action by farmers. Eventually, the SNA also 'modernized' and by 1971 was operating in close co-ordination with CONSEMACH.

VI. Agrarian Reform Institutions under the Christian Democrats

When the Frei government came to power the Christian Democrats, despite a general commitment to create 100,000 new proprietors and to promote rural unions, had few clear or agreed ideas about the kind of agrarian reform they wished to carry out. During 1965–6 a fierce debate went on among party experts and politicians, in which one group advocated the immediate establishment of family farms while another, in which the heads of INDAP, Jacques Chonchol and of CORA, Rafael Moreno, were prominent, preferred a co-operative form of ownership (McCoy, 1969). Not surprisingly, the latter group prevailed, for they controlled the two most important reform institutions, and as a result the right wing of the Christian Democratic Party and many of its rural politicians became estranged from the agrarian reform process. Behind such arguments over tenure institutions, of course, lay different visions of a future agrarian structure: different ideals of a 'peasant economy', different appreciations of the virtues of rapid expropriation, and also an awareness by some that collective institutions could be a useful instrument of political control.

CORA decided, eventually, on the *asentamiento*. The asentamiento was designed as a transitional arrangement which would allow the beneficiaries to receive technical education and, hopefully, to accustom themselves to collective work, under the leadership of an elected Council of five to seven members and with CORA's guidance. Membership was to be decided by the Corporation and at first it was limited to those heads of family or bread-winners who had been working on the expropriated farms, who were to work the land collectively, in a production co-operative. Their numbers were to be calculated in such a way that if, at the time of definitive distribution of the land, they were to decide to distribute it individually there would be enough land to allow each one a viable family farm of about eight standard hectares.[1] CORA would provide credit for inputs and would, above all, pay an 'advance' against profits which would finance essential subsistence during the course of the agricultural year. This 'advance' was seen by the *asentados* as a wage, and when, inevitably, their enterprises did not show a profit, and they were therefore unable to pay back the advance, CORA did not deprive them of or lower the advance in the following year. CORA seems to have attempted, during 1969, to use the advance as an incentive by raising it more from one agricultural year to the next on those farms which showed profits than on those which did not, but as time passed this technique seems to have fallen by the wayside.[2] These advances were between 21 per cent and 51 per cent higher than the wages received by the average farm worker during 1969. The asentados enjoyed more individual pasture rights than before, and the rights were less strictly limited; they also had the use of a plot of land around their house and three-quarters of a hectare (in the Central Valley) for private cultivation in the fields. This is also an expansion of rights enjoyed by inquilinos on the latifundia.

Evidently, the asentados became a privileged minority within the rural proletariat. Furthermore, a substantial proportion of workers on the latifundia did not gain full rights as asentados, and lost the guarantee of daily employment which they had obtained during the last years with the land owners. Thus, according to an unpublished survey carried out by CORA during May 1948 in 225 asentamientos the national average for the amount of work done by hired labour on asentamientos was almost 30 per cent, and in Colchagua the figure was 52 per cent. According to a study of seventeen asentamientos out of the fifty-two already operating in the agricultural year 1967–8, 41 per cent of the days worked on

1. In a *minifundio* area eight standard hectares would be the property of a fairly comfortable rich peasant.
2. Advances were Eo. 10 during the agricultural year 1968–9; according to the President of an Asentamiento in the province of Colchagua in the Central Valley, asentamientos with profits would receive, during the following year, Eo. 15 per day per man whereas those who did not show profits would only receive Eo. 12. (Eo means *escudos*.) But this was not implemented.

these farms were contributed by wage-labour – though the vast variation of the figure, between 0 per cent and 80 per cent, should warn us against taking it too seriously (Jolly *et al.*, 1969). The CORA budget for 1968 shows an average expenditure of Eo. 3,930 per asentado in cash advances, and Eo. 1,340 in wages, the latter referring to wages paid to non-asentados; so about one-quarter of total man-days were worked by wage labourers, taking account of the fact that wages were slightly lower than the 'advance'. But, if the number of man-years worked by wage-labourers is important, it falls far short of the number of wage-workers waiting or expecting to be employed on the asentamiento. In the province of Colchagua (in Region 2 on the map) in 1969–70 I studied fourteen asentamientos and on these farms there were 354 asentados, and 237 *voluntarios*, which referred to a pool of labourers rather than to those actually working full-time. The wage workers did not have rights either to an individual plot of land for subsistence or to pasture rights and received wages which were one-sixth less than the advances given to the asentados in 1968–9 and one-fifth less in 1969–70.

During 1968 CORA sought to put an end to this internal inequality on the asentamiento by incorporating non-bread-winners as full-time workers with the status of *socios*. It took a long time for this decision to be implemented on the ground but by 1972 it could be safely claimed that all permanent workers on asentamientos had the same status and even the same rights to land. Since farms distributed in definitive property to the reform beneficiaries (*fundos asignados*) before the end of 1970 were in fact all distributed in either a co-operative or a 'mixed' form of property under which some of the land is owned individually and the remainder co-operatively owned, possible conflicts arising from the lack of land to distribute to everyone in 'viable' family holdings were avoided. Nevertheless, the beneficiaries remain a privileged stratum, and this has a number of implications for a political analysis of the reform.

CORA's relationship with the asentados was one of clientele, but the clients were far from powerless. The leaders of the asentamientos, intermediaries between the State bureaucracy and their rank and file, were in quite a strong position in bargaining with CORA officials, especially when it was a question of foregoing acquired privileges and benefits. When a big credit for capital investment was sought, the upper reaches of the bureaucracy, removed from the pressures on the ground, could say 'no' without much difficulty. In any case the bureaucratic procedures necessary to obtain such benefits were enough to discourage all but the most persistent asentamiento leaders, and the only way many felt they could obtain them was by applying pressure at the top through a local deputy, senator or other dignitary. But when CORA sought to introduce more workers, say, from other farms into the asentamientos, it met with strong resistance, which it was unable to overcome – although the effort to do so was not intense. Similarly CORA was unable often to recuperate credit, or to control the expansion of private rights. CORA did eventually accord all permanent workers the same status, from the point of view of job security, pay, and individual rights, but this was gained at the price of even greater indebtedness and of a new form of internal differentiation to which we shall come.

Clientelism generated privileged access, especially once national and provincial organizations of asentamientos were set up. The head of CORA, Rafael Moreno, set up a National Confederation as a puppet organization, designed to strengthen political control of the beneficiaries of the reform. At the provincial level, the leaders of this organization had privileged access to offices of CORA, and the knowledge that they had direct access to Moreno probably spurred low-level officials to give them, and their farms, special attention. In Colchagua the provincial leadership sought and obtained a role in the decision to expropriate, and this apparent advance in peasant participation went together with a preference for potential beneficiaries sympathetic to the government. These leaders were mostly of slightly superior social status to the mass of the rural workers and asentados, having been supervisors or office workers on the farms previously, or having had some experience of urban and industrial life. They were thus better equipped than others to find their way through the bureaucratic maze of CORA and other agencies.

This division of the peasantry was a concomitant of the clientelistic application of the Reform Law: the Law did not compel the government to take over all farms falling within the scope, and a bureaucracy staffed overwhelmingly by Christian Democrats was bound to use political criteria in expropriation. Sympathizers among landlords and peasants could hope, at least, for privileged access, though this did not develop into blatant favouritism. However, it is far from clear that the party gained more than it lost out of the process; while asentados seem generally to have backed it, at least in the areas of Colchagua where I worked, the wage-workers and those in other farms who were excluded and who at the beginning were favourable to the Communist or Socialist Parties, were confirmed in their opposition. Furthermore, there is evidence that workers would attempt to appear to back the government, even if in private and in voting booths they backed the opposition, in order to obtain the expropriation of a farm.[1]

The scope of Christian Democrat reformism was limited by the strong influence wielded in the government by industrialists and other capitalist interests; the benefits to be redistributed were few, and clientelism was bound to divide the peasantry. However, an analysis of the mode of production which arose on the asentamientos, is necessary if we are to detect the interests which the asentados would be likely to defend, and thus the longer-term political implications of the reform.

VII. The Development of the Peasant Economy on the Asentamientos

My purpose in this section is to show how the particular kind of non-capitalist rationality applied by asentados affects the allocation of labour as between individual and collective enterprise; therefore I have adopted the term peasant economy to refer to the enterprise based on individual rights to land both on the latifundia and on the asentamientos.

1. *Peasant Economy on the Latifundia*

The institution of *inquilinaje* contained features typical both of peasant economy and of proletarian labour – whence our term 'proletariat in transition'. Other permanent workers on latifundia, although they may have had hardly any individual rights to land or pasture, still frequently participated in the peasant economy, if their father or other relative had individual rights, and they worked together in a common family economy. The only workers to have no access to a peasant economy are those non-permanent workers who are not owners or tenants of a *minifundio* either.

To judge by union action, these private plots on the latifundia were highly valued by the workers, even in recent years when they were losing them, and when the proportion of inquilinos and

1. Since the asentados are a small proportion of voters, even at the municipality level, it is almost impossible to tell their voting behaviour. Furthermore, one does not know how their rate of electoral participation compares with that of other groups. All we can say is that electoral support for the right has exhibited a general downward trend in rural areas since 1958.

indeed of permanent workers as a whole, in the rural labour force, was diminishing fast. In making wage claims, unions of all political colours would include demands referring specifically to the kind-content of wages,[1] in the hope, no doubt, of preserving their members' purchasing power, while the government, claiming to contribute to an improvement of agricultural workers' conditions, restricted payments in kind by law to 25 per cent of the value of the total wage; the government was seeking to incorporate workers into the market economy, while the workers were more concerned to protect their purchasing power in the market. However, the inquilino's plot and cattle rarely afforded him the opportunity to accumulate resources and expand his enterprise, with the exception of some who engaged in petty trade within the larger farms, buying and selling, sometimes even transporting.

Thus such pressure as there was on land was (largely unsuccessful) pressure for the preservation of usufruct rights within the latifundio, while pressure for expropriation came more indirectly through the general collapse of existing social arrangements arising from a movement largely devoted, at the grass roots, to the classic bargaining role of industrial unions. When explaining why they prefer, or would prefer, to work in asentamientos, workers frequently mention the high level of the advances as compared to their present wages, as well as the sense of being free, in the work situation, from the pressures of supervisory personnel. (Lehmann, 1972.) The demand for higher living standards seems to be sociologically prior to the demand for land.[2] The exception, in Chile, is to be found among the indigenous peoples, the Mapuche, in the south, to whom we shall return.

In recent years, it has become less difficult for farm workers to increase their incomes and status by raising their skill levels, and

1. *Regalías*, or 'perquisites' – rights to land, pastures, sometimes a certain quantity of bread and beans at noon, and of course the house.
2. Reporting the results of an attitude survey in an area of the Central Valley, Raul Urzúa found that *inquilinos* expressed less preference for 'structural' changes (i.e. redistribution of land) than smallholders, sharecroppers and day-labourers, and explains this by the fact that they are more subject to paternalistic authority of landlords than the other types of peasant. This may be so, if we rely on the results of a survey, but, of the four groups he refers to, the *inquilinos* are those who, through their participation in the union movement, have *in practice* done most to further agrarian reform. Even day-labourers' participation in the unions is small – to their cost, it should be added. See Urzúa (1969, pp. 192–3), and also a polemic between myself and the author in *Cuadernos de la Realidad Nacional*, 2, January 1970.

by engaging in various forms of piece-work and incentive systems rather than by seeking an expansion of their peasant enterprise. Nevertheless, this process of organizational change has been slow, and the aspiration to individual rights persists.

2. *Peasant Economy on the Asentamientos*

Given this situation, it would not have been impossible to create organizations which encouraged these proletarianizing trends (which are far from being pauperizing trends). But the ideology of the Law was that of the family farm, and in fact, there would simply not have been enough land available for distribution among 100,000[1] beneficiaries on an individual basis. However, the Law left open the possibility of co-operative forms of work and ownership and it was this line which CORA adopted.

Paradoxical though it may appear, the success of these co-operatives, or asentamientos, required an adoption by the workers concerned, of a capitalist rationality: they were expected to work most of the land collectively, under an elected leadership, and either to distribute profits among themselves according to the number of days worked and the quality of each man's work, or to save them. The role of the advance was to guarantee subsistence precisely so that the asentados, rather than concentrate on their private land in order to feed themselves during the year, would, with cheap credit from the state, seek to enrich themselves while raising productivity and yields on 'collective' land. The model assumed that the asentados would respond according to this rationality, if only because it would otherwise be difficult for them to repay their debts, including the advance, and the veto power of CORA officials on the Administrative Council of the asentamientos was to be a further guarantee. But, what if the peasants would not pay their debts? And, more to the point, perhaps, what if the 'all-powerful' CORA, the so-called 'new *patrón*' had few effective sanctions available to enforce debt repayment?

The asentados were in a good bargaining position. Could CORA realistically threaten to withdraw advances or rights to land, even from asentamientos who either did not pay debts which they could pay, or did not cultivate all the land at their disposal, or refused to accept new members even when they were unable to cultivate that land? The uproar was not worth the risk, and, in any case, the political return probably seemed to justify the social costs of the operation. Estimates of the cost of the reform per family are

1. This target figure was reduced substantially in 1966 and 1967.

very difficult to make: one estimate puts it at around $10,000 (Eo. 90,000 at 1968 values), (Echeñique, 1970; Menjívar, 1969, p. 133),[1] but whatever the cost per family, the total budget of CORA was small: 2 per cent of the national budget in 1967 (CORA, 1948) and furthermore, the Corporation was expected (optimistically), to finance future activities to a large extent from returns not further credits. Economically inefficient, but politically less so.

We have circumstantial and some direct evidence for saying that the individual rights to land have expanded on the asentamiento, on the garden plot around the house and the plot land in the field, as well as in pasture rights for cattle. After 1969 a lot of workers who had previously not possessed the status of inquilinos came to enjoy the same rights as the asentados at first kept for themselves: a piece of land in the field cultivated intensively with corn, beans and potatoes, and rights to varying amounts of cattle which usually exceed two and often reach as many as eight, at least formally. These rights are all free of charge, whereas on the latifundia money wages were reduced by a sum corresponding to the (often negotiated) value of the rights. In practice most asentados do not possess as many animals as they have a right to, but the number of animals privately owned by former inquilinos and wage-earners has risen. According to the unpublished CORA census of 1968 the total permanent labour force on farms increased by some 30 per cent after expropriation, which gives further circumstantial evidence that the total proportion of land controlled by individuals increased. On the basis of internal information, CORA sources gave in 1972 the figure of 13 per cent of total sown area under individual control, but this might well be an underestimate. According to my own observations in ten reformed units in the province of Colchagua during 1972, land under individual cultivation was 10 per cent of total sown and unsown irrigated land; but if we remember that a large part of total irrigated land is under pasture and that these figures do not include land taken up by individually owned animals, the likely proportion of sown area is much greater. My own data are not taken from a random sample, but they nevertheless serve as a corrective to national data collected by a still imperfect statistical system.

Now, the amount of land under individual control is less important than the extent to which the interests of the family enterprise prevail over those of the collective, and influence resource-use and the distribution of income among the asentados.

1. The estimate includes administrative costs.

The family enterprise in general receives free use of machinery, such as a tractor, and sometimes free use of inputs such as seeds and pesticides. Finally, and most important, there is little control over the use of labour; analysis of data on two farms collected by the University of Wisconsin Land Tenure Center project shows a remarkable lack of variation in the number of days worked from month to month by asentados, as declared to CORA, and therefore makes one suspect that there is a lack of realism in the declarations made by the asentamientos to CORA to claim their monthly advances.[1] In another study of sixteen asentamientos in 1966–7, an average of only thirty-eight out of forty-nine asentados appeared for work 'every month' (Jolly *et al.*, p. 41). The Christian Democrats sought to relate the distribution of profits both to the number of days worked and to the quality of the work, but this was hardly implemented at all. In any case the advances which are drawn from profits, in theory, had already been received throughout the year, on a straight day rate and how could they be affected retroactively? Once the asentados have understood that their debts are unlikely to be claimed if they can show somehow that they are unable to pay them, they are also likely to have little compunction in distributing among themselves favours whose cost is borne by the State. In any case, the debts of most asentamientos for capital loans and year to year loans for inputs and advances, are so enormous that their members can hardly be made to believe in a rationality based on future profits. By 1972, it was common practice to sell produce from the collective land to private merchants without declaring these sales, and then to claim that the asentamiento was unable to pay its debts – having distributed the income from the sale; but even this possibility did not channel resources away from the family enterprise.

This is not simply evidence of peasant deviousness – though no doubt there is plenty of that as well. It rather reflects the specific conditions of co-operation on the asentamientos. The government – expecting the asentado to behave like a capitalist farmer – gives each man the same advance, assuming that this will be repaid and the remaining profit will be distributed to each according to the number of days he has worked. But the asentados see the advance as a wage, and its role as an incentive is reduced to nothing since all receive the same per day, however much they work, and – if they can manage it – even if they do not work. Once it is widely understood that debts are not enforced, this latter situation becomes increasingly prevalent. For the advance to

1. I am indebted to Marion Brown for giving me access to these data.

operate as an incentive towards co-operation and collective work, there would have to be a high level of morally based co-operation among the asentados, in the absence of an effective material incentive. In practice, however, it was common to hear the argument that there is no point in a man working hard if another spends his time drinking. My interviews with workers and asentados in 1969, show a very clear concern for a fair return to physical effort expended in work. Thus, where there is a lack of trust among co-operators they prefer to turn their energies to the family economy where such a return is more secure. The clientelistic relationship with government authorities foments this trend by making the State, rather than the asentados themselves, bear the costs of the low productivity of work of others so that internal social pressure to work hard on collective land need not be applied. The advance, intended to guarantee the capitalist rationality of a production co-operative, in fact becomes a subsidy to and encourages the peasant family economy, and this conflict of rationalities makes it increasingly difficult for the State to regain control of what happens on the asentamientos.

The distribution of income which emerges from this situation does not arise entirely from variations in each man's effort. Paradoxically, equalization of the status of all workers, whatever their family responsibilities, has accentuated inequality among families, favouring those with most sons of working age. Each working son brings, in the Central Valley, three-quarters of a hectare of land and free pasture rights to his family's enterprise. In Cautín, in 1972, the asentamientos distributed 300 or 400 kg. of wheat per family member to each family, but this apparently egalitarian measure was an addition to rather than a substitute for individual rights. Equalization of status has been confused with security of employment.[1]

The prospect of a stricter attitude on the part of the State, however remote, is likely to encourage these individualist trends, since they offer the best opportunity for the individual to protect his own family against possibly less benign authorities in the future.

On an asentamiento in Cautín in 1972 there were twenty-five asentados owning a total of seventy-nine cows. This did not appear strange, since they were, by common agreement, allowed rights to pasture for four animals each; however, it emerged that

1. If all benefits in kind were distributed according to family responsibilities, job security could be guaranteed to unmarried sons without generating these inequalities. Cautin is to the north of region 3 on the map.

the president of the asentamiento, almost the only member previously employed as an inquilino, had twenty animals of which most were 'shared' with other members. Under this sharing agreement, they hired to him their pasture rights and in return received half of the increase in the value of the animals at sale.[1] This extreme case indicates how an individual with an initial advantage can increase that advantage under the system of subsidies which prevails on the asentamientos.

The development of the peasant economy seemed to be far less pronounced where the material conditions of production were more akin to those of an industrial enterprise than to extensive farming, where work was more repetitive and easily quantifiable and allowed payment by piece-rates or at least of a realistic attempt to fix a 'fair day's work'. Such is the case in vineyards, and indeed the two vineyard asentamientos I studied in Colchagua had a less pronounced development of the peasant economy: in one case almost all the land available was in a vineyard and land for private use was rented individually from the former landlord, on his *reserva*. Profits on this asentamiento were exceptionally high.

This argument reminds us that changes in the material conditions of production affect peasant culture, peasant consciousness, and peasant rationality. But, there are nonetheless cases of vineyards where the peasant economy flourishes as much as where farming is extensive.

We have seen in this section how difficult it is for the State to control social and economic relationships within peasant society. Controls have backfired and afforded the peasants a means of increasing their independence both of the state and of each other. This arises partly from their clientelistic relationship with CORA, but such a relationship is almost inevitable in a process of agrarian reform. It would appear that the only benign means available to the State to control peasant economies are either the establishment of State farms or the judicious use of the price mechanism, and of fiscal instruments such as taxes and credit. These instruments may seem obvious to Indian economists, but in Latin America there is singularly little experience of their use in the control of the peasant economy. In these countries, heirs to a Spanish statist tradition, recourse is usually had to administrative forms of control, even though it is well known that the State

1. This asentamiento has a debt of Eo. 540,000 only on the loan made to them during 1971–2; a number of members also had a sharing agreement, similar to that with the president, with a butcher from the near-by town.

bureaucracy is an increasingly inefficient and unreliable means of dealing with the people.

VIII. Reform and Conflict under Unidad Popular

1. *The Programme*

The *Unidad Popular* programme[1] of government is not a programme of transition to socialism: it speaks of 'revolutionary changes' and of creating 'the most democratic régime in the history of the country'. It offers little solace for the landowners: all land falling within the scope of the 1967 Law is to be expropriated, and preference is to be given to co-operative forms of property, though individual titles will be assigned where conditions are most suitable for such a form of tenure, after the transition period. Asentamiento land can, 'in qualified cases', be assigned to smallholders, tenant farmers, sharecroppers and supervisory personnel of large farms. Where it is assigned in co-operative form, individuals will be given formal rights of ownership of their house and the garden plot, and 'corresponding rights' in the undivided part of the farm. Indeed, the programme reflects exactly the practices adopted by the Christian Democrats, in particular that of trying to eliminate the peasant family enterprise and thus risking its rebirth within the production co-operative. The difference lies in the speed of application of the reform, and in the accompanying general process of structural change in society.

The main UP programme was largely the work of the MAPU, but subsequently a document was put out entitled *Foundations of the Agrarian Reform of the Unidad Popular Government*, before the government had assumed power, in which it is not difficult to detect a Socialist hand. In this document socialism is still not mentioned by name, but the scope of expropriation is no longer limited to farms of more than eighty basic hectares: 'only small and medium farmers will be exempted', and the right to a reserve is to be subject to the peasants' judgement as to its utility for the development of the peasant community. Forest lands are to be incorporated into the reform process, and all agro-industrial and marketing concerns are to be transferred to the State or to peasant co-operatives. National and Regional Peasant Councils are to be established, elected directly by the entire peasantry

1. Adopted by the Communist, Socialist, and Radical Parties, as well as the MAPU and the personal party of Senator Rafael Tarud on 17 December 1969, prior to the selection of a candidate for the election.

('the 98 per cent of the presumably rural population which lives by and depends on agriculture') and these are to be the organs where, in collaboration with those officials responsible, agricultural policy is decided. Further to these measures, the document foresees a whole gamut of benefits, ranging from town hostels to a comprehensive national pension and social insurance scheme, and housing.

2. *Expropriation*

The contrast between these two documents gives us a foretaste of the divisions within the UP about the agrarian question. The National Agrarian Commission, meeting regularly from the start of the government, could never come to a firm decision on central issues – or if it did, the decision was rarely implemented because it did not have the whole-hearted support of all parties. In practice, the two principal parties – Communist and Socialist – proceeded with their own agrarian policies in those institutional areas which they could control, with the concerned, more intellectual MAPU, more or less aligned with the Communists (until the end of 1972), trying to make sense of the situation and being unable to obtain any coherent agreed policy which the government agencies concerned could carry out. The one process which did go ahead was that of expropriation, and it did so even faster than the government had originally promised: by mid 1972 there were no longer many owners of more than eighty standard hectares in the country, and those remaining were frequently in the limbo period between expropriation and actual transfer of their farms. By May 1972, 44 per cent of all farms with more than forty standard hectares, and 54 per cent of the land (weighted according to quality) in those farms had been expropriated, amounting to 38 per cent of the total agricultural land available. Taking into account the reserves left in the hands of the landowners, this last figure would be reduced to 36·7 per cent, referring to all the land actually redistributed.[1] Between January and May 1972 alone, 1,525 farms were expropriated, in open sessions of the Council of CORA held in provincial capitals all over the country.[2] However, the actual transfer of the land was not

1. Calculations made by Arnoldo Rosenfeld. The estimate of reserves assumes that 35 per cent of owners expropriated received, on average, forty standard hectares.
2. The sessions themselves, apparently, were unspeakably boring: an official would read out the name of each farm to be expropriated, no objection was voiced, and he would read on, and on, down the list.

quite so rapid, and according to one CORA source, perhaps exaggerating somewhat, only 313 of these farms were, by May 1972, actually under the control of the peasants. There were, furthermore, 250 'intervened' farms, apart from some 150 which, having been intervened, had been subsequently expropriated.

Stated thus baldly, the 'end of the latifundio' appears as an essentially administrative process, but although it was on the whole peaceful – indeed perhaps one of the most peaceful reforms ever of such magnitude – it was carried out against a background of intense class struggle. The UP could never have achieved expropriation on this scale without massive support for reform – though not necessarily for the government – in the countryside; the neutrality of the police was a help, since they generally obeyed the order not to use violence on any account against peasants, while landowners could not count on police passivity if they resisted officials on CORA business. However, the judiciary tended, when faced with cases of rural conflict, to be severe with peasants and lenient with landlords, even in the most flagrant cases of landlord violence.

3. *The Peasant Movement in Cautín*

This period saw an upsurge in strikes and farm seizures, and a qualitative change in the agrarian struggle. Early on, during December 1970 and the early months of 1971, a wave of farm seizures occurred in the southerly province of Cautín: these were carried out largely by the mapuches, and aimed at reclaiming land legally belonging to the communities, at obtaining more land to live on, and at putting strong pressure on the government to carry out the reform rapidly. By the end of April 1971, there had, according to the *carabineros* (police) been seventy farm seizures in Cautín out of a national total of 639, since Allende took over the government on 5 November 1970.[1] Despite widespread differences of opinion, largely dependent on political differences, it is clear that a massive movement did take place, and that it

1. Information from Carabineros inserted in the record of debates in the Senate, and published in *El Mercurio*, 5 and 6 June 1972; it was inserted at the request of Rafael Moreno, former head of CORA, and now Senator and prominent opponent of the government from the right wing of the Christian Democrat party. Other provinces in the south had as many, if not more, land seizures, but I have chosen to concentrate on Cautín firstly because of the specific agrarian characteristics of the province, and secondly because I carried out field work there in 1972.

involved almost exclusively the indigenous peoples of the province: there are today some asentamientos, created mostly by the Christian Democrats which have almost no mapuche members, while there are others of more recent origin which are exclusively mapuche, and most of which originated with a seizure or a *corrida de cercos* (see glossary).

In Cautín only 16·3 per cent of the agricultural labour force is composed of wage-workers, as against 49·8 per cent and 46·3 per cent in the fairly typical Central Valley provinces of Aconcagua and Colchagua. The land is rather poor and suitable in the main only for extensive crops and cattle-breeding. The 'large' farms are not latifundia, either from the point of view of the number of people they employ or from that of the labour relations prevailing on them. Permanent labourers are rare, perhaps two or three on an average-sized farm. The term *inquilino*, though it appears in the Census, is barely used at all. The central agrarian problem here is, objectively and subjectively, the land hunger of indigenous groups.

There were an estimated 326,066 mapuches in rural areas in 1966, mostly in Cautín; 226,516 of them lived in 2,961 'reserves' or communities, with a total of 526,185 hectares, while some 76,000 lived on 127,000 hectares outside the communities in the south of Chile (Saavedra, 1971, p. 30).[1] The origin of the communities lies in the adjudication of land at the end of the nineteenth century, carried out in order to 'settle' the indigenous peoples, who, exceptionally for Latin America, had opposed armed resistance to colonization ever since the Spanish colonial period. Thus these communities, backed by legal titles, are creations of the republican State; nonetheless, land has constantly been usurped, and the mapuches have had little legal redress, especially since the special court (*Juzgado de Indios*) established to deal with cases involving their lands, was burnt down, with all the archives, in the 1920s. Land tenure within the communities is individual, and the communities usually comprise a small number of families, descendants of the original assignee, whose name the community still bears. Tenure is highly fragmented, and in many cases there is simply not enough land for the younger generation to work on, if all are to inherit a share from their fathers.

Thus, in Cautín, between 1960 and 1966, there was not one

1. The State agency responsible for the protection of the indigenous peoples, the *Dirección de Asuntos Indígenas*, gave slightly different figures in 1972: 274,000 living in 2,430 communities, controlling 435,000 hectares of land.

wage demand or strike by organized rural labour in the province, whereas 1,001 such demands were presented in the country as a whole, and, in 1966 alone, there were 586 strikes (Affonso *et al.*, 1970, II, pp. 22 and 58). Later the union movement grew from 1,648 members in mid 1968, to 4,516 in 1969, and 13,000 in February 1972, but its character here was radically different from regions where the latifundist system prevailed.

Much controversy has centred round the role of the MIR (*Movimiento de Izquierda Revolucionaria*) in the events of Cautín. It is very difficult to tell whether the sudden radicalization of the peasantry in the province was due to the arrival of a government committed to not repressing violently peasants involved in farm seizures, or to the presence of young revolutionaries from the MIR who had been living among the mapuches since 1968. The MIR was certainly far from indifferent to the movement when it did spring up, and its following, specifically among mapuches on asentamientos and in communities – was quite solid. From the national point of view, the strength of the MIR lay in certain shanty-towns in Santiago and other cities and among the mapuches: among the urban working class and the rural proletariat of the Central Zone its influence was negligible.

The tension created in Cautín was enthusiastically reported in the national opposition press, and Chonchol, now Minister of Agriculture,[1] transferred his office to Temuco, the provincial capital, on 4 January 1971; with the Minister came numerous officials and party militants who set about expropriating farms, and organizing the peasantry into Municipal Peasant Councils (*Consejo Comunal Campesino*), elected by the entire peasantry, area by area. For a short period, it may have seemed that the Cautín peasantry were carrying out a revolution: they had seized land deemed to be theirs (morally and legally),[2] they had usurped the powers of the State, literally taking the law into their own hands, and they immediately began to cultivate, without

1. He had been head of INDAP between 1964 and 1968, resigning when the Reform began to lose momentum, and subsequently leaving the Christian Democrats with a small group of prominent politicians and a large number of younger intellectuals to form MAPU. Chonchol later joined the *Izquierda Cristiana* in 1971 (see glossary).
2. The Chilean and foreign press have made much of the few instances where smallholders' land has been seized. It should be emphasized that these instances were rare, and that they often occurred where the smallholder's land was usurped land – a fact for which he himself might well not be responsible. Note the emphasis on guarantees to smallholders in the declaration quoted below.

awaiting legal expropriation. Now, inspired jointly by the MIR and certain factions of the Socialist Party, the Councils emerged, looking at first like soviets, claiming control over the various State organs and the expropriation and distribution of land.

The idea of the *Consejos Campesinos* was not completely new: already on 21 December 1970, the Minister of Agriculture had created a National Consejo, on which would sit two representatives of each campesino organization. But most of these were controlled by the opposition. The Consejo was to 'transmit to the government the opinion of the *campesinos* with reference to all agricultural matters'. It met a few times, but dialogue quickly broke down since the majority of the Consejo demanded complete control of agrarian policy in order to fight that of the UP.

Local consejos were similarly dominated by the opposition. Soon, however, a new formula was found, known as *consejo elegido por la base*, as opposed to the *consejo por decreto* ('elected by the rank and file', as opposed to the council 'formed by decree'). The socialists and *miristas* promoted this formula, later also consecrated by decree, under which between ten and fifteen members were to be directly elected, by all the peasants, whatever their status, and up to fourteen appointed by the various organizations in the municipality (*comuna*). During the first three months of 1971, sixteen such consejos were formed in Cautín, and in only two of them did the UP or the MIR fail to win a majority of votes. Meetings would be called by INDAP officials or party militants in the various comunas, and frequently a bitter struggle would take place between Christian Democrats, who argued for an appointed consejo, and the Socialists and the MIR. The Communists never became involved on this front, laying more emphasis on the expropriation of farms than the formation of these would-be mini-soviets. That such ambitions existed can be seen in the declaration of the first peasant Assembly at comuna level in Lautaro (*Asamblea Comunal Campesina*), at the heart of the indigenous region:

a The agrarian reform is the principal instrument for the destruction of the bourgeoisie in the countryside. Therefore it must be directed against all proven enemies of the *Gobierno Popular* [People's Government] and of the rural and urban workers' power which is being constructed.

b In this province, peasant smallholders are one of the principal pillars of the *Gobierno Popular* and one of the most important forces in the country supporting our comrade President. For this reason their land will be respected and if necessary enlarged.

c The land belonging to those medium owners who respect the authority of the *Gobierno Popular* will also be left untouched, and they will receive such credits and technical assistance as are necessary to increase their production. In return, they will be expected to fulfil meticulously their obligations as laid down by the minimum agricultural wage, and other benefits agreed upon for the rural workers.

d Land obtained through the existing mechanisms of expropriation or others defined below will be placed under the control of the *Asamblea Comunal Campesina*, through the *Consejo Comunal Campesino*, and will be cultivated by all the landless comrades in the comuna, for their own benefit and for that of all the workers in the country. Smallholders who wish to integrate their lands into these reformed units will receive rent for the land contributed as well as payment for their labour. Such lands as belong to mapuche communities but have still not been restored to them during the expropriation period will immediately be returned to their legitimate owners.

e Peasant power, expressed in the *Asamblea*, *Congreso* or *Consejo Comunal Campesino*, will direct the struggle against the agrarian bureaucracy, using all political and economic means of defence available. At the same time, social, cultural, and technical education, housing and other programmes will be organized to contribute to the progress of the peasantry and to the emergence of the new socialist man.

This declaration drawn up by fourteen peasant leaders stands in favour of the protection and expansion of smallholding and of property rights and gives this point a good deal of prominence. It also seeks to obtain authority for the organs of 'peasant power' in spheres, such as control of expropriated lands, which had previously been (and were to continue to be) in the hands of State agencies. These two aspects point up the radical differences between the agrarian structure and the peasant movement in Cautín, and in the rest of the country, especially in the Central Valley.

While Socialists and Miristas were concentrating on forming the *consejos por la base*, CORA, headed by a communist, and Chonchol, were expropriating at a very fast rate: twenty-three farms in January 1971, seventy-two in February, but less than ten in the following months. The land available for expropriation in Cautín was exiguous, and when all that could legally be expropriated had been affected, it was still only some 14 per cent of the agricultural land in the province. The quality of the land in the province was so bad that even fairly large farms, up to 600 hectares, could escape expropriation.[1]

1. At the time of the drafting of the Reform Law, the German govern-

It is because the peasant movement in Cautín was seeking to re-establish traditional moral and legal rights to land, that it yielded, albeit momentarily, the beginnings of a rival power to that of the State. Many of the peasants involved had never had much to do with the State in any case, and saw no reason why, when they had seized the land and had begun to work on it, this outside authority should interfere and seek to start the process all over again with expropriation, and furthermore to acquire the land for itself – for the land expropriated becomes the property of CORA, not of the asentados, until *asignación*. When the asentados in Cautín spoke of bourgeois law (*las leyes burguesas*) they were surely using a ready-made phrase to refer to endless procedural wrangles, to the constant interference of officialdom, to rules and regulations so often in conflict with their own conceptions of justice. Yet, as time passed and as this contact with the State machine increased, as they became dependent on CORA and the State Bank for their advances, for inputs and machinery, so they became enveloped in the endless toing and froing to town, in lengthy and legal and administrative procedures, and so the consejos, born in such a revolutionary spirit, devoted their energies more and more to this bureaucratic guerilla; like the old asentamiento leadership, they had to devote time and energy to pressing upon government officials the problems of their rank and file, and then to informing their rank and file of the progress of their various petitions and demands.

The utopia of peasant unity expressed by the *consejo por la base* proved difficult to forge in practice. The asentamientos had special problems of their own; where they or their representatives controlled a consejo they dealt with CORA through the consejo, otherwise they did so directly. Such divisions, as well as divisions between socialists and Miristas (not to speak of those between these and the communists) reinforced the 'pivot' positions of local leaders, who seemed to be developing the same monopolistic control of access to State institutions which had emerged in the union movement and on the old asentamientos.

Elsewhere in the country, especially in the Central Valley, the class struggle in the countryside had different manifestations.

---

ment had put pressure on the Christian Democrats to more or less exempt that region from expropriation. There are many landowners of German origin, descendants of colonizers, in the south of Chile, and the German Christian Democrats had helped Frei to finance his election campaign in 1964. As a result, the 'equivalences' set by the law for a standard hectare were much larger than they should have been in the southerly regions.

Land seizures certainly multiplied,[1] but as a means of putting pressure on the government, rather than of ignoring or substituting it: workers would seize a farm by striking and preventing anyone from entering, until they had obtained an assurance from CORA that it would be expropriated, or until the farm had been 'intervened'; once a farm had been subjected to this latter procedure, an official (*interventor*) replaced the owner as manager and the workers were encouraged to form committees of management as on the asentamientos, while the *interventor* would only appear from time to time. The workers on intervened farms were lucky in that they also gained control of the capital, whereas on the asentamientos, farms were frequently handed over completely decapitalized. Indeed, a number of seizures were made when workers knew that expropriation was imminent and wanted to prevent the landowner from removing all his capital.

In early 1972 about 177 consejos were known to be functioning in the country but 110 of these were *por decreto*, and doubtless controlled by the Christian Democrats (Gomez & Klein, 1972). However, since the consejo as such lacked legitimate authority, a group or party which was in control of the consejo was not in a position to represent any but its own political adherents. Once one group of leaders had a majority, other parties or groups lost interest. Christian Democrat asentados in the Santa Cruz area of Colchagua, said the UP had 'packed' the consejo with sympathizers many of whom were not peasants; they themselves continued to work with the Provincial Federation of Asentamientos – which, of course, was controlled by Christian Democrats and, being also a marketing co-operative, could afford the means of transport which it used to foment opposition to the government.[2] Ever since 1965 agrarian struggles had been strongly politicized, not only in the sense that class conflict was undermining a system of domination, but also in that it always involved links with one party or another. After 1970, however, the rural proletariat and its organizations became increasingly divided over very fundamental issues of the direction of the agrarian reform, the nature of new tenure institutions and the shape of the society which was to emerge at the end of the process under way – issues on which conflicts had not arisen in previous years.

Strike action has probably increased under the UP, but it shows one or two interesting new features: in 1966 the vast majority of

1. According to the *carabineros* report quoted above, 1,767 between November 1970 and April 1972.
2. Such marketing co-operatives, nonetheless, received credit from CORA or the State Bank.

strikes were in support of economic demands – 452 out of 586 – whereas in 1971 38 per cent were solidarity strikes in support of workers involved in other conflicts. Another indication of political motivation is the national rural strike called by the opposition in 1971 against the government's agrarian policies, in which it is estimated that some 30,000 workers participated – a figure to be compared with the total membership of some 95,000 in opposition-controlled organizations. In April 1972 these organizations again threatened to call a national strike, but did not do so, probably because they were unable to muster sufficient support.

But if the UP's agrarian reform was, as we have seen, no different in its effects, if not in its intentions, from that carried out by the Christian Democrats, how was the opposition able to maintain control over such a large – if decreasing – proportion of the organized peasantry? Firstly, there was the ongoing power of the system of political clientilism which had characterized the reform right from the start, as well as the union movement, especially the Christian Democratic unions, and which, by creating self-perpetuating regional leaderships, allowed a party to maintain control over a certain number of its followers come what may. Secondly, there was the great uncertainty generated by the UP's indecision over its agrarian policy: to this we shall come, for the moment it is enough to say that the government's evident dislike of the very comfortable asentamiento model, together with its failure either to produce a clear model of what was to replace it, or even to attempt in practice to create a radically different form of organization on the ground, gave the Christian Democrats much fertile ground on which to sow the seeds of discontent.

For the UP did not wish simply to expropriate; it sought to set the society upon the path to socialism, and to remedy some of the worst defects of the reform. The two intended policies which aroused opposition among peasants, especially among the asentados, concerned employment, and new institutional arrangements. The asentamientos had not contributed significantly to the reduction of the very high rate of rural unemployment, commonly estimated at about 30 per cent, including under-employment. The entry of members of their own families did not arouse opposition among the asentados, especially when they realized it would be subsidized by CORA through the monthly advances. But the government also hoped that those landless labourers who lived in *minifundio* areas, or who were migrant labourers, would be integrated, and reaction among asentados was so strong that the government barely sought to implement this.

IX. New Institutional Forms

The most controversial intentions of the government concerned the new institutional arrangements on the asentamientos. Right from the start, the opposition had been warning the peasantry that the UP would never give them ownership of the land, and that the old *patrón* would be replaced by the State. The Christian Democrats themselves had distributed definitive land titles to only 5,586 members of 109 asentamientos (out of 246 asentamientos which had completed the statutory three years by the end of 1970), and all but fourteen of these were assigned in ownership to a co-operative, of which the asentados were members, and not to individuals. All asentados in these co-operatives were granted the ownership of a house (although, where it was new, they were supposed to pay for it) with a garden plot of about one-quarter of a hectare around it. The UP, by May 1972, had only assigned land to forty-four asentamientos, all of it in co-operative ownership.

In 1971 it was announced that the government would create a new institution to be known as the *Centro de Reforma Agraria* (CERA). The aims of the CERA were numerous: (1) to broaden and deepen participation of the rank and file in decisions by giving all male and female members of the community over sixteen full voting rights in the Assembly and having the Assembly rather than a single elected Council, elect members of various committees; thus concentration of power was to be reduced; (2) to increase employment opportunities on expropriated forms; (3) to eliminate wage-labour once and for all; (4) to rationalize the size of new farming units, allowing the integration of previously separate units; (5) to progressively reduce individual rights, except those covering the house and garden plot and (6) to socialize control of the surplus produced through the contribution of a percentage (variously quoted at 10, 20 and 30 per cent) of profits to a municipal capitalization fund, to be used for infrastructural and other investments. An important change in the internal organization of the CERA was its division into committees with responsibilities for each aspect of its work; the workers in livestock, and those in crop production, or if necessary each kind of crop, would form committees to take collective decisions, and assume collective responsibility, whereas on the asentamiento the president and one or two members of the council were taking all decisions themselves without formal consultations. On the CERA, the function of the leader of the organization, and that of head of production were separated, and a Control Commission was given much emphasis, in the hope of preventing the concentration of power. On the asentamientos there had been provision for something very similar to the Control Commission, but it had never functioned properly.

Various models of the CERA statutes were elaborated, but few have seen the light of day. One which has been published, though bearing no indication of authorship, makes all the points we have made, and a few more.

On paper, this model is impeccable; it deals with many of the defects of the asentamiento, from the point of view of both equity and efficiency. Rather than being distributed individually, profits will finance socialized consumption, through a welfare fund; 'wage advances' being held at the level of the agricultural minimum wage, and distributed strictly for days worked which might provide an improved material incentive. Restriction of individual land to bread-winners and to half a hectare would ensure that families do not benefit unduly from their size and age distribution as would the institution of a rent payment. Equitable treatment and participation for seasonal workers is ensured without burdening the farm with excess labour all the year round. A tax is levied on a part of the surplus (10 per cent of profits) to go to a municipal savings and investment fund. The document does not establish incentives to expand employment, but it does say that the CERA should be 'oriented' towards this aim as its productive capacity improves. Some doubts might be cast by the provision that all relevant decisions are to be taken by the Assembly.[1]

And yet, and yet . . . the model, in the conditions at present prevailing in Chile, is largely unworkable, and the root of its unrealism lies in its very conception, in its dependence on a number of crucial assumptions about the political and administrative conditions prevailing in the countryside. It is a political and administrative model, and not an economic one. It depends for its success on a very high level of egalitarianism, collectivist consciousness and mutual trust among the workers who make up the Assembly. It depicts an organization of a 'transitory character' to be applied while a definitive new structure transcending the agricultural underdevelopment of the country is created, yet it takes as given a profound transformation of the consciousness of the workers involved. In these characteristics, it is a good example of the ideas circulating at the time.

1. This text, *Los Centros de Reforma Agraria* was published by ICIRA around March 1971, although it bears no date nor any author's name. ICIRA does not have 'official' views on this kind of issue.

The persistent attempts to deal with economic problems by administrative and hortatory means shed interesting light on Latin American culture. Peasants, or rural workers, are expected to conform to administrative rules laid down by the bureaucracy, out of 'solidarity' or 'consciousness', as if the laws of economic life did not exist: if peasants break the rules, then there is something wrong, even if those rules demand of them a quite unfamiliar economic rationality – or economic irrationality. If politicians were intentionally seeking to impose institutions operating against the interests of those subjected to them, then the resistance of rural people could be expected; but the paradox is that they seek to favour the interests of many, if not all, the peasants involved with new institutions, and still the people undermine the institutions by stubbornly pursuing what they see as their own interest; by responding to market incentives, by opposing the dead weight of social and political inertia to alien institutions. They rarely say no; they prefer to nod their heads in agreement, so that the long-winded officials will depart soon, and so that they can continue to pursue their interest in their own way. It will be remembered how the asentamiento, as a model, was based on the assumption that the rural workers who became asentados would obey capitalist rationality, as well as co-operate with and trust one another, and how mistaken those assumptions turned out to be. Even more crucial, perhaps, for our present discussion, was the reliance of both the Christian Democrats and the UP (as we shall see) on CORA, on the State Bank and other bureaucracies to enforce the new rationality on hundreds, and now some 4,000 farms. It may not have mattered too much to the Christian Democrats when the rules were not obeyed, but that does not appear to have been the original intention! When rural people do not co-operate, and the government is weak, there seems to be little alternative to the use of market mechanisms in the allocation of resources, especially at a time of social transformation, and especially when the resources are to go to thousands of peasants. Otherwise clientelism, or just the vagaries of disorderly political and bureaucratic access, take over.

We have seen how the State bureaucracy is increasingly unable to carry out the tasks assigned to it by those who direct the various agencies, and that this is due partly to political conflicts within the system, and partly to what can only be called a bureaucratic breakdown. Organizations such as CORA are structured to control the activities of a clientele, and to impose a legal order upon their own activities. Activities which have close connections in practice are separated in their management by numerous strata and hierarchies; officials at regional level are responsible both to regional chiefs and to chiefs of functional divisions at national level – who may disagree about policy. Officials at the bottom of the rung feel obliged to lecture the peasant clientèle on the evils of excessive indebtedness or short working hours, but they do not have the political power to apply rewards and sanctions for good or bad performance. Decisions are often taken at the top on the assumption that the State can more or less order the workers and peasants to do whatever the politicians and bureaucrats think is good for them and the officials at the bottom simply cannot and do not apply these decisions, so a system of institutionalized lying is created. Thus, responsibility for all administered credit to asentados was shifted from an over-burdened CORA to the State Bank during 1972. The State Bank, unlike CORA, is accustomed to lend as a commercial bank, and requires some evidence of future prospects – its banking system was quite unsuited to the system prevailing on asentamientos and CERA's, where losses were being incurred in the majority of cases, and where even if a more rational system of organization had prevailed, many farms would still be showing losses for a good time to come. But, although the government itself had appointed the majority of its directors, the Bank was still insisting on a strict commercial criterion during 1972. Although the Bank proved more successful at debt collection than CORA, CORA officials found that they had to ensure that all Cultivation Plans showed an expected profit, whereupon the Bank agreed to finance them. The 'hole' at the end of the year would be filled by CORA. Almost everyone involved seemed aware of these contradictions, yet the system continued.

The attempt to establish CERA's was yet another case of concentration on moral, political and legal rules and neglect of the rewards and sanctions of the market which continued to offer the best explanation of asentado behaviour, especially where it ran counter to the hopes of politicians and ideologues. Data I collected on twenty-four asentamientos and CERA in Colchagua and Cautín (presented in full in Lehmann, 1973), shows that the difference between the two is largely one of name. The important differences among these farms lay in quality of political leadership, but this was independent of their labels. The pattern of institutional forms adopted in practice showed the indecision of the government in the face of distrust, opposition or doubt. In 1971 some 120 CERAS were established, as against 246 asentamientos and 628 *Comités Campesinos* (literally, Peasant Committees). Comité is a transitional name adopted when those concerned do not want to establish a CERA and officials do not want to establish an asentamiento, at least before they have had more time to persuade the peasants to think again; the prevalence of Comités is a symptom of indecision within the UP as to the characteristics of a CERA, and the few possibilities of persuading the workers to adopt those forms of organization and rewards which might distinguish the CERA from the asentamiento.

Certain people in very influential positions were talking of the use of taxes in agricultural strategy, but this was not receiving the same publicity as the CERA. Prices emerged as a tool of policy in July and August 1972, in a speech by Allende (which spoke of bonuses for overfulfilment in the context of a system of production contracts with asentados and individual producers) and in a remarkable speech by Luis Corvalán, Secretary General of the Communist Party.[1] Of course, it is very difficult indeed to use prices in a planned and controlled manner (not, of course, the prices given by 'free' market forces): the calculation of the prices of a wide range of products, taking into account not only the need for incentives, but the relationships among the prices and the constraints imposed by scarcities and bottlenecks in the supply of consumer goods, poses classic problems; my argument is simply that reliance on moral and political incentives may *appear* easier, but it distracts from the simple and observable fact that the question of material incentives is left to chance, and it is to these incentives that the peasants concerned continue to respond.

Thus it is not surprising that, despite some changes in names, the basic trends analysed earlier for the asentamientos were observable on the CERAS as well: the dominance of the interests of the family enterprise in decision-making, and its expansion on the basis of individual rights to land, the lack of an incentive system which linked earnings on collective land to the individual's effort, and so on. The financial subsidy to the sector was becoming uncontrolled, reaching some 30 per cent of gross agricultural product and probably changing substantially the terms of trade between agriculture and industry. In the past, the terms of trade were unfavourable for the sector as a whole, but because of the extremely unequal distribution of income, they were not unfavourable for the landowners; now the purchasing power of the peasantry, both independent and in asentamientos and CERAS, in terms of industrial consumer goods, was increasing at a much faster rate than agricultural production, though there were in 1972 signs of a slight reversal of this trend.

1. Speech to the special Plenary Meeting of the Central Committee on the agrarian situation, reprinted in *El Siglo*, 14 August 1972.

In this context two separate, but related issues arise: one concerns incentives within the asentamientos where, as we have seen, the flat-rate 'advance' offers little realistic incentive to maximise 'profits' for the enterprise as a whole, provoking rather distrust among the workers, and a consequent retreat to the more secure benefits of the peasant family economy. The other concerns the instruments available for the state to control and orient production on the asentamientos. Administrative means such as the Cultivation Plans, backed by no economic or other sanctions, are ineffective; a price policy, combined with measures such as a tax on differential rent and a judicial use of interest rates and of the prices of those inputs on whose supply the State has a monopoly, might be more effective, as an incentive to production but it must be added that if taxes and debts are not collected, all is lost. Thus certain kinds of price policy might allow an escape from the problems of non-enforcement of debts. However, such instruments are unlikely to provoke the desired productive response on asentamientos and CERA's operating as we have earlier described them. For this reason, although the recent recourse to prices as an instrument of policy, at a time when divisions over future institutional patterns are as deep as ever, may reinforce the peasant economy, it may only compel that economy to raise production above present levels if uncontrolled subsidies come to an end, and if the asentados are left free to divide all their land if they so wish.

The drawbacks of such a trend lie in the danger of 'perverse response' (see Bell's note on the subject) and in a renewed turning of terms of trade against industry. On perverseness, all one can say is that the Chilean campesinos are more accustomed to selling in the market, and to seeking to expand their activities through market transactions, than the poorer Indian peasants appear to be. The terms of trade may remain unchanged for the moment, since they are already so heavily in the peasant's favour, and at least the initial possible rise in production would be a response to a 'tightening of the screws' within a very 'untight' context, thus not requiring further tipping of the terms in agriculture's favour. Turning them back in industry's favour, however, would raise complex issues.

The present situation does not seem to permit of further lowering of the size of expropriable farms to forty standard hectares; UP's electoral programme for the March 1973 parliamentary elections provides for this, but everyone knows there is little prospect that the new Congress will allow it through. Thus rural capitalists should benefit from the situation, from high prices and from security, as will the peasants. The difficulty will lie in the cities, where the working class is likely to be deprived of the industrial consumer goods going to underpin a hoped-for rise both in agricultural production, and in the government's popularity among the peasantry.

Yet whatever the UP does, the asentados and smallholders might still feel that the parties of the right offered them more security in the future. On balance, if, as Petras and Zeitlin (1970), have claimed, the core of communist and socialist support lies among male members of the industrial working class, then maybe it is best to protect the supply of food above all. But again, it may be that these will vote for the left in any case, and one must then ask how far it is possible to win over the women, and the middle classes. The Communist Party has sought to win them over all along, but, writing in January 1973, after the shopkeepers' strike it does look as if their support is lost for ever. Paradoxically, if attitudes are so impervious, then the government has more freedom of action than might otherwise be the case, unless it alienates Congress excessively.

X. Socialism

Those in the leadership concerned with agriculture are perfectly aware that the achievements of the agrarian reform so far have little to do with a transition to socialism. The key to such a transition, many claim, lies in the industrialization of agriculture: the establishment of agro-industries for food and fruit-processing and packing, with a view to the export market. This would involve the intensification of the use of land, converting it from extensive crops such as wheat in particular, to the cultivation of fruit and certain vegetables such as tomatoes. The increase in employment needs, would be so great if the programme is carried through that it would be necessary to actually reverse the direction of rural-urban migration. The industrialization of agriculture will allow a proletarianization of the peasantry – and this does seem to be the only road towards a transformation of peasant consciousness which would provide firm rural support for the transition to socialism. Few of the UP's supporters in the countryside understand what is meant by socialism, and if they did understand this, they might pull back. At the moment they are supporting a government which has given them access to land, and has subsidized them so that those benefited by this process can enrich themselves on the basis of the family economy. The effect of industrialization, bringing with it the establishment of many more State farms or regional co-operatives under effective control of agro-industrial units, is that it would eliminate these 'peasant' trends, while probably raising substantially the standard of living of many rural workers and others so far excluded from the reform process. The asentados thus incorporated would not perhaps experience such a substantial increase in their standards of living, if only because this standard is already so relatively high. Experience has already shown that incomes on the few State farms which have been established, usually by vertically integrated enterprises such as the National Seed Enterprise, are much higher than on asentamientos and CERA's. The bargaining power of workers in conflict with a government such as UP is very great, and that is why State farms on a large scale should await substantial technological change.

The erroneous solution seems to be that advocated by certain factions in the Socialist Party, who seek to collectivize, along the lines of the CERA, without any consideration for the relevance of the technological environment. The experience of the past seven years of reform demonstrates, surely, that where the industrial process does not impinge upon the agricultural, and where the agricultural produce can easily be sold at the farm gates to any small trader, collective forms of work breed subterranean peasant family enterprise, and the control of such collective units involves the multiplication of bureaucratic effort to little good. In Chile, it would seem, the socialization of agriculture will have to follow upon that of industry, unless a confrontation with the peasants is sought – and of this there is little evidence.

Unidad Popular has succeeded in exhausting the provisions of the 1967 Agrarian Reform Law, and the character of that Law – as of so many others of its kind – is well demonstrated by the fact that Chile's agriculture remains very much a capitalist one. Furthermore, the inequality of distribution of land has not been eliminated largely because of the relatively high ceiling and because the *minifundio* areas have hardly been touched, and the *minifundistas* have hardly been benefited by the redistribution of land. Some 80 per cent of units of ownership, with less than five standard hectares each, comprise some 10 per cent of the farm land. However, the top 2 per cent of farms which comprised 55·3 per cent of the land in 1965 have been reduced to 0·1 per cent and now cover only 3 per cent of the land. The reform has raised the number of family farms, if we are permitted for these purposes to consider the reformed sector to comprise such units: the stratum between five and twenty hectares would include this sector, where the average number of irrigated hectares per beneficiary is slightly more than eight. This stratum would have risen from 11 per cent to 46 per cent of total agricultural land, while, if each beneficiary is counted as equivalent to one farm, it would comprise about 42 per cent of farm units; this at least gives an order of the magnitude of the change in distribution that has come about since 1965. The stratum between twenty and forty standard hectares comprises 3·3 per cent of farms and 11·6 per cent of land, while that between forty and eighty hectares comprises 4·1 per cent of farms and 27·3 per cent of the land.

I do not put these figures into a table, for their basis is far from precise, due largely to the way in which the 1965 Agricultural Census was taken, but they do give an indication, and they leave little room for doubt about the possibilities and the limits of this kind of reform.

No one is more aware of these limits than the UP leadership, and it is fairly clear that further gains in the elimination of unwarranted inequality must wait upon substantial socialization of marketing and of work. I have discussed whether I think this is a first priority, and it would appear that there is very little choice in the matter, for the political conditions for further socialization, especially in *minifundio* areas where the worst social problems remain, are not yet mature. The conventions would demand of the writer a prediction of future directions, but that is a very difficult task indeed, for it depends so much on the evolution of a highly uncertain political situation. The evidence presented here certainly shows that it is very difficult indeed to 'bring the reformed sector under control' and that it would be difficult to do so for any government, especially if it sought to orient the asentados towards capitalist co-operation or socialist collectives, without setting about the industrialization of agriculture.

Unidad Popular would like to set Chilean society on the road to socialism, and it may be successful. In the meantime there can be no doubt that Chile has become 'ungovernable', ungovernable perhaps for any government, but certainly for governments of the centre or the right. The working class is too strong, the peasantry too independent, to be easily controlled: this is not an unambiguous achievement, but it is certainly a notable one. With most of the options closed all one can do is hope that *Unidad Popular* will take up a historic opportunity to engage in massive political education. Progress in that direction is far more valuable than any number of perfectly fixed prices.

References

Unless otherwise stated, all books are published in Santiago, Chile.

Affonso, Almino, Sergio Gomez, Emilio Klein and Pablo Ramirez, *Movimiento Campesino Chileno*, 2 Vols., ICIRA, 1969.
Chayanov, A. V., *The Theory of Peasant Economy* (eds. Basile Kerblay, Daniel Thorner and R. E. F. Smith), American Economic Association, Homewood, Illinois, 1966.
Corporación de la Reforma Agraria, *Cuatro Años de Reforma Agraria*, 1968.
Echeñique, Jorge, 'Las Expropriaciones y la Organización de Asentamientos en el período 1965–70', *Reforma Agraria Chilena: Seis Ensayos de Interpretación*, ICIRA, 1970.
Echeverría, Roberto, *The Effects of Agricultural Price Policy on Intersectoral Income Transfers*, Ph.D. thesis, Cornell University, 1969 (also published in Latin American Studies Programme, *Dissertation Series*, **13**, Cornell University).
Gomez, Sergio, *Los Empresarios Agrícolas y la Reforma Agraria*, ICIRA, 1969 and 1972.
Gomez, Sergio and Emilio Klein, *Informe Sobre el Estado Actual de los Consejos Comunales Campesinos*, ICIRA, 1972.
Jolly, Arthur, Omar Brevis and Oscar Lefeuvre, *Estudio Ecónomico de los Asentamientos*, ICIRA, 1969.
Kay, Cristobal, 'Theory of Agrarian Change: Manorial or Hacienda System', Ph.D. thesis, Sussex University, 1971.
—, 'The Development of the Chilean Hacienda System, 1850–1972', paper presented to the Cambridge Symposium on Landlord and Peasant in Latin America and the Caribbean, December 1972.
Lehmann, David, 'Hacia un Análisis de la Conciencia de los Campesinos', *Cuadernos de la Realidad Nacional*, **2**, January 1970.
—, 'Political Incorporation versus Political Stability: the Case of the Chilean Agrarian Reform, 1965–1970', *Journal of Development Studies*, **7**, 4, July 1971.
—, 'Peasant Consciousness and Agrarian Reform in Chile', *Archives Européennes de Sociologie*, **8**, November 1972.
—, 'La Agricultura Chilena y el Período de Transición', *Sociedad y Desarrollo*, **4**, January 1973.
Loveman, Brian, *El Mito de la Marginalidad: Participación y Represión del Campesinado Chileno*, ICIRA, 1971.
McCoy, Terry, 'Agrarian Reform in Chile: A Study of Politics and the Development Process', Ph.D. thesis, Wisconsin, 1969.
Menjívar, Rafael, *Reforma Agraria Chilena*, ICIRA, 1969.

Oficina de Planificación Nacional (ODEPLAN), *Antecedentes Sobre el Desarrollo Chileno, 1960–70*, 1971.

Petras, James and Maurice Zeitlin, 'The Working-Class Vote in Chile', *British Journal of Sociology*, **21**, 1, March 1970.

Saavedra, Alejandro, *La Cuestión Mapuche*, ICIRA, 1971.

UNDP-FAO-ICIRA, *Diagnóstico de la Reforma Agraria Chilena* (Noviembre 1970–Junio 1972), 1972.

Urzúa, Raul, *La Demanda Campesina*, Ediciones de la Universidad Católica de Chile, 1969.

Glossary

Area de Propiedad Social (APS): 'Area of Social Property', denoting all enterprises wholly owned by the State.

asentado: fully fledged member of an *asentamiento*, having rights to ownership of the land once it is 'assigned' (see below, under *asignación*), and to daily employment.

asentamiento: agrarian reform settlement. This name refers specifically to the transitional arrangement in force until land is 'assigned', as established by the Christian Democrats.

asignación: The 'assignation' of land to reform beneficiaries in definitive ownership, under individual or co-operative arrangements.

campesino: a generic term referring to all peasants and rural workers.

carabineros: police.

CERA **(Centro de Reforma Agraria):** Agrarian Reform settlement designed by *Unidad Popular*, with different arrangements from those prevailing on an *asentamiento*.

Comité de Reforma Agraria: A provisional institution on recently expropriated farms, in force while the beneficiaries concerned decide whether they wish to establish an *asentamiento* or a CERA.

Comuna: Municipality. (Includes both urban and rural areas.)

CONSEMACH **(Confederación Nacional de Empleadores Agrícolas de Chile):** The National Confederation of Agricultural Employers.

Consejo Campesino Comunal (Consejo): Municipal Peasant Council.

Consejo por la base: *Consejo* with in practice a majority of members directly elected by all the *campesinos* in a *comuna*, apart from delegates of organizations.

Consejo por decreto: *Consejo* composed of delegates of *campesino* organizations only.

CORA **(Corporación de Reforma Agraria):** Agrarian Reform Corporation.

Corrida de cercos: Usually clandestine removal or shifting of fences of farms deemed to have usurped land belonging to indigenous communities. Carried out by organized *mapuches.*

fundo: farm.

fundo asignado: an 'assigned' farm (see above under *asignación*).

ICIRA **(Instituto de Capacitación e Investigación en Reforma Agraria):** Agrarian Reform Research and Training Institute.

INDAP **(Instituto de Desarrollo Agropecuario):** Institute of Agricultural Development. This is a State credit agency, charged also with the organization of the peasantry into unions and co-operatives.

Inquilinaje: A form of sale of labour whereby the worker, a permanent worker on a farm, is remunerated partly in cash (theoretically 75 per cent, according to the Law) and partly with rights to a small piece of land (about three-quarters of a hectare) and pasture rights for two to five animals, as well as receiving a house and a garden plot around the house. These arrangements are prevalent in the Central Valley and obviously they vary a good deal in practice.

inquilino: the individual employed under the terms of *inquilinaje* (see above).

Izquierda Cristiana (IC): the Left Christian Movement consisting of Christian Democrats who left their party in 1971 to support the Allende government.

JAP **(Juntas de Abastecimiento y Precios):** Supply and Price Boards; a form of mass organization to struggle against speculation and black market, and to organize distribution, mostly of food and meat.

latifundio: a large farm employing some of its labour on the lines of *inquilinaje.*

latifundista: owner of a *latifundio*, but the term is used more generally to refer to the large landowning class.

libre: a type of worker on large farms where *inquilinaje* is also prevalent – same as *voluntario* (see below).

MAPU **(Movimiento de Acción Popular Unitaria):** Movement for United Popular Action, formed by a group of Christian Democrats who left that party in 1969 when the party chose not to seek an alliance with the left in the 1970 Presidential Elections.

mapuches: the indigenous people of the South of Chile.

minifundio: smallholding (see *minifundistas*).

minifundistas: people living in smallholding communities. In Chile it is used to refer specifically to those whose holdings are insufficient to employ a family. In this paper it is used to refer to peasants living and working in a smallholding community, most of whom own some land, but many of whom are tenants, sharecroppers, or, in a few cases, landless labourers within the community.

MCR **(Movimiento de Campesinos Revolucionarios):** Movement of

Revolutionary Peasants, the 'peasant arm' of the MIR (see below).

MIR **(Movimiento de Izquierda Revolucionaria):** Movement of the Revolutionary Left.

obligado: another term for *inquilino* (see above). The term denotes the worker's 'obligation' to work every day for the *patrón* in return for the kind payments he receives.

patrón: an employer; literally: 'master'.

socio: literally a 'member' or 'partner' in a business concern or co-operative. In the present context it refers to unmarried workers on *asentamientos* who, because they are not bread-winners, do not in theory have rights to land at the time of the assignation of the land. At first they had no right to vote in *asentamiento* meetings or to daily employment either, but this was subsequently changed.

SNA **(Sociedad Nacional de Agricultura):** National Agricultural Society, the body which had traditionally represented the interests of large landowners.

Unidad Popular (UP): The Coalition which forms Allende's government. It comprises the Communist and Socialist Parties, the MAPU (see above), the *Izquierda Cristiana* (see above) and the Radical Party. (Two other 'Radical Parties' are in opposition, one of them having broken away to support Alessandri during 1970, and the other having broken away in 1972.)

voluntario: a type of worker on large farms in Central Chile. In theory, these workers are not permanently employed, but are relatives of *inquilinos* living in the houses of the *inquilinos*, unmarried and available for work when required by the *patrón* (see above). However, today, they are protected by job security legislation and are permanently employed, but they have no rights to land or pasture, as a rule, and often, despite being married with a family, they have to live in the house of an *inquilino*, who is most likely not a relative (see also *Libre*).

Map 3. China, administrative units

Four

Land Reform and Peasant Mobilization in Southern China 1947–1950

Geoffrey Shillinglaw

The object of this essay is to describe the strategies successively adopted in land reform in Southern China during a crucial period of revolutionary growth and consolidation. Nationwide liberation came in 1949, and it is on the period between 1949 and 1950 that we shall concentrate. China is not only a very large country – it also exhibits widely divergent social and cultural characteristics, from one region to another, and to treat it as a whole in such a short space is to give an inevitably false impression of homogeneity. Furthermore, our aim is not simply to give an account of events: it is also to point out how the changes in strategy – which varied sharply almost from one year to the next – arose from a confrontation between the constraints imposed by the agrarian structure prevailing prior to land reform, and the level of peasant mobilization and party control.

We shall see in particular how an analysis of land tenure in late Republican China suggests at least some of the factors leading to a renewed, if partial, radicalization before the end of 1950. This experience sheds some light on the difficulties which might be faced in comparable situations, and on the starkness of the choices which the Chinese Communists faced in their search for a strategy.

I. The Background: the Outline Land Law of 1947

The government and Party which came to national power in October 1949 had had some two decades of experience in formulating and implementing land policies, in a variety of social contexts and political environments. During the Kiangsi soviet period, in the central south-east from the late twenties to the abandonment of the soviet in 1934, land policies were formed, renounced and reformulated under the impact of peasant response, disputes within the Party leadership, the pressures of the wider political environment, and directives from the Comintern; there were wild fluctuations on such questions as the criteria for class determination, on the rich peasantry, on the formation of collectives, and on the criteria for distribution of land (see Hsiao, 1969). Indeed a case might be made that it was the sheer *rapidity* of changes in policy on fundamental issues during this period that contributed to the failure of the soviet to withstand the Nationalist encirclement campaigns.

From 1937 to 1945, during the Yenan period in North China (Selden, 1971; Chao Kuo-chun, 1960), land policy was to change again, this time in a decidedly moderate direction, under the impact of the Japanese War and the (increasingly disunited) United Front with the Nationalist government. With the thrust of policy towards social stability and a growing output rather than rural political revolution, rural class warfare was largely suspended, and emphasis was placed on rent and interest reductions for the peasantry, and the organization of simple mutual aid teams and co-operatives.

During both these phases land policy was formulated under conditions of a garrison state. It was only in 1947, as the final round of the Civil War commenced, that the Party could with any realism start to formulate a land redistribution policy related to national goals of growth and development, with any hope of applying it nationally.

Even here, however, the initial moves were heavily conditioned by the necessity of securing recruitment of the peasantry into the Communist armies, poised in the north for what was to be their final broad offensive across China. The aims of social stability and increasing production of the Yenan period were replaced by political mobilization and the rapid elimination of oppositional élite strata in rural society, both behind the Communist lines and in those areas soon to come under the Party's control.

This policy found expression in the Outline Land Law, published in October 1947 (reprinted in Hinton, 1966, Appendix). In both intent and application it was markedly radical, and a brief examination illustrates how far the Party was forced to move by the time it formulated the national Land Reform Law of 1950, in the post-liberation period.

The Outline Land Law decreed the pooling of the entire land resources of the rural community, and their re-allocation on an equal and uniform basis among all villagers, landlords and rich peasants included:

'... all landlord's land and public land in the rural areas will be taken over by the rural peasant association and, *together with all other land in the rural area, will be equally distributed in a uniform way* on the basis of the population of the whole area, without regard to sex or age; quantitatively, take surplus to make up deficiences; qualitatively, use (rich) land to supplement poor, so that the population of the whole area equally obtains the same grade of land.' (Article 6. Emphasis supplied.)

Although the Law merely decreed the 'abolition of the feudal and semi-feudal land exploitation system' (i.e. the land of landlords, rich peasants, and of associations and lineages), its emphasis on egalitarian distribution of land and the implied pooling of all the community's land resources, meant that even middle peasant farms, in villages where there were large numbers of poor or landless peasants, could well be reduced in size by the redistribution process. As a result of the political and economic consequences which were to ensue, it was not long before the Party was forced to explicitly buttress the position of the middle peasant against the land poor.

The second important feature of the Law concerned the unit area within which redistribution would take place. This is a crucial problem, especially where villages are small and nucleated and landlords are essentially locally resident with their holdings concentrated in one or several adjacent villages, as was the case in Southern China – a point we shall raise below. If redistribution only occurs *within* the basic village settlement (the 'natural village'), the conflict over access to land may more easily be cast in purely class terms. However, where equal distribution is attempted over wider areas embracing a number of village settlements, the process immediately tends to invoke fierce inter-village antagonisms whose basis may range from traditional access to water rights, or lineage loyalties, to a hostility whose origin is long since forgotten, and in such circumstances village solidarity may re-emerge under the leadership of the traditional, local élite. Yet without this second scale of redistribution, foci of village-based loyalties may persist which militate against social and political integration such as that sought by the Chinese leadership.

With the 1947 Law, the Chinese policy-makers were attempting this second type. The unit of distribution was declared to be the *hsiang*, the lowest administrative level (although some provision was made for smaller geographical units of distribution in areas of scattered population). *Hsiang* varied enormously in area, numbers of constituent villages, and village population. Data in Buck (1937, pp. 464–72) indicates that, in the northern provinces, a 'village' could number anything from a handful to well over a thousand farm families. Although it is difficult to know to what extent this stipulation was enforced, it allowed a potentially enormous transfer of land as between component 'rich' and 'poor' villages in a *hsiang*, and this would have led to intense inter-village political conflict.

Flowing naturally from these provisions, there is no mention in the 1947 Law of maintaining tenants, or peasants generally, in the occupancy of their existing farm units – a consideration which was to be central to the 1950 conception of land reform. And, in a similarly radical line, although several different types of peasant organizations – from 'peasant congresses' embracing the whole village population with the exception of landlords and rich peasants, to the more narrowly-based 'poor peasant leagues' – were designated as the political institutions controlling land reform, it was in fact the poor peasant leagues which in the North China land reform of 1947–8 became the core of the whole process.

Finally, in an attempt to restrain the growth of a new class of land *rentiers* after the reform, an embargo was placed on the renting out of land 'except under specially determined circumstances', although sale and purchase of land was unrestricted.

Thus, land reform was conceived as a radical levelling of the social hierarchy, involving the destruction of rural élite groups, and the creation of a political base. Land reform as a process inducing the growth of output was seemingly not a *primary* concern of the leadership at this point.

Within three months of the publication of the Outline Law, however, the Party was forced to come to grips with the consequences of the rural revolution it had unleashed, for widespread poor peasant action had resulted in the confiscation or destruction of rural manufacturing and commercial establishments operated by landlord or rich peasant families, which in principle were to be left in the hands of existing owners. Furthermore, the attack on middle peasant assets had grown as the land revolution gathered force. This latter tendency was seen as specially dangerous, since some 30–40 per cent of the Communist military forces were of middle-peasant status (Jen Pi-shih, 1948); the Party regarded the relatively self-sufficient middle peasant as, historically, a crucial element in the leadership of peasant revolts and to alienate this stratum would pose serious problems with regard to its political base.

Behind this lay the violence of the mobilized poor. Time and time again over the following months, the leadership was to inveigh against local cadres and members of land reform work teams who permitted 'widespread beating and killing' and a diffused attack which threatened to engulf their rear areas in chaos. In fact, local cadres, all too often, were being called upon to implement social change in a way that ran counter to the thrust of formal policy.

Unable, perhaps, to change policy fundamentally so soon after its adoption, the Party was obliged from the end of 1947 (i.e. within three months) to make changes in the complex criteria governing class determination and the institutions for peasant participation which would, it was hoped, limit the scope of the economic and political revolution. These, in broad outline, covered:

a expanding the category of the middle peasant, so that farms where up to 25–30 per cent of income came from 'exploitation' would still be classified as middle peasant, as opposed to the previous limit of 15 per cent ('exploitation' included hiring of labour, renting out of land, and loan activity);

b diluting the composition of Poor Peasant Leagues by formal provisions for middle peasant participation in these new political organizations of the village;

c a series of complex provisions bringing into consideration the *length of time* peasants had occupied a certain economic position, such that downwardly mobile landlords and rich peasants, and upwardly mobile poor and middle peasants were spared expropriation.

Further technical modifications were to follow through the first half of 1948,[1] all of which effectively modified the egalitarianism of the Outline Land Law. At the heart of them was the Party's difficulty in preventing the violence and destruction entailed in what Jen Pi-shi called 'the poor and hired peasants taking over everything' with the consequent attrition of the Party's base among the middle peasantry, and the destruction of rural manufacturing and commercial enterprises.[2]

1. See, for example, the 'Central Committee directive on carrying out land reform work and Party re-organization in the old areas and semi-old areas'. (22 Feb. 1948, reprinted in *Mu qian xing shi* . . ., 1949, pp. 74–85.) The foregoing pages represent a highly abbreviated account of a complex and painful move to the right during this period.
2. During 1948 a formal provision was written into the Outline Land

By July, 1948, seven months of experience had forced the Party leadership back to a conception of land redistribution which would be very close to the moderate policy of June 1950: 'thoughtless adherence' to 'absolute egalitarianism' was mistaken; and redistribution, while supplementing the holdings of the land poor, must nevertheless take account of the effective use of resources 'so as to benefit production'. 'Utopian agrarian socialism' was reactionary, because it strove to create socialism on the basis of an egalitarian small producer economy by by-passing capitalist development; it denied the inevitability of fresh class divisions after land reform resulting from different abilities and command of resources, seeking instead to maintain a uniformly egalitarian community. Furthermore, the creation of a socialized agricultural sector was only possible after industry had become capable of supplying the peasantry with agricultural machinery. Meanwhile, land reform was *not* 'distribution for distribution's sake' but for 'the broad development of social productive power'. (See, for example, the anonymous 'Questions and Answers on Agrarian Socialism', reprinted in *Mu qian xing shi* . . ., pp. 163–72.)

II. The Land Reform Law of the Chinese People's Republic, June 1950

The Land Law of 1950 represented the summation of the Party's experience of land policy over more than two decades, as that was seen to apply to the situation and needs of China in the period following liberation. The dominant rationale of the new programme was explicitly economic: 'the system of peasant landownership shall be introduced to set free the rural productive forces, develop agricultural production, and thus pave the way for New China's industrialization'. (Article 1.) In an extended report on the new policy, Liu Shao-ch'i stated that this was 'the basic reason and basic goal for implementing land reform', which differed 'from the view that agrarian reform is only designed to relieve the poor people. The problem of poverty among the peasants can only be finally solved if agricultural production can be greatly developed. . . . Hence, every step in land reform should effectively take into consideration, and be

---

Law allowing middle peasants to retain 'a greater amount of land than the average level of land obtained by poor peasants'. This can be found in *Mu qian xing shi* . . ., 1949, where the Law is reprinted.

closely co-ordinated with, the development of rural production.' The resources released by expropriation would of necessity be insufficient; 'Naturally, the means of production obtained by the peasants by merely [expropriating] the landlords will still be very insufficient; this will necessitate that the peasants work hard and carry out co-operation . . .' ('Report on the Question of Agrarian Reform', *The Agrarian Reform Law* . . . 1950.)

This basic economic perspective on land redistribution entailed a series of further sharp departures from the policy of 1947.

The rich peasant economy was to be preserved: with the exception of *large* amounts of land rented out by rich peasants, their landholdings were generally to be left intact. 'Landholdings' included not only the farm area cultivable directly by the typical numerically larger rich peasant family, but also the additional area which could be cultivated with hired labour. This was not, in Liu's words, a temporary strategy, but one dependent upon the rate of industrialization:

> The policy adopted by us of preserving a rich peasant economy is not of course a temporary, but a long-term policy. That is to say, a rich peasant economy will be preserved throughout the whole stage of New Democracy. Only when the conditions are ripe for the extensive application of mechanized farming, for the organization of collective farms, and for the socialist reform of the rural areas, will the need for a rich peasant economy cease, and this will take a somewhat long time to achieve.

The new policy also expressed a commitment to the minimum disturbance of existing farm units: the redistributive process should seek to avoid the displacement of peasants from the land they cultivated: '. . . land *owned* by the cultivator shall not be drawn upon for distribution'. Not resource pooling, but resource adjustment in the name of its optimal use was the dominant tone of the new policy. Finally, the prohibition on renting out land received in distribution was removed.

Together with these economic measures went a number of changes in political direction. There was a very heavy emphasis on the maintenance of political order and consensus in the village. The coming movement was to be 'guided, planned and orderly'. If 'chaotic conditions' arose, the campaign was to be postponed until the following year. In areas not scheduled for land reform during the winter of 1950–1, 'if peasants spontaneously rose to carry out [land seizures], they should be persuaded to stop'. (Liu Shao-chi, ibid.)

New policy also involved a prohibition on the formation of separate land reform leadership organs for the poor peasantry, that is, of Poor Peasant Leagues. The principal organization for controlling the campaign at the *hsiang* and village level was now to be the broadly based Peasant Association, one third of whose committee would be of middle peasant status. The PA was also open to 'poor rural intellectuals and other working people'; and outside the PA, all 'rural anti-feudal elements . . . including those enlightened gentry who support land reform' were to be brought together 'to form a united front against feudalism'.

The new approach rested on two assumptions. Firstly, it was accepted that land reform could not but issue in an inegalitarian land tenure system, which would itself be the source of a degree of further upward and downward mobility.[1] In so far as the leadership provided an answer to the social and political problems this posed, it consisted of prospective state aid (farm credit, etc.) to the least favoured, and the formation of low-level co-operatives and mutual aid teams. Secondly, Liu Shao-chi's report and other contemporary documents were marked by a considerable degree of optimism as to the possibility of overcoming landlord opposition. Policy, it was argued, would effectively neutralize the rich peasantry; although struggle with the landlords would be 'bitter and systematic', there was the implication that the class as a whole could be fairly readily split, and that in any case many landlords accepted the inevitability of their fate. Those that did were to be 'treated liberally according to the law'. Peasants were therefore to be restrained from forcibly extracting the personal possessions of landlord families, and in this sense the treatment of landlords was 'to be far more liberal than in the past'. Additionally, no real difficulty was foreseen in the determination of the class of the broad peasantry: '. . . the class status of the vast bulk of the rural population is clear and easily determined, and should not produce too many disputes.'

Almost wholly lacking from the contemporary view, then, was the sense of group and class conflict which was to permeate subsequent analyses of land redistribution. Absent also was any real awareness of the social cohesiveness and integration of the villages of the 'new areas'. One may speculate why: perhaps the optimism born of newly-acquired state power led the leadership to believe that control of the commanding heights would give easy access to the valleys of the village. Perhaps the Party's most

1. In contrast to the official contemporary analysis of the outcome of the earlier reform in North China, according to which there had been general 'middle peasantization'.

recent experience with the northern rural areas, much of whose social structure had been shattered by war, created a too sanguine view of the problems of peasant mobilization. Whatever the case, before the year was out, the pendulum was to swing back again, and entrenched landlord opposition, peasant immobility and village cohesiveness were to become central concerns in the campaign.

Why this occurred was related, in at least part, to the type of rural social structure in South China, and particularly to the nature of southern landlordism, which we must now briefly analyse.

III. Landlord and Tenant in South China

(i) Landlordism in Central-Southern China was not, typically, absentee. For the 1930s, data exist for four south-central provinces (*Tenancy System*, 1936 and *Wen Hua Pi Pan*, 1935), indicating that in Hupeh 83 per cent of landlords were locally resident, in Honan 82 per cent, Kiangsi 70 per cent, and Anhwei 62 per cent (see Table I). Although the term 'locally resident' is not without ambiguity, it does indicate residence either in the *hsiang* area where the landlord owned land, or in the same village as his landholding, and this would suggest a considerable degree of direct face-to-face contact between owner and his tenant. This is indicated by the high incidence of tenants assisting their landlords with work during disaster periods, performing services at weddings, and sending gifts. This is certainly not to argue that such relationships were amicable or non-exploitative, but simply that they existed. More specifically, only in very few cases was rent collected by agents or managers – usually either the tenant delivered or the landlord visited his land to assess the crop.

(ii) In 1950, confiscation of land was directed specifically at the 'feudal' stratum of rural society, i.e. the landlords (apart, of course, from the confiscation of lineage and village association land). Since rich peasants also received a considerable proportion of their income from 'exploitation' (including land rent), the central difference between the two strata was defined in terms of work: landlords did not work, rich peasants did. But were the lines of demarcation so easily defined in practice?

During the mid thirties at least, some local landlords in Kiangsi were being forced to take their land back into self-cultivation, due to the absence of potential tenants consequent on the decline of the rural population. Hence, among other reasons, the need in 1950 to introduce complex criteria governing the time during which a farm family had occupied a particular status. Furthermore, and more significantly, rural investigations in the thirties classify the majority of 'locally resident landlords' (who themselves constituted a majority) as 'small landlords'. In the case of Kiangsi province, the land owned by 'small, local landlords' (in half an admittedly very limited sample) was either less than, or merely equivalent to the amount of land owned and/or worked by the 'self-cultivating' and 'semi-self-cultivating' peasant farmers. (*Tenancy System*, 1936, pp. 14–15 and 77–9.)

TABLE 1

Province	*% of locally resident landlords*		*% of cases where rent collected by agent*
	(a)	(b)	(a)
Hupeh	83	—	8
Honan	82	61	6
Kiangsi	70	73	1
Anhwei	62	71	22

(Sources: (**a**) *Tenancy System*, 1936, above. (**b**) 1934 Ministry of Industry survey, cited in (a). Discrepancies between (a) and (b), although considerable, do not upset the basic hypothesis. There seems to be no evident correlation between use of rent agent and absenteeism.)

(iii) Available data indicate that rent as a percentage of output was high, and generally confirm the Party's post-liberation analyses that around 50 per cent of tenant's output went to his landlord.

TABLE 2 *Crop Rent as a Percentage of Output, 1934–5* (*Wet Land*)

		Land Grades		
Province	*Sample*	*Upper*	*Middle*	*Lower*
Kiangsi	14 *hsien* (county)	47	50	50
Honan	1 *hsien*	39	41	47
Hupeh	15 *hsien*	43	43	48
Anhwei	13 *hsien*	41	43	45

(Sources: *Tenancy System* pp. 51–2; and *Wen Hua Pi Pan* (cited above), p. 19.)

However, factors which *might* have mitigated the harshness of these high rent levels must be taken into account. There was a customary obligation on the landlord to reduce rent in times of poor harvest or natural disasters (an obligation which might be written into the rent agreement), and although there is no way of knowing how far this obligation operated in practice, rural depopulation, as in Kiangsi in the thirties and forties, could well have induced landlords to treat defaulting tenants with relative leniency. Further, there is evidence to suggest that landlords might, on occasion, supply some working capital (seeds, implements, fertilizer) to their tenants, as distinct from lending it, and might bear part of the cost of irrigation repairs.

(iv) I have suggested above that there existed an affluent stratum of working farm families whose economic position in terms of land owned and cultivated (if not their social status) surpassed that of the southern landlord. Additionally, the richer peasantry, in contrast to the landlords, appear to have played an important role in rural finance throughout the two decades prior to land reform. Between 1941 and 1947, almost 50 per cent of private cash loans in Kiangsi, for example, came from rich peasants, as compared to 25–33 per cent from landlords, and 18–33 per cent from merchants. In the mid thirties, only 9 per cent of Kiangsi tenants borrowed from their landlord, 14 per cent in Hupeh, 21 per cent in Anhwei, and 22 per cent in Honan.[1] One might conclude, then, that in 'preserving the rich peasant economy', the Party in 1950 was preserving an economically important stratum of rural society, having a considerable role in farm credit, and that this policy accorded well with the then dominant economic rationale of the land reform programme.[2]

By the same token, however, the line of demarcation between the principal strata of the rural élite (landlords and rich peasantry) which the Party sought to enforce was probably less meaningful to the poorest and unemployed in the villages than it was to incoming work teams learned in the formal regulations governing class criteria. Although the poor peasantry could draw sharp distinctions between the richer members of their own community (whether or not they worked actively in agriculture) and evidently rich and powerful large landowners who were more

1. These data are drawn from the contemporary issues of *Nong Bao* and *Zhong Nong Yue Kan*, and from *Tenancy System*, 1936, pp. 84–6.
2. An equally important political rationale also existed for the preservation of the rich peasantry as a class: that only by so doing could the middle peasantry be effectively shielded from the force of poor peasant mobilization.

usually outsiders, could they distinguish intra-élite demarcations within the village? Would the distinction of non-work/work (the criterion distinguishing landlord from rich peasant) have sufficient force to withstand the brunt of poor peasant mobilization, once this was unleashed?

Factors such as these, it is argued, lie behind the particular pattern of peasant response to the land reform campaign. The reaction of the poorest strata swung between two extremes: either they resisted mobilization by Party-led work teams, since they saw themselves as vulnerable to the power of the village élite; or, once assured of permanent political security, they would mobilize, and move to expropriate all village wealth in a wave of egalitarianism. Those middle peasants who rented in land from landlords would be mobilized only on condition that the process did not lead to their own expropriation and the denial of their right to legally acquire the land they had tenanted. Overarching these considerations were the factors of landlord patronage, and the ties of kinship and local residence between tenant and landlord.

It was against this background that the leadership was obliged, once again, to fundamentally re-assess its land policy.

IV. The Renewed Radicalization of Autumn 1950: Prelude

There has been a tendency to see the abandonment of the moderate and optimistic perspectives of the Land Reform Law as a direct outcome of the People's Republic's growing involvement in the Korean War (Vogel, 1969). The evidence, however, indicates that it was the Party's pessimistic assessment of the results of the trial periods of land reform implementation in late summer and early autumn which led to a reformulation of its policy.

In brief, a growing appreciation of the complex nature and entrenched power of local political and social organization in the countryside – a power which threatened to nullify or seriously inhibit the drive towards land redistribution – led the Party part-way back to conceptions and techniques of the pre-liberation period. At the heart of the problem was the manifest ability of the landlord class at the village level to subvert newly established peasant associations to its own interests, to disperse its wealth and land among 'reliable' poor, to resist the efforts of the incoming work teams seeking contact with aggrieved elements, to conceal their own class status behind a wall of silence, or in the last resort to physically intimidate cadre and recalcitrant peasant by the mobilization of 'underground' armed forces of bandits and secret societies.

The beginning of the transition to renewed radicalism is to be found in the fullest report on land reform plans in the central south, by Li Hsueh-feng, Chairman of the Central-South Land Reform Committee, in mid September, 1950.

In the two months prior to Li's report, the central-south area had been engaged in initial work on 'trial point' land reform for testing Party land policies, and in the training of leadership cadres and land reform work teams of students and former 'northern' cadres in the new perspectives and methodology of mid 1950. A series of rectification movements had also been carried out to correct bureaucratic and commandist tendencies among the lower levels. Meanwhile, movements for rent reduction had continued from the autumn of the previous year (*Chang Jiang Ri Bao*, 21 July 1950 and 16 September 1950) and in certain areas the establishment of new, or the reorganization of existing, Peasant Associations and Peasant Representative Conferences (*nong dai hui*) had gone ahead. Land reform plans were only finally assessed and approved after an examination of this work had taken place in cadre rectification conferences at *hsien* (county) and above levels.

It is clear that in the course of the various meetings of leading cadres in the provinces charged with assessing the work-base and with policy planning in their areas, a variety of opinion had begun to emerge over how best to approach the task ahead. As reflected in Li Hsueh-feng's report, opinion was divided over the best methods for achieving the aims of the movement, that is, over the issues of control and violence, and over the use of 'united front' policies for peasant mobilization.

The projected plans for the land campaign of winter 1950–1 (covering 155 of the central-south area's 514 *hsien*, and 50 million of its 120 million population) had produced, Li noted, two types of 'deviation'. One group of those involved in discussing land reform plans clearly saw the 'freeing of the peasants from the political and ideological influences of the old society, and the overcoming of dispersal and diffusion and the organizing of mutually alienated (*ge ai*) lineages and villages into class troops capable of carrying out the land reform struggle, as an extremely simple matter'. Such comrades 'treated the appearance of one peasant representative conference as representing the level of consciousness of the broad masses' and were taken in by what appeared to be a 'uniform demand for land reform'. Where the landlords were concerned, these comrades failed to distinguish between the acceptance of land reform by a few 'enlightened gentry' and the phoney demands for 'rapid land reform, quickly over the hump, rapidly settle things' by those landowners who planned to take advantage of the lack of preparatory work among the masses to disperse their land and property. In this view, landlords had essentially accepted policy and bowed to the new government. Cadres with this orientation advocated 'an arbitrary enlargement of land reform plans'.

Against this group, Li pointed to the 'general phenomenon' of destruction of economic resources and of the activation of political ties between politically reactionary landlord groups and 'land bandits and special agents' which had occurred in the area since the publication of the Land Reform Law (June) and 'especially since the publication of the texts on class determination' (26 August). Landlords were also making use of 'natural disasters and the fighting in Korea to create rumours widely and stir up chaos'. Thus it was clear, Li argued, that the implementation of land reform would be far harder than assumed by the 'optimists', and that only a policy of organizing and mobilizing the peasantry into an 'anti-feudal united front' for 'resolute and appropriate struggle against reactionary landlords' would secure the obedience of the landlord class to the law.

Yet Li also argued against certain leading cadres who apparently felt that land reform plans had been pitched too high, and that only after the peasantry had been fully prepared and educated, and sufficient cadres fully trained, could land reform go ahead. This group advocated an extreme reduction in plans, or even postponement for the present. Li said simply that no formal training process would ever be complete, that cadres and masses would be forged in actual land reform struggle and that excessive conservatism on the part of the leadership could well produce a 'spontaneous settling of accounts' by the peasantry which would pass out of its control.

Despite his criticism of the 'conservatives' it is evident, however, that Li's position was closer to theirs than to that of the 'optimists'. An accurate assessment of the situation in the central-south gave no cause for complacency. Although there were some 20 million Peasant Association members in the area, at the most in the provinces south of the Yangtse, only some 20–30 per cent of Associations had sufficient leadership and organizational strength to be able to carry out the campaign. A similar proportion were either front organizations for oppositional groups or were 'basically impure', and over half needed basic reorganization. In addition, the time had been too short for thorough cadre training and rectification, and the number of 'old cadres' was insufficient. The autumn grain levy, and preparation for winter and spring production also imposed strains on existing personnel resources. Given these factors, plus the fact that central policy had laid down that two particular deviations were to be avoided – 'serious chaos' and 'half-cooked phenomena' (i.e. incomplete implementation of land reform) – Li concluded that the only policy open to the leadership in the south was one of caution and tight control over the campaign. Liu Shao-ch'i's interdiction on spontaneous mass movements of the peasantry in non-land reform areas was to be closely observed, as was his directive to postpone land reform until the following year in areas in which 'chaotic conditions' developed which could not be rapidly corrected. Li also added a condition of his own to the effect that any area which found that its preparation for land reform was beginning to clash with spring production, should reduce its plans accordingly.

Thus Li Hsueh-feng's report begins to acknowledge the dimensions of the problem of organizing the peasantry in a context of 'dispersal and diffusion' and 'mutually alienated lineages and villages'. It is less sanguine than that of Liu Shao-ch'i in regard to landlord opposition – but even here Li notes that it is incorrect not to accept 'the possibility of striving for the majority of landlords to hand over their land according to the law'. The situation dictated extreme caution, and like Liu, Li's whole emphasis is on order and control. He also similarly stresses the overriding economic rationale of land reform, and the 'petty-producer' orientation of the peasantry: '. . . the peasants' demand for land is the demand to work and produce for themselves on their own land. To overlook that land reform is to develop production . . . is extremely erroneous.'

Thus land distribution must not allow the concern for 'those without labour power' to reach the point where the means of production were wasted. Policy had to pay attention at every stage 'to all measures for the restoration and activation of the rural economy'.

Although there was debate within the leadership of the central-southern provinces over the relative weight to be accorded to socio-political as against economic factors, there is no evidence that, *at this stage*, there was disagreement over the economic goals of land reform as such. But clearly there *was* a division of opinion on how far this goal could or should be reconciled with social and political goals, as well as on the most appropriate methods for achieving the end. In a situation of acute shortage of resources for distribution, did either considerations of social justice or the need for political support dictate that the demands of the poor and hired peasants for land and capital weigh equally with, or even outweigh, considerations of 'economic rationality' as expressed in the Land Reform Law and Liu Shao-ch'i's report? In June, Liu had scarcely touched upon the question. By September, Li Hsueh-feng would explicitly throw far more weight than Liu on the necessity of satisfying the poor and hired peasants, who constituted 'over 50 per cent of the rural population'. Since, he argued, agricultural development depended so largely on a labour-intensive strategy, it was of vital importance to meet the demands of the majority of the agricultural labour force. 'To this end, the poor and hired peasants' demands must be looked after first when distributing the landlords' land and means of production.'

At the same time, however, Li gave scarcely less weight to the necessity of protecting the middle peasant, 'whose numbers are only slightly inferior to those of the poor and hired peasants'. They constituted a 'social force whose productive power is relatively strong'. In areas where rich peasant land was being requisitioned and middle peasants rented out some land, or in areas where there were no landlords at all and relatively little land rented out by rich peasants the temptation to redistribute middle peasant land was particularly strong; and here, especially, any tendency to move against middle peasants or classify them upwards was totally prohibited. Politically, the middle peasant was to be drawn into all decision-making in relation to land reform, to the distribution of tax burdens in the village, and to the provision of food-grain loans and mutual aid in production, in accordance with the general line laid down by Liu Shao-ch'i. For the middle peasant was 'part of the battle-line of the peasant class, and (the) so-called unleasing (*fang shou*) of mass mobilization referred to the poor peasants, the hired peasants *and* the middle peasants'. The so-called 'poor and hired peasant line' of some areas in the 1947–8 period was mistaken precisely in underrating the anti-feudal united front. Policy, quite specifically, was 'to combine the two aspects of mobilizing the masses and . . . organizing an anti-feudal united front'.

It was precisely over the question of the form and limits to mass mobilization that considerable differences of opinion were expressed in the preliminary land reform meetings, if we can judge by Li's report. The central-south authorities' policy on 'struggle with the enemy' as presented by Li represented a compromise between 'some comrades' who had advocated a policy of 'legal control' (*fa zhi*) and were thus 'unwilling to support [even] legal struggle', and a contrary group who had doubted whether any form of *legal* struggle could arouse the masses. The former group believed allegedly that 'one must control the masses' and were unwilling to undertake painstaking mobilization; they failed to see, however, that without mass struggle there could be no policy implementation. The latter group failed to appreciate that through 'reasonable and legal struggle' (*he li he fa dou zheng*) they could both avoid the chaos and violence of the past, and secure policy implementation.

We quote at some length Li's rationalization of the policy of *he li he fa* struggle, both for what it indicates of the central-south authorities' expectations about the likely progress of the campaign, as well as for the slight emphasis it gives to certain methods of execution – such as 'speak bitterness' – which were later to occupy a central part in implementation:

In handling the enemy under a democratic administration, only reasonable and legal forms of struggle should be used, and not illegal struggle forms – because it is now no longer a question of seeking and making use of legal opportunities under a reactionary administration, but a new situation where it is completely possible to fully use legal forms with full justification and without fear to handle the enemy rationally and legally. Nor is it like the tense war period of the past, but a new period in which time is available for orderly treatment of the enemy. . . . By national policy, the Land Reform Law and other laws and decrees we have laid down the organs which guarantee the masses the legal implementation of land reform, and have guaranteed [them] the opportunity for legal activity within a broad scope. We also decided to announce the organizing of people's tribunals, adopting a dictatorial spirit of dealing with the enemy. This will be even more effective in organizing the masses to carry out struggle. (So) why still hanker after certain past and inappropriate forms (of mass action)?

Those who still 'hankered' after the past called for continuance of methods of 'the fearless intimidation of the crowd' (*qun dan qun wei*), of 'face-to-face and speak-bitterness struggle'. But they did not understand that,

in reality the best struggle experience of the past can be incorporated in the various forms of legal struggle, and even better developed, while it can avoid many errors that might occur.

The various methods of legal struggle combined with the use of the people's tribunals, are all even more organized manifestations of the 'fearless intimidation of the crowd' and 'face-to-face' struggle, and all can be combined with speak bitterness (if necessary, and if the masses naturally have such a demand) and with accusation, to arouse the masses' deepest feelings and sense of righteousness. By means of the Peasant Association and all types of internal peasant conferences, and having been forged in this type of struggle, the authoritative power of the masses can manifest itself fully, and there will be no need for merely formalistic shouting or disorganized intimidation and even beating and cursing [as a means of] manifesting violence. . . . Mass congresses with large numbers of people should be used for the goals of mobilizing the masses, reviewing their power, passing decisions, announcing results and summing up and proclaiming victories, but they must not be used for speak bitterness struggles or public trials. . . . All blind slogans and behaviour which [too] easily arouse the masses should be avoided to the utmost.

From this review of Li's report a number of points emerge. Firstly, the Military Administrative Committee's perception of the political and social environment has shifted somewhat from Liu Shaoch'i's assessment of the summer: that is, while asserting that existing policy provided the authorities with sufficient instruments to carry out their programme, there is a growing appreciation of the complexity of rural society, of the strength of landlord opposition, and of certain inadequacies in the leadership resources (Peasant Associations and cadres) at the disposal of the authorities. It was the first two of these factors which, I suggest, led Li to lay considerable stress on the necessity of methods of controlled mass mobilization as against the largely 'instrumentalist' view of Liu – whose report is noteworthy for not mentioning mobilization at all. But if there has been a shift towards more mobilization in carrying out the programme, it remains strictly within the framework of legal struggle, and the Liuist aversion to disorder and inchoate mass action remains. 'Speak bitterness' (*su ku*) is not presented as a central method of arousing mass action; and, importantly, heavy stress is laid on the use of united front tactics. The primacy of economic goals remains.

One further element in policy which must be noted concerns the 'requisition' of land rented out by rich peasants in the area under central-south jurisdiction. The Land Reform Law and Liu's report provided for the mandatory confiscation of those large amounts of land rented out by 'semi-landlord style' rich peasants, but other rich peasants who rented out only *small* amounts should not 'generally' have that land confiscated, except in special areas where poor peasants would not get 'an appropriate amount of land' under normal policy. In Li's report of September, it is announced briefly that this exception to normal policy is to be fully utilized :that is, apart from the normal confiscation of land rented out by 'semi-landlord style' rich peasants, 'it is further necessary *over relatively large areas* to requisition land rented out by *general* rich peasants' (emphasis supplied). The question of how to treat such rented-out land had apparently been one of the main subjects of discussion in preliminary meetings on land reform in the provinces. Land surveys made during the summer had indicated that in the 'old soviet areas', because of the relative dispersal of landownership, a more radical policy of confiscation would need to be pursued against the rich peasants to ensure sufficient transfer of land to the poorest strata. ('The state of rural social classes and tenancy relations in each province of the central-south', CJRB, 18 August 1950, p. 3.) Thus by mid September, the scope of land confiscation had been extended to embrace part of rich peasant holdings 'over relatively large areas'.

The fact that Li's report was not published until several months later indicates that policy was still in a considerable state of flux in September, and that the line he espoused could not gain agreement among the several hundred delegates at the conference. But evidence in support of his view on the costs of unrestrained peasant mobilization could be found in a retrospective analysis of preparatory land reform work over the preceding six months, by Tu Jun-sheng, Vice-Chairman of the Central-South Land Reform Committee. ('Report on preparatory work and the state of land reform implementation over the past half year', CJRB, 21 September 1950.) Tu, who two months later was to lead the attack on the earlier moderate policy, noted that 'bandit elimination' (presumably referring mainly to remnants of Kuomintang forces) had been moderately successful. The movements for rent reduction and return of rent deposits had, however, been far less so. Begun in Hunan and Hupeh in March, and expanded to the whole area at the beginning of April, they had resulted in the organization of some 25 million peasants (i.e. about a fifth of the population) into Peasant Associations. But violent deviations had developed as peasant and cadre sought to extract grain or cash from landowners, spring cultivation work had been threatened, and on 18 April the MAC had brought the deposit-return movement[1] to a halt with the publication of 'ten great policies on spring production' (which found it necessary to specifically forbid 'undisciplined compulsion, beating and

1. Tenants were often obliged to pay a deposit as a guarantee to landlords; this refers to a movement for the return of these deposits.

arrest'). If the central south authorities needed a reminder of the degree to which campaigns in the countryside could beget violence and affect production, the rent and deposit movements seemingly provided it.[1]

V. Radicalization sets in

The two months following this September conference, which had manifested both indecision and the beginnings of a more radical approach to land reform, were given over to further extension of the rent reduction movement, to reorganization and 'purification' of peasant associations, to the autumn grain levy (i.e. the collection of grain tax), to the intensification of propaganda in land reform policies, to training and rectifying new and old cadres – of whom some 100,000 were training in autumn, including 50,000 members of land reform work teams – and finally to further trial-point work in selected *hsiang* as a means of settling final work methods for each province.

It was an analysis of the results obtained in these trial areas which finally and decisively swung policy in the direction of radicalization. It is possible to date the definitive policy change to early November, when the Central-South Land Reform Committee called in lower-level cadres to report on the condition of land reform work in a hundred *hsiang* throughout the area.[2]

We have no direct record of the discussions at this second conference. But on 18 November, Tu Jun-sheng (and not the Chair-

1. Tu also admitted that rent reduction to date was 'not general and not deep', due to the pressure of the production season and effective avoidance by landlords. In fact the spring campaign had forced a compromise on the authorities, who changed the existing 37·5 per cent (of output) ceiling on rent to a general 25 per cent reduction in rent payments, which 'took account of landlord difficulties'. A later analysis asserted that at the time, even in the best areas, only 38 per cent of rents that should have been affected by the movements were in fact reduced: (*CJRB*, 8 December 1950 editorial). Subsequent regulations on return of deposits, also provided for a 50 per cent reduction in the amount 'owed' by landlords to tenants, or exemption in the case of hardship, and the process of extraction of rent deposits was to be tightly controlled by the *ch'u* government and Peasant Association.
2. During the 'middle ten days' of November the Committee also inspected work in Hunan and Kangsi, and drew serious conclusions from what they observed. See *CJRB*, 24 December 1950, p. 1: 'The land reform movement is now gradually developing.'

man of the Land Reform Committee, Li Hsueh-feng) summarized the lessons drawn from work in these trial *hsiang*. (Tu Jun-sheng, 'Several problems in the leadership of the coming land reform', CJRB, 3 December 1950, pp.1 and 3.) His message was clear: experimental work had shown that existing policies on land reform were insufficient to secure an effective and full redistribution of land. Of the hundred *hsiang*, only twenty were 'good', fifty were 'not very good' and thirty were 'very bad'. The mass basis of organization was insufficient, in very many villages middle peasants exercised effective power, and 'half-cooked' results existed widely.

The 'principal dangerous tendency' at the root of this state of affairs was identified by Tu as a 'mentality of peaceful land reform' (*he ping fen tian si xiang*) among the cadres. Such 'peaceful thinking' manifested itself in a 'simple production viewpoint', a belief that 'land division is for production and peaceful land division will benefit production'. Cadres with such an outlook were deluded by the general state of 'peace in the land' and failed to understand that, although the fragmentation of the landlord class 'under the general objective situation of [national] victory is possible', the class would not spontaneously fragment unless the full weight of a mobilized peasantry were brought to bear on it. Otherwise, the traditional power structure would prevail, and the redistribution of land resources to the landless would be marginal. Land reform must be seen as a 'revolution to reform the social system, a systematic political, economic and cultural revolution which takes land distribution as its core. . . .' Central to its success was the satisfaction of the land demands of the peasants 'and especially the poor and hired peasants'.

A further manifestation of 'peaceful thinking' among cadres was a failure to realize that peasant demands for land might be misdirected towards the government and away from the local élite. Only a direct demand by the peasants on their local landowners could constitute a 'real rising up' by the peasantry, and this necessitated the full use of struggle methods since 'the landlords will fight to the death'.

Finally, many cadres laid too much stress on the 'several hundred clauses of laws and decrees' governing the orderly conduct of the campaign, which confused the peasantry and overstressed care for the landlords. Correct priorities dictated arousing the poor first, and worrying about the landlords afterwards. 'To explain orderliness without linking it with struggle corresponds to not wanting revolution.'

Cadres, however, did not bear sole responsibility for the poor results of the 'first battle' in the campaign. The tendency towards a technical approach 'was not without connection with the leadership of leading organs' who over the past year had 'concentrated heavily in their discussions of orderliness on drawing up laws to prevent chaos' without explaining how to put them into effect nor what sort of 'order' was required. The result was a 'half-dead stalemate in land reform'.

The way forward from this impasse could only be via a policy of 'unleashing' (*fang shou*) the peasantry in a 'great burning movement . . . to destroy the landlords' political control, using revolutionary procedures, to overthrow their organizational leadership and their economic privileges, as well as all feudal ideology used to control the peasants, such as family rules, lineage, conscience (*liang xin*) and fatalism'. The fully mobilized peasants would inevitably produce 'some over-heated activity' but cadres should guide it into correct paths and not pour cold water on it. For the true definition of 'order' in a revolution was when 'the peasant raises his head and grinds the landlord into the earth.' The threshold of violence had been raised.

The satisfaction of poor and hired peasant land demands became the *principal* content of land reform and, as a corollary, Tu seems to have left the way open for more aggressive grass roots action against rich peasant landholdings than previously. In September the authorities had decided on full utilization of the clause allowing confiscation of land rented out by rich peasants – but the process had always been one requiring provincial approval. Tu, in November, states that 'where the local peasants resolutely demand it, their (the rich peasants') rented-out land must be confiscated (*yao dong*)', and rather defensively adds that this had already been provided for by existing decrees and did 'not negate the principal of preserving the rich peasant economy'. To the extent that locally initiated direct mass action against rich peasants could now be envisaged, this was less than the truth.

The second major and crucial aspect of policy radicalization concerned the organization of the poorest village strata. And here, in virtually direct contradiction of Liu Shao-ch'i's interdiction on the formation of Poor Peasant Leagues, Tu Jung-sheng announced that 'poor and hired peasant congresses' (*da hui*) were to be held at the level of the natural village, as well as 'poor and hired peasant representative conferences', and when necessary 'councils' (*zhu xi tuan*) of these conferences (the latter two at *hsiang* and *ch'u*[1] levels), in order to establish the 'backbone

1. The *hsiang* remained the basic administrative grouping of villages

function of poor and hired peasants in the peasant association'. By these structural changes, leadership in land redistribution would be placed more firmly in the hands of the poor.

With the announcement of the 'unleashing' of mass activity came also the notification that a 'speak bitterness' campaign was both an integral part of and a precondition for successful political mobilization of the peasants. The pouring out of peasant hatred against the old élite's economic and political exploitation would serve to heighten emotional tension in the village and marked for the first time a definitive turn towards the *psychological* goals of securing inner commitment to the new power structure in the village. Thus, the violence of 'mass struggle' activity was not only a structural necessity (that is, directed to securing a redistribution of political power in the village), but also a psychic necessity. The concrete examples of economic exploitation and political manipulation and patronage, revealed in the course of village bitterness meetings, would bring home to the peasant the real nature of power in his village, interpreting to him his existence not in terms of the vagaries of an impersonal fate but as the creation of powerful interest groups determined to protect their privileges at his cost. Thus he would be brought to 'draw lines' between himself and the enemy, and the inner cohesiveness and traditional loyalties of the rural community would begin to crumble. This process of 'self-education' would also operate for the new cadres, many of whom had 'no confidence in this new set of methods'.

The leadership, however, given its experience in the land reform of 1947–8 in North China, could not ignore the risks in the 'new methods' and hence Tu continued to lay considerable stress on the importance of not following 'the masses' spontaneous morale blindly, but standing among them and guiding them forward' (i.e. leadership from within), and on the fact that the middle peasant 'is our permanent ally' and that a 'united front must be maintained with him'.

In fact, Tu's attitude to how specifically 'unity' could be maintained, once confiscation and distribution got under way, between those strata in the village who had only marginal access to land resources and those whose access (through either ownership or tenancy) gave them the self-sufficient status of middle peasants, is not without ambiguity – and this was the crux of the problem of organizing the peasant movement. Land reform, as a

---

during the fifties, with the *ch'u* as an intermediate level between it and the *hsien* (county).

process of distributing land rented out by landlords and rich peasants, had to ensure both that those middle peasants who hitherto had relied effectively on renting in a major part of their holding did not suffer a too severe decline in their economic status, but that sufficient resources were transferred to the poorest strata who hitherto had only marginal access to land. In a situation of high tenancy, relations between the poorest villagers and tenant middle peasants were thus crucial. Tensions between the two strata were, Tu noted, 'manifested very prominently in Kiangnan' (South China). Hence, middle peasants were to be allowed to participate in meetings of the poor peasants, and land was to be distributed 'in resolute accordance with the principle of taking the existing cultivator as the base'. Any rent and rent deposits returned during the course of the campaign were strictly 'to go back to middle peasant ownership'.

In restating that middle peasants were to participate in the councils of the poor (as well as the other restraints noted above) Tu was repeating Liu Shao-ch'i's formulation of the summer. But for many cadres, sensing the drift of policy in late autumn, it must have seemed that the 'moderate' line of summer had been abandoned in favour of a return to the 'poor peasant' line of the civil war period, and that the obligation to 'unite with the middle peasant' might, *à la rigueur*, be downgraded. At least, as subsequent discussion showed, there was some confusion in their minds.

The seal of authority on the new line enunciated by Tu Jun-sheng was a directive of the Central-South Bureau of the Party in December 1950: 'Unleash mass mobilization and thoroughly complete land reform plans'. No text is available but an existing brief summary indicates the line laid down: that only a policy of *fang shou* (unleashing), 'directed especially to the poor and hired peasants' with primary attention given to 'satisfying PHP needs', could achieve land reform. (The land reform movement is now gradually developing, CJRB, 24 December 1950.) Its main targets of criticism were 'peaceful land reform thinking' and 'helplessness' on the part of cadres who had a blind 'fear of chaos'.

Thereafter, a series of editorials in *Chang Jiang Ri Bao* discussed and developed at length the themes of *fang shou* mobilization, the real danger of 'peaceful' deviations, the inevitability of landlord opposition, and the distinction between the new policy and the erroneous 'poor peasant line' of pre-liberation land reform. The first of these editorials, on 8 December, cited Tu's report as 'basic policy' and sought to establish that the government since entering the new areas of South China had pursued a policy of 'liberality' towards the landlords, but to no avail: the attacks of the enemy had only redoubled.[1] Thus, 'although today's land reform must be somewhat smoother than the historical land revolutions . . . this is only to say *somewhat* smoother!' The fragmentation of the landlord class was merely a 'potential condition' which would be actualized only under conditions of mass struggle. The principle obstacles to policy implementation were 'destruction by landlords, the negative passivity of the masses and the helplessness of cadres'. The real problem facing the Party 'is not that mass arousal has produced excesses, *but that the masses are unwilling and don't dare to rise*' (emphasis added). The policy of *fang shou* that had been stressed in the old areas had been 'very successful' and the errors that had been produced could have been avoided if 'ideological boundaries' had been drawn correctly. Finally, although the movement was aimed at the economic base of 'feudalism', the prerequisite for success was the destruction of landlords' *political* power.

Six days later, the paper again took up the discussion of policy in an attempt to clarify the confusion in cadre minds over how exactly they were being asked to act. ('Further discussion on unleashing mass mobilization', CJRB, 14 December 1950.) *Fang shou* did not mean giving free rein to the peasants' 'free flowing' (*zi liu*) activity: it still referred to the guided implementation of policy. Nevertheless, cadres should not 'overstress the prevention of leftism' as soon as the movement started in an area, nor 'pour cold water' on mass activity. *Fang shou* opposed an administrative approach to land reform but not the fact that there was a specific policy to be implemented. So peasants had still to grasp 'the principles of reason, benefit and measure during struggle'. 'Lawful' struggle-means were still to be used, such as the courts, large meetings of combined villages (i.e. 'collective mass power'), but not beating and killing. On the other hand, 'lawful' did not mean just sticking to the various decrees issued in narrow 'textualist' way.

Throughout December feedback from those *hsien* now beginning the campaign indicated that cadres were still uncertain on the direction of policy. New cadres 'in large numbers' showed signs of sympathy towards landlords. But it was particularly the old cadres (i.e. those who had experienced the earlier land

1. Over 3,000 cadres were said to have been killed in February alone. Landlords threatened the peasants with the spectre of past repression: in 1935, 'the Kuomintang was waiting for you'; slaughtered cattle, activated lineage ties to carry out mock class determination, etc.

reforms) who had 'ideological blocks' over the new policy. On 26 December the subject was analysed at length, since in certain areas 'struggle has fallen into a chaotic condition, work must be stopped, and cadre conferences held before re-establishing the movement.' (Get rid of misinterpretations, correctly implement the *fang shou* mass mobilization line, CJRB, 26 December 1950.) Old cadres saw little difference between the thrust of policy now and that of the pre-liberation campaigns – but they remembered that for the latter they had been severely rectified. If they were being asked to give priority to mobilization of the poor and hired peasants, would they not be led ineluctably 'to commit errors of the "poor and hired peasant line" and then be criticized?' They believed that 'stressing unilateral action by the poor and hired peasants necessarily will infringe on the middle peasants'.

Clearly their pre-1949 experience had instilled in old cadres a view of the dynamics of land revolution, the logic of which the central-south authorities were attempting to resist. These cadres saw themselves faced with a situation where the campaign must be either strictly controlled from above or else left to run its own course, with all the attendant violence and destruction. In the latter case it was wishful thinking to expect that the spirit (let alone the letter) of policy pronouncements would be observed by the mobilized poor. The political behaviour of the Chinese peasant was to be understood in terms only of stark alternatives: either passive obedience to orders, or violent extremism for which cadres could not be held responsible. 'If you want *fang shou*, you shouldn't rectify us; if you want to stop deviations, we must take over everything ourselves.'

To this view of peasant political behaviour neither the editorial in question nor other discussions of the period could offer a convincing reply. It could assert that the dichotomy posed by the cadres between 'policy and *fang shou*' was a false one; that the choice was not just between cadres 'taking over everything themselves' (*bao ban dai ti*) to ensure that policy was strictly observed, or giving the poor peasantry their heads and accepting that past violence would be repeated; it could argue that what the Party wanted was a process of controlled mobilization of the dispossessed which yet took account of the interests of the middle strata of rural society and did not destroy valuable social assets in rural industry and commerce. Yet in the end, it was reduced to reassuring cadres that their fear of rectification was baseless so long as they stuck to policy, without attempting to refute their implicit view of the nature of peasant political response, as they had experienced it in the past. Thus the possibility of a campaign of considerable violence persisted.

VI. The Seal is set

Evidently, these short weeks saw a very fierce debate on fundamental issues of policy. The period was crucial, for the full land campaign was due to begin at the end of December. The final, decisive intervention came from a member of the highest party (not government) body in the region, in the form of a broadcast speech by Teng Tzu-hui, third secretary of the Central Southern Bureau of the Central Committee on 26 December (published in CJRB the following day).[1] The themes enunciated by Teng were developed with such force and clarity as to make his speech rank with that of Liu Shao-ch'i as one of the two authoratitive statements on policy of that year. And they constituted a direct critique of the assumptions underlying Liu's report.

Teng's principal theme, and opening assertion, was quite simply that land reform was pre-eminently a political movement: 'first change politics and then economics'. Whereas 'some comrades' saw the reform as simply land distribution and 'one-sidedly understood [it] as only for developing production', it was in fact an integral part of a long historical struggle against feudalism and imperialist encroachment on China. Land reform was a two-edged sword which, by striking at the traditional rural élite in all its political ramifications, struck both at the internal allies of imperialism and at that class which would always and totally block the implementation of rural change. Land reform was therefore to be seen not as the *direct* precondition for economic development, but as an indispensable condition of the establishment of a new *political* order in the countryside which alone could guarantee subsequent economic change.

Teng articulated a view of counter-revolutionary political structure which had received scant attention in the six months since Liu's report:

This landlord class is not a powerless enemy, but has had two thousand years of political power. Militarily, it not only had a national KMT regular army, local security corps and *hsiang* security troops, but also had land bandits, secret society forces acting outside, hangers-on for rough

1. 'Some basic problems in Land Reform', CJRB, 27 December 1950. The broadcast was prefaced by the authoritative 'To be carefully studied by all responsible and land reform cadres'.

work, and so-called 'self-protection' troops. After their defeat, underground armies were organized in many areas. Politically in the past, not only was there a vertical organizational system of KMT state power, but also a *bao jia* system stretching into every corner of the *hsiang* and village. After we destroyed the *bao jia*,[1] feudal power immediately changed form and took advantage of its running dogs or simple trustworthy peasants to act as village heads, and organized puppet (*wei*) peasant associations – so that in fact it still held village power and (could) guarantee its political superiority in the village. In Central-Southern China, this type of village is relatively widespread. . . . Organizationally, not only did it have the KMT, the *San Qing Tuan* [the rural youth organization of the thirties] and special agent organizations, but now still uses all types of feudal forms such as associations (*bang hui*), sects, etc., to organize the peasants. . . .

The existence of this entrenched network of political control dictated that land reform could only be conceived of as a series of 'interlocking' attacks on each of these structural manifestations of landlord power. For

although today the people's power has been established, in the shadows in many villages, the ratio of class power is reversed and power still belongs to the landlords; or the landlords are still supporting illegal forces (land bandits) and secret troops, or they control our militia, and *hsiang* and village administration is still openly monopolized or secretly manipulated by landlords . . . so the economic system is not changed, or only superficially. In many places, rent reduction is not thorough, or is secretly not done. . . . If landlord forces are not transferred to the peasants and the landlord-manipulated peasants' associations, militia and village power not transformed so that the class power ratio changes basically, then even if success if ours in the province and the *hsien*, in the shadows we will be powerless to carry out land reform.

This analysis of the local power situation, fifteen months after victory at the national level, forms the background for an attack on unspecified advocates of the perspective enunciated in summer. Faced with the actual disposition of power in the countryside, to 'posit simple land distribution and purely technical work' was 'the ideological root of peaceful land reform everywhere', and a 'very great political mistake on the level of principle'. But a further cause of the belief that a peaceful redistribution was feasible was 'one-sidedly taking land reform as

1. A traditional form of local military organization resurrected by the KMT for 'self-defence and policing functions'. (Schurmann, 1968, p. 411.)

having the goal of establishing production and not grasping that when land reform overthrows the enemy politically and sets up the peasant dictatorship it is precisely to create the conditions for the widespread development of production. Only when feudal power is destroyed can agriculture be greatly developed and industrialization become possible.' During the phase of destruction, '*that some disorder should occur . . . and some drop in production power* [*take place*] *for a period after land reform due to dispersal of land, is certain.*' (Emphasis added.)

This was the first occasion in six months that a direct and explicit challenge had been issued to the priority accorded to economic considerations in summer. And in support of his position, Teng cited Lenin's words of 1920: 'The proletariat must not fear to produce the temporary phenomenon of falling back. . . . For the bourgeoisie, the most vital thing is production for production's sake. For the proletariat, the most vital thing is to overthrow the exploiters . . . the first task of the proletariat is to guarantee its own victory.' The accusation had been made that the economic priorities of summer were 'anti Marxist-Leninist' and represented political errors 'on the level of principle'. Teng pursued his comparison with the newly-established Soviet State:

> Despite the apparent dissimilarity between Lenin's wartime situation and our own victorious situation – so that seemingly we should not stress the political factor – such thinking is only apparently correct. Although the national revolution is victorious and internal fighting has basically finished, we must realize that the people's government in the new areas is still not consolidated. We only control the upper levels, the lower levels are still in feudal hands. The danger of a third war (which imperialism is actively preparing) still exists, despite the increase in power of the democratic forces, and the fighting in the Korea area is still not resolved. Such internal and external situations demand a thorough extirpation of feudalism in land reform.

Where, to Liu Shao-ch'i in June the 'national task' had been 'economic construction, restoration and development of the social economy', now (as defined by Teng) 'the basic task of the revolution (was) to oppose imperialism and feudalism', in a context of war crisis and domestic political insecurity not dissimilar to the Soviet State encircled by the Western Powers. This represented the first occasion, on the available record, when the international context of the Korean War had entered so directly into an analysis of the domestic opposition to land reform.[1]

1. War, of course, had lain at the root of rural destruction and violence

Following this general analysis of the context of land reform, Teng moved to a discussion of certain specific problems. Since much of what he said had been foreshadowed in Tu Jun-sheng's speech in November, we shall note only certain points of emphasis. As with Tu, the centre of gravity in the campaign has shifted heavily towards the poorest strata of the rural population: the one 'basic demand of land reform' was to satisfy the demands for land and means of production of the poor and hired peasants. Priority was to be given to basing political organization on the poorest peasantry before bringing those of middle peasant status into village organization. The poor and hired peasants were to constitute the 'leadership core' with a separate organizational identity:

In areas where there is still no peasant association, we must first start by organizing the poor and hired peasants . . . and then absorb the middle peasants. . . . Where peasant association organizations already exist, we should first only summon poor and hired peasant congresses (*da hui*) or . . . representative conferences where everything is first discussed by them, and then passed on to the peasant association for discussion and passing, so as to establish a leadership core of poor and hired peasants and *guarantee that* (*they*) *have a current organization* [emphasis supplied]. And without provoking the middle peasants, a council (*zhu xi tuan*) can be created by the poor and hired peasants to be the current leadership organ.

Similarly, a greater degree of tolerance was expressed towards the violence of direct mass action:

In areas where the masses are mobilized and they still demand a political attack on the landlords, then they should be allowed to demand respect openly, and vent their anger on someone. Mass activity should not be hindered; cold water should not be poured on a little ultra-left activity so long as it is the masses' own anti-feudal action . . .

Only 'afterwards' was it to be 'explained and rectified'. Faced with the inevitable 'howls' of protest of landlords, and of notables 'inside and outside the Party', cadres should remain calm and not correct excesses 'prematurely in public' in a way which would affect the dynamics of the movement.

Yet Teng experienced the same difficulties as Tu Jun-sheng

---

before 1949, and so had a second factor which Teng mentioned – 'insufficiency of cadres': 'our cadres fall far behind the demands of objective conditions, especially in Central-South China where the area is vast . . . and those with experience in mass work and land reform are even fewer.'

over the problem of how to avoid driving a wedge between the middle and poor strata of village society. 'Unity' with the middle peasant was still to be maintained, via his participation in the leadership of the peasant association. The 'successful' experience of pre-liberation land reform was adduced not, significantly, as being generally inapplicable to the campaign in the central-south but as showing the specific dangers of excluding the middle peasantry:

The mistake of the hired-poor (*gu pin*) line carried out in certain areas in North China in the past was essentially that it sloughed off the middle peasant; it was not mistaken, but correct, in resolutely depending on the poor hired peasants, in mobilizing the poor and hired and in its method of starting by organizing (them). We must understand that the middle peasant is the reliable ally of the proletariat. Whoever rejects him will fail.

Immediately, however, Teng offered an analysis of middle peasant political behaviour which in fact questioned that very reliability and highlighted the crucial problem of the source of endogenous rural leadership in land reform which we have raised above.

But we must understand that the middle peasant is weak and has a compromising nature, and during land reform is basically a fence-sitter (*bu jin bu chu*),[1] economically speaking. So middle peasants cannot become peasant leaders, and especially we cannot hope that they will lead land reform. But speaking of their position in the old social economy, very often the middle peasants could easily become peasant leaders in peasant movements, especially in their initial stages.

This 'traditional' propensity to leadership by middle peasants, which found expression in the leadership role they played 'in possibly the majority' of current peasant association organizations, was adduced to justify the deliberate attempt to create a countervailing force of poor peasants by means of the device of the 2:1 leadership ratio in their favour. Only in this way could genuine 'joint leadership' be secured. But what was the meaning of 'joint'? In underlining the 'compromising nature' of the middle peasant, Teng was throwing doubt on the credibility of one element in that joint leadership, drawing attention to the clash of two interest groups in the village – and, again, increasing the possibility of downgrading middle peasant interests.

Once again, the resolution of a situation fraught with contradictions was to be left to the cadres' skill in managing conflict

1. 'He does not come in and he does not go out.'

between poor and middle peasants. Hence, as in earlier analyses, the exhortations to cadres to control poor peasant radicalism:

But the poor and hired peasants should be told that their demands can only be solved in opposing feudalism, vis-a-vis landlords' land and property and the land rented out by rich peasants, but that they cannot make plans on the middle peasant's position, nor on those in industry and commerce, nor on rich peasants' self-cultivated land and other property. Landlord property is limited and the poor and hired peasants' demands are difficult to satisfy completely, so they should be restricted to within the scope of laws and decrees and not develop into egalitarianism. . . . We must unleash legal struggle, . . . (not) illegal struggle – and this boundary must be clearly explained to cadres and the poor and hired peasants. Certainly, the ultra-leftist behaviour of the land reform in North China and Shantung – with its unexpected and widespread unearthing of property, general encroachment on industry and commerce and its irregular sweeping of everything out the door – cannot be repeated.

Yet 'legal struggle' was to be sharply distinguished from the legalistic 'textualism' of cadres who regarded 'legal clauses as binding' – and so the tension at the heart of policy remained:

Laws and decrees . . . in land reform should be treated as weapons in the struggle against landlords. . . . Many things cannot be decided in a text – and here the majority of poor and hired peasants should be allowed to express their opinions. . . . Texts can be interpreted in every way, and should be interpreted to the advantage of the poor and hired.

Cadres were thus being called upon to manage competition for endogenous leadership in the village as between the poor and middle peasants, arising from a campaign which sought to 'unleash the poor' within a framework of specific policy, whilst regarding the legal expressions of that policy as mere instruments in class struggle. Inevitably, many cadres (in the light of past experience) saw themselves caught between the hammer of policy and the anvil of the extremism of the mobilized poor, and they clearly recalled earlier rectification when a similar radicalization had occurred. Inevitably, therefore, the question of future cadre rectification loomed large – and here Teng could only attempt to play down the 'question of cadre deviations': '. . . explain that cadres will be further corrected and restrained, but do not publicly bring up names for criticism or high-hat them.[1] If it is not a serious deviation it should not be so treated.'

1. I.e. ridicule them.

Teng Tzu-hui's broadcast raised the crucial problems in, and set the guidelines for, the land reform campaign in Central-Southern China. It may be seen as the final statement in a long and tense debate over the correct strategy for land reform, as the centre of Party work shifted from North to South China, and the leadership grappled with questions of basic economic and socio-political priorities in a changing political context. The following three years would see the working out in practice of the aims and tensions inherent in that policy. Although that period lies outside the scope of this essay, the Chinese experience of 1947 to 1950 may serve as warning and exemplar of the problems of mobilizing a peasantry to achieve basic change in its relationship to land. In the mythology of peasant revolutions, the Chinese land reform has often been presented as the archetype of a radicalized peasant monument – 'a force so swift and violent that no power . . . will be able to hold it back'. The land reform debate, seen from within, alerts us to the complex calculus of costs and opportunities in land reform; to the necessity of a concrete analysis of social structure, of conflict of class interest within the peasantry, and of the nature of leadership resources available to the land reformers; and finally to the enduring problems of ordering economic and political priorities and goals.

References

Chinese

Chang Jiang Ri Bao (CJRB), 21 July 1950, 16 September 1950, 8 December 1950 (other articles cited under their titles).

'Central Committee directive on carrying out land reform work and Party reorganization in the old areas and the semi-old areas', in *Mu qian* . . . (see below), 22 December 1948.

'Further discussion on unleashing mass mobilization', CJRB, 14 December 1950.

'Get rid of misinterpretations, correctly implement the *fang shou* mass mobilization line', CJRB, 26 December 1950.

Jen Pi-shih, 'Some Problems of Land Reform', 12 January 1948 (reprinted in *Mu qian* . . . (see below)).

'The land reform movement is now developing', CJRB, 24 December 1950.

Li Hsueh-feng, 'Strive to complete land reform plans for this winter and next spring', *Yi jiu wu ling nian zhong guo jing ji lun wen xuan* (*Selected

Essays on the Chinese Economy for 1950), Series 2, I, Peking, 1951, pp. 42–63.

Mu qian xing shi he women de ren wu ('The Present Situation and our Tasks'), n.p.i., *Xin hua shu dian*, November 1949.

Nong Bao (Agricultural News).

'Questions and answers on Agrarian Socialism', 27 July 1948 (reprinted in *Mu qian* . . . (see above)).

Rural Reconstruction Committee, *Kiang su sheng nong cun diao cha*, 1934.

'Several problems in the leadership of the coming land reform', CJRB, 3 December 1950.

'The state of rural social classes and tenancy relations in each province of the Central South', CJRB, 18 August 1950.

Teng Tzu-hui, 'Some basic problems in land reform', CJRB, 27 December 1950.

Tenancy System . . . (See *Yu-Ou-Huan-Gan* . . ., below).

'The tenancy system in Kiangsi', *Wen Hua Pi Pan* (*Critique of Civilization*), II, 2–3 January 1935, pp. 10–38.

Tu Jun-sheng, 'Report on preparatory work and the state of land reform implementation over the past half year', CJRB, 21 September 1950.

Yu-Ou-Huan-Gan si sheng zhi zu dian zhi du (*The Tenancy System in the Four Provinces of Honan, Hupeh, Anhwei and Kiangsi*), Nanking, 1936.

Zhong nong yue kan (Chinese Agricultural Monthly).

English

Buck, J. L., *Land Utilization in China: Statistics*, Shanghai, 1937.

Chao Kuo-chun, *Agrarian Policy of the Chinese Communist Party*, Asia Publishing House, New York, 1960.

Hinton, William, *Fanshen: a Documentary of Revolution in a Chinese Village*, New York, 1966; Penguin, Harmondsworth, 1972.

Hsiao Tso-liang, *The Land Revolution in China, 1930–1934*, University of Washington Press, 1969.

Liu Shao-ch'i, 'Report on the Agrarian Reform Law', *The Agrarian Reform Law of the People's Republic of China*, Foreign Languages Press, Peking, 1950.

Schurmann, Franz, *Ideology and Organization in Communist China*, Berkeley, 1968 (revised edn. 1971).

Selden, Mark, *The Yenan Way in Revolutionary China*, Harvard University Press, 1971.

Vogel, Ezra, 'Land Reform in Kwantung', *China Quarterly*, **38**, April–June 1969.

Abbreviations employed

CJRB *Chiang Jiang Ri Bao* (Yangtse Daily).
KMT Kuomintang (Nationalist Party).
MAC Military Administrative Committee.
Except for place and personal names and administrative units, Chinese terms are romanized according to the *pin yin* system.

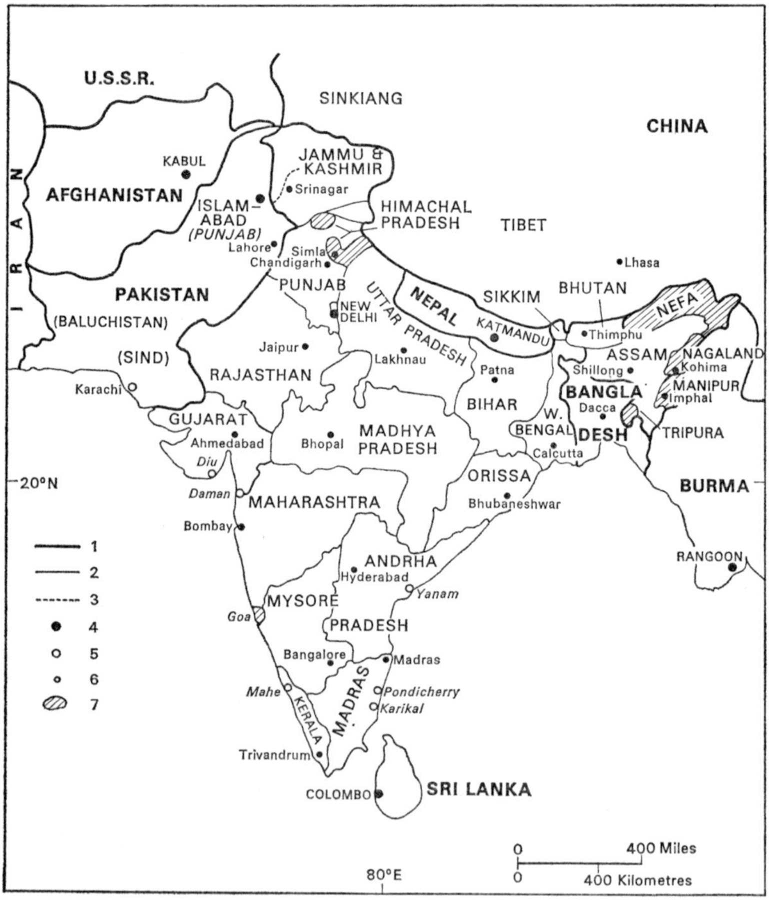

Map 4. India, Pakistan and Bangla Desh

Five

New Technologies and Income Distribution in Agriculture

D. P. Chaudhri

The relationship between agricultural performance and economic growth is deep and intricate. A dynamic agriculture ushering in structural change would gladden the heart of any growth planner. His enthusiasm is completely understandable if the dynamism appears dramatic. This is precisely what the 'green revolution' seems to be doing.

'Narrowly defined, the "green revolution" is the rapid growth in Third World grain output associated with the introduction of a new package of tropical agricultural inputs. The package consists essentially of a combination of improved grain varieties, mainly rice and wheat, heavy fertilizer usage and carefully controlled irrigation. Without fertilizer or without controlled irrigation the new varieties usually yield no more and sometimes less than traditional strains. With them they give substantially higher yields per acre.' (Cleaver, 1972, p. 171.) In this paper we attempt to examine the distributional effects of the 'green revolution'. In Part I we discuss the theoretical aspects; Part II is devoted to the examination of the Indian experience, and in Part III the policy implications of our theoretical reasoning and of the Indian experience is outlined.

I

We look here at received economic theory not because we can set up an empirically testable econometric model – data limitations obstruct such a course of action – but to separate out various components which influence the 'direction of effects' of changing technology and relative input prices on the pattern of income distribution.

I.1 *Input Substitution*

According to standard neo-classical economics,[1] changes in factor shares between any two input factors, say capital and labour, would depend upon the underlying aggregate production function and the pace of technological change on the one hand and supply conditions of the input factors on the other. As long as the production function remains stable the relative shares of the factors would depend upon:

a their elasticity of substitution – the percentage by which their relative proportions change in response to a 1 per cent change in relative prices with output held constant.

b their relative prices and supply conditions.

In most situations a falling purchase price of an input, say capital, will reduce the demand for its substitute, say labour. The exact magnitude will depend upon the price of output; the extent of changes in the relative prices of inputs; and the magnitude of the elasticity of substitution between the input factors.

The falling relative price of capital may have an effect on the income distribution within agriculture. According to Ferguson and Saving (1969) the direction of change in the output at which average cost is minimized, as a result of change in the price of an input, is determined by the expenditure elasticity of demand for the input. Like income elasticities, an expenditure elasticity refers to the relationship between percentage change in expenditures on an input and percentage change in total cost, holding all input prices constant. An input has an expenditure elasticity of greater than one if its quantity rises relative to costs as output expands. Ferguson and Saving show that if the price of an input (capital) falls, the quantity at which average cost is minimized will increase only if the input is expenditure elastic and will decline if the expenditure elasticity is less than one. Thus, as the prices of purchased inputs fall, farms relying most heavily on purchased inputs (farms with greatest ratio of purchased input to product) will realize the greatest drop in average costs and in this sense will gain relative to other farms. Furthermore if purchased inputs are expenditure elastic, then 'large' farms will gain relative to small ones as the price of purchased inputs falls since they devote a larger share of their costs to purchased inputs.

1. Those who do not believe in neo-classical production functions need not get restive; we are just looking at the possible direction of change using conventional techniques. In the later sections of the paper we look at the problem from other angles.

I.2 *Technical Change in the Neo-classical System*

The determinants of technical change are the least understood areas of economic theory. One can ascribe to the 'embodiment' hypothesis, to the 'learning by doing' approach or simply treat the process as a function of time in separable homogeneous production functions. None of them is satisfactory and yet the state of the art does not go any further (Kennedy and Thirlwall, 1972).

If we consider purely neutral productivity advances within an industry such that the productivity of all factors is increased by the same proportion, movements in the shares of factors are inversely related to input supply elasticities, and the direction of the effects is determined by the associated change in total revenue to the industry.

The effects of purely neutral technical progress on input prices are determined by the direct revenue effect, but in the case of non-neutral technical change with differential augmentation of inputs there is also a substitution effect. The growth rate of total factor productivity, r, is then a weighted average of the growth rates of the two inputs:

$$r = K_a r_a + K_b r_b,$$

where K_a and K_b are the input shares.

Thus we generate the following conclusions:

a if labour and capital are complements, the substitution effect will tend to increase the price of labour relative to the price of capital, when technical change necessitates a larger use of capital.

b if labour and capital are competing, a more rapid rate of augmentation of capital will tend to reduce the relative price of labour through substitution.

c if labour and capital can be used only in fixed proportions the distinction between neutral and non-neutral technical change is meaningless.

The impact of technical change on the relative shares of different input factors, according to the neo-classical production theory, would depend upon the rate at which the productivity of each factor is increasing and its supply conditions, including relative input prices. Some of the very demanding assumptions in this line of reasoning are that all farms, irrespective of the size of holding, would be on the same production function, would have the same factor intensities and, given identical input prices, would choose the same technique – a unique one. In the 'real world' these assumptions do not hold. Large farms would have certain advantages in terms of access to the capital market, while family labour on small farms might have a lower opportunity cost than the market wage rate; we examine these in the next sections.

I.3 *Farm Size and Information*

As technical progress occurs through the introduction of new inputs, uncertainty of productivity response increases. This is because the farmers are less familiar with the productive characteristics of new inputs. Yet, the maximization of profits depends critically on the farmers' ability to evaluate correctly these responses. Even if the farmers have perfect knowledge of the input and output prices, the imperfect knowledge about the characteristics of the new inputs would make achievement of an optimum combination of inputs difficult. Those farmers who acquire such information would be able to reach the adoption frontier while those lacking such information would still be operating inside the new production possibility frontier – for a while at least. There is ample evidence to suggest (Chaudhri, 1968; Harker, 1971) that large farmers, who invariably have formal education, are always among early adopters of yield-raising, cost-reducing innovations, while small farmers, who are generally illiterate in most developing countries, are among the laggards.

I.4 *Farm Size and Cost of Credit*

Reasoning based on received economic theory in Sections I.2 and I.3 implicitly assumed that input prices are the same for all producers. Nominal input prices are likely to be the same but real input prices are most likely to be different. It is well known that the borrowing rate in the unorganized agriculture sector in less developed countries has a wide range, usually from 6 per cent to 75 per cent per annum. Those producers who are able to get access to official agency loans through co-operative societies or other government bodies are able to borrow at 6 per cent to 10 per cent, while others have to go to the traditional money-lenders, who usually charge much higher rates. In countries like India, where official agencies provide less than 30 per cent of total rural credit and eligibility for credit depends on the ability to offer security, tenant farmers and small farmers are usually found to be getting the costliest credit, while more credit-worthy large farmers are able to borrow at the lowest rate of interest. Thus the real price of inputs is different for large and small farmers.

I.5 *Farm Size and Lumpy Inputs*

Adoption of new 'green revolution' technologies requires assured and timely irrigation. Having control over the irrigation supply, so as to be able to regulate its timing, has been an important element in the decision to adopt. A number of studies (Nulty, 1972) citing evidence from West Pakistan suggest that ownership of tubewells has almost exclusively been found among farmers with ten acres or more. The theory does not allow us to treat this as an important hurdle to adoption of a new technology because if the technology is really profitable and inputs (even if lumpy) are available, there ought to develop a rental market for such inputs. But, to the extent that the development of such a market comes with a lag, the larger farmers will be able to take advantage of an early start.

I.6 *Farm Size and Cost of Labour*

As the productivity of labour goes up, the operators of large farms who are more dependent on hired labour than small farmers, would find it economically advantageous to supply more family labour. So far as possible, they would seek to substitute family labour for hired labour. This is because the opportunity cost of leisure time has gone up (Becker, 1965). The medium farmers whose dependence on hired labour is marginal and mostly concentrated during the peak periods of labour requirements would not displace hired labour to the same extent, though the tendency would be in the same direction.

I.7 *Implications for Income Distribution*

Technical progress caused by the new technology does not seem to be neutral. Additional variable capital requirements are much higher than additional requirements of other inputs.

Literature on the 'green revolution' points out that the new technology (the seed-fertilizer–irrigation package) is clearly land-saving and definitely need not be labour-displacing (Inukai, 1970; Sing and Day, 1972). In fact, it ought to be complementary with labour. As such, according to our reasoning in Section I.2, the price of labour ought to increase if supply remains constant and with full employment. Even if the price does not go up, due to the existence of surplus labour, the demand for labour as a result of the adoption of new technologies ought to increase.

Even if access to information and capital market is equally distributed, the large farmers are likely to gain more absolutely from the new technologies than the small farmers due to rising productivity of land. Since we know that large farmers have better access to information and capital markets, and thus the benefits of the 'green revolution' would be greater for them.

Unless the rise in the agricultural wage rate compensates for the imbalance, theoretical reasoning indicates a strong possibility of increasing inequality of income distribution within the agricultural sector; large farmers will obtain a greater share of the *increase* in net product than their share in total product prior to the innovation. If landless labourers improve their position this will arise either from increases in the quantity of labour supplied at the going wage rate, or from a rise in the wage rate alone, or from both together.

II

In this section we present evidence from recent studies which seems to have a bearing on the question of the distributional effects of the 'green revolution'.

II.1 *Extent of 'Green Revolution'*

A number of recent studies, for example, Islam (1972), Khusro (1972), Inukai (1970), Dharam Narain (1972), Frankel (1971) and Nulty (1972), clearly point out that the 'green revolution', so far, is restricted to a few crops (wheat and rice mainly) and to areas with assured irrigation. Moreover, the adoption rates, though high in most cases, have not covered all farmers. (Lockwood, Shand and Mukherjee, 1971; Inukai, 1970.)

One does not need elaborate theoretical reasoning or statistical evidence to come to the general conclusion that regions with more favourable endowment have experienced sharply accelerated and very high rates of growth of output, while areas with less favourable endowment have continued on the pre-'green revolution' trend line. Dharam Narain (1972), has brought out some of the economic implications of the growing imbalance in Indian agriculture. For example, in India, the growth rate of agriculture in Punjab, the greatest beneficiary of the 'green revolution', during the pre-'green revolution' period was 5·14 per cent (1951–4 to 1958–61), while the All-India average for the same period was only 3·57 per cent. (Minhas and Vaidyanathan, 1965.) During 1965–71 total agricultural production in Panjab has increased from 3·39 million tonnes to 7·02 million tonnes, an increase of 124 per cent, while the All-India output during the same period increased from 72·34 million tonnes to 107·81 million tonnes, an increase of 49 per cent. (Government of India, 1972.) Thus regions like Punjab, which had a growth rate of agricultural production 50 per cent higher than the national average in the pre-'green revolution' period, have more than doubled their rates of growth, while the national rate is accelerating only slightly.

II.2 *Pre-'Green Revolution' Income Distribution*

Land and income distribution in most Asian countries, with the exception of Taiwan and Japan, have been very uneven. Inequality in income per capita is less pronounced than in the distribution of landholdings in the rural sectors of most of these economies. For example, if we compare Taiwan with India the degree of inequality in landholdings is larger than the degree of inequality in per capita rural income distribution, as is clear from Figure 1. An examination of these figures reveals that:

a The degree of inequality in rural income distribution as well as in land holding is larger in India than in Taiwan.

b The gap between the distribution of landholdings and of rural income distribution is also larger in India than in Taiwan.

This is largely because Taiwan had successful land reforms which led to a reduction in the inequality of land holding and income distribution, while India, in spite of having Land Reform Laws on its statute books, did not take any steps to reduce inequality in the distribution of landholdings (note that these figures relate to the pre-'green revolution' period in India).

It is often argued, with some justification, that computation of per capita rural incomes in traditional agriculture may not truly represent the underlying inequality, and consumption per capita is considered a more accurate measure. If we look at the distribution of per capita rural consumption and the size of landholdings among rural households in India during 1958–9 (Table 3 and Figure 2), and measure the size of landholding on the horizontal axis and average per capita rural consumption on the vertical axis, the relationship, as might be expected, is very strong and positive. Consumption per capita rises sharply with increases in landholding up to ten acres, from ten to forty acres the increase is not very sharp, and at forty acres it again rises steeply. This reinforces our findings (Figure 1) that per capita income in rural areas is highly dependent on landholding.

II.3 *Shifts in Production Function*

Studies based on farm management data relating to 1955–6 and 1956–7 in various states of India indicate (Saini, 1969; Sahota, 1968; Khusro, 1964; Hanumantha Rao, 1966; Sen, 1962; Mazumdar, 1965; and a very interesting interpretation of the data taking into account the risk factor, by Dillon, and Anderson 1971):

a A negative relationship between farm size and output per acre.

b That the output elasticities for chemical fertilizers and irrigation were rather low.

c Returns to scale were said to be constant.

An analysis of the farm management studies data for 1967–8 and 1968–9 for the states of Tamil Nadu, Uttar Pradesh and Punjab as reported by Srivastva, Nagadevara and Heady (1972) have generated the following conclusions (Table 4):

a The partial elasticity of production with respect to seed, fertilizer and irrigation is higher than in the mid-fifties thus signifying the role of modern inputs in increasing production.

b The partial elasticity for farm machinery and implements is very small in the case of Tamil Nadu and Uttar Pradesh but fairly large in the case of Punjab, perhaps showing that modern mechanical inputs have begun to play a significant role in Punjab agriculture.

c Returns to scale in Tamil Nadu and Uttar Pradesh are probably constant and increasing in the Punjab.

d Variations in output per hectare relative to farm size are explained by changes in inputs.

One can postulate that in successive production cycles, large farmers will use more of the purchased inputs. Thus, as argued in Section I, the income disparity among farmers of different size class holdings would increase even with equal access to capital markets and information.

Further recent evidence provided by Uttar Pradesh Agricultural University (UPAU, 1970) from a 'green revolution' area of North-East Uttar Pradesh supports the above findings, as is clear from Table 5, and also indicates fairly clearly the reasons for such a situation.

Larger farms have higher yields per acre. Their use of chemical fertilizers and plant protective chemicals is also much higher than that of small farms. Thus output per acre relative to farm size is probably explained by changes in inputs. This also reinforces our theoretical reasoning in Section I, that the operators of larger farms have higher adoption rates probably due to their access to information and to their higher risk-taking capacity (Chaudhri, 1968, Chapter 8; and Harker, 1971).

Tables 6 and 7 present data relating to intensity of land and labour use in Punjab agriculture (Ferozepur District) for the year 1968–9. Input of labour per acre and intensity of cropping are very stable in the holding size groups of five acres to thirty acres and decline beyond thirty acres. Labour expenses per cropped acre are highest in the ten to twenty acre size group, while fertilizer use per acre is highest in the seventy-five to 100 acre size group. In all probability this is to be explained by labour-displacing mechanization among larger farms.

In another recent study, Singh and Day (1972) examining evidence from Punjab agriculture, estimate output, factor productivities and factor proportions for 1955 and 1965 and project this to 1980 using comparative statics. Their estimates are presented in Table 8. Input per cropped acre for the period 1955 to 1980, according to their estimates, would change as follows: labour (man hours) required would decline from 30·09 to 15·02; for draught animals from 14·91 to 0·82; it would increase for mechanical power (BHP hours) from 34·69 to 206·85 and for working capital (Rupees) from 78·47 to 234·16. The net effect of all this on income shares is difficult to estimate because if rising productivity of all the factors were to raise the price or the employment of labour (or both) due to labour's complementarity with land and variable capital, it would also tend to reduce the price or demand for labour in so far as there is substitutability with mechanical power, as we have argued in section I.2.

II.4 *Post-'Green Revolution' Income Distribution*

It is necessary to distinguish clearly between relative factor shares and rural household incomes. While we cannot say much, without further empirical evidence, about the changes in relative factor shares caused by technological change in agriculture, we can make inferences with a reasonable degree of confidence concerning the household income distribution.

When the productivity of all factors increases, the share of additional income going to different households would depend on the distribution of ownership of these factors among them. We have seen that landholding is concentrated in a small number of households. In Indian agriculture 6·8 per cent of households hold 45·5 per cent of land. When land productivity increases from Rupees 615 per acre in 1955 to Rupees 1604 per acre in 1970 (see Table 9) the magnitude of additional gains for the top 6·8 per cent of the households would obviously be the largest. Ownership of fixed capital and access to variable capital are both closely related to landholding. As pointed out earlier, a rise in labour productivity ought to induce the larger farmers to use a larger quantity of family labour (Becker, 1965). Thus the gains from new technology for about 60 per cent of the households who hold only 7·6 per cent of the land would be largely based on increases either in their real wages or in the quantum of employment, or both. Their relative position would worsen on account of their not owning land and capital, if their wages rose at a rate just equal to the rise in labour productivity. For wages to rise more than the marginal value product of labour, the increase in labour supply has to be relatively low and the degree of complementarity between labour and other yield-raising inputs has to be very high. Recent evidence on the elasticity of labour supply in India's agriculture provided by Herdt and Baker (1972) indicates that (a) 'seasonal patterns in wages were weak tending to support the hypothesis of a perfectly elastic supply of labour in all regions', (b) 'in most parts of India increases in demand for labour are not accompanied by increases in agricultural wages'.

A detailed examination of Table 9 indicates that between 1954–1955 and 1968 real wages in the agricultural sectors of different states of India did not show any upward trend. Even in the Punjab a rise in real wages has occurred only during 1967–8 and 1968–9.

Thus the source of a possible addition to per capita income for the bottom 60 per cent of rural households in India is an increase in employment at a rate faster than the increase in population of this section. The evidence does not seem to indicate that this is in fact happening (Billings and Singh, 1969; Bardhan, 1970).

Dandekar and Rath (1970) provide evidence on changes in per capita consumption from 1960–1 to 1967–8 (see Table 10). During the period, average per capita consumption in all income classes in rural India increased by 3·8 per cent. The increase has been highest in the upper income classes (4·4 per cent) and lowest in the lower income classes (1·6 to 2·6 per cent). In the lowest income class per capita consumption expenditure actually declined by 1·1 per cent.[1] In Figure 2 we had shown that consumption per capita and landholding are strongly related. The change in expenditure from 1960–1 to 1967–8 seems to have strengthened this relationship even further.

Thus fragmentary evidence presented above clearly points towards increasing inequality of household income and per capita consumption in rural India. Non availability of recent data on income distribution makes it impossible for us to bring Figures 1 and 2 up to date, but the evidence cited clearly points to an increasing inequality in rural income distribution, thus reducing the gap between the distribution of landholding and income distribution.

Srivastva, Crown and Heady (1971) come to similar conclusions by using another line of reasoning. They examine cost reductions per unit of output among large and small farms. They conclude that 'the model shows that the income disparity, even among adopters, will grow over time. . . . Thus we have demonstrated, both theoretically and quasi-empirically, that embodied technical change like that of green revolution, will exaggerate existing inter farm income disparities. The gap will grow because the initial pre-technological change income distribution means an unequal opportunity for farmers to attempt to adopt the technology.' (pp. A-171.)

II.5 *Lessons from Japan and Taiwan*

Japan and Taiwan, both have land-labour ratios similar to the rest of Asia. Both have achieved significant productivity rises in

1. The authors of the report themselves put forward reservations about the quality of the data on which they base their evidence, which give us reason to suppose that the degree of inequality is in fact underestimated: 'the (National Sample Survey) estimate of per capita consumption is an underestimate, and it underestimates the consumption of the upper middle and the richer sections much more than that of the middle, lower middle and poorer sections'. In particular the number of items not purchased once a month is bound to be underestimated by the NSS procedure, and it is precisely these items, such as clothing and consumer durables, which are more important in the consumer expenditure of the rich than the poor. Finally, 'it is known that the upper middle and richer households, both in rural and urban areas, have become increasingly inaccessible to the NSS investigators, who are after all Class III government servants'.

their agricultural sectors. An examination of their historical experience indicates (see Table 12) that increasing labour productivity was accompanied by increasing variable inputs, but that in Japan fixed capital did not rise significantly during 1917–1947, nor did man-years per hectare decline to any significant extent after 1917. On the other hand in the case of the Indian Punjab (see Table 9) fixed capital per acre also seems to be rising. We shall explore the reasons in the next section.

Japan and Taiwan achieved agricultural productivity growth through what Hayami and Ruttan (1971) call biological innovations consistent with their factor endowments. This seems to have been achieved because of the following three factors:

a Appropriate choice of technique, made possible by Japan's emphasis on agricultural research dealing with biological innovations, and proper relative input prices in which the relative price of chemical fertilizer and labour was lower than that of farm machinery.

b Availability of artificial irrigation through public investment irrespective of the size of holdings.

c Existence of a highly literate peasantry facilitating the rapid diffusion of innovations.

III

III.1 *Policy Implications*

The input combination thus depends on relative input prices in real terms which are mostly different for different sets of farmers – larger farmers finding capital cheaper than labour. The situation is made worse by the official price policy for farm machinery, particularly of the labour displacing variety.

As I have argued elsewhere (1971), in present-day Asian agriculture (especially in India and Pakistan), the price of capital for an individual large farmer is much lower than its social opportunity cost thus inducing mechanization of a labour-displacing variety. The same holds very frequently in Latin America.

III.2 *Mechanization and Phantom Land Reforms*

In many Asian countries, for example in India, Land Reform Laws provide that 'efficiently run mechanized farms' shall be exempted from ceilings on landholdings. With the price of capital lower than its scarcity value and easily available cheap credit,[1] Land Reform Laws induce large farmers to mechanize not because mechanization is 'essential' for technical reasons but because it provides higher profitability. Though evidence is still scanty, some of this mechanization is surely labour-displacing.

But who is displaced by this mechanization and in which part of the year? Obviously economic rationality would induce the larger farmers to mechanize those agricultural operations which occur during the periods of peak labour demand – a period when casual agricultural labourers earn a major share of their annual income. Thus operations like harvesting and threshing get mechanized first, depriving the casual agricultural labourer of his major source of income.

III.3 *Policy Alternatives*

Dandekar and Rath (1970) believe that redistributive land reforms would reduce output and marketed surplus. Therefore they advocate other measures like rural works programmes for alleviating rural poverty. But evidence from Japan and Taiwan does not suggest that output would necessarily fall. FAO (1970) points out, taking the example of West Bengal (India), that it is possible to reduce inequality and increase output by redistributing land, though this leaves open the question of the marketed surplus. Based on the land distribution patterns of West Bengal in 1960–1, the redistributive land reforms, the imposition of a ceiling of 7·5 acres and a floor of 2·5 acres would create an egalitarian land distribution pattern (Table 11) which would induce more intensive land use increasing both employment and, hopefully, output.

Limited land reforms without changing the working of the capital market and other rural institutions may create a conflict between the reduction of inequalities of income distribution and the maximization of growth. But land reforms with appropriate changes in the capital market and rural institutions would make possible maximization of output and productivity growth completely consistent with reduction of inequalities of income distribution.

Frankel (1971) and Cleaver Jr. (1972) rightly point out that the 'green revolution' has created contradictions inherent in

1. With an inflation rate of about 7–8 per cent per annum, and a nominal interest rate of 6–8 per cent, the real rate of interest comes to approximately zero.

capitalist development, the most important being a sharp increase in inequalities of income distribution. Thus the 'green revolution' seems to be forcing a choice on the policy-makers of the developing countries: whether to have an egalitarian land reform or to accept the consequences of the 'green revolution' in terms of increasing unrest among the rural proletariat. Dismemberments of Pakistan, unrest in West Bengal and Assam, landlord-labourer clashes in Tanjore (India), increasing unrest in North and North-East Thailand, the North in Malaya, West Irian in Indonesia are, in a large measure, the consequences of a changing income distribution caused by the 'green revolution'.

References

Allen, R. G. D., *Mathematical Analysis for Economists*, Macmillan, London, 1960.

Bardhan, P. K., 'The So-Called Green Revolution and Agricultural Labourers', *Economic and Political Weekly*, Review of Agriculture Issue, 1970.

Becker, G. S., 'Economic Theory of Leisure Time', *Economic Journal*, September 1965.

Billings, M. N., and A. Singh, 'Labour and Green Revolution', *Economic and Political Weekly*, December 1969.

Chaudhri, D. P., *Education and Agricultural Productivity in India*, Ph.D. thesis, University of Delhi, April 1968.

Chaudhri, D. P., 'Some Economic Implications of Choice of Technique in Asian Agriculture', paper presented at the Annual Conference of Australian Society of Agricultural Economics, Sydney, February 1972. (To be published in *Australian Journal of Agricultural Economics.*)

Cleaver, H. M. Jr., 'The Contradictions of the Green Revolution', *Monthly Review*, May 1972.

Dandekar, V. M. and N. Rath, *Poverty in India*, Ford Foundation, New Delhi, December 1970.

Dillon, J. L. and J. R. Anderson, 'Allocation Efficiency, Traditional Agriculture, and Risk', *American Journal of Agricultural Economics*, May 1971.

Ferguson, C. E. and T. Saving, 'Long-Run Scale Adjustments of a Perfectly Competitive Firm and Industry', Department of Economics, Texas A. & M. University, Winter 1969. (Mimeographed.)

Frankel, F. R., *India's Green Revolution: Economic Gains and Political Costs*, Princeton University Press, Princeton, 1971.

Government of India, *Economic Survey 1971–2*, Government of India, New Delhi, 1972.

Hanumantha Rao, C. H., 'Alternative Explanations of the Inverse Relationship between Farm Size and Output per acre in India', *Indian Economic Review*, October 1966.

Harker, B. R., *Education, Communication and Agricultural Change*, Ph.D. thesis, University of Chicago, June 1971.

Hayami, Y. and V. W. Ruttan, *Agricultural Development: An International Perspective*, John Hopkins Press, Baltimore, 1971.

Herdt, R. W. and E. A. Baker, 'Agricultural Wages, Production and the High-Yielding Varieties', *Economic and Political Weekly*, 25 March 1972.

Inukai, I.: 'Farm Mechanization, Output and Labour Input: A Case Study of Thailand', *International Labour Review*, May 1970.

Islam, Nur-ul, 'Agricultural Growth in Pakistan: Problems and Policies', in *Agriculture and Economic Development*, Proceedings of a Seminar held in Tokyo, Japan Economic Research Centre, Tokyo, May 1972.

Kennedy, Charles and A. P. Thirlwall, 'Survey in Applied Economics: Technical Progress', *Economic Journal*, March 1972.

Khusro, A. M., 'Returns to Scale in Indian Agriculture', *Indian Journal of Agricultural Economics*, July–December 1964.

Khusro, A. M., 'Structural Change in Indian Agriculture', *Agriculture and Economic Development*, Proceedings of a Seminar held in Tokyo, Japan Economic Research Centre, Tokyo, May 1972.

Lockwood, B., R. T. Shand and P. K. Mukherjee, *The High Yielding Varieties Programme in India: Part I*, The Australian National University, 1971.

Mazumdar, Dipak, 'Size of Farm and Productivity: A Problem of Indian Peasant Agriculture', *Economica*, May 1965.

Mazumdar, Dipak, 'An International Comparison of Low Income in the Agricultural Sector in Selected LDC's', Economic Staff Working Paper 118, International Bank for Reconstruction and Development, October 1971.

Minhas, B. S. and A. Vaidyanathan, 'Growth of Crop Output in India', *Journal of Indian Society of Agricultural Statistics*, 17, 2, 1965.

Narain, Dharam, 'Growth and Imbalances in Indian Agriculture', *Economic and Political Weekly*, 25 March 1972.

Nulty, Leslie, *The Green Revolution in West Pakistan, Implications of Technological Change*, Praeger, New York, 1972.

Reutlinger, Shlomo, *et al.*, 'Agricultural Development in Relation to the Employment Problem', Economical Staff Working Paper, 112, International Bank for Reconstruction and Development, May 1971. (Mimeographed.)

Sahota, G. S., 'Efficiency of Resource Allocation in Indian Agriculture', *American Journal of Agricultural Economics*, August 1968.

Saini, G. R., 'Resource-Use Efficiency in Agriculture', *Indian Journal of Agricultural Economics*, April–June 1969.

Sen, A. K., 'An Aspect of Indian Agriculture', *Economic Weekly*, Annual Number, February 1962.

Singh, I. J. and R. H. Day, 'Capital-Labour Utilization and Substitution in Panjab Agriculture', March 1972. (To appear in an I.B.R.D. monograph *Unemployment and Labour Capital Substitution in Agriculture and Manufacturing Sectors*.)

Srivastva, U. K., R. H. Crown and Earl O. Heady, 'Green Revolution and Farm Income Distribution', *Economic and Political Weekly*, 25 December 1971.

Srivastva, U. K., V. Nagadevara and Earl O. Heady, 'Resource Productivity, Returns to Scale and Farm Size in Indian Agriculture: Some Recent Evidence', *Australian Journal of Agricultural Economics*, XVII, 1, April 1973.

U.P.A.U., *Changing Agriculture in Two Regions of Uttar Pradesh in 1969–1970*, U.P. Agr. University, Nanital, November 1970.

TABLE 1 *Distribution of Farm Holdings and Farming Area by Size Class – Selected Countries*

	Japan		Taiwan		Philippines		Indonesia	
	No. %	Area %	No. %	Area %	No. %	Area %	No. %	Area %
All sizes	100	100	100	100	100	100	100	100
Under 1 ha.	64·4	30·6	66·4	33·1	11·5	1·6	70·1	28·7
1–5 ha.	30·6	53·3	32·9	55·7	69·5	41·5	27·4	47·6
5–10 ha.	3·7	7·1	0·7	11·2	13·4	23·7	1·8	11·2
10–20 ha.	1·6	6·0	—	—	4·6	15·3	0·5	6·9
20–50 ha.	0·1	3·0	—	—	0·8	5·7	0·2	5·6
50–100 ha.	—	—	—	—	0·1	2·1	—	—
100–200 ha.	—	—	—	—	0·1	2·0	—	—
200 and over	—	—	—	—	—	8·1	—	—

	India		Pakistan		U.A.R.	
	No. %	Area %	No. %	Area %	No. %	Area %
All sizes	100	100	100	100	100	100
Under 1 ha.	60·1	7·6	43·3	7·4	49·9	11·5
1–5 ha.	33·1	46·9	44·6	39·4	44·6	44·0
5–10 ha.	4·0	17·3	8·3	22·1	3·5	11·9
10–20 ha.	2·2	17·1	3·8	31·1	1·4	11·1
20–50 ha.	0·6	11·1	—	—	0·4	6·9
Over 50 ha.	—	—	—	—	0·2	14·6

(Sources: *National Sample Survey*, 140 (I.S.I.) p. 11 and *FAO Report on the 1960 World Census of Agriculture*.)

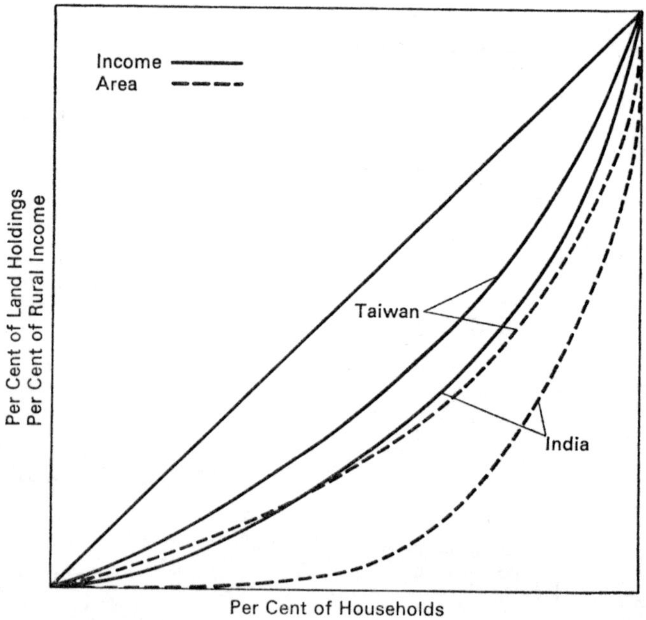

FIGURE 1 *Lorenz Curve Representing Land Holding and Rural Income Distribution in Taiwan and Rural India*

(Source: Table 2.)

TABLE 2 *Distribution of Rural Household Income Given in the Form of Points on the Lorenz Curve: India: 1960, and Taiwan: 1966*

Per cent of Rural Population	Per cent of Total Rural Income	
	India	Taiwan
10·0	0·7	3·39
20·0	4·0	8·25
30·0	8·5	14·14
40·0	14·1	20·97
50·0	20·7	28·75
60·0	28·4	37·53
70·0	37·9	46·65
80·0	50·0	59·77
90·0	66·4	74·81
100·0	100·0	100·00

Note: For India, these estimates were made by the National Council for Applied Economic Research (NCAER) from data supplied by the Planning Commission of India. The estimates pertain to 1960 and refer to pre-tax income. (Source: Mazumdar, 1971.)

For Taiwan: The original data in this table are contained in the *Report on the Survey of Family Income and Expenditure and Study of personal Income Distribution in Taiwan*, 1966 which was undertaken by the Directorate-General of Budgets, Accounts and Statistics, Taipei. The survey is based on interviews carried out in early 1965 and covers the year 1964. (Source: *Personal Income Distribution and Consumption Pattern in Taiwan*, 1964: Chung-li Chang and A. F. Hinrichs.)

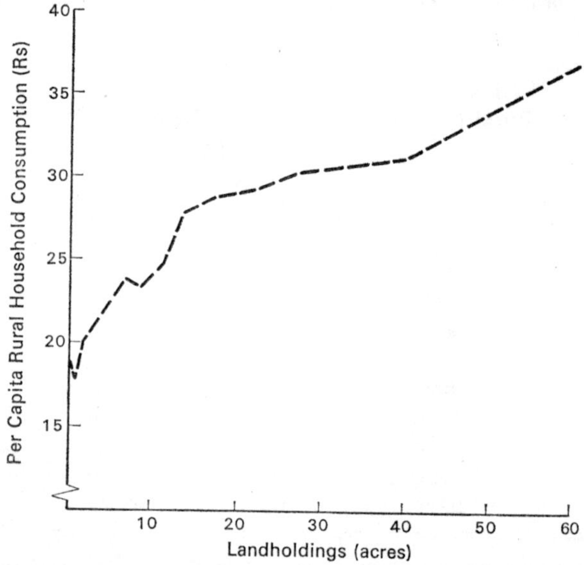

FIGURE 2 *Consumption Per Capita and Size of Landholdings, Rural Households, India: 1958–9*

(Source: Statistical Table 3.)

TABLE 3 *Distribution of Per Capita Consumption by Size of Landholdings, Rural Households, India: 1958–9*

Size Class of Household Holdings	Monthly Per Capita Consumption Class (Rs)						Weighted average Consumption
	Total	0–11	12–21	22–34	35–55	and Over	
Acres	Number of Households						
Up to 0·40	2,127	611	929	382	148	57	18·7
0·50–0·99	375	98	174	81	21	1	17·8
1·00–2·49	1,402	281	652	341	99	29	20·1
2·50–4·99	1,400	226	647	373	114	40	21·5
5·00–7·49	693	94	298	184	85	32	23·8
7·50–9·99	379	67	149	100	54	9	23·4
10·00–12·49	314	45	116	93	44	16	24·8
12·50–14·99	122	9	46	36	22	9	27·8
15·00–19·99	243	21	80	76	44	22	28·7
20·00–24·99	130	11	48	34	20	17	29·8
25·00–29·99	67	4	22	20	14	7	30·3
30·00–49·99	122	9	35	36	28	14	31·2
50·00 and Above	51	2	9	17	11	12	36·7
Total	7,425	1,478	3,205	1,773	704	265	

(Sources: Special Tabulation by NSS 14th Round Data. Data taken from Reutlinger *et al.* (1971).)

(Note: Weighted average consumption reported in the last column is computed by multiplying the midpoint of consumption class by the number of households in that class and dividing the sum of totals of all classes in each sub-category by the total number of households in the respective landholding size.)

TABLE 4 *Production Function and Returns to Scale in Indian Agriculture: 1967–8 to 1968–9*

State	Equation No.	N	Parameters								
			a	α	β	γ	δ	ε	ξ	$\sum_{i=1}^{i=5}$†	R^2
Tamil Nadu	I	300	3·7402	*** +0·3750 (0·0386 ***	*** +0·4828 (0·0518) ***	** −0·0704 (0·0299)	*** +0·0661 (0·0206)	*** +0·1396 (0·0326) ***	*** +0·2375 (0·0337) ***	0·8920 (0·0390)	·9017
Uttar Pradesh	II	300	5·4915	+0·5004 (0·0346) ***	+0·3223 (0·0596) ***	−0·0573 (0·0510)	+0·0218 (0·0162)	+0·2502 (0·0326) ***	−0·3206 (0·1112) ***	1·0376 (0·1604) ‡	·9449
	III	300	5·3694	+0·4893 (0·0332) ***	+0·2813 (0·0473) ***	***	+0·0223 (0·0163) ***	+0·2495 (0·0326) ***	−0·1980 (0·0215) **	1·0425 (·0279) *	·9447
Punjab	IV	299	3·4308	+0·3928 (0·0613)	+0·5097 (0·0763)	+0·0137 (0·00061)	+0·1362 (0·0384)	+0·1417 (0·0420)	−0·2052 (0·0852)	1·1940 (0·096)	·7219

* Significantly different from zero at 10 per cent probability level.
** Significantly different from zero at 5 per cent probability level.
*** Significantly different from zero at 1 per cent probability level.
† The coefficient of dummy variable (X_6) has not been included in the sum of elasticities.
‡ Figures refer to $\sum_{i=1}^{i=4}$

α = Size of farm (hectares).

β = Human labour (Adult man days).

γ = Bullock labour (Bullock pair days).

δ = Interest on fixed capital and depreciation on farm machinery and implements (Rupees).

ε = Value of seed, fertilizers, irrigation charges, owned and purchased (Rupees).

ξ = Year dummy variable. Zero for 1967–8 and one for 1968–9.

(Source: Srivastva, Nagadevara and Heady, 1972.)

TABLE 5 *HYV Wheat Production, Adoption Rate and Productivity in Uttar Pradesh*

	Rabi 1969 – Wheat				*Rabi 1970 – Wheat*				
Class by size of operated area (acres)	<2·5	2·5–7·49	7·5–14·9	15–29·9	30+	<2·5	2·5–7·49	7·5–14·9	15–29·9	30+
% of cult. sowing HYV wheat	—	10	3	52	76	8	25	16	70	91
% of area sown in HYV	—	12	2	20	49	4	14	22	32	53
Area sown per farm (acres)	—	NA	4	5·6	27·2	·8	2·4	9·8	6·7	22·4
Yield per sown acre (quintals)	—	7·1	NA	13	10·5	NA	7·9	9·5	11·7	12·3
Use of Chem. fert. per acre (Rs)	—	20	24	83	143	NA	NA	NA	NA	NA
Use of Plant Protection Chem. per acre (Rs)	—	—	—	66	19	NA	NA	NA	NA	NA

(Source: Adapted from UPAU (1970).)

TABLE 6 *Intensity of Land-Use According to the Size of Operational Holding: Ferozepur (Punjab), 1968–9*

1 Holding Size Group (acres)	2 Average Size (acres)	3 Percentage of Area Irrigated	4 Percentage of Cropped Area to Operated Area	5 Percentage of Cropped Area to Net Area Sown	6 Percentage of Gross Irrigated Area to Net Irrigated Area	7 Labour Input Per Acre Held	8 Output (Rs) Per Acre Held
0–5	4·99	100·00	164·36	164·36	164·36	265·85	1,446·82
5–10	7·90	92·49	148·30	135·06	151·18	305·09	580·67
10–20	15·07	92·61	135·11	144·36	140·44	316·57	823·81
20–30	25·01	86·74	142·09	147·46	149·82	305·89	786·54
30–50	39·24	85·60	128·80	139·00	139·64	215·18	724·61
50–75	58·55	78·17	97·14	117·27	118·16	161·57	579·65
75–100	86·80	89·40	117·16	122·11	130·14	182·64	1,197·41
100–above	129·22	67·28	73·38	121·42	109·07	158·19	669·29
Overall	30·40	85·34	124·19	136·86	137·05	230·92	770·36

(Source: A. S. Kahlon, 'Studies in Economics of Farm Management, Ferozepur District (Punjab), 1968–69', Colleges of Basic Sciences and Humanities, Punjab Agricultural University, Ludhiana.)

TABLE 7 *Expenditure on Labour and Fertilizers and Output per Cropped Area According to the Size of Operational Holding: Ferozepur, Punjab, 1968–9*

Holding Size Group (Acres)	Percentage of Cropped Area under High-Yielding Varieties	Expenses (Rs) on Labour per Cropped Acre	Expenses (Rs) on Fertilizers per Cropped Acre	Ratio of Expenditure on Fertilizers to Labour	Output (Rs) per Cropped Acre
0–5	15·96	109·83	6·34	0·06	880·24
5–10	17·86	127·53	16·53	0·13	391·54
10–20	29·14	132·02	23·69	0·18	609·74
20–30	25·92	130·83	33·54	0·26	553·54
30–50	31·60	106·16	32·40	0·31	562·57
50–75	19·27	111·51	22·04	0·20	596·72
75–100	39·63	93·61	60·91	0·65	1,022·71
100–above	64·06	91·87	35·39	0·39	912·01
Overall	30·43	115·94	32·43	0·28	620·29

(Source: A. S. Kahlon, 'Studies in Economics of Farm Management, Ferozepur District (Punjab), 1968–69', Colleges of Basic Sciences and Humanities, Punjab Agricultural University, Ludhiana.)

TABLE 8 *Estimated and Projected Output, Factor Productivities and Factor Proportions 1955, 1965, 1970, 1980*

	1955	1965	1970	1980
1. Total Output (in millions of Rs. at 1970 prices)	1563·91	2729·94	50·8979	8703·38
2. Market Sales (ditto)	741·23	1859·3	4211·55	7816·97
3. Subsistence Production (ditto)	822·68	870·41	878·25	886·41
4. Degree of Subsistence (3/1)	52·6%	31·88%	17·26%	10·18%
Factor Productivity				
1. Labor (Rs./man day)	15·45	25·20	47·56	91·00
2. Land (Rs./acre)				
Per Cultivate Acre	615·76	989·82	1604·14	2678·87
Per Cropped Acre	464·80	639·63	1034·13	1366·11
3. Capital (Rs./Rs.) (at constant 1970 prices)	5·72	5·35	5·70	5·26
Inputs Per Acre (per cropped acre)				
1. Labour (man days)	30·09	25·38	21·74	15·02
2. Animal Draft (days)	14·91	6·96	5·09	0·82
3. Tractor Use (hours)	0·67	1·30	2·45	4·32
4. Diesel Use (litres)	3·77	6·65	8·63	11·24
5. Electricity (KWH)	5·55	26·24	44·43	69·39

6. Mechanical Power (BHP hours)	34·69	81·81	131·28	206·85
7. Working Capital (Rs.)	78·47	112·27	168·57	234·16
Total Capital Use (in constant 1970 Rs.)				
1. Per Cultivated Acre	107·60	185·09	281·44	509·08
2. Per Cropped Acre	81·22	119·60	181·44	259·61
3. Per Man Day	2·70	4·71	8·34	17·29
4. Per Unit of Output	0·1747	0·107	0·1754	0·19
*Outlays on Variable Non-Farm Inputs**				
(in constant 1970 Rs.)				
1. Per Cultivated Acre	30·04	111·59	197·09	341·78
2. Per Cropped Acre	22·68	72·11	127·06	174·29
3. Per Man Day	0·754	2·84	5·84	11·61
4. Per Unit of Output	0·0468	0·1127	0·1229	0·1275
Water Use (in std. irrigations)**				
1. Per Cultivated Acre	6·43	7·99	9·92	14·91
2. Per Cropped Acre	4·86	5·16	6·39	7·60

* Outlays on fuel, oil, repair and maintenance, electricity, nutrients and canal water.
** Defined as 3 acre inches of irrigation water.

(Source: Singh and Day, 1972, pp. 11–12.)

TABLE 9 *Computation of Annual Average Daily Real Wages from Annual Average Daily Money Wages by Regions, 1954–5 through 1968–9*

Region	Wage Components	1954–5	1955–6	1963–4	1964–5	1965–6	1966–7	1967–8	1968–9
I.	RW	2·40	2·04	2·11	2·11	2·14	1·79	—	—
Bihar/	MW	1·48	1·33	2·11	2·22	2·67	3·18	—	—
West Bengal	D	0·62	0·65	1·00	1·05	1·25	1·78	2·03	1·79
II.	RW	3·35	2·83	2·08	2·09	2·23	2·15	1·98	1·76
Assam/	MW	2·40	2·46	2·08	2·22	2·53	2·66	2·85	3·00
Tripura	D	0·72	0·87	1·00	1·06	1·13	1·24	1·44	1·70
III.	RW	2·72	2·45	1·80	1·82	1·80	1·99	2·99	1·76
Andhra Pradesh	MW	1·62	1·56	1·80	1·98	1·95	2·23	3·12	2·84
	D	0·60	0·64	1·00	1·09	1·08	1·12	1·36	1·62
IV.	RW	1·92	1·70	1·77	1·80	1·79	1·56	1·57	1·58
Mysore/	MW	1·12	1·03	1·77	2·18	2·51	2·31	2·52	2·69
Andhra Pradesh	D	0·58	0·61	1·00	1·21	1·40	1·48	1·61	1·70

V.	RW	2·43	2·10	2·00	2·41	2·93	2·84	2·88	2·61
Kerala	MW	1·76	1·40	2·00	2·50	2·95	3·17	3·82	3·77
	D	0·72	0·67	1·00	1·04	1·01	1·12	1·33	1·45
VI.	RW	2·51	2·43	1·50	1·64	1·74	1·59	1·62	1·66
Bombay	MW	1·57	1·65	1·50	1·94	2·21	2·25	2·46	2·50
	D	0·63	0·68	1·00	1·18	1·27	1·42	1·52	1·51
VII.	RW	1·40	1·73	1·32	1·65	1·58	1·85	2·47	2·50
Madras	MW	0·96	1·25	1·32	1·74	1·65	2·02	2·72	2·71
	D.	0·69	0·72	1·00	1·06	1·05	1·09	1·10	1·08
VIII.	RW	2·81	2·72	2·85	2·56	2·29	2·22	2·90	34·3
Punjab	MW	2·05	2·08	2·85	3·02	3·02	3·57	5·17	6·23
	D	0·73	0·77	1·00	1·18	1·32	1·61	1·78	1·81
IX.	RW	—	—	1·32	1·36	1·46	1·20	1·06	1·05
Madhya Pradesh	MW	—	—	1·32	1·52	1·70	1·77	1·92	1·94
	D	0·63	0·71	1·00	1·12	1·17	1·48	1·81	1·85

Notes: RW = Real wage; MW = Money wage; D = Deflator.

(Source: Herdt and Baker, 1972.)

TABLE 10 *Per Capita Annual Consumer Expenditure by Income Class of Rural Population in 1960–1 and 1967–8 (at 1960–1 Prices)*

Income Class	Per Capita Consumption 1960–1	Per Capita Consumption 1967–8	Index with 1960–1 Base
%	Rs	Rs	Per cent
0 – 5	75·6	74·8	98·9
5 – 10	100·4	102·0	101·6
10 – 20	124·2	126·5	101·9
20 – 30	150·1	153·4	102·2
30 – 40	174·4	179·0	102·6
40 – 50	198·0	205·3	103·7
50 – 60	227·0	236·2	104·1
60 – 70	258·5	269·8	104·4
70 – 80	303·1	316·3	104·4
80 – 90	382·5	399·2	104·4
90 – 95	493·3	514·8	104·4
Average	258·8	268·6	103·8

(Source: Adjusted estimate by V. M. Dandekar and Nilakantha Rath, *Poverty in India*, The Ford Foundation, New Delhi, December 1970.)

TABLE 11 *Estimated effect of establishing a 2·5 acre floor and a 7·5 acre ceiling on operational landholdings in West Bengal State, 1960–1*[1]

Size class of operational holding (acres)	Estimated number of holdings (thousands)	Eastimated area operated (thousand acres)	Area affected by reforms (thousand acres)
up to 0·49	373	89	
0·50 to 0·99	215	153	
1·00 to 2·49	828	1425	
	1416 receiving land	1667 + 1667 = 3334*	
2·50 to 4·99	952	3447	
5·00 to 7·49	425 unaffected	2590	
7·50 to 9·99	179	1538	
10·00 to 12·49	115	1255	
12·50 to 14·99	55	746	
15·00 to 19·99	36	616	
20·00 to 24·99	12	283	
25·00 to 29·99	5	134	
30·00 to 49·99	2	85	
50·00 +	1	48	
	405 giving up land	4705 – 3038 = 1667 available for redistribution	
Overall total	3198	12409	

1. Figures from National Sample Survey, India, Sixteenth Round, 1960–1. (Source: FAO, 1970.)

* There is a small statistical error in the FAO (1970) Study, page 411, table 1. After redistribution of land the floor would come to a holding size of 2·4 acres and not 2·5 acres.

TABLE 12 *Long-Term Changes in Labour Productivity and Labour-Land and Other Input Intensity. Taiwan and Japan*

Taiwan

Year	Labour Productivity[1]		Man-Years per Hectare	Land Irrigated	Fertilizer
	NT$	US$[2]		%	kg./Ha.
1901	1,600	85	1·92	31·1	26·2
1910	2,500	126	1·51	33·6	99·4
1920	2,900	152	1·34	40·7	185·5
1930	4,600	253	1·29	54·3	326·3
1940	4,700	253	1·40	61·6	645·3
1950	4,600	253	1·47	58·4	327·2
1960	6,700	355	1·59	65·7	765·2

Japan

Year[3]	Labour Productivity[4]		Man-Years per Hectare	Fixed Capital per Hectare	Variable Inputs per Hectare
	Yen	US$[5]			
1882	33,600	93	3·12	57·7	11·2
1917	61,200	170	2·38	80·4	27·4
1937	73,400	203	2·22	97·3	32·3
1947	52,700	146	2·86	88·4	19·6
1957	75,700	210	2·38	119·3	58·7

1. *Gross value of output* per man-year in 1952–6 prices. 2. Converted using exchange rate of 18·85 NT$/US$ (1952–6). 3. Five year averages centred. 4. *Net value of output* per man-year, 1955 prices. 5. Converted using exchange rate of 360·8, Yen/R (1955).

(Sources: Taiwan; Yhi-Min Ho, *Agricultural Development of Taiwan 1903–1960*, Vanderbilt University Press, Kingsport, Tennessee, 1966.
Japan; Saburo Yamada, 'Changes in Output and Conventional Inputs in Japanese Agriculture Since 1880', *Food Research Institute Studies*, VII, 3, 1967. As reported in Reutlinger *et al.*, 1971.)

Six

Ideology and Economic Interests in Indian Land Reform[1]

Clive Bell

I. Introduction

To ask what changes in India's agrarian structure are *realistically* foreseeable in the next decade is to put a singularly demanding question. But speculation becomes less idle, and more bounded by an assessment of probabilities, if the variables under consideration are clearly defined. I have therefore ordered the initial discussion in terms of three elements. The first is the existing configuration of social forces and the fundamental interests of various social classes and groups. As different kinds of land reform do not advance all ends to the same extent, the various patterns of shared and conflicting interests, however unlikely some may appear to be, must be sketched out. Moreover, the inescapable presence of class alliance and class conflict provides a reminder that land reform is essentially a question of political power. Secondly, there are historical legacies and trends, out of which the present distribution of power was born. The third element is the influence exerted by exogenous forces. Chief among these are the set of innovations which go under the title of the 'green revolution' and population growth – there being very little scope for increasing cultivation at the extensive margin and no prospect whatever that industrial expansion will

1. My thanks are due to those who attended the conference at which the chapters of this volume were discussed, especially Dharm Chaudhri, Biplab Dasgupta and Lionel Cliffe, for their comments and suggestions on an earlier draft. Robert Cassen wrought a number of improvements in a later version. I owe David Lehmann a special debt for his constant encouragement and a stream of critical ideas and suggestions, so much so indeed that, unlike the others mentioned here, I cannot entirely exonerate him from the errors of opinion and analysis which remain in this paper.

absorb all the new entrants into the labour force over the next ten years. These, then, are the ingredients for a complex and unpredictable alchemy.

II. Relevant Aspects of Class Structure

For present purposes, we need to define social groups in a way enabling us to predict both the pattern of alliances and the issues of conflict which stem from particular variants of land reform. This requires a twofold classification: first, by sector[1] (often loosely referred to as the urban-rural dichotomy); and secondly, by social class. In the urban sector, there are the national bourgeoisie, the petty bourgeoisie, workers and the lumpen proletariat. In the rural sector, there are landlords (ex-*zamindars*) and kulaks, middle peasants, poor peasants and tenants, and landless labourers – though the correspondence is far from exact.[2] As for 'the [populist] assertion that the workers and the toiling peasantry belong to the same class . . . the utter incorrectness of this view is obvious. . . .' (Lenin, 1946, p. 57.) What interests do these groups have which would be affected by each of the range of possible land reform options?

1. *The Urban Sector*

The national bourgeoisie – urban capitalists, the upper crust of the professions and the civil service – have a prime interest in plentiful and cheap supplies of foodgrains, which are the principal wage good. And given the importance of agro-processing sectors in the structure of Indian industry, a fair section of the bourgeoisie also want abundant agricultural raw materials on good terms. (To the extent that fibres and foodgrains compete for land, there is something of a contradiction here.) As agricultural commodities (processed or not) account for the greater

1. 'Sector' refers here not to a geographical entity, but to a branch of the economy producing certain goods. Thus a rice mill located in a rural area is, despite its location, part of the 'urban' sector.
2. Agricultural landless labourers may be divided into those who have 'permanent' contracts (usually on an annual basis), and those who are casually employed (with strong seasonal fluctuations). Nevertheless, it cannot be said that the former correspond to urban workers and the latter to the lumpen proletariat. There is no significant group, in contemporary India at least, which could be called 'sturdy beggars' as were the dispossessed peasants of Elizabethan England.

part of India's export earnings,[1] of which the national bourgeoisie is the main beneficiary, an elastic and assured supply is vital in a wider setting.

Urban money wages are closely tied (with an intervening lag) to the price of food and (to a lesser extent) textiles, so that money profits are dependent on the prices of agricultural commodities – unless capitalists as a whole can set the prices of manufactures on a cost-plus basis without impairing the level of aggregate demand.[2] In the case of manufacturing production for export, world prices are given exogenously. Thus short run money profits from export lines depend on the exchange rate (suitably adjusted for taxes and subsidies), money wages and the prices of intermediate inputs, the last two being related, directly or indirectly, to the prices of agricultural goods. Production for domestic demand, however, is associated with rather more complicated pricing problems. If the prices of manufactures can be increased sufficiently to preserve profit margins in the face of an initial rise in the prices of agricultural commodities (and their subsequent secondary and tertiary adjustments to the movement in industrial prices), then industrial enterprises could always maintain the intersectoral barter terms of trade at a 'normal' level – that is, one which ensures a 'normal' profit margin. But even if this very strong assumption were a fair approximation to reality – which it is not[3] – there would still be the question of

1. Taking the average of 1967–8 and 1968–9, agricultural and allied products together with cotton and jute textiles accounted for two-thirds of Indian exports (India, 1969, p. 40). This figure excludes other manufactured exports with a high agricultural raw material input, such as leather products.
2. In a mature capitalist economy, where imperfect competition, cost-plus pricing and excess capacity coexist, profits are certainly sensitive to the level of effective demand. But agricultural incomes account for such a small proportion of effective demand that though changes in industrial prices (which largely determine urban and rural money wages and salaries) affect them, the resulting impact on aggregate demand is a second order one. In an LDC, however, money wages in the urban sector are, as we have noted, closely related to agricultural prices; and purchases by agricultural households make up a good part of total demand for industrial goods.
3. Taking 1960–1 as base, the price indices of agricultural commodities and finished manufactures for 1967–8 stood at about 210 and 130, respectively (Minhas, 1971, p. 75). Moreover, these adjustments will tend to cause a redistribution of profits within the urban sector because not all industries are equally sensitive to variations in agricultural prices.

what then happens to the level of effective demand. A rise in the prices of manufactures relative to those of farm commodities will raise the aggregate income of industry and lower that of agriculture, unless sectoral outputs move more than proportionately in the opposite direction. (There may also be secondary effects on the distribution of income within each and hence on the level and composition of demand.) Industry would exhibit such 'perverse' behaviour only if the *net* effect of such changes on the level of demand for manufacturers were negative. In some cases of this sort, the fall might be so large as to reduce the utilization of industrial plant to a level at which, even allowing for the initially favourable movement in the terms of trade, the rate of profit would actually decrease. The experience of the past few years indicates that India's industrial structure is sufficiently complex and large for the growth of output to be (occasionally) constrained by effective demand. Thus, unless industrial production can be switched easily from domestic to export markets without a decline in profit margins, there are tangible limits to the efficacy of the intersectoral terms of trade as an instrument for increasing capitalists' incomes.

Over the longer run, industry is subject to increasing returns in three ways: through greater specialization and division of labour, through opportunities to reap external economies, and even in the more limited technical sense; but there must be an adequate expansion in the demand for manufactures if lower unit costs are to be realized. For the capitalist, then, the issue is not solely whether a land reform will change the terms on which a given volume of marketed surplus will be provided by agriculture. It is also intimately linked to the changes in the level and composition of demand for industrial products (both consumer and investment goods) which result from the reform's effects on the level of agricultural output and the distribution of income within the rural sector. In this way, the inducement to invest and opportunities for new lines of investment enter the picture – as indeed they should – but we shall not trouble to pursue them here.

Before proceeding further, it is necessary to add a qualification concerning the nature of the national bourgeoisie, so far assumed to be perfectly homogeneous. In reality, the position is less simple because a substantial part of industry is nationalized, with State corporations clustered mainly in key sectors producing capital and intermediate goods such as steel and heavy engineering. Naturally, the behaviour of public and private enterprises will diverge somewhat, but perhaps there are common interests and objectives among the capitalist class and successive governments. Nor should the disposition of senior civil servants and managers of State corporations, who exercise some discretion in decision-making, be overlooked. Whatever the case, State corporations do predominate in those sectors of industry which are only indirectly linked to raw material supplies from agriculture. Moreover, a greater fraction of their output is sold to other industries (as opposed to agricultural and urban households) than is the case for privately owned enterprises, and transactions among State corporations account for a good part of their aggregate inter-industry deliveries. Indeed, the only substantial bond between the State corporations and agriculture is their wage fund requirements for foodgrains. Thus the State sector is more weakly linked to agriculture than the private sector of industry. Being concentrated in the producer goods sectors, fluctuations in effective demand will affect State-owned enterprises more deeply than those in consumer goods industries. But offsetting this is a strong measure of interdependence among them, so that their expansion is only partly dependent on conditions in the economy as a whole. All in all, therefore, the public sector should have fewer reservations about attempts to engineer favourable movements in the barter terms of trade than the earlier analysis suggests. Of course, if industry were entirely nationalized, the problem of effective demand as a constraint on output would largely disappear (though this does not mean that investment programmes would be error free). The barter terms of trade would then have a pre-eminent role and the setting would be Preobrazhensky's (1965). For the moment, however, it is enough to note that there are sources of friction between the State- and privately owned sectors of industry arising from the levels of indirect taxes and subsidies and agricultural procurement prices.

Turning now to other urban groups, the petty bourgeoisie, which encompasses small traders, artisans, shopkeepers, clerical workers and the like, also has a strong interest in cheap food and in buoyant urban incomes, which are the source of demand for the services they provide. Of course, there are areas of competition between the national and petty bourgeoisies in certain branches of production and distribution, but conditions of high aggregate demand best ensure the small man's chances of survival in the short to medium run. To this extent, therefore, the capitalist and petty bourgeois have immediate interests in common where land reform is concerned.

Similar considerations apply to employed urban workers.

When money wages are sticky downwards, low and steady food prices secure the worker's real purchasing power, and may even hold out the prospect of irregular advances in real wage rates if money wages tend occasionally to drift upwards. The level of effective demand is also important to workers because continuity and security of employment in industry as a whole are closely linked to its fluctuations. Likewise, cheap food and additional employment opportunities are the main preoccupations of the unemployed, the pseudo-employed and other sections of the lumpen proletariat. As most of them survive by exploiting kinship and other ties with employed workers, the generation of extra urban jobs has an important effect on the consumption of both groups.[1] But cheap food does more than provide the capitalists with handsome profit margins; it helps to keep the workers inside the factory gate and the 'lumpen' outside in an acquiescent, if not docile, mood. Plainly, the government of the day also has a stake in the same result.

Thus all urban groups have a shared interest in cheap and assured supplies of food, though in the capitalists' case these must not be at the expense of adequate and cheap raw material flows from agriculture or of strong demand in the market for manufactures. On other, related matters, the coincidence of interest is not so complete or unqualified, but still fairly solid. To sum up, it seems that no urban groups, with the exception of the relatively small number of urban landowners, should oppose variants of land reform which would improve the terms on which the marketed surplus is extracted from agriculture. Only if any of them seek fundamental alliances with classes in the rural sector will the urban-rural dichotomy of interest be overriden.

2. *The Rural Sector*

As with the urban sector, we begin the discussion of rural interests by considering the role of the barter terms of trade. Having cleared much of the ground, we can proceed swiftly. All

1. In a quite different context, Rosa Luxemburg (1951) assumed that the total consumption of the urban employed and unemployed would rise by the full amount of any increase in the wage-bill. As a first approximation it is probably a defensible assumption for contemporary India and perhaps for most other LDCs too. The observed strong inverse correlation between the price of foodstuffs and urban savings in the Indian case, however, suggests that this assumption is stronger than it need be.

producers in agriculture with a net surplus to sell[1] obviously want high prices for their outputs (basically, foodgrains and fibres) and low prices for their industrially produced inputs (chemical fertilizers and pesticides, pumping sets and electricity or diesel fuel). Low prices for certain industrial consumer goods are important for all rural households, be they surplus or deficit – even the most impoverished tenant or landless labourer has to buy cloth and kerosene for his family. In this simple sense, their interests and especially those of the rich rural households are diametrically opposed to urban ones. But the question is not primarily about the level and determination of the barter terms of trade preceding and following the reform. It is about the distribution of poverty rights and control over land. Thus, in the rural sector, the urban-rural dimension of conflict is subordinate to, and derives from, the struggle between opposed rural classes.

As is well known, following Zamindari[2] Abolition, which greatly eroded the power of that feudal class and brought about twenty million tenants into a direct relationship with the State, a class of substantial peasants and petty landlords emerged as the dominant political and economic group in Indian agriculture. With lax implementation of the Ceiling Laws, which specify limits varying from state to state and according to land quality, many households in this group were able to build up or maintain holdings well in excess of the legal maximum. Even the comparatively mild step of implementing fully existing legislation would affect their interests adversely, while the fiercer measures advocated by the Central Land Reforms Committee (CLRC) in 1971, which led to bitter though covert fights, would bite deeply into their economic and political position. The CLRC proposals would in fact affect a much broader stratum of farmers immediately below the rural élite – witness the frantic scurrying and manoeuvring of political forces representing kulak interests. But even if the large, well-organized and vociferous kulak opposition were overcome, the surplus land available for redistribution under any politically conceivable implementation of ceilings would not suffice to gain the support of an overwhelming number of beneficiaries, unless it were doled out in tiny parcels and solely to ultra sub-marginal peasants (operating less than one acre) and landless labourers (Dandekar and Rath, 1971). Such a

1. For a discussion of the forms and behaviour of the surplus, see Byres, *infra*, pp. 224–9, and section IV.
2. A description of the nature and origins of this feudal class is given in ibid., pp. 229–31.

course seems ruled out by official policy, which inclines towards the distribution of surplus land to households already possessing some land and complementary capital (mainly bullocks), so as to make them 'viable' production units.[1] A section of the poor peasantry is to be mobilized against a less numerous (but still large) and much better organized set of kulaks, and the outcome is by no means obvious.

Yet these are only the direct effects of such a redistribution. The middle peasant, though not an immediate beneficiary, on seeing the kulaks being 'cut down to size' – that is, down to *his* size – might try to seize this chance to break their monopoly of local political power and the special access to scarce resources that goes with it. Such perceptions may cause him to side with the poor peasants, though he will undoubtedly weigh carefully the counter-chances that the latter will 'get above themselves'. For the single act of redistribution may precipitate a chain of demands leading to turmoil and working ultimately to his detriment. Small wonder that the Chinese say of the middle peasant: *bu jin bu chu* (see above, p. 151). Yet if his attitude to the advancement of poor peasants is at best ambiguous, the suggestion that the landless should be beneficiaries of redistribution would surely provoke outright hostility. Middle peasants rely very heavily on landless labourers for field labour operations, and if the latter were to be given a little land to cultivate they would supply less labour to other households and might be able to command a higher wage for it. Worse still, as our middle peasant would view it, they might gain self-respect and they might organize. Kulaks would certainly concur in these sentiments, and the poor peasant beneficiaries would do so too. If the admittedly scanty evidence (based on their often heavy use of hired labour) of marked leisure preference among small farmers[2] proves to be solidly and widely

1. Appu (1971, p. 96), the then Land Reforms Commissioner, advocates as a personal view that priority be given to the landless *and* those owning less than a low minimum, 'say one or two acres'. But the marginal cultivators (those owning less than 2·50 acres) outnumber the landless four to one [Minhas, 1970, p. 111], so the standing of the landless remains undetermined. Minhas is more blunt, assuming that surplus land will be redistributed only to those households actually *operating* land (thereby excluding an estimated 22·7M. households in 1969–70). 'The size of the cake is too small [for land redistribution to solve the poverty problem in 1970] and the claimants are far too many' (op. cit., p. 113).
2. In a district of North Bihar, a sample survey of both pure tenants and tenants owning some land of their own revealed that the former paid out on average Rs64 per acre (15 per cent of value added per acre) to

founded, wage rates would be driven up as a result. Reinforcing such opposition to 'land to the landless' is the fact that the landless are predominantly Hindu outcastes or tribals, whereas cultivating peasants are almost invariably at least one rung of the caste ladder above the 'line of pollution'; and the fact that small, middling and rich peasants are frequently drawn from the same caste creates ties crosscutting the divisions of rural class. Despite official protestations to the contrary, and to the chagrin of those who rightly deplore false consciousness, caste continues to exercise a pervasive and baneful influence.

A less dramatic reform involving the nature and conditions of tenure contracts might advance the short-term interests of both kulaks and certain types of tenant.[1] Legislation which sweeps away, or at least alleviates, the exploitation associated with feudal forms of tenure (especially share-cropping) and replaces them with 'efficient' and secure variants (such as fixed cash rent and cost-share[2] leases) would improve resource allocation and

---

hired labour, and the latter Rs87 (22 per cent of value added per acre). The size and age and sex compositions of the two groups of households were similar, but the second cultivated 40 per cent more land. Assuming that the imputed share of all labour inputs (family and hired) in value added was the same for both groups (their cropping patterns and technology were essentially identical), then the difference in their use of hired labour can be explained solely by the difference in group average holding size if the value of family labour inputs were Rs88 in the second case and Rs123 (88 × 1·4) in the first. These figures, if correct, would imply a share of labour in value added around 45 per cent, which on independent evidence is far too high. (These indirect calculations are needed because the sample questionnaire did not deal with inputs of family labour.) It must be concluded, therefore, that the work input from a given family labour supply was larger in the case of the pure tenant group, a result which concurs nicely with that group's lower income level (Rs140 *per caput* compared with Rs210 for the second group) and points strongly to a significant degree of leisure preference (Bell and Prasad, 1972, pp. 27–9).

1. We are more sanguine than Lipton (*infra*, pp. 275–7) about both the importance and the chances of achieving changes in tenancy. The abolition of intermediaries and its subsequent effects provide a case in point.
2. A cost-share lease is one in which the landlord pays a fraction of the variable expenses of cultivation as well as receiving a share in gross output. Resource use becomes fully 'efficient' – that is, identical with that prevailing on owner-operated farms – when that fraction is equal to the landlord's share in gross output (Heady, 1952, p. 600).

productivity, with good chances of achieving some improvements in inter-farm equity (Bell, forthcoming). Changes of this kind would do much to further 'capitalistic' developments in general and the rationalization of the land market in particular, which might even suffice to gain the kulaks' acceptance of a mild distributist reform. These movements away from feudalism would also be in the interests of urban capitalists.

3. *Urban Bourgeois versus Rural Kulaks?*

We can now reconsider the position of the national bourgeoisie in relation to class conflict in the countryside. Let us first take a range of measures all of which would generate a similar volume and responsiveness of the marketed surplus, and among which urban interests would therefore have little to choose. This assumption certainly rules out the subsistence variant, 'land to the landless' which, in any case, would raise the spectre of such a profound upheaval that the bourgeoisie would oppose it irrespective of its 'pure' economic interest.

Now it is often argued that an alliance of bourgeois and kulak interests is 'natural' or at least highly congenial.[1] Together, they control most of the productive assets of the society (capital and land), so the notion that they will submerge their objective differences and make common cause against the dispossessed has considerable intuitive appeal. Crudely, such a compromise rests upon mutually acceptable intersectoral terms of trade and an associated set of taxes and subsidies at the expense of other social groups. It might be possible to distribute some of the benefits thus arising to organized urban workers through a compensatory fillip to money wages, the benefits of which do filter through, albeit imperfectly, to the lumpen proletariat. Thus while the burden of oppression falls partly on this last group, the costs of the compromise would be borne mostly by the rural poor. Such a prospect appears particularly plausible in India, where Congress is based traditionally on a coalition of national bourgeois and kulak interests.

The weakness of this kind of thesis is that the conditions which underpin a class alliance are subject to change. Despite historical ties, the advent of profound structural changes in the situation may unleash objective contradictions of such force that the traditional relationship (and whatever sentiment accompanies it) is eventually discarded. Besides, the national bourgeois-kulak

1. For a forceful statement of this position apropos India, see Lipton (1968; *infra*, p. 311).

alliance has been marked more by mutual suspicion than either rational or sentimental attachment, the principal bond being Gandhian doctrines (Moore, 1969, p. 316). In another vital sense, too, the coalition of Indian urban and rural élites differs from that leading to the rise of fascism in Germany, for example (ibid., p. xi) – 'the marriage of iron and rye'. As a class, Indian kulaks are scarcely comparable with the Prussian Junkers. Whether or not the Indian bourgeoisie is as politically weak as its German counterpart is less clear.

Recent events indicate that the alliance may be undergoing exceptional strains. With the dogged and highly successful defence of inflated foodgrain procurement prices by the farm lobby, the potential contradictions between national bourgeois and kulak interests may rise to the surface. Politicians of the urban élite might decide that the power of the rich peasants must be curbed decisively as was that of the *zamindari* before them. It might prove both easier and not less profitable to impose adverse terms on a large but diffuse middle peasantry than to engage, as at present, in constant haggling with recalcitrant kulaks. The ensuing struggle for power would not be easily won; witness the fact that the cry for lower ceilings brought the riposte, 'no new land ceilings without urban property ceilings'.[1]

III. Burdens of History

There is some danger that in pressing the analysis of shared and conflicting interests, historical factors and new exogenous influences are not given their proper weight. Men may seek their ends, as they perceive them, and yet the final outcome may owe more to legacies of the past and autonomous forces than to the volition of individuals. So it is with land reform.

As we have remarked already, the Congress party is founded on an uneasy alliance of national bourgeois and kulak interests. Gandhi's great contribution was to transform a party of middle-class nationalist dissent into one with a mass base by instilling the desire for Independence into the consciousness of the masses. This was a great gain to the dominant groups in Congress. For

1. After a crucial meeting of Chief Ministers (in July 1972) which discussed the CLRC's proposals, Punjab, Haryana, Rajasthan, Uttar Pradesh and Bihar issued a joint statement to the effect that land and urban property ceiling legislation would be enacted simultaneously (*Commerce*, 29 July 1972, p. 264).

by the time independence was won Congress was established as 'the' nationalist party, and could proceed to a long succession of electoral victories in a political system with universal, but carefully managed, adult franchise. Thus, the bourgeoisie and kulaks found the pursuit of their own interests legitimized and secured. Although Congress rule has tottered and occasionally, if temporarily, fallen in the states, it has rarely been seriously challenged at the centre. With the past continuity of Congress hegemony and its likely future prolongation, a discussion of action on land reform cannot be divorced from Congress policy and hence the shifting balance of power within the party.

An important feature of bourgeois-kulak alliance is that while bourgeois forces are more powerful at the centre, it is the kulaks who dominate State politics. Moreover, not only does Congress ascendancy sometimes falter in the States, but central control over the state Congress parties is far from absolute. Thus kulak interests have had to penetrate the opposition parties as a precaution against the advent of non-Congress Ministries, though as a result they enjoy substantial independence of, and even ability to modify, central policy when it so suits them. Here, their recent successes go well beyond the defence of high procurement prices. The proposals submitted by the CLRC for lower ceilings on 4 August 1971, prompted very little debate on the subject in Parliament, indicating just how powerful the farm lobby is in all parties – both left and right (*EPW*, 6 May 1972, p. 915). One Congress Chief Minister, Zail Singh of the Panjab, went so far as to flout central pronouncements in the following terms: '. . . if the size of a form goes down below thirty acres, we cannot achieve the living standards that we want' (ibid., 8 April 1972).

But while the kulaks and the bourgeoisie continue their battle for ascendancy within the system, there exists an extra-parliamentary tradition which has found occasional expression in peasant movements, and which organized political parties cannot permanently ignore. The resulting outbursts express a potent vein of violence in Indian society[1] and have not been confined to

1. Here we part company with Moore (1969), whose assessment is that Indian society is comparatively pacific. In this connection, it is important not to overlook the fragmentation – Moore certainly does not – which often prevents local incidents from assuming wider proportions. Thus the real question concerns not the weakness of violent expression, but rather the timescale on which the microcosm, the Indian village, is drawn into the mainstream of national politics. Most students will find Chaudhuri's [1965, p. 98] assertion that 'few

the post-Independence period. The Deccan food riots in 1875, fired by blatant injustices in the land tenure situation, were serious enough for the British authorities to set up a major Commission of Inquiry. The Telengana uprisings, which reached their climax in 1947–8 at the very moment of Independence, were suppressed by the Indian army. More recently, there was the 'land grab' movement in West Bengal during the late sixties, some 300,000 acres being seized while the United Front[1] state government remained in power (Dasgupta, 1972, p. 258). The police have since recovered 50,000 acres, and their work continues. In the South, the introduction of new varieties of rice leading to greatly increased yields has occasioned sharp conflict between cultivators and landless labourers. In all these cases, poor peasants and tenants have demonstrated a capacity to carry out sustained mass action – a fitting warning to organized politics and a reminder to social science analysts. Moore (1969, p. 380) tells us that '. . . the instances [of peasant uprisings] involved the peasants' economic grievances quite prominently', but who can tell when their grievances will find political expression? Congress will have to continue oscillating between ritual gestures of radical intent, punctuated by occasional minor concessions to the most dangerous dissenters, and applying the full apparatus of repression at its disposal – or perhaps both at the same time, as seems to be currently the case in West Bengal (Dasgupta, op. cit.). But the contradiction will remain, for the impulse from below has revolutionary potential, whereas Congress has not.

IV. The Effects of Population Growth and Technical Change

The above raw attempts stem from men's direct actions, but they are taking place against a backcloth whose main elements have a dynamic of their own. To grasp better the likely shape of things

---

human communities have been more warlike and fond of bloodshed' too sweeping, yet not easily set aside.

1. The United Front was a coalition of parties of the left, the main force in which was the CP (Marxist). The pro-Moscow wing of the CP and the Bangla Congress (a Bengali splinter group of the National Congress) were also important elements, with the remainder of the coalition being drawn from numerous, small parties. The pro-Moscow CP formed a tacit and successful alliance with the National Congress for the 1972 elections.

to come, it is vital to assess the influence the latter bring to bear on trends already manifest or predictable.

The first element is population growth. Until the comparatively recent past, extra land could be brought under cultivation at the extensive margin to relieve, in fair part at least, growing demographic pressures. But, especially in the last decade, this margin has gradually disappeared, and pressure on increasingly scarce land has been growing.[1] There are two closely related responses to an inelastic supply of land, both of them important in the current situation: one consists of intensified cultivation through a combination of multiple cropping, more careful husbandry and greater inputs of labour and irrigation; the other involves land-augmenting inventions,[2] of which the biological-chemical nexus of the so-called 'green revolution' is a prime example (Chaudhri, *supra*). The obverse of the rising demand for access to land, or 'land hunger', is the failure of alternative income opportunities, principally non-farm jobs, to grow fast enough to absorb the natural growth of the total workforce. Thus a stagnant or barely increasing supply of land has to be set against a rapidly growing number of claimants to rights in its use and ownership.

Now the impact of population growth on the distribution of land ownership (or operation) may be called 'neutral' if the number of households in each holding size category (landless included) in the base year increases by the same percentage over each period of time. In this case, the size distribution of holdings will be invariant over time except for a 'shift' parameter which will move each point of the initial frequency curve to the left in the same proportion, that proportion being the percentage by which the number of rural households increases during the period from the base year to the year in question. (Roughly speaking, the initial frequency distribution will be 'squashed' steadily to the left.) Such a situation would come about if all classes of household had identical rates of natural increase, if there were

1. The area under all crops grew at a compound rate of 1·7 per cent per annum between 1949–50 and 1959–60; and at 0·6 per cent per annum between 1959–60 and 1964–5 (India, 1968, p. 70).
2. An invention is said to augment a 'factor' relative to others if, with the composition of inputs unchanged, it raises the marginal productivity of the factor in question in greater proportion than that of any other. Or, to put it another way, if the relative prices of 'factors' (measured in efficiency units) remain unchanged, the invention will lead to a fall in the augmented factor's coefficient (measured in natural units) in the least cost input bundle.

no net transfers of land between any size category and the rest, and if there were no differences in household (as opposed to personal) rural-urban migration rates.[1] Alternatively, there would exist certain combinations of all three variables, with departures from uniform values in each taken separately for all household categories, which would still produce 'neutrality'. By definition, their effects would offset one another so as to leave the relative numbers of kulaks, middle peasants, poor peasants and landless unaltered. On the face of it, then, the 'neutral' case seems to be an implausible one, though over as short a period as a decade, it might prove to be a perfectly acceptable approximation to reality.

Of the two 'non-neutral' cases, the equalizing sort would entail a higher rate of natural increase among kulak (and perhaps middle peasant) households than the rest and, at most, weakly offsetting effects from land acquisition and migration, or some such combination. In this setting, the number of kulaks would suffer at least a *relative* decline by virtue of an above average rate

1. Suppose there are n_i households having holdings in the range (x_i, x_{i+1}) acres in the base year, there being N_o households in all and p classes of holding. If the number of households in each of p, as well as overall, grows by a fraction g, and total land supply is fixed, there will be $(1 + g)n_i$ households in the class

$$\left(\frac{x_i}{1+g}, \frac{x_{i+1}}{1+g}\right)$$

for all i. The fraction of households in the revised class i is simply $(1+g)n_i/(1+g)N_o$ – that is, the fraction accounted for by it originally. Let x_i approach x_{i+1} closely. Then, denoting the frequency distributions in periods o and t by f^o and f^t, respectively, we have the result that $f^t(x/1+g) = (1+g)f^o(x)$, which defines the 'shifting' and 'squashing' changes in f^o referred to in the text. The acreage held by households in class i is $(1+g)n_i(x_{i+1}-x_i)/(1+g)$, which is the base year acreage held by them. As the total supply of land is unchanging over time, it follows that the fraction of total land held by class i is unchanging too. Thus we have the important result that a 'neutral' population impact will leave the Gini concentration coefficient unaltered. However, the converse does not necessarily hold because a given value of that coefficient does not correspond to a unique frequency distribution. This makes the interpretation of data on the changing distribution of land ownership more difficult, requiring a goodness of fit test between the observed frequency distribution in year t and the appropriate transformation of f^o. By way of interest, the Gini coefficient stood at 0·68 in 1960–1 compared with 0·66 in 1953–4 (Minhas, 1970, p. 112), a change small enough to be consistent with 'neutrality'.

of holding subdivision,[1] with the probable effect of erstwhile kulak households further enlarging the ranks of the middle peasantry. *Per contra*, in the case where population growth has a polarizing effect, kulak households would grow both relatively and absolutely in numbers through net land acquisitions, probably at the expense of poor peasants, many of whom would be reduced to the ranks of the landless. If 'natural' forces were left to operate unchecked, this seems the most likely variant, not least for reasons which are intimately connected with the nature of the 'green revolution' technology and the processes whereby it is diffused among different classes of farmers.

While the 'green revolution' technology is probably scale-neutral in the strictly technical sense of the term, in practice kulaks (and to a lesser extent middle peasants) have adopted such innovations much more readily and intensively than poor peasants and tenants. The main causes of this disparity in their respective propensities to innovate and its consequences are analysed by Chaudhri (*supra*).[2] The safely predictable result over the longer run is that kulaks will have both the means and sufficient reward to evict their tenants and buy out small peasants, thereby further concentrating the pattern of land ownership and operation – unless, of course, legislation to the contrary is effectively implemented.

It is worth remarking here that the 'new' inputs required to exploit these technological opportunities efficiently are produced by industry. And because of the existing structure of inequality in agriculture, which could well be worsened by the spread of 'green revolution' technology (Chaudhri, ibid.), only a comparatively small fraction of the extra agricultural output so generated will go to the rural poor, who consume food relatively intensively. Of the remainder, some will be consumed by the producing households – that is, kulak ones; but a large fraction must be sold either to the urban sector or in foreign markets to pay for 'new' inputs and to satisfy the kulaks' desires for industrial

1. To the extent that kulak holdings are not subdivided but operated jointly, the effects of the above average fertility of such households on some of the formal variables used here will not be visible. But the equalizing effect is still perfectly real because in this class the number of mouths which a *given* acreage has to support is growing faster than average. Of course, this makes no allowance for the rewards of local monopoly (or oligopoly) which joint operation makes possible.
2. For a different approach, though one which arrives at broadly similar conclusions, see Bell (1972).

consumer goods now that their incomes are rising. At the margin, therefore, the marketed surplus is likely to be highly responsive to changes in output. It follows immediately that the form of technical change may have profound political consequences in that it will increase the economic dependence of productive units in agriculture on national bourgeois interests and designs. A further effect is that the growth of intersectoral transactions for the purposes of agricultural production as well as rural households' consumption will further promote capitalist development in agriculture and hence in the economy as a whole.

While the outcome, in the way of cheap food and greater bargaining strength *vis-à-vis* rural interests, is unarguably favourable to all urban groups, the plight of the rural landless might deteriorate even further. In the short to medium run, the land-augmenting aspects of the 'green revolution' may well dominate, and with the extension of the new technology to land previously cultivated by (now landless) poor peasants and tenants, the aggregate demand for labour could rise sufficiently to give agricultural labourers' households more man-months of employment per year – and higher wage rates too, if seasonal excess demand for labour becomes acute enough to give them greater bargaining power. Over the longer term, however, a successful innovative push by kulaks in the field of new varieties and artificial fertilizers will almost certainly lead them to demand the means for mechanizing on an extensive scale, doubtless under a régime of subsidized interest rates and low tariffs on imports. Certain forms of mechanization may be land-augmenting, but overall there remains a strong suspicion that the long run effect will be labour-displacing. The landless labourers will suffer accordingly.

In all this, we see that the two 'autonomous' influences may well work to exacerbate likely future tensions. Their interactions – numerous, complex and simultaneous – make it virtually impossible, at present anyhow, to disentangle the weights of their separate contributions. Yet, because they are seemingly driving in the same direction, that issue is not so important. Much more relevant is their combined tendency to greatly accelerate a process of differentiation and structural change which is already under way. With a rural population doubling every thirty years or so, and output growing at least as fast, largely through changes at the intensive margin, the groups whose potential power is increasing most rapidly are the entrenched élite (gaining in economic ascendancy) and the poorest strata of labourers (gaining in numbers). In principle, such trends should reduce the room for manoeuvre of forces of the centre seeking to alleviate conflict without sacrificing the rules of the Indian political game.

V. Alternative Aims

Before we ask what kinds of land reform may be attempted, we must ask what ends are being sought. There are four major groups of objectives, some of which may be mutually incompatible under certain types of reform. The relative priority accorded to each of them depends, of course, on the nature of the social and political forces which put the reform into effect, and the rather dry taxonomic treatment which follows must be viewed in the light of the discussion in the preceding sections.

1. *To Secure Greater Rural Equity*

There are two dimensions to this objective. First, there may be greater equity among those already holding and/or operating land – that is, a reduction in income disparities between big and small farmers by redistributing land from the former to the latter and/or regulating tenancy contracts to raise the tenant's share in net product. Secondly, there may be improved equity between farmers as a whole, whatever their tenure status, and the landless. If landless labour households constitute a large proportion of all rural households, as is the case in India,[1] then improvements along the second dimension brought about by redistributing land in 'viable' units necessitates a more radical reform (with lower ceilings, among other features) than is required by any

1. According to the 1971 Census, 25·8 per cent of the total Indian workforce are agricultural labourers, compared with 16·7 per cent at the time of the 1961 Census (India, 1970, p. 62). In both cases, the proportion of the total workforce employed in agriculture has not changed much (c. 70 per cent), but the inference that landlessness has been increasing cannot be made – from these figures, at least – because the Census definitions are not quite the same for the two periods. The fact that participation rates are higher among agricultural labour households means that the fraction of all rural households which is made up of landless ones is rather lower than the above figures imply. Using National Sample Survey data, Minhas (1970, p. 110) estimates that about 25 per cent of all rural households would be *operating* no land at all in 1969–70. And households operating less than one acre would still derive most of their income from working on the farms of others, so that the Census figure of 25 per cent may not be very much on the high side.

given improvement limited to those already farming some land. Whether or not a reduction in equality among farm operators increases the inequality between them and the landless is by no means clear. Big farmers certainly enjoy monopoly power in local labour markets, especially over so-called 'tied' agricultural labourers, who are obliged, under the threat of eviction, to offer their labour first to the farmer on whose land they have built their huts, notwithstanding the homestead rights conferred on them by legislation passed in the fifties. The imposition of a low ceiling would erode this monopoly power, perhaps severely, and would thus tend to increase real wage rates. However, big farmers tend to use more *hired* labour per acre than small ones (though less in total). If the ceiling is pitched at a level such that farms of maximum legal size begin to use more family labour than before the reform and the surplus land is distributed to households which continue to cultivate with family labour alone, then the demand for hired labour will be reduced. Against this, to the extent that beneficiaries had formerly hired out their labour to other households, there will also be a fall in the supply of labour for hire. Going further still, if their leisure preferences wax strong with rising incomes, the net effect on demand will be slight. Not surprisingly, the outcome for the rural wage-bill remains uncertain; but there is a fairly certain social outcome: a more egalitarian structure of landholdings and incomes should lead to a more equal distribution of power and respect in the local community, a vital component of any self-sustaining or sustainable reform.

2. *To Raise Output and Improve the Efficiency of Resource Use*

If the marginal returns to inputs vary over farms of differing size, there is a *prima facie* case for redistribution of land on 'efficiency' grounds. Here the criterion for static efficiency is: maximize output per unit of scarce input. If output per unit of (scarce) land on small farms exceeds that on big holdings because inputs of (abundant) labour per unit of land on the former are greater than those on the latter, then redistribution of land from big to small farms will lead to an increase in aggregate output. As above, there is the danger of the beneficiaries' leisure preferences being so marked that their *total* labour inputs per acre fall to the same level as those on big farms.[1] A similar argument for such redistri-

1. This is unlikely if the beneficiaries were formerly landless or nearly so. If, on the other hand, they were cultivating (say) two or three

bution also applies if small farmers employ more careful husbandry practices than richer farmers, requiring greater skill and closer management, but no more inputs of fixed or working capital. Where 'new' inputs are concerned, however, the picture is less clear. As we have already noted, the ability to take and bear risks is crucial when new opportunities arise, and especially when these entail the intensive use of inputs and processes (fertilizers and new crop varieties) which raise the variability of output. The usual contrast between the feckless landlord who under-utilizes his extensive holding and the industrious small peasant who saturates his land with family labour may faithfully characterize a static, 'feudal' system; but the 'progressive' kulak who pursues vigorously a wide range of innovations while the small farmer avoids any such risk presents the distributist reformer with a less comfortable picture – and by no means a completely fanciful one in the more fluid situation brought about by rapid technological change.

Even if the effects of simple land redistribution on aggregate output are uncertain, no such ambiguity attaches to the reform of tenure contracts. Whether the tenant is given the land, or acquires it at a subsidized rate, or his kind rent (almost invariably under sharecropping) is commuted into a fixed cash or cost-sharing arrangement, the net effect on the efficiency of resource use should be favourable.[1] Here, the former tenant's general incentive to produce is certainly enhanced by changes in the contract, and hitherto glaring divergencies between resource allocation patterns on owned and leased land will be narrowed, perhaps to the point of disappearing completely. The greater the importance of non-labour inputs in the production process, the greater the gains in efficiency (to say nothing of equity) stemming from such changes in resource allocation.

All in all, then, the output-enhancing effects of reform may

acres previously, then the chances of significant leisure preference are far from remote.

1. Cheung's (1968) contention that sharecropping is an 'efficient' form of contract sparked off a lively debate, with Bardhan and Srinivasan (1970) weighing in against, and Newbery (1973) supporting him. The emphasis of these authors on labour inputs obscures the fact that sharecropping tenancies are much more than simple labour contracts, even under conditions of traditional agricultural technique. When 'new' inputs enter the picture, a conclusion based on a formulation in which labour is the sole variable input appears extremely dubious (Bell, forthcoming). For an alternative approach to the economics of tenancy contracts, see Rao (1971).

well apply more strongly to tenure contract changes than to pure redistribution as such. For the widening opportunities offered by crop process innovation, the emphasis in earlier literature on differences in labour inputs alone over farms of varying size is surely misplaced. In the longer run, of course, the dynamic effects of the reform – in particular, on the pace and pattern with which technological changes are diffused – may have major repercussions on the welfare of the landless, such as we have already discussed.

3. *To Raise Agriculture's Marketed Surplus and its Taxable Capacity*

Once again, in the currently changing conditions of Indian agriculture, it is necessary to make more careful distinctions than those made by terms in common use. Following Sanghvi (1969), we distinguish the *obligatory* from the *optional* surplus. The former stems from the need to pay direct taxes (mainly land revenue) and to pay for industrially produced inputs (especially fertilizer) used in agricultural production.[1] The latter is the counterpart transaction of rural households' purchases of industrial consumer goods, including the indirect taxes levied thereon. Although these two parts of the surplus are not entirely independent of one another, they cannot be simply lumped together. Any analysis of the likely effects of a land reform on the aggregate surplus must treat them separately because the surplus per unit of gross output is dependent not only on consumer tastes and incomes, but also on agricultural production technology – a major, but unavoidable complication. A second and often neglected effect of a land reform concerns the response characteristics of the marketed surplus. Even if, by fluke, the surplus were to return to its original level after the transient dislocations caused by the reform had died away, its variations with prices and weather might show a completely different pattern from before. Whether or not the post-reform responsiveness of the marketed surplus would be more elastic is a complex question requiring detailed and careful analysis. Its importance lies in the fact that the efficiency of the barter terms of trade as an instrument for extracting the surplus rises with the elasticity of the surplus. All one can say *a priori* is that an elastic production structure is likely to be associated with an elastic surplus.

1. The farmer has the option of buying fertilizer *ex ante*; but once he decides to buy, he is obliged to pay for it *ex post*.

The matter of taxable capacity also has its share of ambiguities. Rises in aggregate real output imply rises in taxable capacity, but if there are accompanying shifts towards a more equal distribution of income in the face of a progressive tax structure, the net effect could be very small or even negative. Suppose, for example, that two farmers have incomes of £200 and £100, respectively, before the reform and £150 each afterwards (an utterly egalitarian reform with no effects on aggregate real output). If the rate is 10 per cent on the first £150 and 20 per cent thereafter, the total tax yield before the reform will be £35 compared with £30 following it. Thus taxable capacity would fall unless aggregate output were to rise to £325 (300+(35−30)/0·20). *Per contra*, with a regressive tax structure, an egalitarian reform will raise actual tax receipts, unless there were an offsetting fall in aggregate output. In reality, however, few States have introduced an agricultural income tax, and even in those where it is levied, revenues are derisory, largely because administrative capacity is wanting. But changes in the burden of (probably regressive) indirect taxation on the industrial consumer goods purchased by rural households which would result from a reform might well be significant.

4. *To Capture or Secure a Rural Power Base*

An élite which is no longer dependent on landed interests and likely to preserve that independence in the future can both bid for 'popular' support and strike at the basis of landlords' power by effecting a redistribution at the latters' expense. In mild reforms, the intention may be more subtle: to get rid of the 'feudal' elements, while giving the emerging agrarian capitalists full rein and improving only temporarily the position of some sections of the smaller and middle peasants. Plainly, the more radical the reform, the greater the spoils to be distributed – and the larger the number of disaffected big and middling farmers. Thus, in the absence of a mass agrarian movement, the reforming élite will probably settle for a less radical option, benefiting enough middle peasants to ensure a solid rural power base and relying upon the post-reform structure to maintain in peaceful acquiescence the unrewarded mass of the peasantry.

In societies where peasants constitute a majority of the population, a secure rural power base is indispensable if long periods of political ascendancy are to be preserved without recourse to a large apparatus of overt repression. Economists tend to be but dimly aware of this, and are often the unwitting apologists for populist ideologies which speak in idealistic terms of the 'desirability of an independent small peasantry operating efficient, family-sized farms'.

VI. Policy Options

Continuing the taxonomic approach of this paper, we now examine briefly four basic land reform alternatives confronting the Indian polity in the light of the objectives we have reviewed.[1] The question of which variant is least unlikely to be implemented is left largely to the concluding section.

1. *Leave Things as They Are*

The prescription is simple: leave legislation on ceilings and tenancy regulation on the Statute Book, make radical noises (at opportune moments) about revising and implementing it – but do nothing. It is difficult to see improvements in equity flowing from such a policy, indeed inequality may worsen as existing tenancies are resumed or made subject to increasingly exploitative conditions. The general uncertainty surrounding official intentions is likely to reduce investment by big farmers and hence future output. The shadow cast over tenancy relationships has an adverse impact on tenants' incentives to produce, such as they are, though resumptions will raise output if yields on land hitherto leased out are increased. All in all, however, the likelihood is that the growth of output and, *a fortiori*, of the marketed surplus will become sluggish.

As for political support in the countryside, that of the kulaks, who have traditionally played a major role in Congress, will be progressively alienated – and Congress' rural power base thereby eroded – if the uncertainties of the situation are not eventually resolved. In the absence of any definite direction to policy, the small and middle peasants are likely to remain suspicious. Tenants, marginal farmers and perhaps landless labourers may

1. The analysis is one of comparative statics under *ceteris paribus* assumptions. Of course, the trend of output, for example, is upwards over time. But the autonomous element in this process is common to all land reform variants, so that it simplifies the discussion considerably to talk of a given variant 'advancing' or 'impeding' progress towards a particular objective on the understanding that these terms relate to a benchmark given by the 'autonomous' movements in that objective.

be encouraged at first, but their continuing support will presumably depend on tangible action being taken sooner rather than later. As the hallmark of this variant is procrastination, early and bold initiatives are ruled out, and in any case, it seems to be official policy to make units operated by tenants and marginal farmers into 'viable' ones before turning to the interests of landless labourers.

2. *'Improve' the Status Quo*

This would entail implementing existing legislation on ceilings and tenure contracts. In the short run, at least, inequality would be tempered and, after some initial dislocation, output would rise. With a ceiling of 25–30 standard (irrigated) acres, the way would be clear for the growth of a large class of capitalist farmers bent upon innovation and certain forms of mechanization. Tenants would be the major immediate beneficiaries of the reform and some marginal groups would gain from the distribution of 'surplus' land through the enforcement of ceilings. In the longer run, however, the position of most small peasants would tend to become increasingly precarious as successful middle peasants built up their holdings to the legally permissible level against the background of a growing rural population and virtually fixed land supply. The effects of these induced changes in the agrarian structure on the supply of the marketed surplus would undoubtedly be favourable.

The effect of this policy on the élite's rural power base is complicated. A numerically small, though politically powerful, group of existing landlords would be severely hit; a somewhat larger group would sustain moderate immediate losses,[1] but if they were perceptive, they would be prepared to bear these losses as a necessary condition for the development of rural capitalism. In the short run, many tenants and the beneficiaries from land distribution would be better off. Thus the immediate outcome would probably be good for Congress, which should reap therefrom a defensible longer run political position with some room for further manoeuvre.

1. On the basis of unweighted acreages (Minhas 1970, p. 111), projections for 1969–70 from 1960–1 data give totals of 0·5M households owning forty-two acres or more and 1·2M owning between twenty-five and forty-two acres. With a ceiling of twenty-five unweighted acres, the former would lose an average of 45·2 acres and the latter 7·2 acres. Taken together, these groups account for about 2 per cent of all rural households.

3. *Undertake a Radical Distributist Reform*

If we are to put numbers on an essentially qualitative assessment, a 'radical' ceiling could not exceed about twelve to fifteen unweighted acres (with corresponding adjustments for land quality on a farm-by-farm basis).[1] This would certainly further the cause of equity but not as overwhelmingly as is sometimes supposed (Minhas, 1970, p. 113). Moreover, the landless would not benefit directly (and might even lose when indirect effects are taken into account) if the present inclination of official policy to bring about only 'viable' units were adhered to. Calculations based on Minhas's projections for 1969–70, which assume – apparently, though not explicitly – a 'neutral' population growth impact, indicate that a fifteen (unweighted) acre ceiling would release about 60 million acres for distribution. If these were distributed among *cultivating* households owning up to 4·2 acres, the minimum holding would be 2·2 acres – barely 'viable'.[2] The effects on output are uncertain for the reasons discussed above, and hence so are those on the marketed surplus.

Despite its limitations, an attempt at a redistribution of these proportions would provoke deep political polarization. Kulaks and some middle peasants would lose out, the former very heavily, and their trenchant opposition to such a reform is only to be expected. Out of a total of some 85 million rural households, about 40 million – mostly tenants and marginal farmers – would gain, and only some 4 million or so rich peasant households would shed part of their assets. Yet, though the latter would lose much power, more than 10 million landless households would remain empty-handed.[3]

The longer run consequences of this policy are intriguing. If, despite the comparatively low ceiling, a capitalistic mode of production were still able to assert itself, the technical dynamism of the sector would be assured – though it might be less striking than under our less radical 'improving' variant. If this dynamism does not set in (and possibly even if it does), the third strategy may well create a substantial peasant rump imbued with a vigorous populist ideology and with possibly reactionary ten-

1. About 20 per cent of the area under cultivation is irrigated, and roughly the same proportion is somewhat marginal and drought-prone. Thus an 'unweighted' acre can be described as one which is unirrigated, but of moderate fertility.
2. These calculations may be had from the author on request.
3. Calculated from Minhas (1970), p. 111.

dencies. This could be important in a post-revolutionary situation if the political and economic position of the rump is strongly established. In particular, there is the likelihood of widespread and bitter opposition to the various forms of collectivization which would be necessary to ameliorate the condition of the landless in a substantial and irreversible way. Nevertheless, this option fits the current rhetoric of Congress, even though its implementation is another matter. It would be opposed by national bourgeois interests (to say nothing of kulak ones), unless these no longer needed the kulaks as allies and were prepared to pay the costs if industrialization were slowed down as a result.

4. *Collectivize*

It is possible to envisage a number of collectivist forms – State farms, collectives (*kolkhoz*), communes and looser co-operatives with significant individual interests in land – though not all of them seem ideally suited to Indian conditions and history affords few examples of undeniably successful collectivization. State farms and, to judge by recent Chinese experience, big communes impose acute demands on very scarce managerial expertise – albeit rather different sorts of expertise. Small communes or collectives and co-operatives embracing both production and marketing appear to offer the most promising lines of development, there being an overriding need to maintain a flexible structure in the face of India's immense diversity in historical experience and her range of climatological/agronomic systems.[1] Either of these lines could secure equity within each collective in a thoroughgoing way, though equity within agriculture as a whole would require that differential rent be taxed and then redistributed – a highly demanding task. Collectivization should also result in a more rational production structure and use of resources, even if the lesson of history is that such expected improvements in input productivity levels are far from 'automatically' achieved in practice. Naturally, if they do rise, automatically or otherwise, output will do so too. The volume of the marketed surplus would still depend on the (possibly implicit) intersectoral terms of trade, though the latter would now be largely determined politically, it being unlikely that a

1. The Nagpur Resolution of 1959, which called for the development of Indian agriculture on the basis of co-operative farming, is important here, not least because it points to traces of collectivist thinking in certain quarters of Congress.

collectivist agriculture could enjoy a stable coexistence with a free enterprise industrial sector.

If the movement for collectivization were to come from the rural masses, the issue of building up a rural power base would be transformed from being a mere effect of the reform into a precondition for it to take place at all. Alternatively, a mass movement from below in favour of an egalitarian distributist reform might bring about a revolutionary situation, in the aftermath of which collectivization might be pushed through from above against the opposition of the mass of peasants whose expectations of important but equal individualist rights to land were subsequently disappointed. On present evidence, the consciousness of the rural masses is such that the latter may well be the more likely 'model' of the two. Yet in both cases the initial impulse must come from below, and in this respect collectivization differs from the first three options, which can be pursued purely from above by a non-revolutionary party such as Congress.

VI. Prospects

What, then, is the prospect for Indian land reforms over the next decade? We have attempted to trace out the separate rationales of various groups in Indian society pursuing particular variants of agrarian change. In the process, there emerged patterns of alliance and conflict that derive from the interests affected by the course and nature of land reform. This line of analysis may not suffice in itself to settle who will take sides with whom, for other partly autonomous influences are at work, which may prove to be of greater importance. Indeed, the issue of land reform may be but a single element of a much wider future struggle for power among the social forces discussed above, and the outcome only weakly determined by the factors we have considered.

Despite all these hazards in making a prognosis, three main features seem to be decisive. First, there is the mounting conflict between national bourgeois and kulak interests, a principal arena for which is the Congress party itself. If the present strains are soothed by some new compromise, the prevailing situation will receive a new lease of life, though the second option of Section V cannot be ruled out entirely. The danger is that uncontrolled explosions of discontent among the rural poor will cause generally unsettled conditions requiring substantial and expensive repression. If, on the other hand, bourgeois-kulak tensions are accentuated – a rather more plausible hypothesis – either slight improvements or a radical redistribution will be attempted, the latter depriving the kulaks of much power and yielding spoils for distribution to a favoured section of the poor peasantry. This matches closely the populist flavour of recent Congress policies and would help to maintain that party's electoral dominance in the face of a largely hostile kulak position. Agreement in principle to proceed in this direction was reached at a meeting of Chief Ministers convened (in 1972) to discuss the CLRC's 1971 proposals. These were watered down somewhat, giving a final result rather closer to the second than the third option discussed above.[1] Moreover, as most aspects of agricultural policy – including land reform – are matters for the individual States of the Union to decide, the implementation of 'radical' measures in West Bengal may be attempted, where present and prospective agrarian tensions are acute and close to the surface, while simultaneously something closer to a thirty acre ceiling is applied in the Punjab.[2] As most of the marketed surplus comes from a mere sixty out of a total of 285 districts, most of which are located overwhelmingly in the States in which population pressure on land is low, a judicious combination of the 'improving' and the 'radical' options could leave the surplus virtually intact.

The second major influence will be exerted by the two exogenous forces: population growth; and the pace and form of technical change in agriculture. The first will excite new pressures by exacerbating land hunger, pressures which seem likely, on

1. The compromise proposals which emerged were as follows:
   (a) 10–18 acres of class I (perennially irrigated) land, with a 1·25 weighting for privately irrigated land subject to a maximum of 18 acres (to appease the Punjab tubewell lobby); or
   (b) up to 27 acres of single crop irrigated land; or
   (c) up to 54 acres of dry land.

   A 'family' is defined to be 'husband, wife and three *minor* children' (italics added to show the crucial departure from the CLRC's original proposals) with increments allowed for further minor dependants. One estimate is that the implementation of these proposals will release 40M acres of surplus land (*Commerce*, 29 July 1972). It should be noted carefully, however, that fifteen standard acres are equivalent to *at least* thirty unweighted ones in productivity and that only 20 per cent of the land under cultivation is irrigated. Thus the proposals fall far short of our definition of 'radical' under option three.
2. This should not be taken to mean that the States can do exactly as they please. A mass uprising leading to the establishment of rural soviets in West Bengal, for example, would be assuredly followed by the summary intervention of the very large (and non-Bengali) Indian army.

balance, to be reinforced by the (probably) unequalizing effects of technical change on land distribution. At the same time, technical change will leave the burgeoning numbers of kulaks so created much more vulnerable to urban pressures than in the past, a rather paradoxical outcome which again points to the 'improving' or 'radical' options, or some combination of the two.

The above analysis points towards a tentative conclusion, but we must first of all consider a third issue: the administrative capacity and will to implement such measures. There would be no cause to go further if the administration were simply the 'neutral' instrument of public policy, but that is rarely so in practice. In structure and primary concerns, the administration at the local level has changed little from the colonial period. The words 'law and order' expressed the central preoccupation of successions of Indian District Collectors[1] well before they became rallying points for conservative opinion in North America and Western Europe in the late sixties. But this is no duumvirate – 'order' takes precedence over 'law' (Bandyopadhyay, 1972). Land reform legislation may be on the Statute Book, but each attempt at implementing its provisions occasions an inflammatory situation, which the Collector, in his other role of District Magistrate, seeks to avoid or damp down. Thus each sally against landed interests on the basis of land reform 'law' is quickly stayed by a contradictory injunction to maintain 'order'. Below the Collector, officials are often closely linked by caste and other interests to the very landlord groups who are the object of the law's provisions. Furthermore, as the process of implementation is rendered futile and vacuous unless up to date and correct records of land-ownership and tenant leases are maintained, the chances of putting even existing legislation into effect require little comment. A glance at what has been achieved since the mid fifties – a mere 1 million hectares of surplus land acquired (and only half of it actually distributed), and some 3 million tenants granted the ownership of roughly 3 million hectares cultivated by them (India, 1969, p. 133) – is enough.

That a separate land reform agency is called for is obvious. Much more vital still is the need to enlist poor peasants as formal

1. In the colonial period, the Collector, as the title implies, was responsible for the collection of revenues (principally, land revenue) in his district and for dispensing justice in his other role as District Magistrate. After Independence, there was added yet a further duty: that of encouraging development. The manifest contradictions of the situation thus created require no comment.

actors in the implementation process, as was done in China in the early fifties. Even then, such attempts to secure grass roots involvement will fail unless the masses acquire a sense of their collective power to overthrow the rural élite – in short, a state of consciousness concerning their objective condition. This is the missing element in the structure of argument developed above, for without it the ranging of pros and cons remains a static exercise. And once social relationships in the countryside are disturbed, the consequences for the existing order may be profound, perhaps even fatal.

References

Appu, P. S., 'Ceiling on Agricultural Holdings', Ministry of Agriculture, Government of India, mimeo, 1971.

Bandyopadhyay, D., 'Bargadars of Salihan', paper presented to the Public Administration Case Workshop, Administrative Staff College of India, New Delhi, mimeo, 1972.

Bardhan, P. K. and T. N. Srinivasan, 'Cropsharing Tenancy in Agriculture: A Theoretical and Empirical Analysis', *American Economic Review*, **61**, 1, March 1971, pp. 48–64.

Bell, Clive, 'The Acquisition of Agricultural Technology: Its Determinants and effects', *Journal of Development Studies*, **9**, 1, October 1972, pp. 123–57.

—, 'Technical Progress and Tenurial Change: The Disappearing Sharecropper', *Journal of Peasant Studies*, forthcoming.

Bell, Clive and S. D. Prasad, 'The Sharecroppers of Purnea District', Report to the Land Reforms Commissioner, mimeo, 1972.

Byres, T. J., 'Land Reform, Industrialization and the Marketed Surplus in India: An Essay on the Power of Rural Bias', this Volume, Chapter 7.

Chaudhri, D. P., 'New Technologies and Income Distribution in Agriculture', this Volume, Chapter 5.

Chaudhuri, Nirad, *The Continent of Circe*, Chatto & Windus, London, 1965.

Cheung, S. N. S., 'Private Property Rights and Sharecropping', *Journal of Political Economy*, **76**, November–December 1968, pp. 1107–22.

Commerce, 'Land Ceiling: a Realistic Way Out', **125**, 3195, 29 July 1972, p. 264.

Dandekar, V. M., and N. Rath, 'Poverty in India II', *Economic and Political Weekly*, **6**, 2, 9 January 1971, pp. 106–46.

Dasgupta, Biplab, 'Gandhism in West Bengal', *Journal of Contemporary Asia*, **2**, 3, 1972, pp. 255–69.

Economic and Political Weekly, 'Tussle over Ceilings', **7**, 15, 8 April 1972, pp. 745–6.

—, 'Land Ceiling and the New Farm Entrepreneur', **7**, 19, 6 May 1972, pp. 915–16.

Heady, Earl O., *Economics of Agricultural Production and Resource Use*, Prentice Hall, Englewood Cliffs, 1952.

India, *Growth Rates in Agriculture 1949–50 and 1964–5*, Directorate of Economics and Statistics, Delhi, 1968.

—, *Fourth Five Year Plan 1969–74 (Draft)*, Planning Commission, Delhi, 1969.

—, *Census 1971*, Series I, Paper 1 of 1971 – Supplement, Delhi, 1971.

Lehmann, David, 'Political Incorporation versus Political Stability: the Case of the Chilean Agrarian Reform, 1965- 1970', *Journal of Development Studies*, **7**, 4, July 1971, pp. 365–95.

Lenin, V. I., *Capitalism and Agriculture*, International Publishers, New York, 1946.

Lipton, Michael, 'Strategy for Agriculture: Urban Bias and Rural Planning', *The Crisis of Indian Planning: Economic Planning in the 1960s* (eds. Paul Streeten and Michael Lipton), O.U.P., London, 1968.

—, 'Towards a Theory of Land Reform', this Volume, Chapter 9.

Luxemburg, Rosa, *The Accumulation of Capital*, Routledge & Kegan Paul, London, 1951.

Minhas, B. S., 'Rural Poverty, Land Distribution and Development Strategy: Facts and Figures', *Indian Economic Review*, **5**, 1, April 1970, pp. 97–128.

—, 'Rural Poverty and the Minimum Level of Living: A Reply', *Indian Economic Review*, **6**, 1, April 1971, pp. 69–77.

Moore, Barrington, *Social Origins of Dictatorship and Democracy*, Penguin, Harmondsworth, 1969.

Newbery, David, 'The Choice of Rental Contract in Peasant Agriculture', paper presented at a Conference on 'Agriculture in Development Theory', Bellagio, May 1973.

Preobrazhensky, Evgeny, *The New Economics*, Clarendon Press, Oxford, 1965.

Rao, C. H. H., 'Uncertainty, Entrepreneurship and Sharecropping in India', *Journal of Political Economy*, **79**, 3, May–June 1971, pp. 578–95.

Sanghvi, Prufulla, *Surplus Manpower in Agriculture and Economic Development*, Asia Publishing House, Bombay, 1969.

Seven

Land Reform, Industrialization and the Marketed Surplus in India: An Essay on the Power of Rural Bias

T. J. Byres

The question we are interested in is whether we have now a pattern of agrarian structure and institutions which could be relied upon for the purposes of rapid growth not only of the agricultural sector but of the total national economy. More pertinently we may inquire whether, when the programme based on current policies is fully implemented, we shall have such a structure or a further radical alteration will be needed.

(M. L. Dantwala, [19], pp. 14–15.)

I. The Two Ends of the Spectrum

One can approach the problem of the 'rural sector' of underdeveloped economies from several different conceptions of the nature of backwardness and of the most appropriate route away from backwardness, most of which concern, implicitly or explicitly, the relationships between agriculture and industry.

At one end of the spectrum is the 'industrializer'. He sees the need for industrialization (and, in India's case, for the creation of a capital goods sector) as compelling; he recognizes that the pace of industrialization depends critically upon the release of resources from agriculture; and he asks himself how best this transfer can be achieved and what obstacles stand in the way. Such an industrializer, indeed, suffers from the 'urban bias' attributed to him, so eloquently, by Michael Lipton ([81], [83]).

Whether 'urban bias' can generate means of siphoning-off the 'agricultural surplus', of which the marketed surplus is one important manifestation, is by no means certain, though this is sometimes implied. That will depend upon the nature and strength of the urban bourgeoisie and its representatives, the power of landlords, rich peasants and capitalist farmers, and upon several other factors. Anyway, one would expect such an industrializer to see land reform in terms of the 'imperatives of industrialization'. Let me confess that I am such a person.

There is nothing necessarily sinister about 'urban bias'. The expression is simply a pejorative way of referring to those who choose the path of industrialization. To categorize this position as 'Stalinist', to dismiss its arguments as 'doctrine' or 'ideology',[1] is to replace logic and argument with what Myrdal aptly calls 'depreciation by terminology' ([93], Vol. 2, p. 962). And in any case the Indian government did embark wholeheartedly upon an industrialization programme geared to heavy industry in 1956 and it is necessary to scrutinize this, the major goal of Indian planning, in relation to other major goals and potential barriers to its attainment.

At the other end of the spectrum we find the exponent of 'agriculture first'. He denies the case for industrialization, at least in the foreseeable future. He argues for a diversion of investible resources into agriculture, and he believes that a severe injustice is being done to rural areas in underdeveloped countries. Such a person, we may say, suffers from 'rural bias', and sees land reform in terms of the 'needs' of agriculture.

II. Difficulties Associated with Analysing Land Reform

For a number of reasons land reform is a peculiarly difficult problem to handle analytically. The meaning of the term varies from country to country, from writer to writer, and from period to period. It is necessary, therefore, to make clear the particular usage we have in mind.

We must start by specifying the precise nature of the pre-reform agrarian structure, which, following Thorner, relates, in its essence, to 'the network of relations among the various groups of persons who draw their livelihood from the soil' ([127], p. 2). In other words, we are concerned here with the social relations of production in agriculture, which, along with the forces of production, allow us to identify the prevailing mode of production in the countryside. Within any given political system there

1. Thus we find Michael Lipton, the most intelligent and persuasive of those who endeavour to root out and expose 'urban bias', writing of 'the . . . ideology of premature industrialization' ([81], p. 147) and of the 'Doctrine of Surpluses' ([83], p. 25). Another writer of the same persuasion tells us that 'the court-philosophy of urbanism is the Doctrine of Surpluses' ([130], p. 12).

will be a variety of means whereby changes in the agrarian structure may be secured, and that range widens if we begin to look at different kinds of political systems. To include all of these within the purview of the term 'land reform' is to dilute it almost to the point of meaninglessness. Thus I shall restrict its meaning to attempts to transform the agrarian structure by altering the distribution of land and the terms upon which land is held and worked. I reject the 'omnibus' notion of land reform, which includes supporting or related measures like agricultural credit policy, agricultural education, extension services, marketing arrangements, a community development programme and so on (as favoured in the first United Nations report on Land Reform, [131], pp. 5–6, in subsequent U.N. documents on the subject, [132], [133], [134], and by a number of American writers, ([25], p. 19, [85], [108], [109][1]). I also reject the narrow definition used by Warriner, which limits land reform to 'the redistribution of property or rights in land, for the benefit of *small farmers or agricultural labourers*' ([142], p. xiv, emphasis added) as excessively restrictive. For example, I would certainly identify as land reform the removal of land from large, 'feudal' landowners and its vesting with *rich* peasants.

A second difficulty in analysing land reform derives from the diversity of aims, set within the rural sector, which are embodied in a proposed land reform programme. These aims are sometimes explicit and sometimes implicit, they are often infuriatingly vague, and they may be contradictory. Their contradictory nature – say a clash between an avowed desire for 'social justice' and the goal of maximum output – may be real in the sense that different aspects of the programme may clash; they also may be more apparent than real inasmuch as one general aim may be expressed in the political rhetoric surrounding land reform, while the programme itself may ignore it completely. There is, indeed, a distinction to be made between land reform as ideology and land reform as a programme (Joshi, [61]), which may be clear at the time of formulation, but usually becomes clearer as implementation proceeds. We shall have occasion to examine some of these contradictions.

If we cast our net more widely we may find, thirdly, a conflict between land reform and major targets set outside the agricultural sector. I shall examine the consistency of Indian land reform with industrialization and we shall see that if we add the necessity for

1. Warriner [142], p. xv, points out how the very wide definition 'confuses the subject' in the U.N. reports.

surplus transfer to the aims of social justice and maximum output, the situation becomes even trickier.

Finally, if we proceed to the actual operation of the programme we find that, apart from the usual headaches associated with establishing causal relationships among groups of factors, land reform raises peculiar difficulties. The true results of a land reform programme may be concealed – because the law has been flouted, or because they are politically sensitive in nature – and one may be tempted to attribute a particular effect to land reform, only to find that the reform has not, after all, taken place in the assumed fashion. One part of the programme may be implemented successfully, while others are disastrously unsuccessful. But even the unsuccessful elements may have an effect, to the extent that fear of their being implemented may have induced changes in the agrarian structure. Or the results may be subject to wide regional variations in a large country like India, so that one must not project one regional pattern upon all regions. One must proceed with caution.

III. The Imperatives of Industrialization and the Broad Questions at Issue[1]

At this juncture we musty identify how the 'imperatives of industrialization' affect agriculture, and the precise role they assign to the marketed surplus. We can do this best by spelling out briefly (and without qualification) the kind of resource flow that is necessary in the 'early years of industrialization' (or the period of primitive accumulation) when the rate of industrial growth is critically dependent upon the transfer of an agricultural surplus.

When a country such as India, chronically short of foreign exchange, embarks upon industrialization and seeks, moreover, to create a capital goods sector, a limit is set by the size of the surplus that can be mobilized from agriculture. It is useful to divide the agricultural surplus into two main parts: a real surplus and a financial surplus. As we shall see the flow of marketed surplus bears upon both the real surplus and the financial surplus, though principally on the former.

The real surplus (real because it is physical in its manifestation) has two components: food and raw materials. Their importance

1. I have not documented the arguments in this section. For some of the relevant documentation see my article [9].

derives from their dual role as industry's working capital and as direct earners of foreign exchange. Food is crucial for the whole of the industrial sector since it is the wage-good *par excellence* (the good which accounts for a very large proportion of working-class expenditure). If the marketed surplus of food is not forthcoming both in sufficient quantity and on favourable terms, industrialization will be held back, and we stress the two-fold nature of the problem. The efficiency of the urban labour force may be reduced, or an unfortunate process may be set in motion, whereby food prices rise, money wages increase, and profit margins are squeezed. Raw materials from agriculture are essential for key industries like textiles and for other agro-based industries, which are important in the early years of industrialization as earners of foreign exchange, employers of labour and producers of consumer goods. Such industries cannot operate effectively if their necessary material inputs can be obtained either not at all, or only on ever-worsening terms. Again, the marketed surplus is of central importance, and we note the very real possibility of a conflict, where food and raw materials compete as crops.

The financial surplus (financial because it is expressed in money terms) represents a 'command over resources' which can be transferred from the agricultural to the non-agricultural sector. Agriculture dominates the Asian underdeveloped economy and must, because of its dominating position, supply a large proportion of the finance for the capital formation inherent in industrialization. The difference between a large and a modest investment rate outside of agriculture will depend on the financial surplus, or, in other words, on the degree to which agriculture relinquishes its command over real resources. The aim is to secure the maximum marginal rate of saving in the agricultural sector, to acquire these savings, and to use them to finance capital formation in the industrial sector. Again movements in the marketed surplus are important. If the terms upon which the marketed surplus is acquired are shifted against agriculture this may have the effect of raising the marginal rate of saving in agriculture; if peasants, indeed, market more in order to buy the same bundle of industrial goods they are, in overall terms, consuming less and contributing more to total savings.

A few words, next, on the so-called labour surplus. Development literature of the 1950s and early 1960s was dominated by the assumption that there existed in agriculture a large pool of underemployed labour, which consumed food but did not add to agricultural output. Agriculture's role was seen to be that of supplying this labour, and supplying it along with its food, as the working force in new and growing industries: labour would move, the marketed surplus would rise and a valuable potential saving would be realized. Now, whatever the truth of this in the past, for other societies, it is not a valid rendering of the Indian situation. With population increasing and high capital intensity in the industrial sector, industry is able to meet its labour needs through natural increase in the cities. Agriculture's role, then, is to *hold* its labour until the industrial sector proves capable of absorbing it (which may be at some distant point in the future) at the same time as increasing the flow of marketed surplus.

Finally, agriculture's market role needs to be spelt out. There is a strong argument to the effect that in the early years industrialization may founder on the rock of an insufficient market in agriculture for industrial products, as a result of too small a marketed surplus (the wherewithal of exchange) or adverse terms of trade (the incentive for exchange). However, if a capital goods sector is the major aspect of an industrialization drive then the problem is not whether a market exists in agriculture: to a large extent, in the early years, these industries supply and sell to one another. In such a context, the problem is, rather, to restrain demand for consumer goods (and certain kinds of investment goods) in the rural sector. It is not a question of ensuring the existence of demand in agriculture. The dilemma, rather, poses itself in reverse: how many 'incentive' goods can the economy afford to supply as a means of eliciting a marketed surplus. Thus, the conflict is not between the 'imperatives of industrialization' outlined already and the need for a market in rural areas, but of another kind.

The agricultural surplus, in its various forms, may be 'extracted' and transferred through a variety of mechanisms. The agrarian structure will assuredly influence the size of that surplus, the manner of its extraction, and the mode of its utilization. Given that a surplus exists – which it certainly does – its transfer and the terms of its transfer will depend, inter alia, upon agricultural taxation, price policy, the nature of marketing arrangements, the effectiveness of controls of one kind or another, the direction of savings and investment flows. And central to the whole process is the behaviour of the marketed surplus, with which we are concerned in this paper.

The agrarian structure will condition the operation of all the aforementioned mechanisms. What we shall examine is precisely how it bears upon the marketed surplus. In order to give some perspective to our enquiry, as well as analysing the initial structure in India I shall briefly outline the various theoretical possibilities for change. This has the merit of suggesting a comparative framework, though we shall do more than suggest it.

IV. The Marketed Surplus and other Key Variables

In the context of the present paper it may be useful, for certain purposes, to work in terms of the marketed surplus of total agricultural produce. If data exist only in this form one may have no alternative, though it may be possible to derive inferences about components of the total marketed surplus from overall figures in conjunction with other kinds of evidence. Concern with the rate of industrial growth and with the manner in which the different manifestations of the agricultural surplus noted above influence the pace of industrialization makes it necessary, indeed, to focus upon the marketed surplus of either a single crop – say jute, or cotton, or rice, or wheat – or of a crucial group of crops – say foodgrains.

It is essential to distinguish *gross marketed surplus* and *net marketed surplus* (called, by Narain [94] respectively the marketed and the marketable surplus). Since we are interested in the proportion of output which reaches urban consumers and export markets, the former should be composed of (1) that part of output – be it total agricultural output, output of a single crop, or output of a group of crops – marketed by cultivating families (or delivered up to monetized exchange); (2) the portion of wages in kind which landless labour may market; and (3) the portion of kind rents which non-cultivators may market. It is, however, the net marketed surplus which the industrializer gives his attention to, or that part of output which is marketed, net of any buy-back. There are many cultivators, landless labourers and even rent-receivers who sell at harvest (or who deliver up on the basis of an agreement made before harvest) to obtain cash for various purposes, only to buy back later in order to meet consumption requirements. Either they market foodgrains and buy back foodgrains, or they market 'commercial' (i.e. non-foodgrain) crops and buy back food. It is this net marketed surplus which reaches urban consumers and export markets though, of course, after it has left the cultivator the activities of traders (such as hoarding for speculative purposes) determine how quickly it reaches the urban consumer and, in part, the price which the urban consumer pays.

There is a range of possible relationships among movements in agricultural output, the marketed surplus, the intersectoral terms of trade, and agricultural prices. In theory at least, there is room for manoeuvre and different kinds of agrarian structure in conjunction with varying degrees of government power may yield diverse results with respect to the marketed surplus. Land reform, by altering the agrarian structure may bring about a new set of possibilities. This, as it has been well put by Bhagwati and Chakravarty, may arise through 'the efficiency and/or the price response of *production* varying under alternative forms of tenure (such as sharecropping or peasant proprietorship) . . . [or through] differences in *consumption* patterns, for any given level of farm output, that may arise from differences in the distribution of the farm income among rents, wages and self-imputed incomes under alternative tenure systems' ([7], p. 38). Furthermore, the altered agrarian structure may make changes possible by allowing government greater access to and control over the rural sector.

The possible combinations of these factors are many, and their configuration depends largely on the response of agricultural producers to changes in the terms of trade. For example, the absolute level of marketed surplus may rise, fall or remain constant while total output grows. In the first case, the proportion of output marketed will rise, fall or remain constant, while in the second and third cases it will be falling, though at different rates, and which of these holds depends on the relative prices of agricultural and industrial goods (terms of trade) and on the nature of producer response, which may be 'perverse'. (A 'perverse' response arises when, in the face of improving terms of trade, a producer markets a lower absolute amount of produce.) Thus favourable terms of trade do not necessarily ensure an increased flow of marketed surplus, nor do unfavourable terms necessarily provoke a declining flow.

When output is falling, the marketed surplus may still be increasing; the accompanying movement in the terms of trade may be either against agriculture or in agriculture's favour. The relationship between the flow of surplus and the terms of trade is difficult to predict when output is falling, but the extraction of an increasing flow of surplus when output is falling probably requires very tight control and an unusual set of institutions whose effects are independent of those which might be expected from the terms of trade. The issue is further complicated by the fact that, at any given moment, there are both peasants who are net sellers and others who are net buyers of food, so that there are two types of response to take into account, and the outcome of their offsetting effects is difficult to predict.

Finally, with a constant level of output, the flow of surplus may increase, decrease or remain constant. But, what all these behavioural possibilities show us is that there is a radical difference between strategies for increasing output and strategies for transferring marketed surplus and resources from agriculture to industry.

V. The Agrarian Structure of Unreformed Indian Agriculture and the Marketed Surplus

I start by giving some indication of the existing forces of production at the time of Independence and in the early 1950s, so that we may have an overall view of the prevailing mode of production.

During this period India was an example of a land-scarce situation, and scope for extending the arable area was small and liable to be exhausted quickly – as, indeed, happened. (See [93], Vol. 1, Chap. 10; [57] pp. 57–59; [107].) Thus it was essential that, after any brief honeymoon period in which output might be added to by extension of the arable area, per acre yields should rise if output were to rise ([43], Chap. 9). Irrigation, a 'leading input', was necessary, but by no means generally available, with only 15 per cent of total arable area and 17 per cent of the sown area irrigated in 1949–50[1] (calculated from data in [38], pp. 14–15, 34 and 39). The application of 'modern inputs' – artificial fertilizers, high-yielding seeds, pesticides, etc. – was extremely limited, as one would expect, given that irrigation was a condition for their success: in 1947–8 and the years immediately thereafter under 1 per cent of the total arable acreage benefited from application of artificial fertilizers (calculated from figures in [89], p. 68). Methods of cultivation were relatively backward. To take but two examples, in rice cultivation the 'traditional' as opposed to the high-yielding 'Japanese' method was overwhelmingly predominant ([30], Chaps. 1, 6, 21; [49], pp. 425–7) while, more generally, the iron plough had made relatively little headway in ousting the wooden one ([118], p. 245). All in all, the development of the forces of production was backward, and this was reflected in and reinforced by the agrarian structure. As a result, yields, per acre and per man, were low and stagnant ([43], pp. 155–6).

As Thorner points out ([127], p. 4), amid significant regional diversity India's agrarian structure exhibited a discernible

1. Arable area equals net area sown plus fallow. Net area sown represents land under crops (double cropped area counted only once). Sown area covers total cropped area or gross area sown (i.e. net area sown plus area sown more than once).

common pattern.[1] The common pattern which I shall identify derives, in part, from Thorner's pioneering work, but differs from it in certain important respects.

At the apex of the agrarian structure was the landlord (or rent-receiving) class, not necessarily 'owners', in the strict sense – they might themselves be 'occupancy tenants' – but with 'superior' property rights in the soil, which permitted them to lease out land to 'lesser tenants, subtenants, or croppers' and to extract from them a surplus in the form of rent ([127], p. 5). Within this class there were two broad groups, which existed in all parts of India, but one or other of which predominated in any particular region. The first was a class of large, usually absentee, landlords, who tended to hold land in more than one village and were most commonly to be found in *zamindari* and *jagirdari* regions.[2]

1. A modern historian of India, Frykenberg, whose chosen brief was to make some sense out of *Land Control and Social Structure in Indian History* (in [27], Introduction, pp. xiii–xxi), tells us gravely, but with the obvious relish of the 'micro' historian, of the 'veritable jungle of overlapping terminologies', of the consequent possibility of 'all sorts of error and misinterpretation' (p. xv), and 'of the fantastic complexity in land relationships' (p. xviii). In one sense, this is assuredly so. In 1947, as a result of survivals from pre-British days in British India ([127]), p. 11), of differing British practice with regard to land revenue settlement (see, for example, [4], [27], [50], [70], [116], [122], [126], [127]), of the seeming diversity existing in princely states ([64], [67]), and of the complex layering of rights in the soil which had emerged in the century and a half before Independence ([127]), there was a veritable 'tenancy chaos' ([116], p. 113) and the juridical forms which overlay and influenced the social relations of production were numerous and confusing. But variety and confusion in this sense do not, of necessity, imply a corresponding plethora of *substantive* and *essential* differences in underlying realities. Frykenberg and his co-authors operate at the level of the district and the province and nowhere is an attempt made to establish all-India perspectives. Moreover, at that level Frykenberg is rather concerned that 'efforts to bring order out of the chaos and confusions of juxtaposed relationships must necessarily become exercises in abstraction and over-simplification' (pp. xviii–xix).
2. In 1793 the British created 'a strange group of great landlords, a class whose annual payments of land revenue to the State were fixed . . . at sums which were to remain unchanged for all time to come – hence the name for this arrangement, the Permanent Settlement' ([126], p. 124). These were the great *zamindars* of Eastern India, who had been the tax-gatherers in Mughul India, and whom the British hoped would become a class akin to the great Whig landed aristocracy, a hope that was rudely shattered. The *zamindars* were for the first

These were the classic 'intermediaries' between the government and the peasant, whose tenants often sub-let to others. ([127], pp. 4–5 and 8, [67] 181–2). Secondly, there was a class of smaller, normally resident 'proprietors', who typically held land in one village, who were most common in *ryotwari* and *mahalwari* areas, and who, like their wealthier counterparts, would also sub-let the land. ([127], pp. 4–5.)

---

time given property rights in land and in return paid revenue to the government. Beneath them were tenants from whom they extracted rents, and the tenantry were themselves composed of several layers, with differing degrees of rights in the soil, some of them rent-receivers themselves. The Permanent Settlement spread to various parts of India and at Independence the *zamindari* areas were West Bengal, Eastern U.P., Bihar, Orissa, and Northern Madras. For the background to the Permanent Settlement see Ranajit Guha's magnificent essay [50] and Eric Stokes's fascinating book [122]; see also [126], pp. 124–5; [127], lecture 1; [67], pp. 182 *et passim*; [70], Chapter 1; [116], Chapter 2.

The British were faced with two broad problems. One was that of land revenue, the need to secure the maximum amount of revenue from the land. The other was a political problem, that of retaining power and authority in India by creating a class of collaborators who would give them their support. The Permanent Settlement solved the second of these problems and the British had in the great *zamindars* loyal allies. It did not, however, solve the first problem. As the Permanent Settlement proved unsatisfactory in this respect, so the British, when they conquered other parts of India, tried other systems of land revenue. The major alternative to the Permanent Settlement was a settlement made with individual cultivating peasants, the so-called *ryotwari* settlement: which was not made in perpetuity but was subject to regular re-assessment. The vision here was that a class of sturdy independent peasants would be created, and it was again not to be realized. In fact, as the nineteenth century progressed peasants began to sub-let their land and two broad classes emerged as population rose and pressure on land increased: a class of large landlords and a class of petty landlord *rentiers*. In the end the *zamindari* and *ryotwari* areas became more and more similar in their attributes, though some essential differences did remain. At Independence *ryotwari* areas included Bombay (later Maharashtra and Gujarat), Southern Madras, parts of Madhya Pradesh and Assam. See [126], pp. 124–5; [127], Lecture 1; [122]; [4]; [67], pp. 182 *et passim*; [116], Chapter 2; [70], Chapter 1.

The *mahalwari* settlement, made in the Punjab and in parts of U.P. was a variant of the *ryotwari* system in that settlement was not permanent, though settlement was made not with individual peasants, but on a village basis. In practice, areas of *mahalwari* settlement seem

It was in the interests of both groups to keep rents as high as possible, and, some landlords, in their capacity as moneylenders, drew from the peasant an interest surplus as well as a rental surplus. This was especially true of the second group, some of whom, or some of whose antecedents, had started as moneylenders, becoming proprietors by buying up or foreclosing ([127], pp. 9–10; [31], pp. 185–6; [110], pp. 102, 167, 169, 171–2; [126], p. 125; [29], pp. 30–1, 161–4, 230 *et passim*). Some landlords used hired labour to work the land that was not leased out, drawing the labour from the ranks of poor peasants and landless labourers (of which more anon), and paying in money or kind, in a range of unfree and free relationships, which, though they had been changing in the previous century, were still essentially pre-capitalist in nature. ([128], [127], p. 6, [70], p. 35.) The landlord class used the surplus which it extracted unproductively: not to invest in agriculture or in industry, but to sustain high levels of consumption in the countryside or in the city ([103], pp. 24–7; [67], p. 187).

India's agrarian structure had two further major components: a peasantry and a class of landless labourers. Among the peasantry some differentiation was fairly evident, varying in degree from region to region and being most marked where commercialization had penetrated furthest and in *ryotwari* and *mahalwari* areas – that is to say, in Bombay (later to become Maharashtra and Gujarat), the Punjab and Madras (as suggested by the data in [31], pp. 188–9). We shall identify and describe the characteristics of three strata within the peasantry – a rich, a middle and a poor stratum – a division whose importance for the marketed surplus we shall later come to stress. Size holding data are obviously a fairly crude way of locating and analysing the charac-

---

to have resembled closely *ryotwari* areas. See [70], pp. 11–12 and [116], pp. 67 and 74.

The *jagirdars* existed in some of the princely states, and especially in Hyderabad (later to become part of Andhra Pradesh) and Rajasthan. In these areas 'vast tracts of land . . . were made over by princely rulers to their courtiers and nobles in return for their military and administrative services. These *jagirdars* were not owners but administrators of the land and extracted high land revenue payment from owners. Most owners cultivated lands directly, but some had tenants. Thus emerged a four-tiered system, with the state granting *jagirs*, and getting loyalty and service, the *jagirdar* conferring ownership and getting revenues, the owner leasing land and getting rent and the tenant paying rent while cultivating the soil' ([67], p. 182). See also [64]. The *jagirdari* system was in several respects like the *zamindari* one.

teristics of differentiation even at a disaggregated level ([80], [101]). At the all-India level the crudity increases considerably, but for my limited purposes the method is useful and, having examined the available data with some care, I take it that, in the conditions prevailing in India at Independence, the following very rough categorization does not do too much outrage to the facts: in most operational (as opposed to ownership) holdings up to five acres we find poor peasants, in most holdings between five and fifteen acres middle peasants, and in the majority of those above fifteen acres rich peasants. Obviously there was significant regional variation in the holding size appropriate to the different categories.

Commercialization touched parts of Indian agriculture long before the British gained hegemony in the sub-continent ([54], pp. 39–52, 61–81 and 118–19) and with commodity production some differentiation of the peasantry in Mughal India has been noted ([54], pp. 120–2, 128–9). Commercialization spread a little in the first half of the nineteenth century, with extension in the cultivation of jute and cotton ([29], pp. 13–15), but it was not until the 1860s and thereafter that it began to penetrate important areas of the Indian countryside, with improved communications and access to export markets being especially important for 'the Punjab wheat area, the jute area of Eastern Bengal and the Khandesh, Gujerat and Berar cotton tracts' ([29], p. 159. See also, op. cit. pp. 16–18, 60–6, 93–100, 158–61, 206–15; [126], pp. 121–5; [28], pp. 450–5). The British had cleared the way for commercialization by adding three new elements to the inherited situation: 'a demand throughout the areas they ruled directly for payment in money; for payment in full each year (i.e. a relatively *inflexible* demand); and within the context of a private property structure of landholding.' ([126], p. 124.) The major aim was to maximize land revenue and one of the major results (which also served British interests) was to force peasants into growing commercial crops in order to raise the necessary cash to pay the tax. Thus the conditions necessary for differentiation were created: commodity production on an unprecedented scale, monetization, profit possibilities and the transferability of land. When harvests were bad or prices low most peasants went into debt, and once in debt they found it difficult to extricate themselves. ([126], p. 125; [31], pp. 185–6; [29], pp. 30–1, 160–5, 227–37.) Two distinct trends could be seen. One was the emergence of a class of moneylender-landlords already noted. The other was increased polarization within the peasantry.

Rich peasants, as we have seen, existed in Mughal India. It was, however, in the century or so before Independence that a class of rich peasants burgeoned in India: most obviously, we have suggested, in Western India, the Punjab and Madras, *ryotwari* and *mahalwari* areas, but discernible, also, in, for example, parts of U.P., West Bengal and Bihar, *zamindari* areas, ([77]; [70], pp. 12, 30–5; [116], p. 73). Rich peasants were part-owners and part-tenants. Thus we find that in 1954–5 in the nine states for which figures exist ([105], p. 28) all operational size-holdings above fifteen acres had rented-in land:[1] in the Punjab, renting-in accounted for between 40 per cent and 50 per cent of total operated area for some of the size-holding groups, whereas in the *zamindari* areas (U.P., Bihar and West Bengal) the figure was for the most part under 10 per cent and sometimes far lower.[2] In these latter areas rich peasants were far from being capitalist farmers and generally rented-out some of their land ([70], p. 35). Significantly, a high proportion of the land leased-in by rich peasants was on a sharecropping basis – 30 to 40 per cent for most areas of India ([105], p. 33)[3] – indicating the essentially pre-capitalist nature of the mode of production. This was shown, also, by findings of the Farm Management surveys conducted in certain States in the mid 1950s ([32], [33], [34], [35], [36], [37]). For example, the widespread fragmentation on rich peasant holdings in all of these States, and the consistently lower output per acre achieved by rich peasants compared with middle and poor peasants.[4] At the same time rich peasants accumulated

1. These are the Punjab, Rajasthan, Madhya Pradesh, Bombay (later to become Maharashtra and Gujarat), Uttar Pradesh, Bihar, West Bengal, Andhra Pradesh and Madras. The size-holdings for which figures are given are 15–19·99 acres, 20–24·99, 25–29·99, 30–49·99, 50 and above.
2. In 1953–4 at the very least 20 per cent of the total operated area in India was rented-out ([95]). My own hunch would be that the figure was nearer 30 per cent. The 20 per cent figure is from the National Sample Survey data. There must have been significant under-reporting by landowners because of apprehension over possible land reform measures and by tenants through fear of reprisals from landowners if they were discovered to be telling the truth. This is briefly touched upon by Narain and Joshi [95], but they are more sanguine about the extent of under-reporting than I am. See also [114].
3. In 1954–5, of the total rented-out land in India the proportion which was sharecropped varied from at least 26 per cent in South India (Madras and Andhra Pradesh) to at least 50 per cent in East India (Bihar and West Bengal). See [105], pp. 32–3. The average for India as a whole was probably around 40 per cent of total rented-out land.
4. The reasons for the inverse relationship between output per acre and size of holding have been explored in a wide-ranging debate among

capital (see, for example, [77]), were market-oriented and, as shown in the Farm Management surveys, were substantial employers of wage-labour (though, as with the landlord class, the relationship with labour was still of a pre-capitalist kind). Figures of operational holdings show that in 1954–5 holdings of more than fifteen acres represented 9 per cent of total cultivating households in India, operating 52 per cent of the cultivated land ([105], p. 3). Rich peasants were not the 'masters of the countryside' at Independence – the landlord class was still very much in command – and they were not to be clearly seen in all parts of India. They were a class of capitalist farmers in embryo, in the womb of the old order.

TABLE I *Distribution of Cultivating Households and Cultivated Land by Size of Holding: India, 1945–55.*

Holding Size	Cultivating Households	Cultivated Land
	%	%
0 – 5 acres	72	17
5 – 15 acres	19	31
Over 15 acres	9	52
	100	100

(Source: [105], p. 3. Derived from National Sample Survey Data.)

The middle peasant stratum made up 19 per cent of families with operational holdings and operated 31 per cent of total cultivated area in 1954–5 (loc. cit.). Middle peasants were part-owners and part-tenants, *owning* a larger portion of the land they worked than poor peasants, but a smaller proportion than rich peasants, this being true for all nine states for which data are given ([105], p. 28) except the Punjab. They were, however, tenants to a fairly substantial degree: most middle peasants renting-in more than 20 per cent of the land they cultivated, and most poor peasants more than 25 per cent, compared with most rich peasants who rented-in less than 20 per cent. The situation with regard to sharecropping, if we can accept the figures, was varied, not to say confused. In North and North-West India (U.P., Punjab and Rajasthan) middle peasants had a larger share of their rented-in land on a sharecropping basis than either rich

Indian economists. For a full list of references and a selection of the contributions to that debate see [10].

or poor; in South and Central India (Madras, Andhra Pradesh and Madhya Pradesh) they had more, proportionately, than poor peasants and less than rich; in West India (Bombay) they had rather less than poor peasants and significantly less than rich; and in East India (Bihar and West Bengal) they had less than poor peasants and more than rich ([105], p. 33). All we can say, by way of generalization, is that in all parts of India middle peasants sharecropped a large proportion of the land which they rented-in. Like all other peasants, they held their land in several scattered pieces; they were decidedly not market-oriented, but geared rather to the needs of the family and subject to the logic of family-based agriculture; they employed small amounts of wage-labour at peak periods. All in all, they enjoyed a rather precarious existence, aspiring to the status and wealth of rich peasants but conscious of the abyss into which they could so easily fall.

In 1954–5 poor peasants constituted 72 per cent of families with operational holdings and worked only 17 per cent of the cultivated area ([105], p. 3). As we have seen they were part-owners and part-tenants and tenants to a greater degree than other peasants. Because a greater proportion of them were tenants of one kind or another, they were more likely to be sharecroppers than others, even where the proportion of rented-in land held on a sharecropping basis was rather less than was the case with the other strata, and they were particularly likely to be sharecroppers in East India (Bihar and West Bengal). Among poor peasants fragmentation was rife; access to credit was via the village money-lender at usurious interest rates and the level of indebtedness was high [110]; market-orientation was absent and the market would be resorted to only in desperation. Poor peasants had, perhaps, more in common with landless labourers than with other segments of the peasantry: in 1950–1, for 15 per cent of rural families with land the major activity was supplying their labour to others ([42], Essential Statistics, Table 1, p. 5), while 50 per cent of agricultural labourer families were, in fact, poor peasant families with land ([42], p. 20). Even so, poor peasants, like middle peasants, did employ some wage labour at peak seasons. In all areas of India the highest output per acre was achieved on their dwarf, 'uneconomic' holdings.

There were landless labourers in Mughal India, notwithstanding the relative abundance of cultivable land ([54], pp. 120–122). There is some dispute as to just how large a class of agricultural labourers existed in India at the inception of British rule, with the earlier view that this class was essentially a creation of the British ([99]) called into question by Kumar ([76]). Certainly this class grew in numbers in the nineteenth and twentieth centuries. In 1950–1, 15 per cent of all agricultural families in India were without land ([42], Essential Statistics, Table 1, p. 5).

I have spent some time delineating India's agrarian structure at Independence since it is very important for the subsequent analysis that we portray it accurately. Let us now relate it to the marketed surplus. No 'industrializer', with his keen eye upon the marketable surplus, could have been happy with this situation. Firstly, at existing levels of production the prevailing system of exploitation did not maximize the net marketed surplus. The 'rental surplus' and 'interest surplus' together amounted to anything between 20 per cent and 40 per cent of total agricultural income, depending on the region ([100] and [103], p. 24), and much of this surplus was used to support 'faithful legions of servants' and those engaged in activities generated by the expenditure of rent-receivers – goldsmiths, artisans building luxury houses etc. ([103], pp. 24–7). To the extent that these activities took place in the rural sector the net marketed surplus was diminished. Secondly, in the unreformed situation there was little capacity to control the terms of trade, and periodic harvest failures, the activities of speculating traders and so on loaded the dice against the urban sector. Thirdly, existing levels of production were low, and were kept low by the logic of the system. The landlord class was parasitic, uninterested in making or encouraging productive investment on the land. Within the peasantry the highest yields were achieved by poor peasants but given their position as sharecroppers, their lack of access to credit on reasonable terms, their crushing burden of unproductive debt, they were most unlikely to indulge in the risky investments that would secure growth. Middle peasants were equally unlikely to do so, while rich peasants were as yet insufficiently strong and as yet not faced with adequately attractive profit possibilities. Even if the proportion of output marketed were high its absolute level, in the static situation, was too low to support rapid industrialization. The 'industrializer', in such circumstances, would want to see such growth in the agricultural sector as would ensure a flow of marketed surplus. The agrarian structure prevented such growth.

If we examine the agrarian structure a little more closely and identify which strata actually produced the marketed surplus, the situation seems even more unsatisfactory. The figures we have are those calculated by Narain [94] and are for gross marketed surplus. They show that in 1950–1 poor peasants marketed 34 per cent of the output they produced, by value; middle

TABLE 2 *Proportion of Output Marketed by Size of Holding in India, 1950–51*

Operational Holding Size	% of output of each stratum
0 – 5 acres	34
5 – 10 acres	27
10 – 15 acres	23
15 – 20 acres	30
20 – 25 acres	32
25 – 30 acres	40
30 – 40 acres	40
40 – 50 acres	46
Over 50 acres	51
India	33

(Source: [94], p. 35. Note: The author provides two sets of estimates. I have chosen the above estimate since he tells us that it probably gives 'better approximations to the true values' (p. 35).)

peasants in the size-groups of five to ten acres and ten to fifteen acres marketed only 27 per cent and 23 per cent respectively; smaller rich peasants (fifteen to twenty acres) marketed 30 per cent while for larger rich peasants the proportion rose steadily to 40 per cent in size-holdings twenty-five to thirty acres and 51 per cent in holdings of fifty acres and above. ([94], p. 35, second set of estimates. These figures are reproduced in Table 2.) For India as a whole the gross marketed surplus was 33 per cent of the value of total output. Poor peasants contributed 26 per cent of the total gross marketed surplus, middle peasants 28 per cent and rich peasants 46 per cent (see Table 3). Thus, just over

TABLE 3 *Contribution to Total Marketed Surplus by Size of Holding in India, 1950–51*

Operational Holding Size	%
0 – 5 acres	26
5 – 15 acres	28
Over 15 acres	46
	100

(Source: [94].) (Note: See Table 2.)

half of the gross marketed surplus was supplied by poor and middle peasants and the other half by rich peasants. Narain further argues (pp. 36–8) that the former half of the gross marketed surplus is a 'distress surplus' and the latter a 'commercial surplus'. The 'commercial surplus' is of the kind which market-oriented rich peasants set out to market regularly. Not so the 'distress surplus'. It emerged from the compulsions to which poor and middle peasants, but especially poor peasants, were prey:

These pressures arise from certain money obligations of the farmer like land revenue, rent and debt service and the need to purchase such necessities of life as salt, kerosene and cloth. They derive their onerous character from the poverty of the farmer and the institutional set-up in which he operates. His weaker economic position is turned to their own advantage by the trading-moneylending community and social considerations compel him to incur expenses on marriage and other ceremonies which in many cases are out of all proportion to his income earning capacities. And once he falls into the clutches of the moneylender it becomes difficult for him to get out of them, so that his debt obligations become a continuing source of pressure to acquire more cash, through a 'distress sale' of his own produce. ([94], p. 36.)

Among the middle peasantry these compulsions ease and the proportion marketed falls.

Now this distress-surplus is less desirable for the industrializer than might appear at first blush. Firstly, a portion – perhaps a sizeable portion, though we do not know precisely how much – of the gross marketed surplus found its way back to the peasants who marketed it 'in distress'. This could happen in different sets of circumstances. Thus, 'in many areas . . . the burden of debt on the average cultivator compelled him to sell the larger part of the crop at harvest and reborrow in grain or cash for domestic consumption later in the year.' ([29], p. 243.) The poor peasant perhaps produced and sold foodgrains, needed the buy-back in order to survive, probably paid more for it than he received originally, and would get into debt in order to obtain it. He might also have financed the purchase through money wages earned by supplying his labour to other peasants (or earned, even, in non-agricultural pursuits) or through remittances sent from the city ([17]), p. 190). Again, as pointed out by Dandeker ([17], pp. 189–90), he might have sold commercial crops and bought foodgrains. Whatever the circumstances, the contribution of this particular kind of exploitation to the net marketed surplus was limited. It benefited the landlord, the moneylender and the trader, but did not necessarily serve to shift food to urban consumers.

Secondly, the nature of the 'distress surplus' was such that it created the possibility of perverse response to price movements. If one half of the marketed surplus were 'normal' and the other half responded perversely to price changes then any price policy designed to induce a larger marketed surplus would run into difficulties.[1]

VI. Differing Possibilities for Changing the Agrarian Structure and their Implications for the Marketed Surplus

1. *Collectivization*

One response to the very unsatisfactory agrarian structure described is that of the socialist countries, especially the Soviet Union and China: collectivization. It is, indeed, the case that: 'It has been the socialist view that a pre-industrial society could not mobilize its surplus effectively without collectivisation of peasant farming. Only then could prices of agriculture be reduced relatively for the benefit of industrial investment' ([53], p. 263).

That is to say, one of the primary aims of collectivization is to ensure that the absolute size of the marketed surplus rises and the flow to the cities and to export markets is smooth, and that the terms of the transfer are in industry's favour. There is no doubt that in the Soviet Union this aim was served, even when agricultural output was stagnant or falling [62], though whether the accompanying brutality was 'necessary' is another matter. There is equally little doubt that the motivation behind Chinese collectivization was similar (see, for example, [139]), and that probably the aim has been realized, though we await a full analysis of the Chinese experience.

However desirable in principle, collectivization has never been a possibility in India – politically, ideologically or administra-

1. This possibility has been suggested, also, by Mathur and Ezekiel [88], and by Khatkhate [63], while it has been questioned, though not wholly rejected, by Dandekar [17] and denied by Khusro [68] – all on *a priori* grounds. Empirical work has tended to be aggregative in nature and has not rejected satisfactorily the possibility of perverse response by poor peasants (the evidence is surveyed by Bhagwati and Chakravarty in [7], pp. 32–8: see [72], [73], [74], [75], [86], [96], [97], [106]). One econometric study, at least, by Krishnan [75], lends substantial support to the distress sales/perversity hypothesis.

tively. It would, of course, require a thoroughgoing political revolution, which India has never had.

2. *Capitalist Agriculture*

Another possibility is to actively encourage the development of capitalist agriculture and to secure its growth as the dominant mode of production. We might call this the British-Western European-North American model. Pre-capitalist forms of exploitation, like sharecropping, would be swept away and sections of the landlord class or of the rich peasant class, or both, would emerge as capitalist farmers. Its characteristics would include, obviously, private ownership of the means of production (land and capital); the employment of free wage labour on a regular basis as an integral part of the production process; production pursued not for subsistence but for the market, to earn profit (i.e. a very high degree of commercialization and monetization); concentration of ownership, the eradication of inefficiencies like fragmentation, and a tendency to larger holdings; a development in the forces of production towards mechanization; and systematic capital accumulation. A land reform programme might help in clearing the ground for such a development, but an appropriate technology with large inherent profit possibilities would have to be available.

Capitalist agriculture would have certain apparently desirable repercussions with regard to the marketed surplus, since it is geared to the production of regular surpluses of food and raw materials for urban and export markets. In principle the flow of marketed surplus would be continuous and its quantity would rise in response to effective demand. Yet the problem of the terms of trade would remain. The free play of the market would not by any means guarantee that they would favour industry; if an attempt were made to rig them, by one means or another, the result might even be a decline in marketed surplus (if the move against agriculture were too great); and if, indeed, capitalist agriculture did grow on any scale, a powerful pressure group would develop, which, while keen to see the growth of agricultural output and a steady rise in marketed surplus, would also press for terms of trade favourable to agriculture.

3. *Meiji Japan*

Another possible institutional form is one resembling that prevalent in Meiji Japan. This was not capitalist agriculture, but to a large extent family-based agriculture characterized by smallholdings, tenancy, no mechanization and improving landlords. Rents were high and the rent burden actually rose, while the marketed surplus flowed to the city and the terms of trade remained remarkably steady. The Japanese landlord class was an unusual one, with its frugality, its interest in the industrial sector, its leadership in developing and disseminating new agricultural practices, and its alliance with the urban bourgeoisie. ([23]; [24]; [98]; [92], Chapter V especially Section 3.)

Without such a peculiar landlord class the system in Meiji Japan would not have worked to sustain industrialization in the manner that it did. India, most certainly in 1947 and equally certainly since then, has not had such a landlord class, and in its absence, the Japanese model had little or no applicability.

4. *Family-Based, Owner-Occupiers*

The final serious broad possibility that we might consider is the John Stuart Mill–Doreen Warriner–Michael Lipton vision of family-based, owner-occupied smallholdings ([84]; [90], Book I, Chap. 9 and Book II, Chaps. 6 and 7; [142], Part I, esp. pp. 30–7). Re-distribute land in smallish parcels, remove the shackles of rent and sharecropping, supply ancillary supporting services, and, with the missing incentives provided, growth and social justice will come.

But what of the marketed surplus? There seems little doubt that in the unlikely event of such a change, even if agricultural output were to increase, the marketed surplus would fall. The poor peasant would presumably use the newly acquired land for subsistence farming, and would increase his self-consumption. Equally certainly, it would be very difficult to manipulate the terms of trade in favour of the urban sector to any dramatic extent: the initial response would be a reduction in the marketed surplus, and eventually there might even be a fall in the sown area.

VII. India's Proposed Land Reform and its Implications

With the aforementioned background in mind we can turn to India's proposed land reform programme and consider its implications, intended and unintended, for the marketed surplus. This is a useful exercise since it allows us to set one major aim of planning in India, industrialization, beside another, land reform, and ask whether there was any consistency between the two.

In very brief compass, the features of India's land reform programme were as follows. First and foremost it was decided to abolish the great intermediaries between the government and the cultivator, the *zamindars* and *jagirdars*, and so destroy the semi-feudal order which persisted over vast tracts of the country. The principle of land-to-the-tiller was enunciated, according to which as many cultivators as possible were to be owner-occupiers. Where this was not possible, tenancy was to be controlled and rendered fair: sharecropping would be eradicated, rents would be set at a just level, tenure would be secure. Land should be redistributed and there should be a ceiling on the size of holdings. Co-operative farming was to be encouraged, especially among those with 'uneconomic holdings', and fragmentation of holdings was to be swept away by consolidation ([1], [43], Chap. 12, [67], [136], [142], Chap. 6.)

Now, to judge from the various key documents in which statements of the proposed land reform programme are made ([1], [43], Chap. 12) the basic drive behind it had nothing whatsoever to do with the 'imperatives of industrialization', or, in particular, with the likely flow and terms of transfer of the marketed surplus. The agrarian structure was to be changed and semi-feudal relations abolished, partly to serve the ends of social justice: social justice is a prominent and recurring theme. On the other hand there was the belief – an article of faith – that if the disincentives associated with sharecropping, high rents, insecure tenure, minute and fragmented holdings, could be extirpated, the springs of growth would be uncovered. The ideology of land reform was that the large landlords were to be dispossessed and *all* peasants – rich, middle and poor – were to be the beneficiaries, equipped by the programme to secure growth. There is nowhere an apprehension that even if growth were to be secured the marketed surplus might, nonetheless, remain obdurately low, or that the terms of trade might be persistently unfavourable to industry.

There were, of course, definite latent implications for the marketed surplus in the land reform programme, and of these I shall examine three: (1) the possible development of capitalist agriculture; (2) the possible effects of ceiling legislation; and (3) the possible results of co-operative agriculture.

1. *The Possible Development of Capitalist Agriculture*

Some writers have seen in the framing of the land reform programme the dim intention of encouraging the development of capitalist agriculture ([11], pp. 20–1; [51], pp. 9–10), the implication being that some regard for the marketed surplus was, after all, present. The growth of capitalist agriculture, it is argued, was to arise from the abolition of the great intermediaries. The large landlords would be deprived of most of their land and, therefore, of their source of income and status; yet they would keep enough land to farm on a large scale (by Indian standards), and compensation would be sufficient to allow them to invest in the land in a substantial way; and they, or at least a significant number of them, would take to farming for profit in order to maintain previous living standards, and would become capitalist farmers.

But, whatever the actual results of the abolition of intermediaries there is no evidence to support the argument that the intention was to encourage the development of capitalist agriculture in India. To argue otherwise is to impute to the framers of the land reform programme a Machiavellian cunning and a foresight that they did not possess. It is to misconstrue their motives. They possessed no urban bias. Their concern was, assuredly, social justice and the needs of agriculture, however great the gap between intention and achievement.

2. *The Possible Effects of Ceiling Legislation*

A line of thought did emerge among Indian economists concerning ceiling legislation and its effects upon the marketed surplus. It was argued that redistribution might have an adverse effect upon production and hence reduce the flow of marketed surplus, and that even if it raised production it would lead to a decline in marketed surplus, 'for small farmers tend to retain a larger proportion of their produce for self-consumption than large farmers' ([71], p. 310; see also [56], pp. 28–9, 64, 68–9, 74, 116).

The argument needs some care. It is unlikely, firstly, that redistribution would lead to a fall in output. It would probably lead to a rise. We have, after all, the unequivocal findings of the Farm Management Surveys that output per acre increases as size of holding falls. There is nothing to suggest that smaller average holdings, consequent upon redistribution, would not imply a rise in output. We also have Narain's demonstration that poor peasants on the smallest holdings market a larger proportion of their output than middle peasants and, even, than some of the smaller rich peasants. These findings gave rise to rather incautious statements and unwarranted inferences. For example, it was asserted that they 'lay at rest the ghost constantly raised in connection with land ceilings, namely, that a reduction in the size of larger holdings will automatically reduce both agricultural production and agricultural disposals in India' (V.K.R.V. Rao in his foreword to [94], p. vi). But, as we have seen, these same poor peasants buy back a not insignificant proportion of the gross marketed surplus, so that the important quantity, the net marketed surplus, might fall after all, notwithstanding a rise in output and even a rise in the gross marketed surplus. No ghost is laid at rest. Indeed, if the feudalistic compulsions of unreformed agrarian society were removed (i.e. if all the elements in the land reform programme were successfully implemented), the gross marketed surplus would also itself fall, insofar as the 'distress surplus' arises partly from these compulsions. Poor peasants would at once eat more and better, the gross and net marketed surpluses would converge, and the services of an exorcist would be even more necessary than previously. Such a reform expresses rural bias with a vengeance.

It would, of course, be theoretically possible to generate fresh compulsions via agricultural taxation. In a nation of 600,000 villages within a federal polity, like India, in which agricultural taxation remained the preserve of individual state governments, the possibility of legislation let alone implementation, would be small.

3. *The Possible Results of Co-operative Agriculture*

In the original Report of the Congress Agrarian Reforms Committee (the Kumarappa Committee) the basic notion seems to have been 'compulsory co-operative joint farming for cultivators whose holdings are below the basic size and who form about 40 to 50 per cent of Indian cultivators' ([1], p. 50).

But nothing is defined, criteria are never mentioned, and the whole idea is surrounded by a cloud of vagueness. However, had such schemes ever got off the ground, in the Indian context, the reaction of poor peasants would surely have been to eat more and market less.

Another concept of co-operative farming ([142], pp. 175 *et passim*) seems to have been in part stimulated by the Report of the Indian Delegation to China of 1956, which expressed admiration for collectivization ([48]). In 1959, at Nagpur, Congress resolved that co-operative joint farming should be the future pattern of agrarian society. This seems to have arisen from a desire to see a dramatic increase in agricultural production and an increased flow of surplus to the cities. Significantly, after the initial flutter of excitement this notion of co-operative farming was quietly dropped. It is not mentioned in the Third or Fourth Five Year Plan documents ([45], [46], [47]; for a detailed account of the precise statements on co-operative farming in the plan documents see [16]). To have persisted with such a proposal in the circumstances prevailing in India would have been absurd. Nonetheless, these are the only Indian proposals for land reform which manifest concern for the 'imperatives of industrialization'.

VIII. Land Reform and India's Changing Agrarian Structure

The assumptions and implications of India's *proposed* land reform programme are interesting in that they demonstrate clearly the absence of 'urban bias'. The ideology of land reform was geared to the interests of the rural sector, and land reform, in its promise to disinherit the large feudal interests and benefit *all* sections of the peasantry (even, perhaps, landless labourers) seemed, momentarily at least, to abstract from the differentiation and opposition of interests which existed among the peasantry. As pointed out by Joshi, ([61], p. 7), this alliance had been a feature of strategy in the struggle for independence and winning political power, and it became part of the strategy of retaining and legitimizing power. More interesting and more important for our purposes, however, are the actual effects of the land reform programme as implemented, upon the agrarian structure, and the influence of the changed agrarian structure upon the marketed surplus.

Land reform legislation and its effects have proceeded in three broad phases in India since Independence. In the late 1940s and early 1950s the abolition of the great *zamindar* and *jagirdar* intermediaries was the central activity, while some attempt at regulation of tenancy was also made; thereafter from the 1950s onwards, starting in Western India and spreading thence to other parts of the country eradication of tenancy, and especially of the most backward tenancy form, sharecropping, was attempted; and currently redistribution of land is the apparent major objective ([138]). In the earlier periods ceiling legislation was passed slowly and reluctantly, in the different state legislatures, with a wide array of built-in loopholes, so that the 'net benefit of ceilings legislation seemed in the end to be negligible' ([67], p. 199, see also pp. 196–8; [136], pp. 151–4; [142], pp. 170–3). Of these earlier periods it has been observed that 'all in all, an excellent opportunity for acquiring surplus lands . . . appears to have been lost for ever' ([67], p. 199). The validity of this observation is borne out by the recent undermining of the proposal for a ten to eighteen acre ceiling per family, under pressure from the well-organized rich peasant lobby ([12], [13], [14], [26], [124], [125]). The present configuration of political forces in India effectively precludes redistribution: it is a configuration which derives from the agrarian structure which land reform, as implemented, has helped create.

The abolition of semi-feudal intermediaries was broadly successful. Despite all the delaying tactics and the devices to retain more land than the law allowed for 'personal cultivation', the largest feudal landlords – the *zamindars* and *jagirdars*, the absentee and non-cultivating landlords who had been the allies of the British in British India and the bulwark of the princes in Princely India – received a blow from which they could never recover. As Daniel Thorner noted: 'India's older agrarian order is on the way out' ([127], p. 84). This was true ([67], pp. 186–9; [64]; [61]) of the *zamindari* and *jagirdari* areas, and from among the hitherto absentee landlords in those areas a small group emerged which was ripe for transformation into capitalist farmers ([67], p. 189, [61], p. 42). The medium to smaller landlords, who were often resident and sometimes cultivating, and common in *ryotwari* areas, received no such mortal blow. Their survival was assured, but on a rather different basis. The attempt to abolish tenancy was unsuccessful and the smaller landlords were able to devise new forms of tenancy which successfully evaded the law ([137], [138], [61], pp. 28–33). However, despite their ultimate lack of success, one effect of the attempts at tenancy abolition was to encourage non-cultivating smaller and medium landlords to become direct cultivators. Here was another, larger group within the landlord class – this time the beneficiary, to a certain extent, of the land reform legislation ([61], pp. 33–5) – which would, if conditions were right, take to capitalist farming.

By far the greatest beneficiaries of land reform, however, have been the rich peasants who have been stabilized as independent proprietors, and whose 'rise as the new dominant class in the emerging agrarian structure' land reform has helped bring about ([61, p. 22]). Legislation to regulate tenancy 'sought to extend protection not to all classes of tenants, but to certain specified sections belonging to the upper layers of the tenantry' ([61], pp. 17, see also 28–38, [64]). There was an increase in more purely commercial, as opposed to feudal tenancy, and a rise in the amount of land rented in by rich peasants, who gained control of a far larger proportion of the tenanted area ([61], pp. 35,

38, 42–3; [137]). These tendencies have been rather more marked in *ryotwari* than in *zamindari* and *jagirdari* areas. The kulaks were well on the way to becoming masters of the Indian countryside. Political and social power has shifted from the old-style landed gentry to the rich peasants, and rich peasants have shown themselves capable of exercising political power not only in the village but also at the level of district, state and centre (see [61] *passim*; [5] Chap. IV and V, [111], pp. 71–4 and 195–8).

Poor and middle peasants and landless labourers, however, have gained very little from land reform. In the earlier years there was a mass eviction of tenants, when fear of the future land reform was strong and efforts were made to secure as much land for personal cultivation as possible ([61], pp. 29–33 [64], [67], [136]). But, in any case, sharecropping continued to exist on an extensive scale, while new and more insidious forms of 'disguised tenancies' began to emerge: tenants-at-will who hold their tenancies as sharecroppers under illegal, verbal agreements and on even more insecure terms than in the past ([18], [22], [61] pp. 31–2, [78], [137], [138]).

Land reform, then, has been a potent force making for the disintegration of the traditional agrarian structure. It has brought about the demise of the old feudal landlords; but, at the same time, it has ensured the continued and strengthened existence of medium and small landlords, though on a rather different basis than hitherto, and its most significant legacy has been to increase substantially the differentiation of the peasantry in many areas of India. Thus, until the mid 1960s land reform was probably 'one of the major impulses for agrarian change' ([61], p. 43) in India, but this change did not represent a shift from a pre-capitalist to a capitalist mode of production in the Indian countryside. Those writers who implied this to be so in the 1950s and 1960s (for example, [6], [11], [51], [52], [70], [129]) were premature in their judgement. However, commodity production and commercialization did penetrate larger areas of Indian agriculture, and land reform did prepare the ground for capitalism by creating social groups – within the landlord class, but mostly in the form of a greatly strengthened rich peasant class – which, given the appropriate technology and substantial possibilities for profit, would respond. The meaning of that response, in the circumstances surrounding the so-called 'green revolution', is well illustrated in D. P. Chaudhri's contribution to this volume (see also my article, [8]).

IX. Terms of Trade and the Marketed Surplus, to the mid 1960s

It has been shown that between 1951–2 and 1965–6, when overall agricultural production grew at a compound rate of 2·7 per cent per annum, the overall net marketed surplus produced by Indian agriculture grew at a rate of 2·9 per cent per annum, rising from 39 per cent to 44 per cent of total agricultural output ([123], especially pp. 98–9). This is hardly spectacular at a time when rapid industrialization is being sought, and the trend is certainly not consonant with the 'imperatives of industrialization'. Growth of the net marketed surplus at a rate somewhat in excess of 5 per cent per annum, double the rate actually achieved, would have been more in keeping with the needs of the industrial sector ([9], [112], [113]).

Moreover, if we disaggregate the net marketed surplus into its component parts, the implications for industrial growth become even bleaker. A study of the net marketed surplus of cereals in the Indian economy – and we recall food's crucial role in the industrialization process – between 1952–3 and 1964–5 reveals that while cereal output grew at 2·7 per cent per annum the amount transferred to the non-agricultural sector showed only a small increase, and the marketed surplus as a proportion of the output of cereals exhibited a definite though mild downward tendency ([3], especially pp. 104–6). If there has been 'urban bias' in Indian planning it has proved singularly ineffective in influencing the flow of marketed surplus. The rate of growth of commercial (i.e. non-food) crops has been higher than that of food – for example, between 1952–3 and 1961–2 foodgrain production rose by 2·5 per cent per annum and non-foodgrain by 3·9 per cent ([39], p. 38) and this trend has continued – the marketed surplus of such crops is significantly higher than that of food crops, and this has given an upward bias to the overall net marketed surplus. The growth of commercial crops includes very substantial rises in sugar-cane, for example, which increased at a rate of 8·6 per cent per annum between 1952–3 and 1961–2, ([39], p. 40). Some of this is exported, but the most reliable authority tells us that export prospects are bleak ([120], p. 227). For the industrializer foodgrains are infinitely preferable.

If we turn to the intersectoral term of trade, we find an apparent controversy over the direction in which they have moved during most of the period we are examining. One school of thought argues that over the period in question the terms of trade have moved against agriculture, and that this is one reason for the failure of agricultural output, and, by extension, of the marketed surplus, to rise ([81], pp. 101–7, [87], [91]). A weaker variant of this argument is that P.L. 480 food imports have been used to depress urban food prices and so have prevented the terms of trade moving as far in agriculture's favour as they would otherwise have done ([2], [87], [104]). The first version of the argument was subjected to critical scrutiny by Dantwala ([20]) and shown to have little or no basis in fact. The second version is valid, but its validity is a qualified one. P.L. 480 imports, rather than preventing a shift in the terms of trade towards agriculture, have merely moderated the degree of that shift.

Dantwala has pointed out that if we examine 1952–3, the base-year for most of the statements about movements in the intersectoral terms of trade, we find that 'cereal prices were not only four and one-half times higher than the pre-war prices, they were also relatively higher than the prices of manufactured articles, broadly indicating favourable terms for agriculture' ([20], p. 4). At that point in time, as plans for an all-out industrialization strategy were being made, Ricardian apprehensions with regard to the industrial sector would have been in order. The experience of the years since then shows these apprehensions to have been justified: urban bias has not succeeded in tilting the terms of trade in favour of the cities. Recent empirical studies of the years 1951–2 to 1965–6 show clearly that since about 1955–56, after the fortuitously good harvests of the First Plan, the inter-sectoral terms of trade have clearly moved in favour of agriculture. All prices have been rising, but those received by agriculture have risen faster than those paid by agriculture. The net barter terms of trade[1] have shifted in favour of agriculture, and the income terms of trade have done so to a substantial degree. ([123], pp. 96–100. See also [135], and the earlier study, [65].)

These movements in the marketed surplus and in the inter-sectoral terms of trade must be understood in relation to the changing agrarian structure produced by land reform. One would expect the disappointing performance of output and of marketed surplus (disappointing in relation to the 'imperatives of industrial-

1. The ratio of prices paid by agriculture to prices received by agriculture: i.e. where N represents the net barter terms of trade, P_X the price index of goods sold by agriculture and P_M the price index of goods purchased by agriculture, $N=P_X/P_M$. 'Income terms of trade' are the net barter terms of trade corrected for changes in export volume: i.e. where I represents the income terms of trade and Q_X the export volume index, $I=N.Q_X$.

ization') from a mode of production ripe for capitalist transformation, but still essentially pre-capitalist in nature. Until the mid 1960s the technology available to Indian agriculture was not yet capable of generating growth at a rate of over 5 per cent per annum, but the existing technology could certainly have been used to far greater effect. It was not so used because the 'progressive'[1] elements in the Indian countryside – sections of the landlord class and rich peasants – brought forth from the womb of the old order by land reform were as yet insufficiently developed. They were ready, but not in sufficient numbers, to counteract, for example, the extensive sharecropping which land reform had not eradicated. Sharecropping deadens incentives and prevents growth in agriculture by discouraging the application of the new bought inputs which will yield growth – an observation which is not inconsistent, in the static situation, with our evidence that a sharecropping poor péasant achieves a higher output per acre than a non-sharecropping rich peasant. At the same time, sharecropping is one of the semi-feudal compulsions which lead to the marketing of a 'distress surplus' by poor peasants – a surplus which adds to gross marketed surplus, but not necessarily, in any large degree, to net marketed surplus. A development of the forces of production (a new technology) and attendant large profit possibilities were the catalysts necessary to complete the work started by land reform, and they will eventually lead to the demise of the sharecropper and the tendency of capitalism to become the dominant form in Indian agriculture. I have argued elsewhere that these changes are inherent in the so-called 'green revolution' ([8]), though, we must stress, they will be fraught with antagonistic contradictions.

The underlying demand and supply conditions would have been enough to shift the terms of trade in favour of agriculture. But they have been reinforced through the exercise of political power by rich peasants and small and medium landlords.

1. I should make clear what I mean by 'progressive'. In a not dissimilar context Christopher Hill makes the point very well: 'The word *progressive* as used in this essay does not necessarily imply moral approval. It means simply that the tendency or social group so described contributed to the expansion of the wealth of the community. The "progressive" (i.e. capitalist) farming of the sixteenth and seventeenth centuries led to expropriation of many small peasants; the wealth produced by the new methods came into the hands of a small group of profiteers; the village community was broken up. Nevertheless, more wealth *was* produced: the alternative would have been economic stagnation or retrogression' ([55] p. 5).

Recently, in 1967, the Agricultural Prices Commission, which was set up to advise the government on agricultural prices and staffed by men like Dharm Narain and V. S. Vyas, who could hardly be described as hostile to the interests of agriculture, had its advice unceremoniously ignored by the government: procurement prices were set 12 per cent to 15 per cent higher than the Commission suggested ([21]). The late D. R. Gadgil (then Deputy Chairman of the Planning Commission) warned: 'we have already reached the brink, and more playing with food prices would make the task of economic recovery in the near future almost impossible' (quoted in [21], p. 1945).

His warning had no impact at all. Again, in 1970 the recommendation of the Agricultural Prices Commission that the procurement price of wheat be reduced was set aside by the Chief Ministers ([79]). And this was repeated in April 1972, when the Chief Ministers of Punjab, Haryana and U.P. once more had their way on the same issue ([13], [14], [26]). 'Urban bias' there may have been, but 'rural bias' won out. It is to be stressed that rural bias operates in favour of rich peasants, and small and medium landlords. It is they who benefit from favourable terms of trade and high procurement prices. Poor peasants and landless labourers have to buy foodgrains and they suffer, therefore, along with urban consumers, from high food prices ([40], [117]).

Let us revert, finally, to the quotation from Dantwala which stands at the beginning of this essay. In a nutshell, my position as an unequivocal industrializer is that the question posed by Dantwala was never uppermost in the minds of those who framed India's land reform programme – they were interested in other things. And, in answer to Dantwala's question, I take the position that, to date, the agrarian structure which has emerged cannot be relied upon for the purposes of rapid growth. The coming of capitalism would go part of the way towards solving the problem, but only part of the way. The problem of the terms of trade would remain. Indeed, the most important contradiction in the Indian socio-economic system in coming decades is that posed by an urban bourgeoisie intent upon industrialization but frustrated by a strong and increasingly powerful class of rich peasants and small and medium landlords, on their way to becoming capitalists and exercising growing political power. If there was ever an alliance between these two classes, it could only temporarily conceal the inherent conflict of interests between them, and the manner in which that conflict of interests is resolved will determine much in the course of India's future.

References

1 All-India Congress Committee, *Report of the Congress Agrarian Reforms Committee*, New Delhi, 1951.

2 Bardhan, Kalpana, 'Do Foodgrain Imports Affect Production?', *Economic and Political Weekly*, **1**, 13, 12 November 1966, pp. 541–5.

3 Bardhan, Pranab Kumar and Kalpana Bardhan, 'Problem of Marketed Surplus of Cereals', *Economic and Political Weekly*, **4**, 26, 28 June 1969, pp. A–103–A–110.

4 Beaglehole, T. H., *Thomas Munro and the Development of Administrative Policy in Madras: 1792–1818*, Cambridge University Press, 1966.

5 Béteille, André, *Caste, Class and Power*, Berkeley, 1965.

6 Bettelheim, Charles, *India Independent*, MacGibbon and Kee, London, 1968.

7 Bhagwati, Jagdish N. and Sukhamoy Chakravarty, 'Contributions to Indian Economic Analysis: A Survey', *American Economic Review*, **59**, 4, Part 2, Supplement, September 1969, pp. 1–73.

8 Byres, T. J., 'The Dialectic of India's Green Revolution', *South Asian Review*, **5**, 2, January 1972, pp. 99–116.

9 Byres, T. J., 'Industrialization, the Peasantry and the Economic Debate in Post-Independence India', *Towards the Socialist Transformation of the Indian Economy* (ed. A. V. Bhuleshkar), Jawaharlal Nehru Memorial Volume 2, Popular Prakashan, Bombay, 1972.

10 Byres, T. J. (ed.), *The Logic of Peasant Agriculture*, Frank Cass, London, forthcoming.

11 Communist Party of India, *Developments in the Agrarian Economy*, mimeo, New Delhi, 1964.

12 Correspondent, '18 Acres Is Too High', *Economic and Political Weekly*, **7**, 19, 6 May 1972, p. 908.

13 Correspondent, 'Land Ceiling and the New Farm Entrepreneur', *Economic and Political Weekly*, **7**, 19, 6 May 1972, pp. 915–16.

14 Correspondent, 'Land Ceiling Talked Out', *Economic and Political Weekly*, **7**, 20, 13 May 1972, p. 963.

15 Dandekar, V. M., 'A Review of the Land Reform Studies Sponsored by the Research Programmes Committee of the Planning Commission', *Artha Vijnana*, **4**, 4, December 1962, pp. 291–330.

16 Dandekar, V. M., 'From Agrarian Reorganization To Land Reform', *Artha Vijnana*, **6**, 1, March 1964, pp. 51–70.

17 Dandekar, V. M., 'Prices, Production and Marketed Surplus of

Foodgrains', *Indian Journal of Agricultural Economics*, **19**, 3 and 4, July–December 1964, pp. 186–95.

18 Dandekar, V. M. and G. J. Khudanpur, *Working of Bombay Tenancy Act, 1948: Report of Investigation*, Gokhale Institute of Politics and Economics, Poona, 1957.

19 Dantwala, M. L., 'Presidential Address. Agrarian Structure and Economic Development', *Indian Journal of Agricultural Economics*, **16**, 1, January–March 1961, pp. 10–25.

20 Dantwala, M. L., 'Incentives and Disincentives in Indian Agriculture', *Indian Journal of Agricultural Economics*, **22**, 2, April–June 1967, pp. 1–25.

21 Dantwala, M. L., 'Growing Irrelevance of Economics in Planning: Case of Procurement Prices', *Economic and Political Weekly*, **2**, 43, 28 October 1967, pp. 1945–7.

22 Desai, M. B. and R. S. Mehta, 'Abolition of Tenancy Cultivation', *Indian Journal of Agricultural Economics*, **17**, 1, January–March 1962, pp. 127–34.

23 Dore, R. P., 'The Meiji Landlord: Good or Bad?', *Journal of Asian Studies*, **18**, 3, May 1959, pp. 343–55.

24 Dore, R. P., 'Agricultural Improvement in Japan: 1870–1900', *Economic Development and Cultural Change*, **9**, 1, Part II, October 1960, pp. 69–91.

25 Dorner, Peter, *Land Reform and Economic Development*, Penguin, Harmondsworth, 1972.

26 *Economic and Political Weekly*, Editorial, 'The Show Goes On', **7**, 2, 20 May 1972, p. 1001.

27 Frykenberg, Robert Eric, 'Introduction', *Land Control and Social Structure in Indian History* (ed. R. E. Frykenberg), University of Wisconsin Press, 1969.

28 Gadgil, D. R., 'Indian Economic Organization', *Economic Growth: Brazil, India, Japan* (eds. Simon Kuznets, Wilbert E. Moore and Joseph J. Spengler), Duke University Press, 1955, pp. 448–63.

29 Gadgil, D. R., *The Industrial Evolution of India in Recent Times, 1860–1939*, O.U.P., London, 1971.

30 Ghose, R. L. M., M. B. Ghatge and V. Subrahmanyan (eds.), *Rice in India*, Indian Council of Agricultural Research, New Delhi, revised edition 1960.

31 Ghosh, A., 'The Impact of Commercial Growth on Agricultural Tenure Systems in India', *The Manchester School*, **23**, 2, May 1955, pp. 184–90.

32 Government of India, Ministry of Food and Agriculture, *Studies in Economics of Farm Management in Bombay State. Combined Report for the years 1954–5 to 1956–7*, Delhi, 1963.

33 Government of India, Ministry of Food and Agriculture, *Studies* *in Economics of Farm Management in Madras. Annual Reports, 1954–5, 1955–6, 1956–7*, Delhi, 1963.

34 Government of India, Ministry of Food and Agriculture, *Studies in Economics of Farm Management in Madhya Pradesh. Combined Report, 1954–5 to 1956–7*, Delhi, 1963.

35 Government of India, Ministry of Food and Agriculture, *Studies in Economics of Farm Management in the Punjab. Combined Report, 1954–5 to 1956–7*, Delhi, 1963.

36 Government of India, Ministry of Food and Agriculture, *Studies in Economics of Farm Management in U.P. Combined Report for the years 1954–5 to 1956–7*, Delhi, 1963.

37 Government of India, Ministry of Food and Agriculture, *Studies in Economics of Farm Management in West Bengal. Combined Report for 1954–5 to 1956–7*, Delhi, 1963.

38 Government of India, Ministry of Food and Agriculture, *Agricultural Statistics of Re-Organized States*, New Delhi, 1956.

39 Government of India, Ministry of Food and Agriculture, *Growth Rates in Agriculture*, mimeo. New Delhi, 1964.

40 Government of India, Ministry of Food, Agriculture, Community Development and Co-operation, *Report of the Agricultural Prices Commission on Price Policy for Kharif Cereals for 1968–9 Season*, New Delhi, September 1968.

41 Government of India, Ministry of Home Affairs: *The Causes and Nature of Current Agrarian Tensions*, mimeo, New Delhi, 1969.

42 Government of India, Ministry of Labour, *Agricultural Labour Enquiry. Volume 1, All India*, Delhi, 1955.

43 Government of India, Planning Commission, *First Five Year Plan*, New Delhi, 1952.

44 Government of India, Planning Commission, *Second Five Year Plan*, New Delhi, 1956.

45 Government of India, Planning Commission, *Third Five Year Plan*, New Delhi, 1961.

46 Government of India, Planning Commission, *Fourth Five Year Plan. A Draft Outline*, New Delhi, 1966.

47 Government of India, Planning Commission, *Fourth Five Year Plan, 1969–74*, New Delhi, 1970.

48 Government of India, Planning Commission, *Report of Indian Delegation to China on Agrarian Co-operatives*, New Delhi, 1957.

49 Grist, D. H., *Rice*, Longman, London, 1965.

50 Guha, Ranajit, *A Rule of Property for Bengal*, Mouton, Paris, 1963.

51 Gupta, S. C., 'Some Aspects of Indian Agriculture', *Enquiry*, **6**, pp. 3–53.

52 Gupta, S. C., 'New Trends of Growth', *Seminar*, **38**, October 1962, pp. 15–29.
53 Gurley, John G., and E. S. Shaw, 'Financial Structure and Economic Development', *Economic Development and Cultural Change*, **15**, 3, April 1967, pp. 257–68.
54 Habib, Irfan, *The Agrarian System of Mughal India (1556–1707)*, Asia Publishing House, London, 1963.
55 Hill, Christopher, *The English Revolution, 1640*, Lawrence and Wishart, London, 1970.
56 *Indian Journal of Agricultural Economics*, Conference Number, **16**, 1, January–March 1961, Section 1, 'Problems of Marketable Surplus in Indian Agriculture', pp. 26–121, fifteen papers and Report.
57 Ishikawa, Shigeru, *Economic Development In Asian Perspective*, Kinokuniya Bookstore, Tokyo, 1967.
58 Joshi, P. C., 'Thinking on Agrarian Policy Before Independence,' *Economic and Political Weekly*, **2**, 8, 25 February 1967, pp. 447–56.
59 Joshi, P. C., *A Survey of Research on Land Reforms in India. Part I. General Survey. Major Problems, Approaches and Insights*, Indian Council of Social Science Research, New Delhi, 1971 (mimeo).
60 Joshi, P. C., *A Survey of Research on Land Reforms in India. Part II. Bibliography*, Indian Council of Social Science Research, New Delhi, 1971 (mimeo).
61 Joshi, P. C., 'Land Reform and Agrarian Change in India and Pakistan since 1947', *Studies in Asian Social Development* (eds. P. C. Joshi and Ratna Dutta), Tata McGraw Hill, Delhi, 1972, pp. 3–64.
62 Kahan, Arcadius, 'The Collective Farm System in Russia: Some Aspects of Its Contribution to Soviet Economic Development', *Agriculture in Economic Development* (Carl K. Eicher and Lawrence W. Witt), McGraw Hill, New York, 1964, pp. 251–71.
63 Khatkhate, D. R., 'Some Notes on the Real Effects of Foreign Surplus Disposal in Underdeveloped Economies', *Quarterly Journal of Economics*, **76**, 2, May 1962, pp. 186–96.
64 Khusro, A. M., *Economic and Social Effects of Jagirdari Abolition and Land Reforms in Hyderabad*, Osmania University Press, Hyderabad, 1958.
65 Khusro, A. M., 'Intersectoral Terms of Trade and Price Policy', *Economic Weekly*, **13**, 4–5–6, 4 February 1961, pp. 289–91.
66 Khusro, A. M., *An Analysis of Agricultural Land in India by Size of Holding and Tenure*, Institute of Economic Growth, Delhi 1964 (mimeo).
67 Khusro, A. M., 'Land Reforms since Independence', *Economic*

History of India 1857–1956, (ed. V. B. Singh), Allied Publishers Private, Bombay, 1965, pp. 181–200.

68 Khusro, A. M., 'The Pricing of Food in India', *Quarterly Journal of Economics*, **81**, 2, May 1967, pp. 271–85.

69 Khusro, A. M., 'Farm Size and Land Tenure in India, *Indian Economic Review*, **4** (New Series), 2, October 1969, pp. 123–45.

70 Kotovsky, Grigory, *Agrarian Reforms in India*, People's Publishing House, New Delhi, 1964.

71 Krishna, Raj, 'Agrarian Reform in India: The Debate on Ceilings', *Economic Development and Cultural Change*, **7**, 3, Part 1, April 1959, pp. 302–17.

72 Krishna, Raj, 'A Note on the Elasticity of the Marketable Surplus', *Indian Journal of Agricultural Economics*, **17**, 3, July–September 1962, pp. 79–84.

73 Krishna, Raj, 'The Marketable Surplus Function for a Subsistence Crop: An Analysis with Indian Data', *Economic Weekly*, **17**, 5–6–7, February 1965, pp. 309–20.

74 Krishna, Raj, 'The Marketable Surplus Function for a Subsistence Crop: Reply to Comments', *Economic Weekly*, **17**, 44–5, 6 November 1965, pp. 1665–8.

75 Krishnan, T. N., 'The Marketable Surplus of Foodgrains: Is It Inversely Related to Price?', *Economic Weekly*, **17**, 5–6–7, February 1965, pp. 325–8. Reprinted in *Readings in Indian Agricultural Development* (ed. Pramit Chaudhuri), Allen and Unwin, London, 1972, pp. 99–109.

76 Kumar, Dharma, *Land and Caste in South India*, Cambridge University Press, 1965.

77 Kumar, Ravinder, 'The Rise of the Rich Peasants in Western India', *Soundings in Modern South Asian History* (ed. D. A. Low), Weidenfeld & Nicolson, London, 1968.

78 Ladejinsky, Wolf, *A Study of Tenurial Conditions in Package Districts*, Government of India, Planning Commission, New Delhi, 1965. Reprinted in *Mainstream*, **3**, 28–29–30, 12, 20, 27 March 1965.

79 Laxminarayan, H., 'Doing Without a Food Policy?', *Economic and Political Weekly*, **5**, 24, 13 June 1970, pp. 949–51.

80 Lenin, V. I., *New Data on the Laws Governing the Development of Capitalism in Agriculture*, in *Collected Works*, Volume 22, Progress Publishers, Moscow, 1964.

81 Lipton, Michael, 'Strategy for Agriculture: Urban Bias and Rural Planning', *The Crisis of Indian Planning: economic planning in the 1960s* (eds. Paul Streeten and Michael Lipton), O.U.P., London, 1968, pp. 83–147.

82 Lipton, Michael, 'Should Reasonable Farmers Respond to Price Changes?', *Modern Asian Studies*, **1**, 1, 1966, pp. 95–9.

83 Lipton, Michael, 'Myths of the Rural Sector', *Bulletin* of the Institute of Development Studies, **1**, 4, May 1969, pp. 23–5.

84 Lipton, Michael, 'Towards a Theory of Land Reform', this Volume, Chapter 9.

85 Long, E. J., 'The Economic Basis of Land Reform in Underdeveloped Economies', *Land Economics*, **37**, 2, May 1961, pp. 113–223.

86 Majumdar, I. M., 'Marketable Surplus Function for a Subsistence Crop: Further Comments', *Economic Weekly*, **17**, 20, 15 May 1965, pp. 820–2.

87 Mason, E. S., *Economic Development in India and Pakistan*, Center for International Affairs, Harvard, 1966.

88 Mathur, P. N. and H. Ezekiel, 'Marketable Surplus of Food and Price Fluctuations in a Developing Economy, *Kyklos*, **14**, 1961, pp. 396–408.

89 Menon, V. S., 'Role of Fertilizers in Crop Production in India', *Studies in Agricultural Economics*, Volume II, Government of India, Ministry of Food and Agriculture, Delhi, 1956, pp. 61–75.

90 Mill, John Stuart, *Principles of Political Economy*, Longman, London, 1891.

91 Millikan, M., 'India in Transition: Economic Development', *Foreign Affairs*, **46**, 3, April 1968, pp. 531–47.

92 Moore, Barrington, *Social Origins of Dictatorship and Democracy*, Penguin, Harmondsworth, 1969.

93 Myrdal, Gunnar, *Asian Drama, An Enquiry into the Poverty of Nations*, 3 Volumes, Allen Lane, The Penguin Press, London, 1968.

94 Narain, Dharm, *Distribution of the Marketed Surplus of Agricultural Produce by Size-Level of Holding in India, 1950–51*, Asia Publishing House, Bombay, 1961.

95 Narain, Dharm and Joshi, P. C., 'Magnitude of Agricultural Tenancy', *Economic and Political Weekly*, **4**, 39, 27 September 1969, pp. A 139–A 142.

96 Nowshirvani, V. F., 'A Note on the Fixed Cash Requirement Theory of Marketed Surplus in Subsistence Agriculture', *Kyklos*, **20**, 3, 1967, pp. 772–3.

97 Nowshirvani, V. F., 'A Note on the Elasticity of the Marketable Surplus – A Comment', *Indian Journal of Agricultural Economics*, **22**, 1, January–March 1967, pp. 110–14.

98 Ohkawa, Kazushi and Rosovsky, Henry, 'The Role of Agriculture in Modern Japanese Economic Development', *Economic Development and Cultural Change*, **9**, 1, Part II, October 1960, pp. 43–68.

Reprinted in *Agriculture in Economic Development* (Carl K. Eicher and Lawrence W. Witt), McGraw Hill, New York, 1964, pp. 45–69.

99 Patel, Surendra J., *Agricultural Labourers in Modern India and Pakistan*, Current Book House, Bombay, 1952.

100 Patel, S. J., 'The Distribution of the National Income of India, *Indian Economic Review*, **3**, 1, 1956.

101 Patnaik, Utsa, 'Economics of Farm Size and Farm Scale. Some Assumptions Re-examined', *Economic and Political Weekly*, **7**, 31–3, Special Number, August 1972, pp. 1613–24.

102 Poduval, R. N., 'Economic Development and Marketed Surplus in Agriculture', *Agricultural Situation in India*, August 1958, pp. 409–14.

103 Raj., K. N., *Employment Aspects of Planning in Underdeveloped Economies*, National Bank of Egypt, Cairo, 1957.

104 Raj., K. N., 'Price Behaviour in India, 1949–1966: An Explanatory Hypothesis', *Indian Economic Review*, **1** (New Series), 2, October 1966, pp. 56–77.

105 Raj, K. N., 'Ownership and Distribution of Land', *Indian Economic Review*, **5** (New Series), 1, April 1970, pp. 1–42.

106 Rao, C. H. Hanumantha, 'The Marketable Surplus Function for a Subsistence Crop: Comments, *Economic Weekly*, **17**, 16, 17 April 1965, pp. 677–8.

107 Rao, C. H. Hanumantha, 'Agricultural Growth and Stagnation in India', *Economic Weekly*, **17**, 9, 27 February 1965, pp. 407–11. Reprinted in *Readings in Agricultural Development* (ed. A. M. Khusro), Allied Publishers Private, Bombay, 1968, pp. 88–101.

108 Raup, Philip M., 'The Contribution of Land Reforms to Agricultural Development: An Analytical Framework', *Economic Development and Cultural Change*, **12**, 1, October 1963, pp. 1–21.

109 Raup, Philip M., 'Land Reform and Agricultural Development', in *Agricultural Development and Economic Growth* (eds. Herman M. Southworth and Bruce F. Johnston), Cornell University Press, New York, 1967, pp. 267–314.

110 Reserve Bank of India, *All-India Rural Credit Survey, Volume 2, The General Report*, Bombay, 1954.

111 Rosen, George, *Democracy and Economic Change in India*, University of California Press, Berkeley and Los Angeles, 1966.

112 Rudra, Ashok, 'Agriculture and Industry: Relative Rates of Growth', *Economic Weekly*, **16**, 45, 7 November 1964, pp. 1773–1787.

113 Rudra, Ashok, *Relative Rates of Growth – Agriculture and Industry*, University of Bombay, 1967.

114 Sanyal, S. K., 'Has There Been A Decline in Agricultural

Tenancy?', *Economic and Political Weekly*, **7**, 19, 6 May 1972, pp. 943–5.

115 Sen, A. K. and Verghese, T. C., 'Tenancy and Resource Allocation', *Seminar*, **81**, May 1966, pp. 28–33.

116 Sen, Bhowani, *Evolution of Agrarian Relations in India*, People's Publishing House, New Delhi, 1962.

117 Shetty, S. L., 'Recent Trends in Intersectoral Terms of Trade', *Economic and Political Weekly*, **6**, 25, 19 June 1971, pp. 1235–40.

118 Shukla, Tara, *Capital Formation in Indian Agriculture*, Vora, Bombay, 1965.

119 Singh, Baljit, *Next Step in Village India*, Asia Publishing House, London, 1961.

120 Singh, Manmohan, *India's Export Trends*, Oxford University Press, 1964.

121 Singh, V. B., 'Agrarian Relations in India', *Studies on Developing Countries*, Volume 2, *Agriculture Land Reforms and Economic Development* (ed. Ignacy Sachs), Polish Scientific Publishers, Warsaw, 1964, pp. 29–48.

122 Stokes, Eric, *The English Utilitarians and India*, O.U.P, London, 1963.

123 Thamarajakshi, R., 'Intersectoral Terms of Trade and Marketed Surplus of Agricultural Produce, 1951–2 to 1965–6', *Economic and Political Weekly*, **4**, 26, 28 June 1969, pp. A–91 – A–102.

124 Thapar, Romesh, 'The Ceiling Is the Sky', *Economic and Political Weekly*, **7**, 20, 13 May 1972, pp. 960–1.

125 Thapar, Romesh, 'A Ceiling on Ceilings', *Economic and Political Weekly*, **7**, 2, 20 May 1972, p. 1005.

126 Thorner, Daniel, 'Long-Term Trends of Output in India', *Economic Growth: Brazil, India, Japan* (eds. Simon Kuznets, Wilbert E. Moore and Joseph J. Spengler), Duke University Press, Durham, N.C.: 1955, pp. 103–28.

127 Thorner, Daniel, *The Agrarian Prospect in India*, Delhi University Press, Delhi, 1956.

128 Thorner, Daniel and Alice Thorner, 'Employer-Labourer Relationships in Agriculture', *Indian Journal of Agricultural Economics*, **12**, 2, April–June 1957, pp. 84–96. Reprinted *Land and Labour in India* (Daniel and Alice Thorner), Asia Publishing House, London, 1962.

129 Thorner, Daniel, 'Capitalist Agriculture in India', mimeo, paper delivered at Cambridge Conference on South Asia in 1968.

130 *Times Literary Supplement:* 'Back to Grass Roots', 19 December 1968. Reprinted in *Bulletin* of the Institute of Development Studies, 4 April 1969.

131 United Nations, *Land Reform, Defects in Agrarian Structures as Obstacles to Economic Development*, New York, 1951.

132 United Nations, *Progress in Land Reform*, New York, 1954.

133 United Nations, *Progress in Land Reform. Second Report*, New York, 1956.

134 United Nations, *Progress in Land Reform. Third Report*, New York, 1962.

135 Velayudham, T. K., 'Price Trends During the Three Plan Periods', *Reserve Bank of India Bulletin*, **21**, 6, June 1967, pp. 740–94.

136 Vyas, V. S., 'Land Reforms in India – Review of a Decade', *A Decade of Economic Development and Planning in India* (ed. M. R. Sinha), Asian Studies Press, Bombay 1962, pp. 138–55.

137 Vyas, V. S., 'Tenancy in a Dynamic Setting', *Economic and Political Weekly*, **5**, 6, 27 June 1970, pp. A–73 – A–80.

138 Vyas, V. S., 'Implementation of Tenancy Legislation', *Economic and Political Weekly*, **7**, 34, 19 August 1972, pp. 1721–3.

139 Walker, Kenneth R., 'Collectivization in Retrospect: The "Socialist High Tide" of Autumn 1955 – Spring 1956', *China Quarterly*, **26**, April – June 1966, pp. 1–43.

140 Warriner, Doreen, *Land Reform and Economic Development*, National Bank of Egypt, Cairo, 1955.

141 Warriner, Doreen, *Land Reform and Development in the Middle East*, Royal Institute of International Affairs, London, 1957.

142 Warriner, Doreen, *Land Reform in Principle and Practice*, O.U.P., London, 1969.

Eight

A Note on 'Perverse' Producer Response to Changes in Prices*

Clive Bell

The very word 'perverse' conjures up pejorative notions, and since one particular sort of 'perverse' behaviour – that involving the response of peasant producers to changes in the prices they receive for their outputs and have to pay for their inputs and manufactured consumer goods – is a major bone of contention between Byres and Lipton, it seems desirable to clarify certain aspects of the matter. Intuitively, one would expect a rise in the prices of outputs relative to those of goods purchased to result in producers expanding both output and (rather less certainly in the case of peasant farms) the quantity sold. If they were to do exactly the opposite when prices thus move in their favour, their behaviour could be called 'perverse' to the extent that it is counter-intuitive; but, as we shall see, it need not be irrational. The significance of these 'unnatural' goings-on is that they may underline the reliability of the barter terms of trade as an instrument for altering the level of the marketed surplus in a predictable way. Paradoxically, though it is Byres who broods over the consequences of such a situation, the absence of 'perverse' peasants is far more crucial to the position of those, like Lipton (*infra*, p. 305), who argue that a smallholder agrarian system can still be 'planned' into producing adequate surpluses which are accompanied by improved urban-rural equity by means of suitable price incentives.

The causes of 'perverse' behaviour considered in the literature deal with rather special, though not necessarily unrealistic, situations. Here is a well-worn example: suppose poor peasants with simple tastes have *fixed* annual cash requirements to pay off

* This note was written at the Editor's request, and neither Byres nor Lipton saw it before the manuscript went to the publishers. As many of the readers of this book will not be economists, the exposition takes little for granted.

land revenue and interest on past debts and to buy customary quantities of cloth and kerosene. Then a rise in the prices of agricultural commodities will cause the volume of the marketed surplus to be reduced in the same proportion. Of course, if land revenue is abolished, past debts written off and formerly simple tastes transformed into avid yearnings for less 'basic' industrial consumer goods, then 'perverseness' should disappear. Other examples in this vein can be provided, all featuring what economists term 'awkward' cases, such as inferior goods and the like. But there is no need to resort to these constructs, for as we shall now demonstrate, a 'perversely' behaved marketed surplus can arise from apparently innocent assumptions coupled with orthodox neo-classical analysis. With his reliance on the efficacy of price incentives, Lipton is logically constrained to accept an approach along these lines (though not necessarily our formulation, nor the conclusions, which depend on the correctness of the logic presented here). Byres is far less sanguine about the validity of most things neo-classical (though he should find our conclusions pleasing). The results depend on two vital characteristics of peasant economic behaviour: the fact that the household is both a consumer and producer unit; and the distinction made above (p. 210) between the obligatory and the optional parts of the surplus.

The assumptions required for the analysis are listed below *seriatim*. They are undeniably stringent, but that is all to the good in an attempt to demonstrate that 'perverse' conclusions may still follow from 'well-behaved' postulates. Besides, some of them can be relaxed later.

A1 Peasants produce a single good,* 'food' say, with labour, land and 'fertilizer', which is purchased from the industrial sector. Land and labour are always fully employed, so that the level of food output is determined solely by the quantity of fertilizer used as input.

A2 Some production of food is possible without inputs of fertilizer; thereafter, fertilizer inputs are subject to (smoothly) diminishing returns.

A3 Peasant households have well-behaved utility functions which have as arguments their consumption levels of food and 'textiles' (a manufactured consumer good).

A4 Peasants are price takers, both for purchases of fertilizers and textiles and for sales of food. This means that the ruling

* The introduction of a cash crop, such as jute or cotton, would complicate the analysis without, I think, changing the qualitative nature of the conclusions.

prices for exchange can be set purely by the 'planner', who decrees taxes (or subsidies) on farm purchases and procurement prices for farm sales.*

A5 Peasant households have the same production and utility functions (up to a scalar multiple), even though their land and labour endowments may vary. This assumption enables us to draw an aggregate, well-behaved production function and a set of convex indifference curves for the rural sector as a whole.

A6 Peasants are utility maximizers.

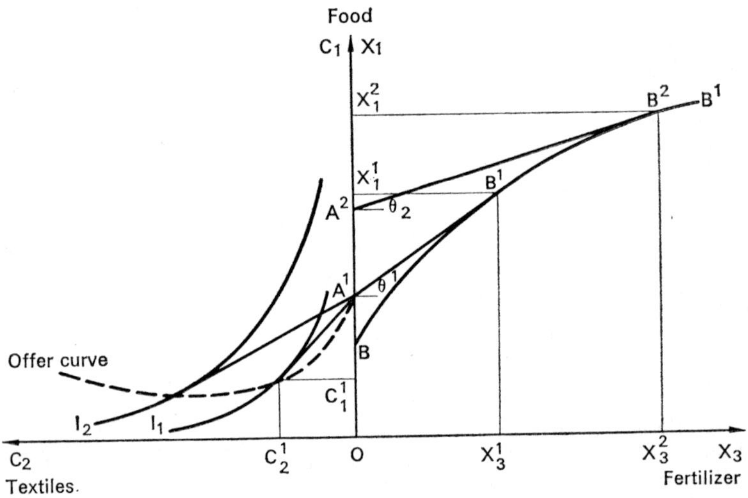

Figure 1

Here, indeed, is an array satisfying the loftiest of orthodox canons. But, formidable though it may appear, the whole structure can be accommodated within the compass of a single diagram for the purposes of answering the question: what will happen to the marketed surplus of food when there are changes in the prices of fertilizer and textiles relative to food?

The right-hand half of Figure 1 shows gross food output (X_1) as a function of fertilizer input (X_3) represented by the curve BB′, where OB is the level of food output when fertilizer input is zero (**A2**). **A6** and **A4** require that X_3 be chosen such that at the corresponding point on BB′, the slope of the curve is equal to the

* Such a *deus ex machina* is all very well for our present purposes, but it should be noted that there is also an industrial sector in the background.

fertilizer-food price ratio (tan θ_1 in Figure 1). Thus X_1 is also determined. If the tangent to BB′ at a point B^1 (say) is projected back to cut the vertical axis at A^1 (say), then $A^1X_1^1$ ($=X_3^1 \tan \theta_1$) is the obligatory surplus – that is, the quantity of food output which must be sold to pay for the optimum input of fertilizer at the ruling fertilizer-food price ratio. The residual, OA^1, is the net output (income) of the sector measured in terms of food.

The left-hand side of the diagram shows the quantities of food (C_2) and textiles (C_1) consumed by rural households along the horizontal and vertical axes, respectively, and a set of convex indifference curves I_1, I_2, . . . After the obligatory surplus has been sold off, leaving a net output (income) of food, some part of the latter will be exchanged for textiles. How much is thus sold depends on the level of net output of food and the ruling textile-food price ratio. **A6** and **A4** demand that C_1 and C_2 be chosen such that the indifference curve passing through (C_1, C_2) is tangential to the price ratio projected from the given level of net output of food. With C_1 thus determined, the optional surplus is simply net output less consumption of food – that is, $A^1C_1^1$ (say). The behaviour of the optional surplus as the price of textiles falls relative to that of food is mapped out by the points of tangency to the set I: made by a ray pivoted at A_1 (say) as it swings progressively NW. This 'offer' curve may well be U-shaped, so that while the optional surplus at first increases as the terms of trade move in agriculture's favour, beyond a certain point, it goes into ('perverse') decline. Whether or not this happens depends, of course, on the characteristics of the indifference curves and hence on the utility functions underlying them.

Although the total surplus is simply the sum of the obligatory and optional surpluses ($A^1X_1^1 + A^1C_1^1 = C_1^1X_1^1$), it is easier analytically, as well as more realistic, to assume that the 'planner' can fix the prices of fertilizer and textiles independently of one another. First, keep the price of fertilizer relative to food (and hence the obligatory surplus) constant, at tan θ_1 (say). Then a fall in the price of textiles relative to food will lead to a rise in the optional (and hence total) surplus provided the offer curve slopes down to the left and OA_1^1 exceeds the subsistence requirements of the sector (if it does not, the surplus will be completely insensitive to changes in the barter terms of trade). Now keep the price of textiles constant and let that of fertilizer fall (the complications begin). A fall in tan θ will cause a rise in X_3, so that the obligatory surplus rises or falls according as the proportionate increase in fertilizer input outweighs, or is outweighed by, the reduction in its relative price. Which effect prevails depends on the nature of the production function in the neighbourhood of B^1B^2. If BB' begins to flatten out towards some maximum, the obligatory surplus will eventually fall as the terms of trade continue to move in favour of agriculture.* Suppose it does fall. Then as X_1 has increased by virtue of the rise in X_3, net output measured in food must increase too. As the relative prices of food and textiles are fixed by assumption, the fraction of the resulting extra net income measured in food which is consumed within the rural sector is determined solely by the income elasticity of demand for food over that range of income. The greater it is, the smaller will be the associated rise in the optional surplus and hence the higher the probability that the overall surplus will (perversely) fall. In a kulak-landless system, the former will have a large income share and a low income elasticity of demand for food; however, while higher, the said elasticities for landless and small farmers will also be similar. It follows that, *ceteris paribus*, an egalitarian, small peasant agriculture is more likely to show perverse response than one dominated by kulaks. (The reader should note that the chances of perverseness depend on technology as well as utility functions.) Of course, if textile prices were also lowered, the situation *might* be rescued (see below) – at the cost of 'buttering both sides of the peasants' bread', or paying them what Lipton calls 'fair' prices. If, on the other hand, the obligatory surplus rises with a fall in the relative price of fertilizer, then net output (income) must increase too† (and hence the optional surplus). Although there is no perverseness in this case, the lower is the income elasticity of demand for food, the greater is the rise in the optional surplus. Thus, the change in the obligatory surplus being determined by technology alone, the marketed surplus in a kulak agrarian system will tend

* Let $X_1 = F(X_3)$, then $\tan\theta = F'(X_3)$ and the obligatory surplus is Z (say) $= X_3F'(X_3)$. Hence $\frac{dZ}{dF'} = X_3 + \frac{F'}{F''}$. By **A2**, $F' > 0$, $F'' < 0$ over the relevant range of X_3 (> 0), so that dZ/dF' may change sign for certain classes of production function. If $dZ/dF' < 0$ for all fertilizer-food price ratios, then the obligatory surplus is well-behaved everywhere, and conversely for $dZ/dF' > 0$. In particular, if F is of the form $X_1 = AX_3^\beta + B$, where β is a positive constant, $dZ/dF' < 0$ for all positive X_3.

† Net output Y (say) $= X_1 - Z$. Hence, $\frac{dY}{dF'} = \frac{F'}{F''} - \left(X_3 + \frac{F'}{F''}\right)$

$$= -X_3 < 0 \text{ for all } X_3 > 0.$$

to have a greater elasticity with respect to the barter terms of trade than that prevailing in a smallholder system.

It has become increasingly difficult to keep apart the prices of fertilizer and textiles, so to round matters off we now fix one in terms of the other (it does not matter which way round). The fertilizer-food price ratio is now identical with the textiles-food price ratio (subject to an alteration in the units in which either textiles or fertilizers are measured), so that the tangent at B^1 (say) may be projected into the left-hand side of the diagram (redrawn as Figure 2 to avoid a plethora of confusing lines) to give a point

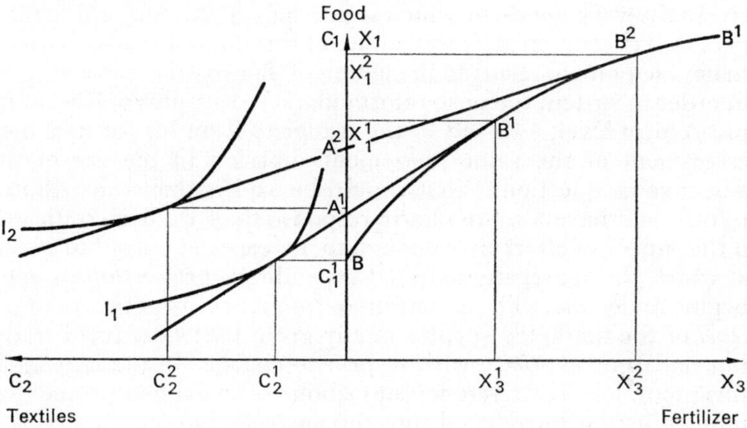

Figure 2

of tangency on one of the indifference curves. Outputs, inputs, consumption levels and surpluses are determined as before but simultaneously. The condition for perverseness is simplified by the elimination of one price variable, but it is formally similar to those derived above, the likelihood increasing with the marginal expenditure proportion on food and any tendency of BB′ to 'flatten' suddenly.*

* In an unpublished paper which goes into this whole problem in some detail, I show that the condition for the marketed surplus to be perversely sloped is $X_3 + \left(1 + \frac{\alpha_2}{\alpha_1}\right)\frac{F'}{F''} > 0$, where α_1 and α_2 are the utility elasticities of food and textiles, respectively. This condition is less likely to come about than that for a perverse obligatory surplus alone because of the income and substitution effects tending to raise the optional surplus along with net output.

By way of final comment and summing up, the comparative statics developed above, while limited in scope, do point to a more elastic response of the marketed surplus in kulak systems and bigger chances of perverseness in smallholder ones. The root cause of these findings is not difficult to grasp. A redistribution of income away from rich and towards poor households – in this case, through a distributist land reform – will probably depress the formers' consumption of food by much less than the latters' is enhanced. Thus one important effect will be to raise the rural sector's propensity to consume its own output, a close analogy in international trade theory being a country which consumes intensively the very goods in which it specializes. Lipton, a fine (and persuasive) economist, is well aware of this difficulty, which seems to have led him to resort to the notion of 'fair' barter terms of trade in order to sustain the post-reform marketed surplus at least at its pre-reform level. It is left to the reader to form his (or her) own assessment of the value judgements implicit in the use of the adjective in question. What should be said is that a distributist reform will have a more elastic response than we have indicated if the supply of effort rises enough to increase net output to a level at which the aggregate marginal expenditure proportion on food begins to decline. (The effects on output alone are germane to the *level* of the marketed surplus at any given barter terms of trade, but not to its *elasticity* with respect to changes in the latter.) At this point, leisure preference and labour as an explicit production input must be introduced into the analysis, but such complications will not be pursued here.

Nine

Towards a Theory of Land Reform*

Michael Lipton

I. Definitions

Definitions can go wrong in three ways. First, they may be insufficient, e.g. 'A chair is a piece of furniture'. An insufficient definition allows foreign bodies to slip in, e.g. tables can be counted as chairs just because tables are furniture too; and an insufficient definition of land reform permits some things not correctly or normally[1] counted as land reform to slip in. Second, definitions may be more than sufficient, e.g. 'A chair is a four-legged piece of furniture designed for sitting on'. A more-than-sufficient definition excludes some things that should be included, e.g. three-legged chairs. A more-than-sufficient definition of land reform excludes some things correctly or normally counted as land reform. Third, a definition can be plain wrong, specifying characteristics that do not really belong to the object defined, e.g. 'A chair is something used to eat from'. A plain wrong definition of land reform would both exclude things that should be in, and include things that should be out.

All three sorts of mistake are extremely common in defining land reform, for three reasons. Firstly, a definition must both connote and denote; and the expression 'land reform' is misleading as to connotation. 'Land reform' looks as if it connotes the reform of land – the moving of mountains – but it obviously does not. 'Land reform' does not even connote 'reform of the basic relations between man and land', which could be achieved

* I am grateful to Clive Bell and David Lehmann for critical comments on an earlier draft.

1. Philosophers will recognize these adverbs as rather clumsy signposts for the 'essentialist' and 'nominalist' views, respectively, of the relationship between a definition and what it defines. In this context I prefer a third adverb, 'usefully', signposting an intermediate position: that it is not *useful* to extend the meaning of 'land reform' to cover all sorts of agrarian change, or to restrict it to include only collectivization, or to alter it to 'rent restriction'.

by the use of a new plough. 'Land reform' in fact connotes 'reform' of basic relations among tillers of the land, and of basic relations between them and other direct beneficiaries from the land-tiller interaction. This, however, is at once sufficiently *recherché* and sufficiently open to conflicting interpretations – what is basic? – to produce genuine confusion. Secondly, people seeking to avoid land reform may find it politically convenient to have a more-than-sufficient definition that makes land reform look impossibly difficult by adding extraneous requirements, e.g. confiscation. Thirdly, each of the three errors may be due to a wish to 'define' as land reform only those agrarian changes that seem to the definer to be desirable; for instance, an insufficient definition excludes naughty land reforms, and a more-than-sufficient definition includes nicely-behaved non-land-reforms.

* * * *

Before examining these three errors, I must present my own (not very original) definition:

Land Reform (agrarian reform, *reforma agraria*) comprises (1) compulsory take-over of land, *usually* (a) by the State, (b) from the biggest landowners, and (c) with partial compensation; and (2) the farming of that land in such a way as to spread the benefits of the man-land relationship more widely than before the take-over. The State may give, sell or rent[1] such land for private cultivation in smaller units than hitherto (*distributivist reform*); or the land may be jointly farmed and its usufruct shared, through co-operative, collective or State farming (*collectivist reform*).

Land reform, so defined, is by definition an equalizing policy, at least in intention. It may also foment growth, but its primary motivation is to reduce poverty by reducing inequality, though not necessarily through helping the very poorest, or all the poor. This may be achieved by distributist or collectivist means. Collectivization may be used solely to extract a cheap food surplus for the cities, but this is not a necessary concomitant, and it may serve other aims.

The Chinese experience shows that – whatever the intentions –

1. The distinction between land rented from the State and land owned privately (e.g. after gift or sale) is not clear. Land revenues or rates are often collected on 'privately owned' land, and their distinction from rents paid to the State is purely verbal. Nor is the State's right to repossess a clear dividing line: it is often legally, politically or administratively difficult to exercise such a right on land 'rented' from the State. Conversely, just by calling land 'privately owned' the State does not forswear the right or power to repossess it.

the consequences were rather the reverse.[1] In China collectivization was accompanied by measures turning the terms of trade in the farmers' favour *and* enabling the rural sector to keep a larger share of its surplus – not easy things to do at once, as we shall see (Bardhan, 1969, showed that both happened). In the special case of State farming,[2] admittedly, the equalization may be intended to benefit the urban poor by facilitating the compulsory extraction of cheap food; or tomorrow's poor, by using such food to nourish more producers of investment goods that will raise tomorrow's output. However, since such objectives are usually (and probably more efficiently) achieved by means other than land reform,[3] it remains reasonable to see the normal objective of land reform as that of increasing intra-rural equality. This is attempted, in a more permanent manner than by taxes and hand-outs, by the redistribution or collectivization, in the interests of some poor people, of some of the main productive resource of some rich people: land.

Changes in landholding structures that do not reduce inequality, such as the conversion of 'feudal' holdings into capitalist holdings of the same size (Byres, on p. 223 *supra*) are neutral with respect to the equalizing motive underlying land reform, and hence fall outside our definition. This applies more forcibly to such unequalizing structural changes as the enclosure of common land by rich farmers in eighteenth-century Britain, however growth-fomenting or 'inevitable' they may be.

To say that land reform is to be the main path towards greater intra-rural equality is to assume that land is the main scarce resource and hence the main source of rural inequality and power.

One might challenge this view that poor countries are 'landist', by saying that the seed-fertilizer 'green revolution' puts special emphasis on *working* capital. Certainly its importance increases relative to land in the 10–20 per cent of farm area where such change happens, and it is arguable that there a class of 'capitalist

1. In 1956–7, following the 1955 collectivization campaign, grain reaching the central government through taxation or purchase declined 13·5 per cent while grain sold to villages rose 11 per cent. Net grain surplus fell by 33 per cent. (Information from G. Shillinglaw.)
2. Of course, collective farming is often State farming in disguise, notably in the U.S.S.R.
3. See below, pp. 289–93; an *initial* fall in marketed surplus, and some disruption of the (very price-sensitive) methods by which commercial farmers market their produce, are not to be ruled out as possible effects of land reform.

farmers' emerges; but as a rule these are precisely members of the old landist dominant class, who use the power conferred by land to secure privileged access to the two *sine qua nons* of 'green-revolutionary' capitalism: cheap credit and subsidized irrigation (cf. Epstein, 1973).

It may be argued that in arid areas it is access to water, not to land, that provides the key to power; but one can give Wittfogel his due in our context by conceding that land should be measured in 'efficiency-units' (indicating its capacity to yield net-value-added per acre in conjunction with optimal hirings of non-land inputs) rather than in crude acres, both when one assesses the degree of inequality and when one designs a land reform.

Both Byres's account of the Indian situation and Shillinglaw's discussion of Chinese reforms indicate that rural social justice, broadly conceived, formed at least the overt motive for land reform proposals. Such justice can be defined as absence of exploitation, but exploitation cannot reasonably be assumed to end with the abolition of sharecropping or wage-labour: even if families of identical size inherit *and farm with their own effort* vastly different amounts or qualities of land, the accident of birth confers greatly different incomes, i.e. claims upon commodities produced by the effort of others. Hence 'rural social justice' has to involve equalization of claims upon the usufruct of land, even if constraints and other goals limit its scope.

* * * *

The first of the three definitional sins, discussed above, is over-liberal definition, allowing some pseudo-reforms to acquire the kudos of real reforms. Alternative methods which claim to increase rural equality share certain characteristics with land reform, and it is tempting to frame definitions that let them in. This is particularly true of the two Great Evasions of land policy: settlement schemes and reform of tenure conditions. Both are often included in a too-weak definition, such as 'any basic change in the conditions of landholding designed to increase intra-rural equality'. Such programmes fail to achieve their stated goals because they do not attack the rural power structure, which is rooted in an extremely unequal distribution of owned land (see Section II).

Even less is it likely that intra-rural equality can be advanced by 'green revolutions', or in general by injections of *capital* in the hope of reducing the productive importance of *land* (and hence of inequality of landholdings), without major redistribution of land (Section V); yet there are definitions of land reform so wide as to include such purely technical improvements in farming. There are, of course, changes in land use, affecting both the consolidation of fragments and cropping patterns and sequences, that would improve efficiency within almost any structure of land tenure and distribution; but such measures, while often desirable ancillaries to land reform, do not themselves involve any land redistribution. Another way in which definition can be over-liberal is by including, in the reform itself, allegedly necessary conditions for it, notably a full cadastral survey and the registration of rights.[1]

The second definitional sin is over-rigorous definition. For a passionate collectivist, reform seeking to redistribute land to small private holders is an evasion; he may even interpret it as a deliberate attempt to create a conservative peasantry, opposed to the replacement of competition by co-operation, and of individualist by socialist motivations in farming.[2] Conversely, a passionate distributivist may argue that collectivist land reform merely transfers to the State (or the leadership of the commune) the oppressive power formerly wielded by the big farmer, and forgoes the advantages of small-scale farming normally associated with distribution in land-scarce situations (Section III). Each side is right given its values – mine incline to the distributivist position – but it is absurd to exclude major methods of land redistribution, whether distributivist or collectivist, from the definition of genuine land reform, for both involve radical equalizing change in the land-based structure of rural power. Not only is such redefinition poor logic; the attitude behind it makes the

1. This permits a government to evade the issue of land redistribution in several ways. It may say that redistribution has to wait till registration, etc., is complete; that registration etc., is part of the reform, which is therefore under way; that registration, by making farmers aware of their rights (and of the inequalities to be opposed), actually *is* the reform; or that the task of a full cadstral survey is too great, so that subsequent reforms dependent upon it are impossible. Some governments try those arguments one after another, or even, carelessly, all at once.
2. The inclusion of landless labourers in a distributivist reform, on this reading, makes things worse, by enlarging the conservative rural mass, at the expense of potential (revolutionary) supporters of collectivist reform. For a conscious advocacy of land reform in this conservative sense, see the practice of Stolypin, and the theory of S. Huntington (1968). (See also Lehmann, 1971.) In my view the notion that the appetite for change is stilled by demonstrating its practicability is, to use P. Streeten's phrase, 'paradoxical yet false'.

best the enemy of the good, and plays into the hands of landlord-politicians. A favourite piece of public dishonesty, by 'socialist' ministers eager not to alarm people with big landholdings, is to reject specific distributivist proposals – which they know are practical and a serious risk – as a capitalist evasion of the need for unspecified future collectivist reforms, which they know to be impracticable. An analogous trick is to claim that democratic land reform implies the payment of full compensation, which is impossibly costly; or that, given past extortions by landlords, only expropriation *without* compensation (which is of course politically impossible) constitutes real land reform. Perhaps the most common of all these over-rigorous evasions is the argument that only 'integral reform', with full-fledged systems of credit, etc., ready for the beneficiaries, is 'really' land reform: don't do anything till you can do everything, so do nothing. All these over-rigorous definitions share one feature: they let the rich farmers keep their land, fertilized with the crocodile tears of *soi-disant* frustrated reformers.

The third definitional sin really combines the first two: it is over-liberal in letting in things that are not land reform at all, *and* over-rigorous in leaving out genuine reforms. There are politicians, even 'authorities', who regard consolidation of fragments as real land reform while excluding collectivization, which they regard as not reform but bloody revolution.

II. Alternatives

It is often genuinely believed that the equalization sought by land reforms can be attained with less political disruption by such measures as reform of tenancy conditions, settlement of new lands, direction of new inputs to small farmers, or progressive taxation of landholdings. This belief is refuted by the now abundant evidence that, once rural power is concentrated in the hands of big landowners, these alternatives cannot work unless the State first diminishes that power through redistribution of land. This is true, whether the big, powerful farmers are true feudal barons (Ethiopia), or big landlords (Madras), or commercial farmers (Punjab). It is true, whether their power is underpinned by the traditional patronage powers of caste and *jajmani*, of tribal chiefs, of sheiks or other religious leaders, or of kings and princes. The machinery and the conduits of rural power vary, but its basis in land stays the same. For in pre-capitalist (and even in early capitalist) agriculture, land ready to farm is the scarce resource. Water, or money for working capital, can sometimes be the constraint on 'readiness to farm'; where land is plentiful, riches can sometimes consist not in owning land but in being able to pay people to work it; but even in these cases control over farmland is usually found in fairly fixed proportions to access to other resources, and such control still confers rural wealth and power. True, in those few situations where landowning is fairly equal, moneylender credit is the main constraint in raising the net output of almost all land, and is not provided by or in conjunction with the landowners; but these situations are uncommon and probably transitory, since fairly equal landholdings reduce both the supply and the demand for loans, whereas the foreclosure of debt will produce increasingly unequal landholdings. Land is normally power and equalizing change must first attack the power base. Can this be done without real land reform?

1. *Tenancy Reform*

Tenancy reform normally comprises the granting to the tenant of one or more of the following rights:

a limited rents, typically (assuming no landlord share in inputs) to one-third of the value of gross output, instead of the prevailing levels of 50–75 per cent;

b conversion, at the tenant's discretion, from crop-share to fixed rental:

c security against eviction, save for bad farming or non-payment of legal rent;

d first option to purchase the property, should the owner sell.

Such reforms have limited scope. First, dispersed and largely illiterate tenants must be told of their rights; but the *indirect* means of local and sometimes national communication (radio and the press) are highly responsive to the preferences of big landlords, while land reform officials taking the news *direct* to the tenants are in danger, and do well to go armed. Second, the landlords tend to control political and legal institutions and are usually the source of many types of rural patronage, including protection, consumer loans, contact with officials, marketing channels, and part-time employment; so a small tenant will seldom insist on his rights. The State probably cannot replace all the important services landlords have to offer. Third, administrative scarcity is inherent in the very definition of underdevelopment, and tenancy reforms make particularly heavy demands on the administration: the situation must be kept under permanent watch, and rent controllers must be paid and supervised enough to prevent their corruption by landlords.

Theoretically tenancy reform can achieve some of its objectives if the initial disparities of rural power are small, and it may discourage landlordism where rich and powerful rural families have promising alternative activities in politics, industry or trade. A secure tenant agriculture, without sharecropping,[1] and with adequate access to credit, is much less unequal, less exploitative and (as Bell's paper argues) less inefficient than existing cropshare systems. Despite the fact that evasion is so easy and administrative costs are higher than in once-for-all redistribution, tenancy reforms can make small tenant farmers more aware of the possibility of legal redress, and their very failure can expose the power structure, thereby strengthening those in and near government (including some spokesmen of the urban and industrial interest) who argue for genuine land reform. These arguments, rather than the prospects of general enforcement, provide a tactical case for the tenancy reform now under discussion in Ethiopia.[2]

However, landlords may well see unenforced or unenforceable tenancy reform as a welcome substitute for effective land redistribution. The almost complete failure, in Ceylon, to enforce the 1958 Paddy Lands Act (in respect to its provisions limiting the right to evict) is a typical example of this. In some cases, rent control coexists with genuine land reforms legislation affecting

1. S. N. S. Cheung (1969) has produced theoretical and empirical arguments against Alfred Marshall's argument that under sharecropping the tenant – because he gets much less than the full addition to product due to his outlays on extra inputs – cuts such outlays down. A forthcoming paper by Dipak Mazumdar (1974) essentially refutes Cheung and re-establishes Marshall's common-sense case. One might, however, argue that rational landlords will be concerned to raise tenant output if they share in it, and therefore to share with tenants the cost of providing optimal input levels. For organizational, security and political reasons, however, landlords seldom do this to anything like the extent one might expect.
2. After many years of talk about reforms, Ethiopia since 1972 has a strong and determined Ministry (and Minister) of 'Land Reform', and (partly due to pressures from aid donors) the Emperor has asked the landlord-dominated parliamentarians to give its tenancy reform proposals top priority in the current session, November 1972–July 1973. The proposals centre on security from eviction and limitation of crop-share rents; but earlier laws against tithe (10 per cent of gross produce paid to landlords before rent was calculated) are dead letters, so the value of rent restrictions presumably lies less in the prospect of enforcement than in the tactical considerations mentioned in the text.

operated holdings (ceilings legislation), and the landowner can in effect opt for whichever law is easier to evade; in several states of North and West India, ceilings on an individual's holdings are easily evaded by *mala fide* transfers, but rent control is harder to evade in face of an increasingly mobile and politicized tenantry. Thus landlords take over the land of potentially troublesome tenants, divide it into several bogus sub-ceiling holdings (for wife, children, cousins, aunts)[1] and resume personal cultivation – effectively turning tenants into labourers.[2] Similarly tenancy reforms may induce them to shift around tenants every year or even every season, so that no single tenant cultivates a piece of land long enough to establish a claim to rent reduction, prior right of purchase or security of tenure;[3] this is tolerated because tenants dare not imperil their access to patronage (loans, jobs, intercession with officials).

In general, tenancy reform in the 'soft states' of the Third World breaks upon the rock of landlord power, and the effects of evasion can include insecurity that worsens both rural income distribution and the standards of capital and land acquisition and maintenance on tenant farms.

This counter-productive result arose in Ceylon, where the 1958 Paddy Lands Act (designed to bring rents down and to render eviction difficult) was followed by more evictions and higher share-rents, largely because the landlords were able to destroy or subvert the Cultivation Committees intended to implement the Act. In most poor countries, landlords' strength rests upon the scarcity of land, so that tenancy legislation alone has to fight both market forces and political power; small wonder that, backed by underpaid and undertrained civil servants, such legislation is usually ineffective. To oversimplify: if you can do a land reform you don't need tenancy reform; if you can't, tenancy reform won't work.

1. Or, in one of Ladejinsky's memorable field observations in Kosi, when a man ran out of relatives, for 'Fatki, the horse'.
2. Usually paid by share of crop – in Latin America these would be called 'labour tenants'. There are other ways to escape ceiling legislation, notably by dividing one's owned land among separate (and unco-ordinated) administrative districts; often such division is bogus, by arrangement with a landlord in the other district.
3. If, as sometimes happens, long-standing tenants of a particular plot are entitled to buy it (especially below market price) in a land-to-the-tiller programme, the landlord's incentive to shift them around is even greater.

2. *Settlement Schemes*

Settlement schemes seem a natural way to proceed where spare land is available. Why confront the difficult politics of land redistribution, if the inequality in the size of holdings can be reduced simply and gradually as new areas are settled in roughly equal smallholdings?[1] In practice, however, the costs relative to benefits of clearing, preparing and settling new land are usually high (and almost invariably higher than forecast), and they compare very unfavourably with carefully selected intensification. Furthermore, since it is sensible to settle lands enjoying low cost/benefit ratios first, only higher ratios are available later (ILO, 1971). Technical progress associated with the 'green revolution' raises, over time, the benefits both of intensification and of new lands farmed; but there is no similar process to cut the cost of settlements, so the heavy fixed burden of such costs looms proportionately larger, when compared with the declining costs of working capital per unit of extra grain on older lands. Attempts to lower the costs of social capital (such as houses, schools and roads) on the new settlements by reducing standards have usually failed: even a landless labourer will not be lured by a smallholding to move hundreds of miles into a void; the attempt to cut building costs by do-it-yourself tactics fails, because once the poor labourers realize that the benefits of social capital (e.g. roads to market) go disproportionately to precisely the rural élite who contribute least by way of free labour, they become increasingly reluctant to work at less than the full market wage.

Apart from these considerations, the land-holding structure on new lands often replicates the inequalities prevalent on old lands. The physical success of the Gezira scheme in the Sudan has been well documented,[2] but not so its human failure: that the farmers with their ten to twenty acres had by 1962 become country

1. On pp. 288–93 I argue that *where land is scarce* the case for small-scale farming to increase output, 'employment' and (with care) marketed surplus, is strong. Whether land is scarce or not, however, a huge dispersion in holding size (under roughly similar physical farming conditions) *must* mean that many of the holdings are far from the optimal size. And land *ready to farm*, i.e. together with the fixed and working capital to farm it, is never so plentiful in poor countries that its wastage in big owned holdings with their low labour inputs-per-acre – whether this is caused by the owner-farmer's lack of sufficient family workers or by the share-tenant's lack of incentives – can be a matter of indifference.
2. Notably by A. Gaitskell (1959).

gentlemen, paying near-subsistence wages to the few Western and Southern Sudanese (and North Nigerian) migrants who get jobs at all.[1] In Ceylon, ten-acre or even five-acre settlements soon 'settled' into the pattern of 50 per cent share-rent, or of gentleman-farming with landless labour. Attempts are under way to reduce the holding size, at least on new settlements, but there is no reason to believe that credit, inputs, and soon enough the power to control land will not accrue to the farmers with initial monetary advantages, as they have done on older lands. Indeed, it is surely the men with power conferred by existing rural land, and their relatives and urban counterparts – rather than the very poor – who are likeliest to obtain entitlements to the newly settled lands.[2]

To reform tenancy conditions and to settle new lands: these, then are usually Great Evasions. They can sometimes usefully complement, or show the need for, distributivist or collectivist land reform as a route to greater rural equality; they can seldom provide an alternative route.

3. *Special Aid to Small Farmers*

Special aid to small farmers, like land reform, is supposed to have advantages for efficiency as well as for equality. Whatever form it takes – special credit facilities, input subsidies, marketing or delivery arrangements – it is intended to shift agricultural capital towards those with more 'underemployed' family labour, who are likely to use new capital at higher levels of labour per unit and thus to raise its yield. Conversely, though, unless the small farmers also get extra land (Section IV), such a policy also involves reducing the amount of land upon which the typical unit of new capital operates, and hence also the yield of new capital. Furthermore, unlike land reform, special aid to small farmers *necessarily* leaves landless labourers unaided, and if it is at the cost of large

1. In 1962 I saw the appalling conditions in which these workers live: chronically undernourished, crowded into practically unfurnished, leaky, bare fieldhuts, with no community or social life (they dared not appear in the villages of the gentlemen-farmers) and worked desperately hard. In recent years, labour shortage – not legislative change – has compelled some amelioration as migration slowed down.
2. Colombia is a case in point, as it is also of the hostility of governments in poor countries to 'squatting', and their propensity to evict even efficient and poor farmers from otherwise unused public lands; this does not suggest that the model of settlement schemes as a generous equalizing device to help the rural poor is a realistic one.

farmers[1] these labourers may find themselves further impoverished through a dwindling demand for their wage-labour (see Bell's paper). What is more, these benefits tend not to reach the really small farmers for whom they are designed; secretaries of credit co-operatives, for example, notoriously are big farmers or money-lenders or their relatives or clients, and credit intended for small farmers thus finds its way via the rural élite into the high-interest private-moneylending cycle. The heavy administrative burden of reaching really small farmers, especially in an agrarian system dominated and structured (as regards credit, inputs, extension and marketing) by big commercial farmers or landlords, predisposes governments to accentuate such biases[2] by confining even small-farm support, in effect, to the medium-sized. In the Kosi district of Bihar, the 'Small Farm Development Agency', by excluding farmers cultivating less than two and one half acres, leaves out the worst-off 40–60 per cent of farm operators! Marginal-farmer programmes are tiny (Jodha, 1973).

4. *Progressive Land Tax*

This last major alternative to land reform is understandably popular with the economists and unpopular with politicians and administrators. Since it is the larger landholdings that are farmed least labour-intensively, progressive taxation will at once penalize offenders, encourage them to sell their land to smallholders,[3] raise revenue and reduce inequality. Why not let the market do the land reform, instead of the government? Again, this is a *cul-de-sac*. Land valuation is always a difficult task, and all the more so when rapid agricultural change, only some of it due to the farm operator or owner, requires fair revaluation. These difficulties become critical when the injustices of error are amplified by tax progressivity. Even more seriously, progressive land taxation recruits just the same determined, powerful opposition from big landlords as does land reform, but can rely on none of the active popular support that could be mobilized

1. Either by reducing their share of a fixed total of new agricultural capital formation or by so increasing small-farm output as to reduce demand for large-farm output.
2. As does governmental predisposition to help those (biggish) farmers who contribute substantially to the urbanized food surplus that provides the wage-goods for 'industrialization'; see below, p. 311.
3. Or to rent it out, if the tax is on operated rather than owned holdings; but then the danger of high-rent sharecropping creates a new policy problem.

from the potential beneficiaries of a land reform; most of these will actually or potentially suffer, albeit mildly, from a progressive land tax, and in this case their grumbles can easily be mobilized by the big farmer in his role of patron. It is hard to point to a single successful progressive land tax in the Third World; even unprogressive ones have been abolished, despite their usefulness as revenue-raisers, in several Indian states since 1967.

III. Objectives and Implications

Most poor countries have in the past quarter-century enjoyed unprecedented growth of income per person; substantial 'development' as measured by the *per caput* availability of doctors and teachers, roads and electricity, steel and fertilizers; but nevertheless, little or no improvement in the living standards of the worst-off 40–50 per cent of the people, certainly in the countryside, possibly even in urban areas. (Lipton, 1974, Chap. 1.) The growing emphasis on land reform is mainly a response to this platitudinous but still shocking[1] paradox. We shall argue that land reform can contribute positively to other developmental goals: both to primary objectives (*overall* equalization, growth, the improved composition of output) and to intermediate objectives (improvement of the balance of payments, mobilization of savings). The impact on some other intermediate objectives, notably the generation of a bigger marketed surplus in the process of intersectoral trade, is less clear, but can be improved by the use of suitable ancillary measures (Sec. IV). But it is by its impact on intra-rural income distribution and hence on mass rural poverty that land reform stands or falls.

This might seem odd. Intrasectoral inequality is greater in industry than in agriculture, and intra-regional inequality in urban than in rural regions – in Africa especially, but also in Asia and Latin America. So why the emphasis on reducing intra-rural rather than intra-urban inequality? There are three reasons. First, the average rural income is so far below the average urban income that, despite the lower degree of rural inequality, the rural poor are usually worse off than the urban poor; hence it seems more important to enrich the rural poor. An urban-biased power-structure is reluctant to imperil itself (or to slow down 'industrialization') by doing this through the allocation of adequate

1. It shocks even aid donors (who are far from egalitarian with regard to the domestic or international policy of rich countries) that 'their' aid does so little to relieve poverty in recipient nations.

resources to farm development or through transferring urban resources direct to the rural poor, so that land reform, unless impeded by a marriage of convenience between urban industrialists and rural surplus farmers (p. 311), seems the easiest route to an ethically defensible and politically manageable rural scene.

Second, while, as we shall see, the break-up of large farm units usually leads to a more efficient use of scarce capital and land, the break-up and redistribution of large industrial units in poor countries would usually sacrifice genuine economics of scale, notably in administration and marketing, and lose valuable learning effects.[1] Finally, insofar as Third World economies are governed by, from and for the cities, the power of urban capitalists to resist distribution or collectivization of their property exceeds the power of rural landlords to offer similar resistance. Hence land reform but not capital reform. Similar political obstacles impede a transfer of resources from city to village – a transfer which could contribute much to equality.[2]

Thus intra-rural equalization seems the least unlikely concession to equality to flow from most governments in the Third World; and it is also the main objective of land reform. Yet I can find no rigorous treatment of the relationship between the two. A mere sketch of such treatment is all that can be presented here (pp. 282–6).

Let us suppose that all land is of identical quality and potential, and that all farm families are of identical size and composition.

1. This remains true despite the fact that 'collectivist reform' of industry, by nationalization, has not been strikingly successful in mixed economies in the Third World. This failure has been due not to the lack of scale economies, but to the high propensity to take over or pioneer chronically problem industries; to the public sector's reluctance to charge full market prices to powerful industrial consumers; and to governmental reluctance to compete with such consumers for top management by offering the wage levels needed, in such an economy, to attract them.
2. In the 1950s and 1960s in most LDCs, an extra unit of capital was associated with about twice as much extra output inside agriculture as outside it (Szczepanik, 1970) despite prices generally so set as to make farm inputs appear unduly costly and farm outputs unduly cheap; the Indian experience of the mid-1960s exemplifies the self-defeating nature of attempts to finance industrialization by neglecting agriculture; and as pioneering work by Ishikawa (1967, Chap. 4) and T. H. Lee (1971) has shown, both Japan and Taiwan financed agricultural take-off by initial resource inflows from urban areas, well before making any attempt to industrialize by transfers in the other direction.

Then rural equalization is clearly maximised, in the case of a distributivist reform, by dividing acreage by number of families, taking away all land in excess of the average, and using it to make all sub-average households up to average size – or in the case of a collectivist reform, by sharing the surplus product among families in proportion either to need or to the share of their available labour time that they choose to put in.

1. *Constraints on Achieving Equality in Distributivist Reforms*

Even on these simple assumptions, there are limitations on the procedure, which we shall examine first with reference to distributivist reform.

First, 'viability' sets a lower limit to desirable farm-size. That limit should presumably be a viable 'livelihood holding' that will permit an average farm family to enjoy a decent minimum level of income; for a family of five, paying no rent and providing its own labour, the Ceylon Employment Mission of ILO (ILO, 1971) estimated that such a holding averaged two acres of rice land, varying in accordance with soil fertility. There are many parts of the world, notably Java, where completely equal redistribution of land would leave no livelihood holdings at all, and it is hard to see this contributing to the creation of an innovative or happy peasantry.

Second, the output effects of bringing mini-farms up from one-quarter of an acre to half an acre would also be very disappointing. Most Censuses of Agriculture show that labour-intensive practices which raise the efficiency of land and capital use (natural manuring, weeding, rice transplanting where choice of broadcasting exists, etc.), while increasing in incidence as farm size falls to about three-quarters of an acre, fall off thereafter. This is perhaps because mini-holdings are associated with part-time farming, which may militate against proper or direct supervision, especially since incentive patterns lead the farmer to concentrate increasingly on obtaining non-agricultural earnings.

A third argument is that there is some evidence that, below about half an acre, the rate at which further declines in holding size compel the family to buy in food accelerates sharply and thus depletes the marketed surplus, net, sold to the cities.

A very delicate political question then arises: to whom shall the scarce above-ceiling land be distributed? and the equally political answer is that it is best to make small farmers up to viable holdings rather than to turn landless farmers into sub-viable mini-farmers, unless the land available is so abundant that this conflict does not arise – as in Latin America. To take an example of extreme land hunger: in Bangladesh a very severe (ten-acre national average) ceiling on land ownership would free about 2·3m. acres. One might divide it among about 2·5m. landless families, one-fifth of Bangladesh's 60m. agriculturalists (Bose, 1973.)[1] It would be indefensible to jump them up above equally poor mini-holders with half an acre or so; but if the land were distributed to both, 2·3m. acres would be divided among at least 5m. families. The choice would be between an arbitrary and offensive selection process and a reform which offered beneficiaries insufficient land to provide a livelihood even with best practice. From the economic point of view, distribution to the landless would further contribute to buy-back of food, and would also worsen output response due to their lack of farming experience.

Another group of limitations on the degree of equality brought about by distributivist reform arises from the political impossibility of fixing the maximum permissible holding at the same level as the livelihood holdings. Decisive action against the top 5 per cent of landowners is much easier than against the top 10 per cent and may not yield very much less land above the ceiling. In Bangladesh, if the ceiling were cut from ten acres to seven acres, the number adversely affected would be quadrupled (from 2 per cent to 8 per cent of rural families) but the amount of land obtained not even doubled.[2] The relevance of political bargaining emerges from the case of the riceland in Ceylon, where the ILO team judged the best relationships between ceiling and livelihood

1. A similar calculation for India is found in Bell's paper.
2. Bose, *loc. cit.* The data for Bangladesh and Ceylon, like most estimates of land distribution based on agricultural censuses, are for operational holdings and probably somewhat understate the inequality of distribution of owned holdings, and hence the land made available by any given ceiling; too much hope should not be placed in this, however, especially since K. N. Raj's demonstration that each major size-group of operational holdings in India rents in about as much land as it rents out. More spare land may be available too, in that micro-surveys show somewhat greater inequality of both owned and operated holdings than macro-surveys on which availability estimation is based, but which are usually done too quickly to detect under-reporting of large holdings. Furthermore, reform *increases* the number of *efficiency-units* of land (because small farmers produce more per acre), and this effect is enhanced if consolidation is possible (p. 305). Conversely, the tendency of bigger holdings to be on worse land, and to support bigger families, reduces the *efficiency-units* of land available, above a fair ceiling, for redistribution among *consumer units*.

holding to be 5: 1, but the reforms now under discussion seem to imply a disparity closer to 12½: 1. If the disparity becomes very large, the whole exercise can be called into question, given the vast administrative effort involved and the frustration of the many excluded peasants.

The extent of desirable equality may be limited by some managerial considerations. In theory, if all farmers had equal natural gifts, there would indeed be a single optimum size of farm; but differences in managerial skills, innovativeness and spatial position do justify some actual difference in the operated holding size, as measured not in even acres per family but in 'efficiency acres' or productivity equivalents of land per consumption-unit. Of course, it would in principle be possible to go for wholly egalitarian redistribution, allowing renting-out to establish economically desirable divergences among *operated* holdings; but it is a time-wasting (and output-wasting) procedure, and contrary in spirit to the 'usufruct-to-the-tiller' motivation underlying reform. A 5:1 ceiling-to-livelihood ratio would keep down both the damage to those existing big landowners who are also good farmers and (given the reduced power of the bigger farmers) the incentive to an inefficient farmer to hang on.

The final and, to my mind, most serious group of limitations on intra-rural equalizing, desirable in distributive land reform, arises from the position of the landless labourers. Let us not consider 'easy' cases with very large average holdings and tremendous inequality (such as Cuba where the government was thought radical when it set a ceiling of eighty hectares). I write in Bangladesh, where in 1968 the top 7·8 per cent of farmers owned only 30·6 per cent of land, by virtue of having ownership holdings of over 7·5 acres only.[1] Even the most egalitarian imaginable reform would fail to create viable holdings for more than about 90 per cent of the 12m. or so farm families. But whatever the ceiling, to whom should the spare land be redistributed? If to the landless labourer, it will be possible to create only a few viable holdings, because each landless family – in Bangladesh 20–25 per cent of farming families – must be made up from nothing to the full amount needed to maintain a family at minimum viable income level (normally two acres for a typical family of five). But, by making up to the two-acre livelihood those farming families already near to it, we would create the largest possible viable, egalitarian peasantry composed of full-time farmers without, however, helping landless labourers. In Ceylon this is, at

1. Government of Pakistan, *Master Survey of Agriculture 1968*, Islamabad, 1970, Table 1.

least arithmetically, a viable policy; a 5:1 ceiling-to-livelihood ratio would free enough land above the ceiling to bring all farmers holding above one-quarter of an acre up to the two-acre viability level. Below one-quarter of an acre we are among mini-farmers. The dilemma is a cruel one and its name is poverty. My own preference is for this solution, however. To distribute non-viable holdings to the landless is a sentimental but ineffective method of improving their situation. There are many other ways to help them, notably by rural works, such as supplying the irrigation maintenance needs of the new class of viable small farmers (could the landless co-operatively *own* such capital?). But one must admit that by abolishing big holdings one abolishes also the landless's main source of employment, and substitute sources must be created if the mass-equalizing effects of distributive reform are not to be a hollow mockery for the poorest of all.

I have identified three types of constraint upon the extent to which distributivist reform can be equalizing: the holdings created must be viable (not 'economic' or 'optimal' – see below): the gap between the ceiling and viable holding size must not be too small to be sustainable politically, or to rule out *justified* managerial diversity; and something has to be done to improve the position of the landless, which except in the land-rich countries of Latin America will not be universal distribution because of the first two constraints. What is now needed is a rigorous analysis, for which the above provides a mere skeleton. We need, first, distribution functions of land owned among farm families – or, ideally, of 'efficiency units' of land owned, adjusted, however crudely, for soil fertility, among consumer units. (The latter is usually less unequal, for many of the big holdings feed big families, or are on bad land, or both.) Second, we need to examine the impact, upon the numbers of families that can be brought up to a viable floor holding, of (a) adjusting it downwards, which can always be achieved, to some extent, by raising public investment in improving farming on the new units; (b) adjusting the ceiling downwards, which involves setting the gain in families settled against the political resistance from middle farmers, who may actually be below national average income-per-head; (c) various compromises between settlement priority for the landless and enlargement priority for those not too far below the viable holding. Third, we need to estimate the severity of the reduction in available wage-labour for the residual landless, and (in the context of specific rural situations) the prospects of improving matters through programmes of rural works. More empirical work is (as always) needed. Such important tasks as identifying at micro-level the realities of ownership distribution requires prolonged residence in a single rural community. But there is quite enough information to attempt the above analysis for quite a wide range of rural areas.

2. *Constraints on Achieving Equality in Collectivist Reforms*

This cannot, I fear, be said of countries that have undertaken major collectivist land reforms. Except perhaps in Tanzania, it is not usually possible to undertake field-level inquiries into distributional effects with the normal criteria for scientific research that can be applied to land reform in more open societies. Scientific rigour and self-expression for the articulate and privileged are not obviously preferable to improved life chances for the rural masses through the equalization of rights in land (if there is a trade-off!). But, until Cuba, China, North Korea, North Vietnam, Algeria and Eastern Europe and the U.S.S.R. open their rural sectors to objective scholarly inquiry, it will not be possible to state whether such equalization has taken place, let alone to what degree and with what results.

The little information we do possess is not favourable to the impact of collective or joint co-operative farming on intra-rural equality. In the U.S.S.R., China and Eastern Europe, collective farmers prefer to put their effort into their own smallholdings; and often, if they are able to choose, we find collective farmers prefer the status of wage-labourers on State farms. We know little of the impact of either system on economic equality, but we do know that there is substantial political inequality. Indeed Stalin chose collectivization as a method of supporting an already privileged industrial sector, though this result is not inherent in or special to collective farm systems. In India, co-operative joint farming proved to be easily exploited to enrich the traditional holders of rural power (Thorner, 1960), and, as Byres shows, was quietly abandoned despite the Nagpur Resolution of 1959. Hitherto, the disease of gentleman-farming with landless hired labourers, as a form of reformist inequality, was thought to be limited to distributivist reforms setting up over-large farm units, and to similar errors we have mentioned on settlement schemes, but Allende's reforms in Chile showed that production co-operatives are not immune to it either. If collectivist reform not only (as we shall suggest) hinders the efficient use of farm resources, but even has dubious benefits for equality, we must be chary of advocating it merely because it *may* be *one* way to achieve the questionable desideratum of easy extraction of cheap food for rich townsmen.

Provided there is enough land to settle the landless, to produce 'enough' farm output despite any resulting inefficiency, and to make small and mini-holders up to viable size – as in most of Latin America and many parts of Africa – an egalitarian, or any opponent of exploitation need feel no qualms about distributivist reform. Even in South Asia it may well be that the landless can be absorbed in a non-exploitative way in supplying rural works and ancillary services to the new class of viable, non-hiring and non-renting, family farmers (the landless might well jointly own the capital). Collectivist reform may assist the turning of agriculture into an underfed milch-cow for an over-privileged urban sector in some situations; but especially under capitalism it is neither necessary nor sufficient for intra-rural equality, and has proved less able to produce it than distributive reform.

3. *Other Aims*

The bulk of this discussion of objectives has been confined to intra-rural equalization, or more precisely intra-agriculturist equalization, since I judge this to be the central aim of reform. But what of other aims? Since farm output, and more especially retained on-farm output, will rise in most cases (see below), agriculturists will get better off relative to other richer villagers such as craftsmen, goldsmiths and moneylenders, at least on the first round, so that rural as well as agricultural equality benefits from distributivist land reform. Also the rural sector should benefit relative to the richer urban sector: at present an underpriced food surplus is extracted from agriculture as a whole, by subsidizing only the biggest farmers, so that the small surplus farmer and his employees bear much of the cost of – often inefficient – industrialization. This would become more difficult, while an urbanist policy to turn the terms of trade against farmers would become more unattractive on account of its downward impact on the net marketed surplus (p. 293). It is of course possible to use State farming to increase the underpricing and extraction of the farm surplus, but this is neither a necessary nor a special feature of it.

Sometimes a radical concern for equality will drive out growth and leave little to equalize, but this risk hardly applies in the case of land reform. There is now abundant evidence that 'output per unit of land is inversely related to farm size'.[1] Part of

1 See Dorner (1972), p. 120; R. Krishna (1965); ILO, op. cit.; Government of Pakistan, *Census of Agriculture 1960* and *Master Survey of Agriculture 1968*; the Indian Farm Management Surveys cited by Byres in his essay; and Dayal (1971).

this relationship is spurious (because holding size is usually smaller on good soil), but much of it survives even in micro-studies where the soil quality can be held constant. Small family farms can saturate the land with plenty of labour per acre, as there is little else for the labour to do (except perhaps at seasonal peaks). Large commercial farms must supervise labour and pay it the full market price, which is likely to rise if they buy too much of it. Another and more surprising fact is that, as Colin Clark has often emphasized, all the careful micro-work shows that *capital* per acre also increases as farm size declines (Dorner, 1972, p. 102).

It is often claimed that small farmers do not save and that land reform therefore dries up the source of growth, though making a once-for-all contribution to output; but micro-studies which identify non-monetized investment show that any static short-fall in the small farmer's savings propensity will normally be out-weighed by the dynamic incentives to labour-intensive formation of labour-complementing capital associated with a larger (but still small) family farm, and by the acquisition of tangible assets and income sources which reduce the need to divert potential savings to pay usurious interest. The opposite criticisms are more interesting: if small farmers use more capital per acre than large farmers, will not their high output-per-acre be counterbalanced by the adverse general effect of high capital requirements per unit of output? If land is scarce, so is capital. But the reply is that (1) output per unit of capital seems to be slightly higher on smaller than on larger farms, since output per acre rises more markedly with falling farm size than does capital per acre; (2) much more important, there is capital and capital. The big farmer's capital (tractors, weedicides) tends to be financed by hard-won (and often undervalued) foreign exchange or monetized saving, both of which could be put to alternative uses. The small farmer's capital is financed by the direct diversion of his own effort from inactivity or growing food towards digging field channels, making a compost pit, or building a shed to protect his implements from rain; this hardly affects capital formation elsewhere, and is almost no drain on the nation's resources for financing growth elsewhere. Often small farms raise output faster than large ones (Dayal, 1971).

Let us now consider several counter-arguments, against the proposition that the comparative-static association between rising farm size and falling output per acre implies that distributivist reform assists the growth of farm output. First, it is argued that the initial disruptive effects of land reform reduce farm output. This is plausible enough, but the evidence is not univocal: the reverse was true in the West Bengal reform of 1968, which was carried out by grass-roots forcible occupancy of land held above the ceiling. Second, it is claimed that the association holds only for cereal crops; but even for crops such as tea and tobacco, where apparent economies of scale do exist they are usually pecuniary or due to pseudo-indivisibilities rather than technological, and can thus often be overcome through the (profitable) provision of private or co-operative services. These services normally involve the control of cashcrop quality and the provision of extension through buying agencies such as bought-leaf tea-processing plants and tobacco-curing barns, so that the basic linkage between high labour-availability per acre, small farm size and high output per acre can re-assert itself. Third, it is sometimes claimed that the argument for redistribution into small family farms applies only in 'Asian' situations where land/labour ratios are low: but first, the capital needed to bring 'spare land' under the plough is scarce in any poor country, and needs to be worked labour-intensively; second, under-farmed giant holdings are a clearly damaging part of the Latin American farm output scene; and third, if there is an optimum farm size (Section IV) it surely lies between the smallest and the largest in most or all poor countries, and does not justify an enormous diversity of acreage in any, even where land is plentiful. Fourth and most plausibly, it is argued that land reform, even if it helps output to grow, diverts desperately scarce administrative resources away from *more* output-enhancing uses, notably input provision; but this assumes, wrongly, that land reform must wait upon full and administratively burdensome cadastral surveys and records of rights. Paradoxically, an equalizing land reform can help the public sector to reduce administrative personnel and supervision in the distribution of fertilizers, seeds, pesticides and water; insofar as such people are supposed to ensure that services go to small farmers, the new power of such farmers and the reduction of intra-agricultural inequality renders their work superfluous, and its decentralization or even 'privatization' less dangerous.

So, for two of the three primary aims of economic policy – growth and equalization – the impact of distributivist land reform is beneficial. We have already hinted that collectivist land reform does not, on the limited scientific evidence available, help farm output; the Soviet record and that of Eastern Europe speak for themselves, as does the fact that most South Asian collective and co-operative farm experiments fail to show a profit even after many years of special favours from the government. The very size of large holdings – private, public or co-operative – induces farmers and farm managers to prefer inert machinery, notably tractors, to troublesome workers, who are more easily organized when concentrated in large units. This may advance 'modernization', but is not suited to the factor endowments of poor countries with many workers per unit of land.

Will distributivist reform improve the composition of output? In other words, will it raise the proportion of measured GNP comprising items 'undervalued' by market prices that reflect either income maldistribution or monopolistic (or, especially for foreign exchange, governmental) price manipulation? Production of poor men's foodgrains such as millets and maize, and pulses, is likely to rise relative to rice and dairy products; the effects of substituting import-saving self-consumed cereals for export crops are ambiguous. Then there are those goods and services, and styles of life, that increase happiness and elegance and beauty, perhaps neither for buyer nor for seller but for third parties whose external benefits do not affect prices; the reader must decide for himself whether I am right to say that an egalitarian peasantry is good for the quality of life in this way.

We have made some reference to the impact of land reform on two intermediate aims: saving and marketed surplus. These are intended to increase, respectively, the resources for future growth and the capacity to provide wage-goods and inputs for industrialization; and they will contribute to the struggle against demand inflation. In both cases the logic is similar: land redistribution may possibly reduce the *proportion* of income saved and of output marketed, but it will certainly increase the total amount of income and of output available as a source of savings and marketings respectively. Hence the *volume* of savings, and marketings, may rise.

It is often argued that, because big farmers save a bigger share of income than small ones, saving will decline when land is redistributed. Apart from theoretical arguments against this in a static framework, in practice it is the dynamic effects which count. First, land reform will provide the new class of viable farmers with a whole set of new outlets for embodying savings in productive investment; the incentive to save will rise for the beneficiaries. Second, in the traditional village system, the big savers are the moneylenders, who are often big farmers too, and the most profitable use of their savings is to lend to deficit farmers, who cannot make ends meet on their own land, for consumption purposes at 30–60 per cent per annum. Thus in a highly unequal system of rural land-ownership, with its typical supporting credit system, the saving of the rich finances not investment but the dissaving of the poor. Land reform, especially with the necessary ancillary credit institutions,[1] can reduce the demand for such financing, and compel the bigger remaining farmers to seek investment outlets for their savings, instead of lending them for the consumption of the poor.

The argument on marketed surplus looks very similar. There is no doubt that, net of buyback, marketed surplus is a larger proportion of output for big farmers than for small ones. But it need not follow that total marketed surplus falls after a distributivist land reform. First, the farmers who move into viability thus become able to produce net marketed surpluses for sale to the cities (as opposed to gross surpluses of distress sales to meet debts). Incentive is added if, as is likely, food prices increase owing to short-term disruption of marketing channels and of the old urban alliance by which huge farmers provide cheap food in exchange for selective subsidies. Second, if we are concerned, like Adam Smith, with food surpluses to feed more and more industrial workers then we must consider a food-cycle quite like the saving-dissaving credit cycle of the village and similarly broken by land reform. That part of the big farmer's surplus which in the traditional village is eaten up by the small farmer's frequent food *deficit* will, after reform, be almost entirely available for the cities. Finally, as we have seen, output per acre is bigger on smaller farms, with the following result: although marketed surplus is smaller in relation to output per acre on small farms, and thus constitutes a smaller proportion of total village output after distributivist reform, output per acre is itself larger and so, therefore, is total village output. Hence it is not at all clear that the village's marketed surplus will fall, especially if the appropriate marketing institutions are provided. If the city has to pay more for its surplus than before, that is not self-evidently bad: poor villagers have perhaps been bled long enough in the interests of protected, capital-intensive, perpetually infant industries.

1. It is important to decide whether one wishes rural credit provision to move from rural moneylenders to other institutions more likely to reinvest rentier income in *agriculture* or towards urban sources likely to transfer what was formerly moneylender expenditure to the creation of investment and consumer (and subsequently multiplier) incomes in *urban areas*. This transfer is described in a brilliant and prophetic passage in K. Kautsky, *Die Agrarfrage*, Dietz, Stuttgart, (1899). Advocates of financing the industrialization of the wealthy out of the forcibly extracted 'savings' of the poor might pause to consider Kautsky's unequivocal chapter title for his discussion of the above-credit-transfer process: 'The Exploitation of the Countryside by the City'.

Hence Byres may be too gloomy in his assertion (p. 242) that distributivist reform would produce even an 'initial . . . fall in the marketed surplus' – certainly it need produce no lasting fall in net deliveries to the city. If there were a short-run fall, the consequent rise in food prices would normally reverse it. Byres is doubtful about the responsiveness of the net marketed surplus to price increases, though he is careful to insist only that the response is not 'necessarily' normal (p. 228) and upon the 'possibility' (p. 240) that it 'may' (p. 228) be perverse. The only systematic inquiry into the true net surplus sold by villages to cities – presumably the surplus of industrializable inputs and wage-goods that concerns Byres – suggests that in India it responds normally to price, with a supply elasticity close to unity (Bardhan, 1971).

An important consideration is that distributivist reform is likely to reduce the chances of a perverse response of net marketed surplus to price, and to increase the size of a normal price response. Bell correctly reminds us of the distinction between optional and obligatory surplus. The price response of the latter depends on a number of complex factors, including the effect of price change upon the rents, interest rates, and propensities of rural landlords and moneylenders to prefer cash or kind. But a positive price-elasticity of demand for urban goods, and low leisure preference, probably ensure normal price response with regard to changes in the price of the optional surplus. Now a distributivist reform brings a number of deficit farmers into surplus and hence (especially if linked with the reduction of tenancy) reduces their need to pay consumer loans and rents with an obligatory surplus; reduces the riches that can supply money-lending and sharecropped land, the poverty that must demand them, and hence the capacity of rents and loans to boost transactions involving the obligatory sacrifice of surplus by small farmers; and transfers land to small, poor farmers with more workers for each acre, i.e., to farm units with (presumably) lower leisure preference than the pre-reform larger farms. All these changes seem certain to make marketed surplus more price-responsive after reform than before.

This does of course suggest that the way to *ensure* that land reform benefits net marketed surplus is to allow the terms of trade to move in favour of agriculture (see Section V below). This will in turn reduce the savings fund available to support industrial investment. But the predominance of spare capacity in industry in poor countries, together with the low yields on even operated industrial capacity, do not suggest (*pace* Byres) that it is a constraint on investment finance that holds back industrialization in poor countries. It is, rather, a constraint upon the availability of wage-goods and inputs from agriculture, and of imported spares and raw materials that might be financed by import-substitution in cereal farming. If this view is correct, it is self-defeating to attempt to industrialize by financing further under-used, low-yielding industrial capacity by forced saving extracted from agriculture (or, which amounts to the same thing, by turning the terms of trade against agriculture). Especially after land reform, an efficient industrializer would encourage marketings by ensuring high levels of *agricultural* investment and terms of trade at least fair to agriculture.[1]

This discussion of objectives cannot end without some clarification of the issue of employment. More work is not an end in itself, but a means to the twin ends of growth and equalization. It helps growth in poor countries, because labour is their only abundant resource and should be used to saturate scarce resources; even 'spare' land needs costly capital to bring it under the plough. It helps equity by raising the share of labour, and the chance of poor people productively to become less poor. Distributivist land reform certainly raises the amount of productive effort put in per acre, because the small family farm has – and uses – more of its own, highly motivated effort per acre; big farms, often with some degree of local monopsony of labour, sometimes face (1) a rising supply price, and always (2) a market wage reflecting much more than (and hence much higher than) the opportunity-cost of unpaid family labour on small farms, and (3) rising unit supervision costs. Hence they feature lower labour-input per acre. But only if there is enough spare land to permit the landless to be given viable holdings to a substantial degree will land distribution reduce *un*employment, rather than just allowing the partially employed to find more work. Indeed the employment prospects of the landless may suffer, as the bigger farmers (their main employers[2]) are dispossessed. That is why it is important to

1. To anticipate Section V, and to reassure readers of pp. 249–50 of Byres's paper, let me say now that this is *not* the same as seeing that the terms of trade do not move against agriculture. In Pakistan during the 1960s the terms of trade moved sharply in favour of agriculture, so that the farmer in 1968 received two-thirds of the world market value of his net marketed surplus (in terms of bought industrial goods) as against only half at the beginning of the decade (S. P. Lewis, *Pakistan: Industrialization and Development*, OECD 1970, pp. 148–50); one-third theft, while less than half theft, remains theft.
2. Several micro-surveys indicate that this effect is less overwhelming than it may seem.

incorporate programmes of rural works in which the landless have prior claims to jobs, as discussed in Section IV.

In contrast, we have little evidence that collectivist reforms will increase labour-input per acre. Non-individual farming often has a perverse similarity with sharecropping, in that effort is deterred by the knowledge that its usufruct must be shared with others whether they work or not. Moreover, those responsible for management are prone to evade the difficult problems of labour relations by introducing labour-replacing capital, notably tractors. These may also be used (as in the U.S.S.R.) as instruments of control, to secure the desired pattern of crops (and marketing); but the effect is the same: to reduce work-per-acre, save in exceptional cases. In mobilized societies, where the 'desired' amount, and type, of farmwork can be enforced by a Pharaoh or a commissar, a labour-intensive collective is conceivable, and sometimes it might be briefly induced by political enthusiasm. But on available evidence the prospects of long-lasting, voluntary, yet labour-intensive collectives or joint co-operative farming seem bleak (BARD, 1972), especially in those societies where powerful bureaucrats or middlemen benefit from tractor and weedicide subsidies.

It has been argued in this section that distributivist, but probably not collectivist, reform can increase equity, while probably benefiting growth and other subsidiary targets. In industry, because of scale economies and the possibilities of supervision, the approach to socialism through self-management, after the Yugoslav model, is viable even in quite large units. In agriculture, such large units have high capital costs. But why worry? The small family farm need neither a hirer nor a renter be; it need exploit nobody. Socialism is often felt to require planning, but small family farms have shown their rapid (often too rapid) responses to price incentives, new inputs and cropping patterns, and even extension. If the small, fairly equal family-farm system can change as the economy develops and grows less labour-intensive; if it can be provided with suitable ancillary services; and if the system can decently accommodate agriculturalists who cannot be 'given' farm units – then I can see no reason why a politically viable, distributivist land reform should not give rise to a contented, prosperous and by no means 'reactionary' rural population, whether in a socialist or a capitalist framework of political and economic advance. The small family farm is after all the only form of agricultural producer co-operative that is a proven success.[1] But is it flexible enough?

1. Though, like other forms, it is often unduly influenced by its

IV. After the Reform

One of the participants in the IDS' 1971 Land Reform Study Seminar graphically pointed out that 'to create thousands of small farms, without providing them with ancillary services of credit and extension and marketing, is like putting newborn kittens upon a snowy mountain-top and expecting them to fend for themselves'. The participant was from Latin America, where there is ample land for a land reform to benefit the landless as well as the small farmer – and enough mass literacy and political consciousness to imperil any reform that does not. Neither is true in South Asia, and if a land reform does not benefit the landless the need for ancillary services is less acute. A farmer made up from three-quarters of an acre to two acres does not become a different animal. He already knows about farming; he can now innovate and devote more time to his land, so he needs some extension, but he probably knows how to get it and whether it is worth the effort. Similarly, when his marketing needs change as he moves into surplus, he has some relevant knowledge. Two or three neighbouring two-acre viable farmers are likely to have, or to acquire, a pair of bullocks or a bullock-cart among them, and to arrange to swap assets and implements according to their marketing and other needs, in exactly the sort of *ad hoc* informal co-operative with which family farms have always met such needs, whether in the Mutual Aid Teams of early revolutionary China or in the *varengula* (labour exchanging) arrangements in parts of contemporary rural Maharashtra.[1]

One of the advantages of the unhappy situation where there is sufficient land only for the small farmer to be made viable is therefore that marketing and extension services will to some degree look after themselves. But in so doing they will provide new opportunities for local monopoly, new chances for the rural élite to retain its threatened dominance; and credit will not 'look after itself' at all. The newly viable farmers will need less consumer-credit, and less will be available from the bigger landlord, who has lost land and hence the capacity to lend. However, they will undoubtedly need more producer credit; and

stronger elements, in this case the father; but how many women serve on the management committees of conventional co-operative or collective farms?

1. It is precisely because small individual farmers choose to co-operate in suitable activities that they are not keen to be compelled to co-operate in activities picked by outsiders.

in the very first season after the reform, they will need an enormous amount if they are to finance input for, say, two acres with the spare income, if any, from the pre-reform holding of perhaps half or one acre. Having neither seed nor savings from earlier crops, they will still require – for the last time – the traditional amount of consumer credit as well. At the same time the mini-farmers and landless labourers, if they are to receive little or no benefit from the reform, will face the same consumer-credit needs as before, with fewer sources of loans and perhaps fewer prospects of employment.

It must be remembered that no land reform so far has been fully equalizing; and there will inevitably be evasion. The small number of families left with sizeable holdings can, in the situations outlined above, acquire enormous monopoly power over ancillary services, especially credit. It thus becomes very important to develop a policy for supplying such services to the new farm units, both to permit efficient input acquisition and output production and disposal, and to maintain the thrust towards rural equalization.

1. *Credit*

No attempt has to my knowledge been made to estimate the impact of any particular land reform on the number of persons needing credit, or on the size-timing and size-distribution of their loans. As suggested above, after the first difficult season, demand for consumer credit will fall sharply (as will supply), but demand for producer credit will rise, though not much if it was substantially used before the reform in order to pay hired labourers. As for timing, it is fairly clear that cropping intensity (mainly due to higher incidence of double-cropping) increases substantially as farm size falls from about fifty to about 0·5 acres, being responsible for perhaps half the variation in output-per-acre with holding size. Hence the inflow of credit in normally slack seasons must rise – and with it, presumably, the rate at which credit organizations recover loans in the main season. But the principal problem lies with the distribution of loans: inevitably, there will be a major shift from Agricultural-Bank-type lending to the bigger farmers, on medium term, towards Co-operative-type lending, intended for small farmers on short term. Such lending, if not well organized in public or private institutions, will again be concentrated among – and will enrich and strengthen – the traditional holders of rural power.

Despite much evidence – anecdotal and other – of the failure of co-operative credit, three considerations might restore some faith. First, in India, co-operative credit does very much less badly in areas where initial land distribution is not too unequal, such as Maharashtra. Second, in Bangladesh and probably elsewhere, those who default on the largest portions of their loans from credit institutions are the bigger farmers; land reform will erode their power and will to default in this manner. Third, the best guarantee against default by borrowers, defalcation by officials, and destruction by rich farmers is the presence of an interested body of fairly equal and politically strong borrowers with an interest in the success of the credit institution – ideally, perhaps, a hundred or so small farmer borrowers, electing and overseeing a co-operative credit committee (with powers to borrow from the government and to lend to members) in a single village, and insisting, as a condition of borrowing, that each borrower buy shares in the society, say of 10 per cent of the value of the loan.

'Liberal credit' should mean that credit is ample to provide for farm-family needs, and that there are no tedious formalities to determine the purpose of the loan. It should not mean that defaults are permitted (unless the weather is especially harsh), still less that, as in Ceylon, politicians promise to tolerate them in order to win elections. Nor should it mean that interest rates are set unrealistically low, impeding both efficient credit rationing and the organization's prospects of building up sufficient reserves. A co-operative must cover inevitable defaults and expand its lending; a rate of 15–20 per cent would reflect roughly the true cost of capital, especially given inflation, in most poor countries, and still substantially undercut the moneylender; indeed, by making possible a much higher volume of institutional lending than would be possible at lower rates, it would threaten the position of the moneylender correspondingly more.

To succeed, credit institutions should not drive small clients to moneylenders by refusing to provide institutional consumer credit, provided the borrower's repayment record is good. The concept of 'purpose of loan' is anyway an accounting fiction: available cash is used for the purpose with the highest return, and a farmer can well use a loan, obtained for the purchase of fertilizers that he would have bought anyway, for the next-highest-return activity of paying off the village moneylender, without offending against either the formal rules or economic rationality. Elaborate attempts to channel loans to stated productive activities create ill-feeling everywhere, help moneylenders where they succeed, and supply little credit where they fail.

2. *Extension Services and Marketing*

There are few examples of successful extension in poor countries, partly because farmers often know much more than extension officers, partly because the latter receive neither the pay to attract good personnel in the first place nor proper performance incentives. Extension workers who receive classroom training only, are paid less than clerks, and have no career structure, will do little good. Rather than swamp and dilute an already inadequate service in order to maintain a fixed extension-worker/farmer ratio after reform, it would be better to ensure that inputs are available on time, and that incentives favour their adoption. Under such circumstances farmers do much of their own extension.

There is little to be said for separating what extension workers advise farmers to do, what credit agencies lend for, and what government price and marketing policies make possible. Therefore it often makes sense to supply credit against the security of the crop at a guaranteed price (reflecting a realistic annual interest), and to see that the credit is in the form of approved local innovations in the form of seeds or fertilizers. There is seldom much of a case for extending labour-replacing inputs such as tractors or even weedicides; or for diverting scarce credits towards such inputs and away from water, seeds and fertilizers. After a reform, all these ancillary services have to be directed to new recipients, and the learning period will involve risks and losses; these will need to be kept down by abandoning some of the policy mistakes of the past.

3. *Input Delivery, Rural Works and Administrative Distortions*

I turn now to two under-researched areas of ancillary policy which are commonly in a far more parlous state (as regards both efficiency and equity) than the three so far discussed, yet which possess even more importance: the delivery of current farm inputs, and the provision of simple fixed-capital services, especially small irrigation and drainage facilities. Such services are particularly crucial for small farmers unused to obtaining modern inputs for themselves. They can also form the basis for programmes of rural works, and of co-operative supply on a commercial basis, that can do much to employ the landless, who may not benefit from reform where there is too little land.

Even those, like myself, who believe that planned public action is essential for equitable development, must recognize that ineffective input delivery, especially to small farmers in most poor countries, arises from two phenomena: public monopolies, which are often maladministered and sometimes corrupt; and subsidies which fulfil no function as incentives, and seldom reach their intended destinations. The urgency of ending both these abuses increases as the delivery system comes to deal with the heavy burdens of supplying a new class of small surplus farmers. This task can easily become high-cost, both because of the larger numbers of outlets for inputs, and because the increased input of labour will lead to greater use per acre of most inputs, and certainly water and fertilizer, provided credit is available.

There is a case for subsidies on grounds of efficiency if an input carries greater benefits than the farmer realizes, so that he must at first be persuaded to adopt it; but this does not apply in the vast bulk of poor countries, where water and fertilizers are in excess demand even at market prices. There is a case for subsidies on grounds of equity, if they go to poor people, and if they are a more administratively practicable means of enriching them than direct income supplementation; but, where there is excess demand for a scarce commodity such as fertilizers, a subsidy on it is likely to benefit not the final users but those who can administer, transport and, in effect, ration it, and indeed it frequently creates local scarcities that *raise* the price to poor users. In practice, extensive input subsidies have encouraged waste and brought little or no benefit to poor farmers. They merely allow governments to persuade themselves and their electorate that they are transferring resources into agriculture, whereas in reality those resources are usually being transferred to their own administrators and to private importers and distributors. Where the subsidized input is labour-replacing (as with tractors and weedicides) the inequity is graver still, and where such inputs are imported the fact of subsidy is often concealed by overvaluation of the currency. Even where the subsidy does reach the farmer, it is inequitable, because those fortunate enough to be able to benefit from modern inputs are subsidized at the expense of those less fortunately placed.

The second main defect of input delivery in many poor countries is its frequent concentration in the hands of an overworked, understaffed, underpaid and internally non-competitive public sector. The adjectives are not chosen for purposes of rhetoric; if a government chooses to staff its input delivery services adequately, to give them wages and career structures that raise the costs of dismissal relative to the benefits of corruption, and to provide performance bonuses and competing input sources within the public sector, then that sector can be entrusted with the crucial task of delivering modern inputs. But if governmental commitment to 'socialism' is to exclude any intention to provide resources efficiently through the public sector for low-status sectors such as agriculture then it is better to turn the delivery system over to the private sector: better for equity as well as efficiency. I favour the former solution, but the latter is preferable to supplying a new, post-reform class of small and weak farmers with corruption and rhetoric disguised as subsidies, State monopoly and socialism.

The final issue regarding ancillary services lies in the provision of small items of fixed capital, labour-intensive in construction and in use. These can be sold to the new small farmers individually or (more usually) jointly. They can be managed by village-level bodies who sell their outputs (e.g. water, if selling pumps direct to the peasant is excluded). These items – small embankments, run-off and feeder channels, well and tubewell bores, installations for traditional and intermediate irrigation – are naturals for construction in a rural works programme, and can show high returns; an unpublished World Bank study showed a benefit/cost ratio in Bangladesh of 2·2 on drainage and irrigation in such a programme – much higher than for roads. The usual defect of rural works programmes is that the deficit-farmer and landless-labourer families, as in settlement schemes, have to provide most of the (cheap off-season) labour, and become increasingly reluctant to do so as they find that the benefits are steered towards the bigger and more powerful farmers. This arises from both the political power and the size of holdings belonging to these larger farmers; thus a road to market is of greatest benefit to those who sell most in the market. This defect is lessened by a land reform, especially if the landless can be covered.

In the more challenging and difficult South Asian situation, rural works programmes acquire special importance. As we have seen, they can do much to relieve the plight of the landless, who (with mini-farmers not benefiting from reform) deserve priority in employment on them. Works programmes, of course, also supply capital to raise yields for the beneficiaries, and should concentrate on constructions with high and quick yields, recoverable from small farmers – drainage and small irrigation repair and construction – rather than on transport. There is almost no limit to the schemes of this sort that can be profitably undertaken in South Asia, especially in the context of the improved cereal varieties that so hugely increase the pay-off to reliable water-control.

Schemes of rural works whose organisers are ill-trained or

ill-paid degenerate into political patronage (like the 'land army' of Ceylon's UNP in 1968–70) or into pure hand-outs (like the Bangladesh scheme in 1971–3), discredit the idea itself, and require costly rescue operations. As with input-delivery, good administrators for an effective rural works programme are scarce and expensive, and have to be acquired by the public sector for agriculture at the cost of other, lower-priority activities in public or private sectors. But in the case of rural works, to abstain from a major public-sector effort is to renounce both efficiency and equity after reform: efficiency, because of the high potential pay-off to these labour-intensive installations, which are, however, usually beyond the resources or risk-bearing capacities of individual (or even co-operating) small farmers after the reform; equity, because of the need to do something for the very poor who cannot be given land.

The big landowner within a village, even within an extended family, is seldom *simply* a Wicked Exploiter; he owes his position as patron to his readiness to provide consumer loans, jobs, help with (or against) outsiders and in particular officials, and, in general, security against disasters. Unless the reforming agencies can provide replacements for these services, or help the community to provide them for itself, the old power structure will continue to be sustained by its special capacity to meet the need for them.

4. *Structure of Holdings under Growth and Change*

The reader may well have been irritated by the treatment, so far, of land reform as a movement from an old, static situation to a new one. Even if the latter is economically superior, can it continue to be viable during the major shifts likely to affect a developing agriculture, population, growth, adaptation to planning, new pressures towards concentration of landholdings, eventually the replacement of labour by capital? To answer this question, we need to make more precise in what the alleged superiority of smallholdings consists.

(a) *'Optimality', 'Economies of Scale' and Population Growth* It is not argued that land reform creates holdings of 'optimum' size, which in most poor countries would be the size maximizing net value added in agriculture at very high valuations of capital and land, and rather low valuations of labour, corresponding to their opportunity-costs. 'Optimum size' would depend on cropping patterns and managerial skills; political realities are not the only consideration that leads me to suggest a ceiling-to-viable-holding ratio of perhaps 5 : 1 in efficiency-units of land per consumer unit. Furthermore, 'optimum size' may well be less than enough to provide a livelihood for a family of average size (five to six in rural South Asia); in Ceylon, rice output per acre seems to be maximized around half to one acre, whereas the minimum viable holding for a family of five is about two acres.[1] All that is claimed is that distributivist land reform, by creating viable family holdings, improves the efficiency of farming as compared with the pre-reform situations.[2]

This disposes of the objection that any such optimum would alter with time, requiring reforms to adapt farm size; no optimality is claimed, only substantial improvement. The superiority of the family farm to other farming arrangements is a different issue, to which we shall return.

The second point is that the superiority of small family holdings over the present pattern of massive holdings and mini-holdings is *not* alleged to consist in any capacity, on the part of the small farm, to achieve lower average costs purely on account of its reduced size. Attempts to discover either economies or dis-economies of scale, in agriculture in poor countries, by means of traditional production-function analysis have usually failed; apparent scale-economies turn out to be either pseudo-indivisibilities (e.g. tractors, if they make sense at all, can be hired even by a half-acre farm) or pecuniary rather than technological dis-economies (e.g. the effects of power-structures that deny the small farmer access to credit at rates obtainable by the big farmer, even when the risks and administrative costs are no higher per acre or per dollar loaned).[3] Our claim for smaller family farms is

1. ILO, op. cit., Vol. 2 (Technical papers), Nos. 10 and 12.
2. In using the notion of 'viable holding size' (clear, but complex because it implies a notion of tolerable minimum family income) in preference to 'optimal holding size' (also clear but complex), we reject the term 'economic holding', usually a meaningless propaganda term to justify the setting of target farm sizes, and *a fortiori* ceilings, well above the optimum.
3. For pseudo-indivisibilities, see T. W. Schultz (1964); for pecuniary external economies, see T. Scitovsky (1954).

Absence of scale economies means that, if all inputs are doubled, output exactly doubles (at most). However, in national planning, the presence or absence of 'social' scale-economies should be estimated by measuring input and output costs at shadow prices reflecting true scarcities, and seeing whether, with such pricing, average social cost of production varies with scale, assuming that total net value added is

not that they benefit from diseconomies of scale to produce higher levels of output than bigger units with *similar* inputs of labour and capital on an acre. Rather it is that they select *higher* labour-inputs and hence produce higher output-levels from given inputs of land and capital, thereby economizing on what a poor country is short of (land and capital), using up what stands idle (labour), and producing more of the goods wanted (food). This is true even if total cost of factors of production, per unit of output, is independent of farm size (as is likely *if* all inputs and outputs are valued at market prices).

There is no obvious reason, in the new technologies becoming available to agriculture, why the advantages of higher labour-intensity should cease to matter for the small farm. On the contrary, these technologies offer the chance of higher cropping-intensity – sometimes of multiple cropping – and require higher levels of fertilizer and weed control, all of which are likely to be undertaken to a greater extent by farm units with plenty of spare labour per acre farmed. Moreover, the rising levels of nutrition, as output per acre goes up, relieve the biological constraints upon higher labour inputs and are likely to increase the small family farm's advantage even further, as greater will to work and lower marginal utility of leisure are reinforced by greater capacity to work and more muscle-power per family member. Nor are the new inputs of seed, fertilizer and pesticide likely to give rise to new production functions featuring economies of scale – there are neither genuine nor pseudo-indivisibilities here. Where the 'green revolution' does impart pseudo-indivisibilities – in the field of new irrigation devices such as tube-wells and pump-sets – these difficulties can be overcome by private hiring, or by formal or informal co-operatives; these latter, however, will encounter new difficulties if they are pressed to extend their activities beyond the management of the devices that evoked them.

Under these circumstances one must not exaggerate the risk that population growth may turn viable post-reform holdings into unviable ones. Given the pattern of incentives to produce and the new inputs becoming available, there is little reason why net farm output should not at least keep up with population

---

maximized (by the appropriate choice of inputs and outputs) at each scale. To my knowledge this has not been done, but the argument (and the abundant underlying evidence) suggests that it would yield sharply decreasing 'shadow returns to scale' as against the constant return finding of the standard production-function approach.

growth, while the extra incentives provided by land reform (and the associated higher labour-intensity) should eventually produce a considerable improvement on this. Hence after twenty-five years, even if rural population doubles, a one-acre holding should certainly produce more than two acres today. This is not said to downgrade the importance either of family planning or of enabling workers to find non-farm jobs, but merely to show that all is not lost for distributivist reform just because population growth on the land causes average holding size *later* to fall below the level considered viable *now*. Indeed it could be argued that only the push to yields given by land reform can provide the necessary safeguard against the impact of population growth. Moreover, if consolidation within the new viable smallholdings is possible, a further favourable tilt is given to the land-population balance, both because the reduction of walk-to-work time further increases the incentive to labour intensity, and because less land is wasted in partitions. Hence there is no reason to believe that population growth would compel a new land reform in each generation – unless the first land reform accelerates population growth, for which there is no evidence. It is even possible to use the reform to *retard* population growth, e.g. by not adjusting the viable holding offered in such a way as to compensate fully for variations in family size, or (more ruthlessly) by refusing to distribute land to families with more than two children unless the father has a vasectomy.

(b) *Planning* A further worry about the post-reform dynamics of the new, just-viable family smallholdings concerns their 'plannability'. It is sometimes said that, although such a pattern of holdings may end or greatly reduce 'exploitation' in agriculture, it nevertheless retards 'socialism' and development by reducing planning to mere forecasting, since the physical-input and output-disposal decisions of millions of small farmers cannot possibly be controlled. This, however, is valid only for an economy unable, for ideological reasons or because it cannot control smuggling, to use price incentives or disincentives for both inputs and outputs. Small farmers have shown themselves highly responsive to such incentives – probably more so than the pre-reform large farmers, for whom the marginal utility of income is presumably less. We have analysed this for the particular case of marketed surplus. Nor is planning limited to price-incentives: the new viable farmers will need all sorts of services, and the capacity of the State, for example, effectively to tie credit to approved crops and practices is surely greater than it was with the pre-reform large farmers, with their political power and their ability to get credit elsewhere or do without it.

(c) *Renewed Pressures Toward Concentration Arising From Technologies* This Marxian problem is in practice the most important. There is no doubt that both the economics and the politics of the 'green revolution' produce pressures towards an increased farm size: the economics, not because of technological scale economies, but because of the big farmer's easier access to credit and greater willingness to take risks, and because the landlord finds it increasingly profitable to expel tenants and resume personal cultivation; the politics, because of the large farmer's special ability to obtain access to and even subsidies for new inputs. Hence there is some danger that distributivist reform merely holds back, from time to time, a technologically induced (though not justified) tide of concentration. However, even if true, this does not qualify as an argument against such reform. If the concentration coefficient of land owned or operated is tending upwards over time, the marginal social benefit of any success in reducing that coefficient (e.g. by distributivist land reform) is actually increased, both because inequality has rising marginal disutility and because more (or poorer) poor people increase the disutility associated with any given coefficient. As with population growth, so with pressures towards concentration of landholdings: although they do not weaken the case for distributivist reform, there is every reason to orient the reform to their prevention or at least to their reduction.

(d) *The Very Long Term* A basic theoretical objection to the small family farm is this: a holding of two or three acres may be better than a pre-reform large holding when land and capital are ample and labour scarce, but will not the converse eventually also be true? When rural labour becomes scarce and capital ample, and (thanks to land-augmenting capital) labour-intensive use of the land becomes a very low priority, family holdings will still be viable, and perhaps stubbornly unwilling to amalgamate, though they will now fall far below the optimum size. For most poor rural economies, however, this future lies so far away, and is likely to be made even more distant by population growth, that an incredibly low rate of time-preference would be needed before it could outweigh the benefits from land reform – equalisation, and swift output gains from more intensive land use. Nor is policy inflexible. Around 1964, Taiwan began to experience rural labour shortages, and a diminishing pressure on land, as multiple-cropping spread; a deliberate decision to reduce disincentives to tractor use was therefore taken, and small farmers began to hire them more and more. Such a policy might make sense in Ceylon around 1980, and in the sub-continent around 1985–1990. The experience of the United States demonstrates the remarkable flexibility of family farming in face of incentives and technical change. As millions of workers have left the land, and as capital and land have become increasingly plentiful and cheap relative to labour, both cropping patterns and techniques have responded so dramatically that a family with two or three workers, hardly any hired labour, and several hundred acres of efficiently (and capital-intensively) farmed land is quite typical. In other words, as and *if* labour leaves the land and development makes capital plentiful, it is possible that (progressively bigger) family farms will *continue* to be a method of agricultural production that is both efficient and non-exploitative.

V. The Political Dynamics of Land Reform

1. *The Homogeneity of Initial Situations*

Byres, following Thorner, convincingly shows (pp. 229–35) that the apparent legal complexity of the pre-independence tenurial structure in India masks a small number of simply definable and none too dissimilar sorts of agrarian relationship. The universal characteristic of the small-farmer group is that they are beholden to the large-farmer group, often for land, and almost always for security, input purchases, output outlets, consumer credit, intercession with outsiders (especially officials), and jobs to enable them to live despite inadequate land.

The multiplicity of such ties of dependence of client upon patron constitutes the central feature of almost all pre-capitalist and proto-capitalist rural social structures, including those miscalled 'communal tenure systems'. Yet dependence almost always centres upon the inequality of rights in land. The small farmer is usually a deficit farmer whose consumed and marketed output cannot meet his family's food needs; he is almost always driven into, or at least within sight of, a deficit situation by population increase which, while raising his family's needs, makes it harder for him to meet them by saving enough to buy increasingly expensive extra land or extra land-enhancing capital. This land inadequacy makes the small farmer dependent on the big farmer for loans and jobs, and increasingly so as the man/land ratio grows. It follows from this analysis that, despite the bewildering variety of legal forms, radical land reform (distributivist or collectivist) is almost always a necessary condition for producing a more equal sharing of rural power and prosperity. It is not always, or even nearly always, a sufficient condition; monopoly power in the fields of credit and job-provision, at least, must normally be attacked too, but if there is a fairly drastic land reform this need not require measures as radical as might otherwise be required. Provision of viable co-operative credit systems, and (through a right to work on rural works schemes) of alternative sources of employment, may suffice.

This fairly polarized initial situation has certain implications for the political viability of a reform. The big farmers will have much power, and the strategy must be to split them. This can be done (1) by adopting a ceiling which adversely affects only 2–5 per cent of rural families – usually enough to release 10–25 per cent of farmed land if ceilings legislation is fully implemented; (2) by offering reasonable compensation terms. To some extent these will be bonds eroded by inflation – but perhaps one can be less sly and more imaginative: K. N. Raj's suggestion, of compensating owners with some form of monopoly rights in the supply of new inputs (subject to price control), is worth investigating as a way to tap entrepreneurial skills; in Taiwan, compensation was largely by shares in the less successful nationalized industries. No ethical position is being taken here: it is merely pointed out that very ungenerous compensation will stiffen resistance, and evasion, by a strong and subtle group of landlords.

The polarized initial rural situation also means that rich landlords will almost monopolize access to good lawyers. This above all makes evasion easy. Dealing with it requires rapid implementation, with legal authority in case of disputes vested by Parliament in special *ad hoc* bodies, if possible outside the range of the law's delays and the lawyers' pressures.

We have so far implied that land reform is something made by governments – inevitably, urban governments – for villagers. It may be argued that reforms are best made (or can only be implemented) under pressure from effective mass peasant movements; conversely, perhaps such movements are less unlikely to evolve if reforms are in the making. Should just and efficient reforms wait upon the mass organization of the most dispersed and least articulate section of the community? Whether or not the pressure of peasant movements counts for much – and if it does the role of the landless labourer may be very muted indeed – land reforms are in general decided, legislated and implemented by townsmen. It is to the interests of the urban élite that we must finally turn in seeking to explain why there has been so much law, and so little action, in land reform in non-communist poor countries.

2. *Rural Power Structures and Urban Bias: A Reply to Terry Byres*

'The expression' ['urban bias'], writes Byres (p. 222), 'is simply a pejorative way of referring to those who choose the path of industrialization . . . to dismiss [the] arguments [for it] as "doctrine" or "ideology" is to replace logic and argument with . . . "depreciation by terminology".' In my (I believe consistent) vocabulary, that is not how the words Byres quotes are used. It is as well to recall that there are not two positions (pro- and anti-industry) but four: neglect agriculture and develop industry (crude Mahalanobis); squeeze agriculture to finance industrial wage-goods and investment but be prepared simultaneously to develop a squeezable agriculture (Preobrazhensky); divide resources between agriculture and industry as indicated by optimality conditions regarding efficiency and by equity valuations (this usually means developing agriculture first because it shows higher returns on investment and lower initial income-per-head, and only later using its, efficiently growing, wage-goods surplus, traded at fair prices, to fuel industrialization – Adam Smith–Kautsky–Chayanov); and develop agriculture to stay rural for ever (hippy-Gandhian). The two middle positions are easily caricatured by conflating them with the two extreme positions, but the Smith-Kautsky-Chayanov position – to which I hold – though it may be hard to define precisely,[1] does have the merit of giving unbiased norms with regard to which sectoral bias can be defined. In any economy there exist (if one can find them) an *efficiency norm* and an *equity norm* for the distribution of any allocable resources – be they savings, teachers, administrative capacities, or price-incentives – between rural and urban areas (or between agriculture and industry in some cases). The efficiency norm will maximize the present discounted value of all future net income streams, pricing inputs and outputs at the scarcity values that would prevail at the desired distribution of incomes. The equity norm will optimize interpersonal income distribution over all points of time (not necessarily in any one period), and is subject to variation according to the person making the decision.

1. An attempt is made in Lipton (1974).

Now an allocation of resources between urban and rural areas that gives less to rural areas than corresponds either to the efficiency norm, or to almost anybody's idea of the equity norm, is urban-biased. One that gave more to rural areas than corresponded to either of these norms would be rural-biased. Many allocations fall under neither heading; some are widely believed to discriminate against the rural sector too much to be equitable, but nevertheless to push rural investments in relief of need far enough for marginal returns to fall so sharply that an efficiency-optimality norm is violated. But it was closely argued, not just asserted, in the papers of mine to which Byres refers (p. 222, Fn. 1) that substantial and unambiguous urban bias exists in the Indian economy, at least until 1967–8. In subsequent work (1971), I have attempted to measure the scale of resource transfer from rural to urban areas in India in the mid-1960s, and (1974) to show that unambiguous urban bias is a feature of allocation for many types of resource in most poor countries – with India, though still plainly urban-biased, in fact less so than most. All this is 'value-loaded' only in the sense of assuming that efficiency and equity are good. Urban bias refers to the sacrifice of efficient and equitable growth to rapid urban advance; it characterizes statements such as the following; 'The aim is to secure the maximum marginal rate of saving in the agricultural sector, to acquire these savings, and to use them to finance capital formation in the industrial sector' (Byres, p. 225). To describe this statement as urban-biased seems to me descriptive, unemotive and useful. If 'industrial' and 'agricultural' were reversed the statement would be rural-biased, and just as open to attack. It is growth in income for, and equity among, *people* that counts – not priority for arbitrarily selected *sectors*. To prejudice the former by insistence on the latter is indeed only explicable in terms of doctrine and ideology.[1]

Byres argues that objective urban bias in India is disproved by the failure of the terms of trade to move against agriculture since 1953, and by the failure of the marketed surplus to rise much. But (as Dandekar showed in the paper in the *Economic and Political Weekly* refuting the Dantwala paper that Byres cites) the *movement* of the terms of trade is irrelevant. What counts, in assessing whether there is urban bias, is the *impact* of total government action upon the intersectoral terms of trade. Given the sluggishness of food supply consequent on rural under-

1. To me, incidentally, these are not abusive terms. We all have beliefs. (Empiricism itself is such a belief.) Most beliefs have ideological bases.

investment in India, it is surprising that the terms of trade have not moved hugely in favour of agriculture; but one's surprise is lessened when one examines the whole gamut of public policy, from PL 480 to subsidies of industrial inputs, from currency overvaluation (favouring the import-intensive industrial sector) to failure to control industrial monopoly. The sluggishness of net marketed surplus – and indeed of the pace of industrialization in India – does not prove the non-existence of urban bias either; on the contrary, under-investment in agriculture, and unattractive prices for farm marketings, ensured both inadequacies. In the medium term, indeed, surplus-extracting urban bias, by rendering agriculturists both unable and unwilling to meet industry's needs, is a self-defeating route to industrialization; but to point to the internal contradictions of a phenomenon is not to show that it does not exist.

Finally, then, if urban bias exists, it would affect land reform precisely, I would argue, by swinging it to the advantage of the better-off, surplus peasants, in the way Byres describes! The main feature of Indian land reform after *Zamindari* abolition has surely been the built-in opportunities for evasion in the legislation itself: the setting of individual rather than family ceilings, the granting of exemption in the case of vaguely defined 'resumption for personal cultivation', above all the subjection of the whole proceedings to long, tortuous and landlord-influenced legal processes. Now how would an urban-biased legislator look at land reform? He would wish to ensure, just as Byres indicates, that it produced, or at least did not imperil, a substantial and cheap urbanised surplus of wage-goods and industrial inputs; and that it did not weaken the ability or the will of the rural sector to invest its savings in the urban sector, even though rural investment offers a higher *social* rate of return. Efficiency and equity are secondary to such considerations, in the mind of the urban-biased legislator, whose natural procedure is to build an *urban alliance* with the part of the rural élite needed to provide surpluses: the big farmers.

The procedure is natural, because it is these few big farmers who – at whatever cost to efficient and equitable rural resource allocation – supply most of the net, urbanised marketed surplus, and of the urbanised rural savings. Very crudely, the urban alliance works as follows: the big farmers get subsidized inputs and are allowed to retain (and, in the selective wake of the 'green revolution', to strengthen) their exploitative position within the rural sector; in return they provide the urban élite of industrialists and proletariat with wage goods at artificially low prices.

Of course a redistribution of land, from big farmers to make sub-viable farmers viable, would upset this balance. When the smoke had cleared, the net marketed surplus *at unrigged prices* might well, as we have argued, be higher; but it might well fall back at the old prices. (Incidentally, the cost of subsidies on inputs would rise greatly for the urban sector, as much more would be demanded by the new, more labour-intensive farm-structure, and a greater proportion of it would be devoted to producing food consumed on the farm – *ipso facto* of no interest to the pure industrializer – thus endangering the whole process of urban resource inflow from the villages). Hence, if one would not expect most urban-biased policy-makers to support radical land reform save under severe political pressure, this is not because it would reduce the flow of marketed surplus, but rather because it would compel them to allow its price to rise towards fair levels.

A few urban-biased policy-makers, however, do support land reform: some take a longer view of agricultural development, some wish to placate the small peasant, some (despite the selectively-subsidizing urban alliance) take an exceptionally unfavourable view of the surplus-delivering capacity of the existing tenure system, as Byres does. Hence the Indian situation: verbal reforms, catching some of the biggest farmers with idle or very badly farmed land, but full of loopholes for those who provide the surplus; verbal concessions for the peasantry; dormant take-over clauses providing an ultimate legal weapon in case the big farmers insist on higher prices; but no change (however efficient or equitable) that might imperil industry's power to move the internal terms of trade in its own favour.

None of this is intended as a comment on human selfishness, still less as an attack upon India: all élite groups are biased in their own favour and India's élite has made more concessions than most to equity and efficiency. Rather, I offer a description of how people, without conspiracy, will form alliances in pursuit of their own interests. If such alliances imperil the prospect of land reform – as I fear they do – it is the function of the scholar to say so. As Keynes remarked, the long-run power of analysis should not be underestimated.

* * * *

The term 'utopian' has been applied to the advocacy of radically distributive land reform. Yet such reform has been applied, with striking success, in areas of extreme land hunger in Japan and Taiwan; and the distribution of land that it seeks to create is similar to that of many places in Java and Western India. I have presented evidence and theoretical reasons for believing that the family holdings created by such reform are favourable to efficiency and employment as well as equity; I have also shown that quite possibly, and especially after the very short run, the size of the marketed surplus will be favoured as well, albeit not the urban sector's capacity to get it on the cheap. Thus neither experience nor theory suggests that radically distributive land reform is 'utopian'. Such a criticism, moreover, sounds strange in the mouth of an advocate of collectivization, co-operative joint farming, or alternatively of the preservation of the *status quo*. The first two are fiercely unpopular, and proved by almost universal experience to be highly inefficient[1] and far from egalitarian. As for the *status quo*, its supporters (if inequality does not move them) should compare food output per person in South Asia, Africa, and Latin America in 1957–9 and now, after the so-called 'green revolution'. Under-farming by large landholders and under-capitalization of smallholders are not only exploitative but also unproductive. Radically distributive land reform is no panacea, but there is no evidence that anything short of it will substantially or lastingly amend these deficiencies.

References

BARD (Bangladesh Academy for Rural Development), *Cooperative Farming*, Comilla, 1972.

Bardhan, P. K. and K., 'Agriculture in India and China: output, input and prices', *Economic and Political Weekly*, Annual Number, 1969, pp. 54–9.

—, 'Price Response of Marketed Surplus of Foodgrains', *Oxford Economic Papers*, July 1971.

Bose, S., 'The Strategy of Agricultural Development in Bangladesh', *Development Dialogue*, 1, 1973.

1. The prevalence of myth appears once more to make itself felt in the remark of an able and sincere Minister of Overseas Development that 'land reform on the principle of collectivism is *developmentally* the best method, because it is the most effective method.' (Judith Hart's italics, in *Aid and Liberation*, 1972.) It needs re-emphasizing, plainly, that there is a great deal of evidence against this statement, and almost none in its favour. Maybe, of course, a 'developmentally . . . effective' (or even productively efficient or socially equitable) mode of collectivist land reform will be discovered tomorrow . . .

Chayanov, A. V., *The Theory of Peasant Economy* (eds. Basile Kerblay, Daniel Thorner and R. E. F. Smith), American Economic Association, Homewood, Illinois, 1966.

Cheung, S. N. S., *The Theory of Share Tenancy*, Chicago and London, 1969.

Dandekar, V. M., 'Agricultural Price Policy: a Critique of Dantwala', *Economic and Political Weekly*, **3**, 11, 16 March 1968.

Dayal, R., and Elliot, C., 'Land Tenure, Land Concentration and Agricultural Output', in U.N.R.I.S.D., *Social and Economic Factors in Agricultural Development: Report no.* 5, Geneva, 1966.

Dorner, Peter, *Land Reform and Economic Development*, Penguin, Harmondsworth, 1972.

Epstein, T. Scarlett, *India: Yesterday, Today and Tomorrow*, London, 1973.

Gaitskell, Arthur, *Gezira: a study of development in the Sudan*, London, 1959.

Hart, Judith, *Aid as Liberation*, Gollancz, London, 1972.

Huntington, Samuel P., *Political Order in Changing Societies*, Yale U.P., 1968.

ILO (International Labour Office), *Matching Employment Opportunities and Expectations: a report on Ceylon*, Geneva, 1971.

Ishikawa, Shigeru, *Economic Development in Asian Perspective*, Economic Research Series No. 8, Hitotsubashi University Institute of Economic Research, 1967.

Jodha, N. S., 'Special Programmes for the Rural Poor', *Economic and Political Weekly* (Bombay), 31 March 1973.

Kautsky, Karl, *Die Agrarfrage*, Dietz, Stuttgart, 1899. Translated into French as *La Question Agraire*, Maspero, Paris, 1970.

Krishna, Raj, 'Some Aspects of Land Reform and Economic Development in India', *Land Tenure, Industrialization and Social Stability* (ed. Walter Froehlich), Marquette U.P., Milwaukee, 1961.

Ladejinsky, Wolf, 'The Green Revolution in Bihar: the Kosi Area', *Economic and Political Weekly*, **4**, 39, September 1969.

Lee, T. H., *Intersectoral Capital Flows in the Economy of Taiwan, 1895–1960*, Cornell U.P., New York, 1971.

Lehmann, David, 'Political Incorporation versus Political Stability: the Case of the Chilean Agrarian Reform, 1965–1970', *Journal of Development Studies*, **7**, 4, July 1971.

Lenin, V. I., *Capitalism and Agriculture*, International Publishers, New York, 1946.

Lipton, Michael, 'The Transfer of Resources from Agricultural to Non-Agricultural Activities: the Case of India', *Report* of the Fifth Interregional Planning Seminar (Bangkok, 1969), U.N., New York, 1971.

—, *Why Poor People Stay Poor: Urban Bias in Underdeveloped Countries*, London, 1974.

Mazumdar, Dipak, 'The Theory of Sharecropping With Labour-Market Dualism', *Journal of Development Studies*, forthcoming, 1974.

Pakistan, Government of, *Census of Agriculture*, 1960, 1962–4.

—, *Master Survey of Agriculture, 1968*, Islamabad, 1970.

Schultz, T. W., *Transforming Traditional Agriculture*, Yale U.P., 1964.

Scitovsky, Tibor, 'Two Concepts of External Economies', *Journal of Political Economy*, April 1954.

Szczepanik, E., 'Agricultural Capital Formation In Selected Developing Countries', *Agricultural Planning Studies*, II, FAO, 1970.

Thorner, Daniel, *Agricultural Co-operatives in India*, Asia Publishing House, London, 1960.

Index